SEASONS OF FAITH

SEASONS OF FAITH

A WALK THROUGH THE HISTORY OF THE
ROMAN CATHOLIC DIOCESE OF MARQUETTE
1900-2000

ANGELA S. JOHNSON

Published by the Roman Catholic Diocese of Marquette
117 West Washington St., Marquette, MI 49855.

Copyright © 2006
by the Roman Catholic Diocese of Marquette
117 W. Washington St.
Marquette, Michigan 49855

All rights reserved.
No part of this book may be
reproduced in any form without
written permission from the diocese.

Unless otherwise noted, all photographs
are the property of
the Diocese of Marquette.
Endpaper artwork by Daniel Pemble.
Upper Peninsula map by Aaron Peterson.

Library of Congress Control Number: 2006930430

ISBN-13 978-0-9786970-0-6
ISBN-10 0-9786970-0-6
ISBN-13 (3 book set) 978-0-9786970-3-7
ISBN-10 (3 book set) 0-9786970-3-0

Printed in the USA
by Thomson-Shore, Inc.
Dexter, Michigan 48130

Contents

Map of the Diocese of Marquette   xi
Foreword   xii
Preface and Acknowledgments   xvi

Introduction 1

Clergy and Religious
    Bishops   4
    Men's Religious Orders   8
    Women's Religious Orders   12
    Permanent Diaconate   17
    District House, Sisters of St. Paul de Chartres   18
    Monasteries
        Monastery of the Holy Cross, Discalced Carmelite Nuns   20
        Holy Transfiguration Skete   22

Ecclesial Lay Movements   25

Diocesan Sponsored Services
    Diocesan Curia   31
        Office of the Bishop   31
        Communication   31
        Faith Formation and Education   32
        Finance and Administration   32
        Ministry Personnel   33
    Catholic Social Services   34
    Cemeteries
        Holy Cross, Escanaba   35
        Holy Cross, Marquette   36
    Orphanages
        St. Joseph Home, Assinins   37
        Holy Family Orphans Home, Marquette   38
    Retreat Centers
        Marygrove Retreat Center, Garden   39
        Camp Plagens, Watersmeet   40

Institutions
    High Schools
        Sacred Heart, Calumet   43
        Holy Name, Escanaba   43
        St. Joseph, Escanaba   44
        Ironwood, Ironwood   45
        Bishop Baraga, Marquette   46
        St. Paul, Negaunee   47
        Loretto, Sault Ste. Marie   47
        Ursuline Academy, St. Ignace   48
    Home for the Aging   49
    Hospitals
        St. Francis, Escanaba   50
        St. Joseph, Hancock   51
        St. Mary, Marquette   52
        St. Joseph's-Lloyd, Menominee   53
        Divine Infant of Prague, Wakefield   53
    Seminaries   55

Photo section 57

Parishes and Missions
Denotes that the church's history is included under the "mission" heading of the mother church.
    Ahmeek—Our Lady of Peace (Sacred Heart)   214
    Alpha—St. Edward   75
    Amasa—St. Mary Mission   77
    Assinins/Zeba—The Most Holy Name of Jesus/Blessed Kateri   79
        Tekakwitha (St. Catherine)
    Atlantic Mine—St. Mary Star of the Sea Mission   82
    Au Train—St. Therese of the Infant Jesus Mission   84
    Banat—Holy Rosary Mission   86
    Baraga—St. Ann   87
    Barbeau—Holy Family Mission   89
    Bark River/Perronville—St. Elizabeth Ann Seton   91
    Bark River—St. George   92
    Bay Mills—Blessed Kateri Tekakwitha Mission (St. Catherine)   94
    Beacon Hill—Holy Trinity Mission   96
    Bergland—St. Ann Mission   98

Bessemer—St. Sebastian   99
Big Bay—St. Mary Mission   101
Brimley—St. Francis Xavier   103
Calumet—Sacred Heart   104
Calumet—St. Anne   106
Calumet—St. Anthony*   109
Calumet—St. John   107
Calumet—St. Joseph   109
Calumet—St. Mary   111
Calumet—St. Paul the Apostle   112
Caspian—St. Cecilia   113
Cedar River—Sacred Heart Mission   115
Cedarville, Holy Cross Mission*   165
Champion—Sacred Heart   116
Channing—St. Rose   118
Chassell—St. Anne   120
Cooks—St. Mary Magdalene   122
Copper Harbor—Our Lady of the Pines Mission   215
Crystal Falls—Guardian Angels   124
Curtis—St. Timothy Mission   134
Daggett—St. Frederick   126
DeTour—Sacred Heart   128
Dollar Bay—St. Francis of Assisi Mission   130
Donken—Immaculate Heart of Mary Mission   131
Drummond Island—St. Florence Mission   132
Eagle Harbor—Holy Redeemer Mission   215
Engadine—Our Lady of Lourdes   135
Escanaba—St. Anne   137
Escanaba—St. Joseph   139
Escanaba—St. Joseph and St. Patrick   141
Escanaba—St. Patrick   142
Escanaba—St. Thomas the Apostle   144
Ewen—Sacred Heart   145
Faithorn—St. Mary Mission   147
Fayette—St. Peter the Fisherman   149
Flat Rock—Holy Family   151
Foster City—St. Joseph Mission   153
Franklin Mine—Our Lady of Mount Carmel Mission   155
Gaastra—St. Mary   157
Garden—St. John the Baptist   159

Gay—St. Joseph Mission   216
Germfask—St. Therese Mission   161
Gladstone—All Saints   163
Goetzville—St. Stanislaus Kostka   165
Gould City—St. Joseph Mission*   136
Grand Marais—Holy Rosary   167
Greenland—Saints Peter and Paul Mission   169
Gulliver—Divine Infant of Prague Mission   171
Gwinn—St. Anthony   172
Hancock—Church of the Resurrection   174
Hancock—St. Joseph and St. Patrick   175
Harvey—St. Louis the King   177
Hermansville—St. Mary   179
Hessel—Our Lady of the Snows Mission   181
Houghton—St. Albert the Great   183
Houghton—St. Ignatius Loyola   185
Hubbell—St. Cecilia   187
Indian Point—St. Lawrence Mission*   266
Iron Mountain—Immaculate Conception   189
Iron Mountain—St. Joseph   191
Iron Mountain—St. Mary   193
Iron Mountain—St. Mary and St. Joseph   194
Iron River—Assumption of the Blessed Virgin Mary   196
Iron River—St. Agnes   198
Ironwood—Holy Trinity   200
Ironwood—Our Lady of Peace   202
Ironwood—St. Ambrose   204
Ironwood—St. Michael   206
Isabella—St. Ann Mission*   266
Ishpeming—St. John the Evangelist   208
Ishpeming—St. Joseph   210
Ishpeming—St. Pius X   212
Isle Royale—St. Rachael*   186
Kingsford—American Martyrs   219
Kingsford—St. Mary Queen of Peace   221
Lake Linden—Holy Rosary   223
Lake Linden—St. Joseph   225
L'Anse—Sacred Heart of Jesus   227
Little Lake—St. Henry Mission*   173
Loretto—St. Stephen   229

Mackinac Island—Ste. Anne de Michilimackinac   231
Manistique—St. Francis de Sales   233
Marenisco—St. Catherine Mission   235
Marquette—St. Christopher   236
Marquette—St. John the Baptist   238
Marquette—St. Michael   240
Marquette—St. Peter Cathedral   242
Menominee—Epiphany   244
Menominee—Holy Redeemer (Holy Trinity)   245
Menominee—Holy Spirit   247
Menominee—Resurrection   249
Menominee—St. Adalbert   250
Menominee—St. Ann   252
Menominee—St. John the Baptist   254
Menominee—St. William   256
Metropolitan—St. Lawrence Mission*   153
Michigamme—St. Agnes Mission   257
Moran—Immaculate Conception   259
Mohawk—St. Mary Mission   217
Munising—Sacred Heart   261
Nadeau—St. Bruno   263
Nahma—St. Andrew   265
Native American Missions   267
Naubinway—St. Stephen Mission   136
Negaunee—St. Paul   268
Newberry—St. Gregory   270
Northland—St. Joseph Mission   272
Norway—St. Mary 274
Ontonagon—Holy Family   276
Painesdale—Sacred Heart Mission   277
Palmer—Our Lady of Perpetual Help Mission   278
Paradise—Our Lady of Victory Mission   280
Perkins—St. Joseph   282
Perronville—St. Michael   283
Phoenix—Church of the Assumption Mission   217
Quinnesec—St. Mary Mission   285
Ramsay—Christ the King   287
Rapid River—St. Charles Borromeo   288
Rappinville—St. Mary Mission*   135
Republic—St. Augustine   290

Rockland—St. Mary   292
Rudyard—St. Joseph   294
Sagola—St. Margaret Mission*   119
Sault Ste. Marie—Holy Name of Mary   295
Sault Ste. Marie—Nativity of Our Lord   297
Sault Ste. Marie—St. Isaac Jogues Mission   299
Sault Ste. Marie—St. Joseph   300
Schaffer—Sacred Heart   302
Seney—Mission Chapel*   161
Sidnaw—St. Francis Xavier Mission   304
Sobieski—St. Mary Mission   305
South Range—Holy Family   306
Spalding—St. Francis Xavier   308
Spalding/Hermansville—St. John Neumann   310
St. Ignace—St. Ignatius Loyola   311
St. Jacques—St. James Mission*   266
Stambaugh—Blessed Sacrament   313
Stephenson—Precious Blood   315
Sugar Island—Sacred Heart Mission   317
Trenary—St. Rita   319
Trout Creek—St. Anthony Mission*   146
Trout Lake—St. Mary Mission   320
Turin—St. Charles Borromeo*   173
Verona—Sacred Heart*   287
Vulcan—St. Barbara   321
Wakefield—Immaculate Conception   323
Watersmeet—Immaculate Conception   325
Wells—St. Anthony of Padua   326
White Pine—St. Jude   327

Index of priests and men religious   329

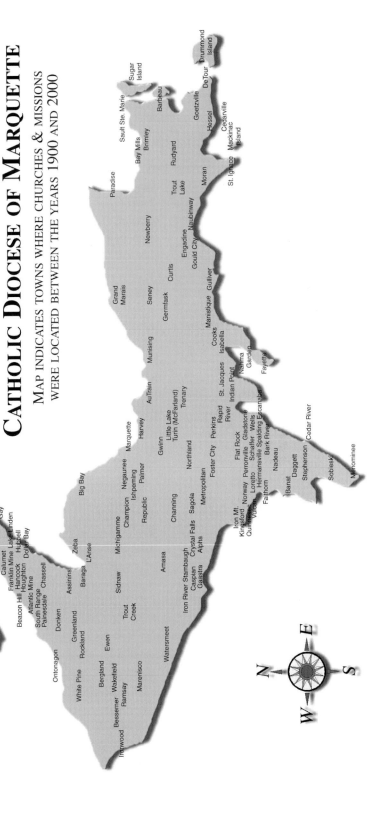

Foreword

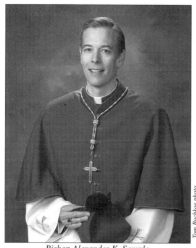
Bishop Alexander K. Sample

Praised be Jesus Christ, now and forever! It is with this sentiment of praise that I express my great delight at the completion of this third volume of our diocesan history, following in the grand tradition of Monsignor Antoine Rezek and his monumental two-volume history published 100 years ago. I remember when my family first moved to the Upper Peninsula in 1978. We became members of the historic parish of St. Ignatius of Loyola in Houghton with its beautiful church. I saw the name "Monsignor Rezek" above our parish hall and wondered who this revered pastor was. Only many years later, during my days of seminary studies, did I come to know of his great contribution in preserving our history as a Catholic people in the Upper Peninsula of Michigan.

I am especially grateful to Bishop James H. Garland for commissioning the production of this third volume in celebration of our sesquicentennial anniversary as a diocese. His wisdom and foresight in helping us celebrate and preserve our more recent history will long be remembered. I am grateful also to Angela Johnson for her tireless efforts to produce this work, which will surely educate and delight many.

Anytime we pause to formally record and celebrate our history, especially at significant milestones such as a sesquicentennial, we have an opportunity to reflect upon our past and remember the many people who have gone before us and who have passed on the faith to us. It is a celebration of the people of God in this local church of the Marquette diocese. Our history is a history of real people—clergy, religious and laity—who have labored long and hard in the vineyard of the Lord in order that those of later generations could enjoy the fruits of their labor and fully live the faith that comes down to us from Christ through the Apostles. We celebrate our one, holy, Catholic, and apostolic faith as it has been lived and experienced in the beautiful north woods that surround us. From the days of the heroic early missionaries, through the sacrifices of our first bishop, Frederic Baraga, and down to our own day, we must reflect with grateful hearts upon the sacrifices and faith of those who have helped build up the church in the Diocese of Marquette.

The production of this volume is not just an opportunity to reflect upon the past, however. Rather, it is an opportunity to be inspired by our history and rededicate ourselves to the work of proclaiming and living the Gospel of Jesus Christ as committed Catholics. Our Holy Father of beloved memory, Pope John Paul II, in his apostolic letter, *Novo Millennio Ineunte*, reminded us that it is the church's task to reflect the light of Christ…to make His face shine before the generations of the new millennium. Having contemplated His face in our history as a diocesan church, may we now move forward in the new millennium and let the light of His face shine upon the future generations, in order that our labor in the vineyard of the Lord will bear fruit for those who will follow us.

SINCERELY YOURS IN CHRIST,

MOST REV. ALEXANDER K. SAMPLE
BISHOP OF MARQUETTE

Bishop James H. Garland
Joe Sullivan photo

IT is a good thing for us who comprise the local church of Marquette to recount the deeds of our forefathers. In studying their efforts to proclaim and live the Gospel in the Upper Peninsula of Michigan, we can see the presence of the Holy Spirit whom the Savior sent to create, vivify and sanctify the world and the church. The history of the Diocese of Marquette from Bishop Frederic Baraga to Bishop Frederick Eis, who led our diocesan church into the 20th century, has been carefully inscribed in two volumes by Monsignor Antoine Rezek. Now with this third volume, and following Monsignor Rezek's approach of focusing on the parish to record our church's years in the previous century, Angela Johnson has brought us into the 21st century. By doing so she has given a gift that complements Monsignor Rezek's heroic effort and serves as an aid for celebrating the sesquicentennial of the Diocese of Marquette.

Two qualities serve the excellence of recorded history. First is a transparency that opens up the truth of the past for the benefit of those of the future. Pope Leo XIII opened the Vatican Archives in 1883 with the words, "The first law of history is not to dare to utter falsehood; the second not to fear to speak the truth." When successive generations are ignorant of history they are subject to the repetition of the errors and failures of the past.

The second quality necessary for understanding the historical past is context. Hilaire Belloc wrote in the last century the following words: "Now the most difficult thing in the world in connection with history, and the rarest of achievement, is the seeing of events as contemporaries saw them, instead of seeing them through the distorting medium of our later knowledge." Writers and readers of history should be guided by the context of the historical events.

I am grateful to the Diocesan Finance Council for giving enthusiastic consent for underwriting this project in 2002 with a keen interest in the value of our diocesan history. Secondly, I need to express my gratitude to Angela Johnson, then a reporter with the diocesan newspaper, *The U.P. Catholic*, for undertaking the writing and editing task with similar enthusiasm, an enthusiasm she maintained even though in the process she assumed the responsibilities of wife and mother.

May God bless this publication for the benefit of future generations of the Diocese of Marquette and the whole church.

✝ James H. Garland

Most Rev. James H. Garland
Bishop Emeritus of Marquette

Preface & Acknowledgements

IN anticipation of the Diocese of Marquette celebrating its sesquicentennial in 2007, Bishop James Garland commissioned this work to document the history of the Catholic Church in the Upper Peninsula in the 20th century. The history of the diocese's first 50 years, beginning in 1857, was written by Monsignor Antoine Rezek in a two-volume compilation, *The History of the Diocese of Sault Ste. Marie and Marquette*, published in 1906 and 1907.

This commemorative volume is titled "Seasons of Faith" to reflect the ever-changing role of the church among the people of the region. Just as they do during the four seasons of the Upper Peninsula, the people adapt well and continue to thrive in constantly changing conditions, even in extreme circumstances. The book's subtitle, *"A Walk through the History ...,"* explains that this publication provides a glimpse, rather than an in-depth account, of the many church entities within the diocese.

The book is divided into five parts: "Clergy and Religious," "Diocesan Sponsored Services," "Ecclesial Lay Movements," "Institutions" and "Parishes and Missions." Each section reflects different aspects of the church in the Diocese of Marquette.

The largest of the book's five parts provides brief sketches of the parish and mission churches that existed primarily between 1900 and 2000. Church entries include information about their founding, the construction of the church buildings and major renovation projects, and the development of parochial schools. Some insight is given into the involvement of the laity and parish organizations, parish traditions, and the celebration of significant parish milestones in each of the churches. The location of church records for merged and closed parishes is also provided.

Within each parish and mission entry is a list of the pastors who served there. This is the first time an attempt was made to list assignments of pastors by parish. The task proved very challenging. In some cases the information was not available; therefore gaps exist. At the end of the book is an alphabetical listing that contains, to the best of our knowledge, the names of the priests and men religious who have served the diocese. The names of those who have served as parish pastors have been indexed. Some of the men listed have left the ministry for various reasons, including those who fell under the provisions of the 2002 U.S. Bishops' Charter for the Protection of Children and Young People.

While collecting the information for the churches section, many people said to me, "Remember that it is the people who make up the church, not the buildings." What I found in my research is that parishioners are very proud of the church structure—the tangible, recognizable feature of the parish. Great sacrifices and large contributions of time, talent and money are made by individuals and parish organizations to support improvements to the churches. The church building is the place where the faithful meet regularly to share in the sacrifice of the Mass, gather in fellowship with one another, and celebrate the most sacred times of life—such as baptisms, marriages and funerals. Much has been documented about the development of the church buildings. Many churches were literally constructed by the parishioners themselves. When we speak of building additions that accommodate a growing membership and the contribution of elaborate furnishings, statues and stained glass windows paid for by parishioners, we are also hearing the stories of the people who make up the parish.

Seasons of Faith also includes brief descriptions of the Catholic institutions that operated in the diocese during the 20th century: high schools, a home for the aged, hospitals and seminaries. "Diocesan Sponsored Services" includes the history of the administration and ministries of the diocese, as well as the two diocesan cemeteries, orphanages and retreat centers. "Ecclesial Lay Movements" lists many of the organizations within the diocese and gives a brief history of them.

The histories of parishes and institutions have been organized alphabetically by town. Some churches, for which only a very limited amount of information could be found, are included under the heading of "missions" with the mother church.

For the most part, this history spans the years 1900 to 2000. It was necessary to go back to the 1800s in order to profile the founding of many of the parishes. The pastor list that follows each of the church histories is up-to-date through 2005. In addition, efforts were made to include significant events between 2000 and 2006, such as a church fire, a parish merger and closure, and the ordination of Alexander Sample as the diocese's 12th bishop in January 2006.

Due to the nature of the book as a resource, and given the large number of subjects included, much of the detailed information pertinent to the history of individual parishes and institutions could not be included here, and would be more appropriate for individual parish histories. Many parish histories are so rich that they are worthy of entire books of their own.

In compiling this information, every attempt was made to give reference to additional sources, such as parish anniversary booklets and other previously published works. A 126-page centennial issue of *The Northern Michigan Edition of Our Sunday Visitor*, published in 1953, served as a foundation for research for *Seasons of Faith*. Much of the historical data predating 1905 was originally printed in Msgr. Rezek's books. In addition to drawing extensively from these two earlier works, *Seasons of Faith* is the product of four years of researching diocesan archives, including *The U.P. Catholic* newspaper files, parish records and annual reports, and the *Official Catholic Directory*.

The archivists of men's and women's religious orders provided invaluable historical data, as did parish personnel and individual church members. Historical societies and organizations throughout the Upper Peninsula were also eager to participate by supplying documentation.

This project would not have been possible without the further support and participation of many pastors, pastoral coordinators, deacons, parish secretaries and lay members of the parish who answered the call for information by agreeing to personal interviews, filling out questionnaires and supplying the documentation for the information included in these pages. Deserving special recognition for their willingness to provide access to records are Elizabeth Delene, diocesan archivist, and Pat Peterson, secretary to the bishop. Joseph Zyble, editor of *The U.P. Catholic* newspaper, also contributed a great deal of support and was an invaluable resource through the entire process.

Special thanks goes to James Carter and Gerald Waite of Marquette who, from the beginning, provided vision for the project and continuing support and encouragement. This project would not have come to fruition without the expertise of these two men in the fields of writing, editing, proofreading and printing. Thanks also to Loreene Zeno Koskey, who oversaw the project from its inception, and to the entire diocesan staff for additional assistance.

I extend my deepest gratitude to Bishop James Garland for entrusting me with the honor of this task. The work has been an incredible journey. I have come away a humble servant of Christ with a full appreciation for the sacrifices made in order that we of the 21st century may continue to grow in the Catholic faith.

In the foreword of his first volume, Msgr. Rezek notes: "'Not one in a thousand' says a writer, 'halts to consider the various obstacles which strew the path of a historical writer; not one gives a thought to the responsibility which attaches itself to him, but all join in searching for errors.'"

The information in this new volume is as accurate as the collected documentation would support. If the effort of compiling this information into one source can be appreciated, and if the volume is found useful—and if the obvious gaps can be filled by newly-surfaced information and conflicting data can be clarified—then *Seasons of Faith* will be considered a success. I hope that the faithful will be inspired to document and preserve the records that will write the history of the seasons that lie ahead.

Angela S. Johnson

Introduction

As early as the 17th century, Jesuit missionaries from France began spreading the word of God to Natives of the Upper Peninsula. St. Isaac Jogues was the first to offer Mass in the U.P., in Sault Ste. Marie in 1641. In 1668 missionary Jacques Marquette became the first resident pastor to the tribes of Chippewa and Sault Indians here. For nearly 350 years the presence of the Jesuits remained constant in the region.

Father Frederic Baraga settled at L'Anse in 1843 and devoted the rest of his life to evangelization of this region. The present-day Diocese of Marquette, encompassing all of the Upper Peninsula of Michigan, was named a Vicariate Apostolic within the ecclesiastic Province of Cincinnati in 1853. In 1857 it was established as the Diocese of Sault Ste. Marie, and the saintly Baraga was named its first bishop.

Baraga moved from his devoted missionary efforts at L'Anse to Sault Ste. Marie to carry out this new charge. However, he found Sault Ste. Marie too remote a location and moved the seat of the diocese to Marquette in 1865. The name was then changed to the Diocese of Sault Ste. Marie and Marquette. In 1937 the title was changed again to the Diocese of Marquette.

Throughout the 20th century Bishop Baraga's successors strived to continue building the church by promoting church vocations and exhorting men and women to join the religious life, increasing the number of parishes, missions and Catholic schools throughout the diocese, and encouraging involvement from the laity.

In 1953, on the 100th anniversary of the diocese being named a vicariate apostolic, 93,560 Catholics were counted in the U.P. Diocesan clergy numbered 143 and 24 religious were serving at 96 parishes, 42 chapels and 38 missions. The diocese had six high schools and 28 grade schools. A Centennial Mass was held Aug. 30 at Memorial Field in Marquette. Seven additional observances were held in various regions of the U.P. in September and October 1953.

The diocese began the celebration of the Jubilee Year 2000 at Midnight on Christmas 1999. Jubilee-year events included a U.P.-wide Confirmation at the Superior Dome in Marquette, where 656 young people were confirmed. Also, an estimated 2,500 people took part in a Eucharistic celebration Aug. 20 at the Mattson Lower Harbor Park in Marquette.

In the year 2000 the number of registered Catholics in the diocese was 65,500. Fifty-eight diocesan priests and 11 religious were serving the people at 74 parishes and 23 missions. There were 10 parish grade schools. Sixty-three women religious were also in service to the diocese.

The reduction in the number of Catholics and Catholic institutions in this diocese now compared with its peak years in the mid-20th century mirrors a trend that has occurred throughout the United States over the past several decades. There are many factors that have contributed to this decline. Indeed, entire books have been and continue to be written about the waning of organized religion in this country.

That said, the Diocese of Marquette today is a church that is optimistic. We believe that our nation, perhaps now more than ever, needs the Gospel message. We are a church that believes in evangelization, beginning with our own membership and extending to the broader community. We are optimistic as we work to return to the basic principles, focusing on the Eucharist as the source and summit of all our efforts. We minister to the poor, defend the innocent, the weak and the infirm. We recognize the integral role of parents in their children's faith formation and we work with them in their children's development.

One hundred fifty years since its founding by Bishop Frederic Baraga, the Diocese of Marquette remains steadfast in a world that has witnessed dramatic change.

Clergy and Religious

BISHOPS

BISHOP FREDERIC BARAGA. Called the apostle to the Native Americans, Bishop Baraga was born in Krain, Austria (Slovenia) on June 29, 1797. He came to the United States in 1830, and moved into northern Michigan and the Lake Superior region soon thereafter. He was consecrated a bishop and named Vicar Apostolic of the Upper Peninsula Nov. 1, 1853 in Cincinnati. The Diocese of Sault Ste. Marie and Marquette was established in 1857. Baraga served as bishop until his death in Marquette on Jan. 19, 1868. The cause for his Beatification has advanced to Rome.

BISHOP IGNATIUS MRAK. Born in Austria (Slovenia) on Oct. 16, 1810, Bishop Mrak served as Vicar General of the diocese under Bishop Baraga and was consecrated Bishop of the Diocese of Marquette on Feb. 7, 1869 in Cincinnati. He resigned as bishop in 1878 to return to work among the Native American missions, while continuing to assist the clergy in the growing lumber and mining towns. He died Jan. 2, 1901 in Marquette.

BISHOP JOHN VERTIN. Born July 17, 1844 in Krain, Austria, Bishop Vertin completed his schooling in the U.S. and was ordained in Marquette Aug. 30, 1860. He was consecrated the diocese's third bishop on Sept. 14, 1879 in Negaunee's St. Paul Church. He died Feb. 26, 1899 in Marquette.

BISHOP FREDERICK EIS. Born in Germany and ordained in Marquette Oct. 30, 1870, Bishop Eis was consecrated the fourth Bishop of Marquette Aug. 24, 1899. He resigned July 8, 1922 upon being named an Assistant at the Papal Throne. He served as bishop of the diocese for 23 years. He died May 5, 1926 in Marquette.

BISHOP PAUL J. NUSSBAUM. The first of the diocese's bishops native to the United States, Bishop Nussbaum was born in Philadelphia Sept. 7, 1870. He was ordained May 20, 1894 in New Jersey and consecrated Bishop of Corpus Christi, Texas May 20, 1912. Bishop Nussbaum was installed as the fifth bishop of Marquette Feb. 6, 1923. He died June 24, 1935 in Marquette.

BISHOP JOSEPH C. PLAGENS. Born in Posen, Poland on Jan. 29, 1880, Bishop Plagens was ordained July 4, 1903 in Detroit. He was consecrated Sept. 30, 1934 as Auxiliary Bishop of Detroit, and was installed as the sixth bishop of Marquette Jan. 29, 1936 at St. John Church in Marquette. He was named Bishop of Grand Rapids Dec. 16, 1940 and died March 31, 1943 in Grand Rapids.

BISHOP FRANCIS J. MAGNER. Born in Wilmington, Ill., on March 18, 1887 and ordained May 17, 1913 in Rome, Bishop Magner was consecrated a bishop Feb. 24, 1941 in Chicago. He was installed as the seventh Bishop of Marquette March 20, 1941 at St. Peter Cathedral. He died just six years later, on June 13, 1947, in Marquette.

BISHOP THOMAS L. NOA. Born in Iron Mountain on Dec. 18, 1892, Bishop Noa was ordained Dec. 23, 1916 in Rome. He was consecrated Coadjutor Bishop of Sioux City, Iowa, March 19, 1946. He was transferred to Marquette Aug. 20, 1947 and was installed the eighth bishop of the diocese Sept. 24. He retired Jan. 10, 1968 but served until March of that year as Apostolic Administrator. He died March 13, 1977 in Marquette after having served more than 60 years as a priest, 30 as a bishop.

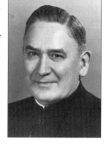

BISHOP CHARLES A. SALATKA. Born Feb. 26, 1918 in Grand Rapids, Bishop Salatka was ordained Feb. 24, 1945 and consecrated March 6, 1962 as Auxiliary Bishop of Grand Rapids. He was installed the ninth Bishop of Marquette March 25, 1968 in St. Peter Cathedral. On Dec. 15, 1977 he was installed as Archbishop of Oklahoma City and served there until his retirement on Jan. 22, 1992. He died March 17, 2003 in Oklahoma City.

BISHOP MARK F. SCHMITT. Bishop Schmitt was born Feb. 14, 1923 in Algoma, Wis. He was ordained May 22, 1948 in Green Bay. He was installed as the 10th bishop of the Diocese of Marquette May 8, 1978 after having served as Auxiliary Bishop of Green Bay. He retired as bishop in November 1992 and lived in the Big Bay area before moving to Green Bay, Wis., in 2005.

BISHOP JAMES H. GARLAND. Born Dec. 13, 1931 in Wilmington, Ohio, Bishop Garland was ordained Aug. 15, 1959 in Cincinnati. On June 5, 1984 he was appointed to the Episcopacy by Pope John Paul II and ordained Titular Bishop of Garriana and Auxiliary to the Archbishop of Cincinnati on July 25, 1984. Bishop Garland was installed as the 11th bishop of the Diocese of Marquette Nov. 11, 1992. He retired Dec. 13, 2005 and resides in Marquette.

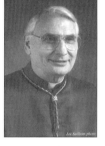

BISHOP ALEXANDER K. SAMPLE. Bishop Sample was born Jan. 7, 1960 in Kalispell, Mont. He was ordained a priest on June 1, 1990 at St. Peter Cathedral in Marquette. After receiving his Licentiate in Canon Law in Rome in 1996, he returned to the Diocese of Marquette to assume duties in the Chancery Office. He was installed as the 12th bishop of the diocese on Jan. 25, 2006.

MEN'S RELIGIOUS ORDERS

The following is a list of priestly orders that sent members to serve in the Diocese of Marquette in the 20th century. Men religious belonging to orders in addition to those listed did serve—either in smaller numbers or for shorter periods of time. The service of the religious orders listed is representative of the countless works undertaken for the faithful of the Upper Peninsula in the past 100 years.

CAPUCHIN FRANCISCANS-OFM, CAP. Capuchin Franciscans of the St. Joseph (also known as Calvary) Province began serving in the Diocese of Marquette as early as the late 1870s to the early 1880s. Through the 1970s Capuchins served as parish pastors, hospital and prison chaplains, and as spiritual directors at Northern Michigan College and Bishop Baraga Central Catholic High School in Marquette.

On Aug. 24, 1956, the former St. Joseph Orphans Home in Assinins was converted to a friary for the Capuchins. In 1957, it was formally dedicated as a novitiate. The facility operated as such until 1968.

Capuchins also resided at St. Fidelis Friary in Marquette from Sept. 2, 1960 to Aug. 1, 1976.

Since 1979 a few friars have maintained individual assignments within the diocese.

FRANCISCAN FRIARS MINOR-OFM. Members of the Franciscan Friars of the Province of Saint John the Baptist, from Cincinnati, Ohio, served parishes and Catholic communities throughout the Diocese of Marquette from 1900 to 2000. Franciscans served as parish priests, held mission retreats, taught religious and secular subjects at Catholic schools, served as hospital chaplains at St. Francis Hospital in Escanaba and as chaplains of the Carmelite Monastery in Iron Mountain.

The service of the Franciscans in the U.P. began in August 1883 when Bishop John Vertin welcomed the assistance of Father Eugene Butterman, OFM, as pastor of St. Joseph Church in Escanaba. Many more friars followed and many more Delta County communities were touched by the devoted service from men of the order.

In the 1890s Franciscans also began a century of service to the Keweenaw Peninsula, assuming the pastorate of St. Joseph Church in Hancock and Sacred Heart Church in Calumet. In 1905 the Franciscans accepted responsibility for several Keweenaw County missions. Efforts there thrived and resulted in the establishment of parish schools and new churches and missions.

Throughout the 20th century Franciscans continued to have at least one member serving as pastor in a diocesan church. This trend came to an end in July 2001 when care of several parishes was given back to the diocese. A few Franciscans have remained to serve in other capacities.

INTERNATIONAL PRIESTS. Like many of the men's religious orders with headquarters in the United States, priests from Ireland, Poland and Germany—to name a few—have also served as devoted ministers to the faithful of the Diocese of Marquette.

Some of the international priests who have served the diocese applied to come to this country and then began their studies here. They later became sponsored by and were ordained for the Diocese of Marquette. These would especially include priests from Poland. Others have been ordained in their native land and have come to the U.P. to serve as missionaries.

Without the service of priests from the Diocese of Kerala in India that began in 1995, the Diocese of Marquette would likely have had to drastically alter operations to overcome the steady decline in the number of priests. Beginning in the late 1960s and continuing through the 1990s, the number of men ordained to the priesthood in the diocese fell far short of the number needed. But when Father Joseph Nagaroor arrived from the Diocese of Kanjirapally, he inspired a wave of Indian missionaries to serve the U.P. well into the beginning of the 21st century. Some 15 Indian priests from the dioceses of Kanjirapally and Chanda, the Archdiocese of Tellicherry, the Missionary Society of St. Thomas the Apostle and the Missionary Congregation of the Blessed Sacrament, were serving as pastors and pastoral associates in 2005. In fact, the diocesan plan for pastoral ministry through 2010 relied heavily on this continued relationship.

The missionaries are invited to serve here only after direct communication between the bishop of the Diocese of Marquette and the bishop or religious superior of the Indian diocese or religious congregation. Bishop James Garland visited India to meet one-on-one with the bishops and religious superiors of those serving here in January of 1998.

The Catholic priests from India are not of the Latin Rite, but rather the Syro-Malabar Rite, a Catholic Eastern Ritual Church. In order to acclimate these men into the customs of the Church in the United States, the Diocese of Marquette developed an orientation program on education and formation about the Church in the United States and the diocese, on the local customs and culture. The first year of the three- to five-year ministry here is spent in orientation working as an associate pastor. The priests are then assigned as pastors as the need arises.

In general the international priests are very well accepted by the faithful of the diocese. People are grateful for the service of these devoted men and extend great kindnesses and generosity to them. Overcoming barriers such as language difficulties and major differences in culture are just some of the challenges facing the international priests.

The service is often a two-fold mission. Since priests in America are compensated up to 10 times as much as priests in India, many of the missionaries serving here are able to send money back to their home dioceses. There is a great fraternity among the Indian priests and, although they are devoted to the work here, they almost all look forward to returning to their homeland upon completion of their appointments.

PREMONSTRATENSIAN (NORBERTINES)-OPRAEM. Norbertine Fathers, from Saint Norbert Abbey in DePere, Wis., served the Diocese of Marquette as parish pastors and hospital chaplains from 1906 to 1968. Their service included stints at St. Francis de Sales, Manistique; St. Mary Magdalene, Cooks; St. John the Baptist, Garden; Sacred Heart, Ewen; St. Joseph Medical Center, Hancock and St. Joseph's-Lloyd Hospital, Menominee. More than a dozen Upper Peninsula men also joined the Norbertine order.

SALVATORIANS-SDS. Members of the Society of the Divine Savior (Salvatorian Fathers) served the Diocese of Marquette as parish priests, hospital chaplains and operated Jordan College, Seminary and Novitiate in Menominee. The Jordan facility was sold in 1968. The last Salvatorian in the diocese was transferred out of the area in June 1974, ending the order's long-standing apostolate in the U.P.

SOCIETY OF JESUS-SJ. Jesuit missionary St. Isaac Jogues from France was the first person to offer Mass in the Upper Peninsula. He arrived in Sault Ste. Marie in 1641 via the St. Marys River. Twenty-five years later, in 1668, missionary Father Jacques Marquette became the first resident pastor to the tribes of Chippewa and Sault Indians there.

From the 17th century until modern times—a span of about 350 years—Jesuits have almost always had a presence in the Diocese of Marquette.

Jesuits in the U.P. during the 19th century included Father Jean Baptiste Menet, Father R. Chartier and Father John Chambon. These men learned the language and customs of the Native Americans. They built mission churches and traveled throughout the eastern regions of the diocese teaching and preaching among the people.

Since 1900, Jesuits have been responsible for new churches in Bay Mills,

Drummond Island, Hessel, Hannahville, Stonington and Zeba—to name a few.

"Traveling" missionary Father William Francis Gagnieur spent more than 40 years, from 1895 to 1937, visiting mission stations, offering the sacrifice of the Holy Mass, hearing confessions, baptizing and marrying Catholics. He died Feb. 7, 1937 and is buried at Sault Ste. Marie. Father Gagnieur's successor, Father Paul Prud'homme, has been deemed the "building" missionary for encouraging the construction of new churches. He served the diocese until 1968 and spent much of his 30-plus years of ministry among people living in the western and central U.P.

In 1946 Father Joseph Lawless arrived in the U.P. from the Detroit Province of the Society of Jesus to assist Father Prud'homme. The two men split responsibility for serving the missions. Father Lawless resided in the Sault and served the Eastern U.P. for the majority of his active priestly ministry. Even after his retirement in 1992, Father Lawless made himself available to those in need. Father Lawless died Sept. 5, 1995.

In 1992 the long standing alliance of the diocese and the Jesuits came to an end when the last few men of the order still in the U.P. were reassigned elsewhere. A shortage of available men and a greater need for Jesuits elsewhere led to the decision. Bishop Mark Schmitt held a farewell service to mark the end of an era and the order's departure from the diocese June 23, 1992 in Sault Ste. Marie.

Women's Religious Orders

BENEDICTINE SISTERS-OSB. Benedictine Sisters from Duluth, Minn., served at Holy Rosary Church in Lake Linden in 1956 and 1957.

DISCALCED CARMELITES-OCD. Sisters from the Carmel of the Holy Cross monastery in Grand Rapids, Mich., at the request of Bishop Noa, came to the Upper Peninsula and established their first residency in Iron Mountain in 1950. Members of the cloistered, contemplative order describe their apostolic service as that of prayer and sacrifice for all of the people of the Diocese of Marquette and for the whole church. The sisters celebrated their Golden Jubilee in April, 2001.

DOMINICAN SISTERS (ADRIAN, MICH.)-OP. The Adrian Dominicans began ministering to the Diocese of Marquette in 1914 with the opening of Sacred Heart School in Munising. Those beginnings eventually led teams of sisters to bring the Gospel to 21 different locations in the diocese. The sisters continued serving in 2000 in the areas of religious education, pastoral works and social, physical and mental health care.

DOMINICAN SISTERS (GRAND RAPIDS, MICH.)-OP. The Grand Rapids Dominicans describe their ministerial endeavor as living the Gospel by empowering people spiritually, intellectually, socially and materially and by promoting justice through prayer, study, community and service. Members of the order served the diocese in 1993 and 1994 in the diocesan Justice and Peace offices.

DOMINICAN SISTERS (RACINE, WIS.)-OP. The Racine Dominicans define prayer, study, community and mission as integral to their way of life. According to its mission statement, the order seeks to build relationships wherever its presence can make a difference toward creating a just world. Service to the diocese spanned from 1979 to 1997.

FELICIAN SISTERS-CSSJ. The apostolic works of the Felician Sisters include education, nursing, social work and mission work. Members of the order served the Diocese of Marquette at Holy Family Parish in Ontonagon from 1955 to 1992. Over the years, their ministry extended to include Donken, Bergland, White Pine, Rockland and Greenland. In the early to mid-1980s the sisters also served the Church of the Resurrection in Hancock.

FRANCISCAN CLARIST CONGREGATION-FCC. From March 2003 to October 2004, three sisters from the Franciscan Clarist Congregation in India served the Diocese of Marquette. The women first lived and worked in Ontonagon. Then, having attained their Michigan nurse's licenses, they moved to Escanaba to work at St. Francis Hospital.

FRANCISCAN SISTERS OF CHRISTIAN CHARITY-OSF. The Franciscan Sisters of Christian Charity began their work in the diocese in 1887 at St. Mary School in Norway. The sisters' ministry expanded to include additional Catholic schools, parishes, diocesan service and outreach efforts. At the beginning of the 21st century, service continued at Escanaba, Manistique, Marquette, Menominee and Republic.

FRANCISCAN SISTERS OF PERPETUAL ADORATION-FSPA. From 1974 to 1982 Franciscan Sisters of Perpetual Adoration served the diocese through work at *The U.P. Catholic* newspaper.

INSTITUTE OF THE BLESSED VIRGIN MARY-IBVM. More commonly known as the Loretto Sisters, the order began its work in the diocese in 1886 at St. Mary Parish in Sault Ste. Marie. Service there continued until 1985. In 1899, after much hard work of raising funds, the sisters saw the opening of a secondary school—the Loretto Academy. Pastoral work expanded to Baraga, Bay Mills, Menominee and Brimley. At the start of 21 century the sisters were still working in Stephenson.

LITTLE SISTERS OF MARY. Sisters of the order from Quebec, Canada, served the diocese from 1907 to 1923 at St. Ann Parish in Menominee.

MISSIONARY SISTER SERVANTS OF THE HOLY SPIRIT-SSpS. The apostolic work of the Holy Spirit Missionary Sisters is primarily with nonChristians. The sisters focus on areas where faith is weak, in education, health care, pastoral ministry and social work in the U.S. and abroad. The sisters came to the Diocese of Marquette from Techny, Ill., at the request of Bishop Magner in 1942 to offer services to Immaculate Conception Parish in Iron Mountain. In just two years, 330 students were enrolled in a catechetical school there. By 1955, the parish established a parochial school. Ministry continued to the mid-1980s and included work in Norway and at the Native America mission in Harris.

OUR LADY OF VICTORY MISSIONARY SISTERS-OLVM. Our Lady of Victory Missionary Sisters' main thrust in serving the people of the diocese was in religious education, social work and healthcare. Members of the order served the people of the Upper Peninsula in this capacity from 1959 until 1995.

SCHOOL SISTERS OF NOTRE DAME-SSND. The School Sisters of Notre Dame strive to meet the needs of others through Christian education, pastoral ministry, Catholic schools and community service. Their work in the Diocese of Marquette began at St. Joseph Parish in Escanaba in 1884. Members of the order continued to serve there for 100 years. The sister's ministry expanded across the diocese throughout the 20th century. At the beginning of the 21st century women of the order remained in Escanaba, Iron Mountain, Marquette and Menominee.

SCHOOL SISTERS OF ST. FRANCIS-SSSF. The School Sisters of St. Francis are an international community of more than 1,300 women serving in the United States, Europe, Latin America and India. They serve in educational, healing and pastoral ministries in 21 states and 10 countries. The sisters served the Catholic school system in the Hubbell area from 1903 to 1971. Escanaba and Watersmeet were also served by School Sisters of St. Francis.

SISTERS OF THE HOLY CROSS. Sisters of the Holy Cross served the diocese at St. Joseph Parish in Lake Linden from 1886 to 1889.

SISTERS OF JESUS AND MARY. Members of the order from Montreal, Canada, served St. Joseph Parish in Lake Linden from 1893 to 1895.

SISTERS OF MERCY OF THE HOLY CROSS-SCSC. Members of the order strive to build communities of justice and eradicate poverty. From 1952 to 1988, sisters served in Ironwood, Houghton and Chassell.

SISTERS OF NOTRE DAME-SND. The Sisters of Notre Dame devote themselves to serving the people of God in education and other ministries including catechesis and responding to the needs of the poor. Members served in Watersmeet in 1982 and 1983.

SISTERS OF THE PRECIOUS BLOOD-CPPS. One sister from the order came to the diocese in 1992 and served Bishop James Garland in the area of culinary arts and housekeeping.

SISTERS OF THE PRESENTATION OF THE BLESSED VIRGIN MARY-PBVM. From 1984 to 1995 one member of the order offered pastoral ministry at St. Louis the King Parish in Harvey.

SISTERS OF ST. AGNES-CSA. Mainly teaching sisters, members of the Sisters of St. Agnes began serving in schools of the diocese in the fall of 1876 and continued to do so at the beginning of the 21st century. Responding to the call for teachers in the Menominee, Houghton, Marquette, Gladstone and Iron Mountain areas, the sisters have worked alongside members of other religious orders.

SISTERS OF ST. JOSEPH (NAZARETH, MICH.)-SSJ. From 1980 to 1990 two Sisters of Saint Joseph, from Nazareth, Mich., served the diocese in the areas of pastoral ministries and administration.

SISTERS OF ST. JOSEPH (CONCORDIA, KAN.)-CSJ. The Sisters of St. Joseph, from Concordia, Kan., began their educational apostolate at St. Anne Parish in Escanaba in 1891. From 1896 to 1971 sisters ministered at St. Joseph Parish in Lake Linden. From 1911 to 1972, the sisters staffed All-Saints School in Gladstone. In 2000, one CSJ sister was serving in the Diocesan Department of Education and Faith Formation.

SISTERS OF ST. JOSEPH (CARONDELET, MO.)—CSJ. On Aug. 6, 1866, 13 Sisters of St. Joseph, from Carondelet, near St. Louis, Mo., arrived in the Diocese of Marquette to serve at Sault Ste. Marie, Hancock and L'Anse. At the beginning of the 21st century, five CSJ sisters continued their devoted efforts in the areas of education, pastoral ministry, jail ministries, family spirituality and parish team ministry.

SISTERS OF ST. JOSEPH-SSJ-TOSF. Sisters of St. Joseph of the Third Order of St. Francis, from Stevens Point, Wis., began administration of the Divine Infant of Prague Hospital in Wakefield in 1946. The facility was closed in 1978. Women from the order also served at Immaculate Conception Parish in Iron Mountain from 1961 to 1971.

SISTERS OF ST. PAUL DE CHARTRES-SPC. The Sisters of St. Paul de Chartres engage in all forms of activity in the areas of education, health care and social services. The order came to Marquette in 1963 at the request of Bishop Thomas L. Noa and established the order's first United States district in Marquette. The order's headquarters remains here. In the 1960s the Sisters of St. Paul de Chartres also started the Bishop Noa Home for the aged and retired priests. Their service to the diocese also included serving at St. William School in Menominee and at the parishes and schools of St. Christopher and St. Michael in Marquette. At the start of the 21st century, the women of the order continued staffing Bishop Noa Home, as well as working in Native American ministries and at Menominee.

SISTERS OF THE THIRD ORDER OF ST. FRANCIS-OSF. In 1884, five sisters from Peoria, Ill., were sent to take charge of the Delta County Hospital at the request of Bishop Vertin. In 1915 the sisters purchased the building and named it St. Francis Hospital. Members of the "hospital" sisters continue serving there. Additional hospitals in the diocese that had been managed by the Franciscans included St. Joseph in Menominee from 1889 to 1974 and St. Mary in Marquette from 1890 to 1973.

SISTERS SERVANTS OF THE IMMACULATE HEART OF MARY-IHM. The Sister Servants of the Immaculate Heart of Mary came to the Diocese of Marquette in 1972. Work first began at Holy Name Central School in Escanaba and later extended to religious education at Holy Spirit Parish in Menominee. Service also branched out to Northern Michigan University in Marquette and St. Isaac Jogues Parish in Sault Ste. Marie, where the women were still serving at the beginning of the 21st century.

URSULINE SISTERS-OSU. The first sisters to offer service to the Diocese of Marquette were the Ursulines, whose history here began June 1, 1853 and spanned nearly 150 years. Assistance was first requested from the order for a school in Sault Ste. Marie. Sisters of the Ursuline Order also conducted a school in Ontonagon's Holy Family Parish Convent for more than 100 years, from 1862 to 1967. Members of the order served in many areas of the U.P. until 1984.

Permanent Diaconate

In addition to sharing with bishops and priests the ministries of service, word and liturgy, the permanent deacon also serves as a symbol to all parishioners that they, too, are called to be servants of Christ. A man ordained a deacon may be married and likely is not hired by the church, but rather is employed in the secular world, yet he still devotes himself to service of the church.

A permanent deacon is a member of the clergy, ordained to holy orders, who makes a lasting commitment to serve the church. The office is called "permanent deacon" to distinguish it from the "transitional deacon," who is a seminarian ordained to the diaconate as the final step in his pastoral preparation for the priesthood. The ministry of the permanent deacon is threefold: ministry of service (charity and justice), ministry of the word (preaching, teaching and counseling), and ministry of liturgy (assisting at the altar, witnessing marriages, baptizing, presiding at wakes and funerals, leading prayer services, benedictions and other liturgical rites).

Pope Paul VI authorized the restoration of the order of Permanent Deacon in 1967, following the recommendation of the Second Vatican Council. The U.S. Bishops petitioned the Holy See for permission to restore the order in 1968.

The Diocese of Marquette began investigating the potential advantages of a permanent diaconate ministry in 1980. The first director of the Permanent Diaconate Program was appointed in June 1983. Between 1980 and 1989 three men were ordained permanent deacons for the diocese following the completion of training received elsewhere.

Beginning in 1989, the diocese began offering a deacon formation program in cooperation with neighboring dioceses. Essentially, the accepted candidate received his first two years of formation in the Diocese of Marquette and the remaining two years in the neighboring diocese. Upon completion of this program, the candidate was recommended to the bishop for ordination.

After the first seven years, the program was studied as to its future viability and coordination with the neighboring dioceses for the academic, spiritual and theological preparation of candidates. At that time, a three-year moratorium on new candidates to the diaconate was put into place. The examination of the program resulted in higher standards for evaluation of prospective candidates, more intense education and additional mentoring and supervision.

As of 2000, the diocese had 20 active permanent deacons in 20 parishes and 11 candidates. In 2004, there were 31 active permanent deacons in 24 parishes, one retired permanent deacon and 18 candidates. The program is in a continual state of growth and development. It is anticipated that there will be 50 permanent deacons in active ministry by 2010.

SISTERS OF ST. PAUL DE CHARTRES DISTRICT HOUSE, MARQUETTE

The Sisters of St. Paul de Chartres established their first United States district in the Diocese of Marquette in 1963. The congregation was born in France in the 17th century. Serving primarily in the fields of teaching and caring for the sick, the order is now in more than 30 countries.

The sisters came to the United States at the invitation of Bishop Thomas L. Noa, who wanted a novitiate established here so that women wanting to become a religious would not have to leave the Upper Peninsula. Bishop Noa was also looking for sisters to staff a home for elderly priests and others from the diocese. The first Sisters of St. Paul to arrive were nine women of French, Irish, and Canadian descent. Three of them began working immediately at the Bishop Noa Home in Escanaba. The other six took up residency at the Holy Family Orphanage in Marquette.

A novitiate was opened Jan. 25, 1964 in the Holy Family Orphanage. There were only two orphans waiting for their adoptions to be finalized when the sisters first arrived. The Sisters of St. Paul, Cuban refugees and Catholic Social Services offices each occupied separate floors of the building. The Sisters of St. Francis who were working at St. Mary's Hospital nearby also lived there. In 1966 the diocese's use for the former orphanage building changed and so the Sisters of St. Paul were dispersed to the St. John's Convent in Ishpeming and the St. John the Baptist and St. Michael Convents in Marquette while their current district house was being built.

The district house and novitiate located on the old Pinten Farm on County Road 492 near Marquette was completed in 1968. Bishop Charles A. Salatka blessed the facility July 14 of that year. Two council members of the congregation from Rome were present at the ceremony. The facility has a chapel, an oratory, living quarters and 20 bedrooms.

The sisters' service to U.P. Catholic schools and parishes began in 1964 when one Canadian and six Filipino sisters began staffing St. William's Catholic School in Menominee. Sisters continued to serve there through the consolidation of St. William's into the Menominee Catholic Central School System in 1972. The sisters served in Menominee until 1992.

From 1967 to 1987 Sisters of St. Paul also staffed St. Christopher's School in Marquette. Upon closure of that school, the sisters stayed on to administer in religious education and pastoral care. From 1987 to 1997 the sisters also responded to an invitation to serve St. Michael Parish and St. Michael School in Marquette.

After having served the needs of the Bishop Noa Home for 25 years, the community assumed full sponsorship of the retirement home in July 1988.

Additional contributions made to the diocese by the Sisters of St. Paul de Chartres include Native American ministry, prison ministry, summer religious education programs, youth ministry, adult faith formation, vocation promotion and visitation and care for the elderly and shut-ins. Since coming to Marquette, the sisters' service has also expanded elsewhere in the United States. In Washington, D.C., the sisters serve in the areas of religious education and as hospital chaplains.

As of 2004 there were 20 Sisters of St. Paul in the United States: four Americans, one Irish, one Thai, four Filipinos, two Koreans and eight Vietnamese.

MONASTERY OF THE HOLY CROSS, DISCALCED CARMELITE NUNS

In January 1949 Bishop Thomas L. Noa requested a Carmel be established in the Diocese of Marquette. At the time it was anticipated that a house in Escanaba, left to the diocese by the late Catherine Bonifas, would become the new home of the Carmelite Nuns. But the house was situated in a district not zoned for such a purpose. The bishop was unsuccessful in overcoming opposition to bring the nuns there.

Instead, the City of Iron Mountain—Bishop Noa's birthplace—welcomed the notion. An empty house on East B Street in that city would become the first U.P. monastery for the cloistered contemplative nuns.

On Nov. 21, 1950 four of the seven religious chosen as foundresses for the new Carmel left their Mother-Carmel in Grand Rapids, Mich., to oversee the remodeling necessary to transform the little house into a suitable monastery. The work was completed in about four months. On April 5, 1951, the three novices who had been waiting in Grand Rapids came to join the other nuns, making the community complete. Bishop Noa dedicated the new monastery on April 11, 1951.

Daily life within the monastery reflects St. Teresa's wish to preserve the eremitical spirit of the early hermits on Mt. Carmel within the loving and supportive setting of community life. Their schedule includes the Holy Sacrifice of the Mass, two hours of quiet prayer before the Blessed Sacrament, the entire Divine Office in Choir, the Rosary and Litany of the Blessed Virgin Mary, manual work and joy-filled recreation together. The silence observed throughout the day, except for the hour of recreation after both lunch and supper, is meant as an aid to the spirit of recollection so helpful for prayer. From Sept. 14 until Easter Day, the nuns keep a monastic fast. According to their rule the nuns do not eat meat unless health needs require it.

As a cloistered contemplative community, the nuns willingly embrace the obligation of papal enclosure, which they see as an important means of safeguarding that atmosphere of silence and solitude necessary for their life of prayer. Therefore, they do not leave the monastery except for medical attention, nor do they watch television or listen to the radio. While their chapel is open to the public for daily Mass, the nuns remain within the cloistered section of the chapel, separated by a metal grate reaching from floor to ceiling. Visitors who come to speak with the nuns are greeted from behind a wooden grate in their parlor.

Many renovations in those early years on East B Street allowed the nuns to live out their mission there. They supported themselves by baking and packaging altar breads for many U.P. churches, sewing vestments, laundering church linens and printing religious cards and invitations, as well as gardening to provide, as much as possible, the vegetables needed during the winter months. Another helpful means of support continues to be unsolicited gifts from many generous people.

As the community grew, the original house became unable to accommodate its needs. Fifteen years after the founding of the Carmel, a new monastery was built. Located at the intersection of Highways M-95 and U.S. 2 three miles north of Iron Mountain, the new site allowed the growing community to live in greater solitude and silence. The dedication of the Monastery of the Holy Cross was held July 16, 1966. Built in the shape of a cross, the new monastery included a simple chapel, choir for the nuns, refectory, and various workrooms, a small separate cell for each sister, a library, community room and classroom for the formation of new members.

An outdoor Way of the Cross was erected within the cloister in 1975. Bishop Charles A. Salatka formally blessed the stations in a ceremony held on Sunday, Oct. 26. On March 25, 1976 the Carmelites celebrated the 25th anniversary of the founding of the monastery with a special Mass of Thanksgiving at which Bishop Salatka was the principal celebrant. About 55 priests and a good number of the sisters' many friends participated. Later that year, on Aug. 22, Bishop Salatka once again celebrated a special Mass after blessing a new cemetery for the nuns.

On Sept. 15, 1978 the diocese's new bishop, the Most Rev. Mark F. Schmitt, came to the monastery to solemnly bless the newly-completed hermitage dedicated to St. Joseph. The area was erected at the edge of the woods inside the enclosure and allows the nuns to spend periods of time in even greater solitude and prayer.

The Chapel of the Holy Cross Monastery was designated a place of pilgrimage in 2000. Bishop James Garland, at the request of the Carmelite Nuns, deemed the chapel a place for gaining the Jubilee Indulgence in the Diocese of Marquette for those unable to travel to Rome and the Holy Land.

MONASTIC CHURCH OF SAINT JOHN THE THEOLOGIAN AND HOLY TRANSFIGURATION SKETE, EAGLE HARBOR

The Society of Saint John was founded as a Michigan non-profit corporation in April 1983 and established itself on the shore of Lake Superior near Eagle Harbor in late August of the same year. In 1995 the community came under the jurisdiction of the Ukrainian Catholic Eparchy of St. Nicholas in Chicago, receiving the designation Holy Transfiguration Skete. The founders were invested as monastic novices according to the Byzantine Rite at that time and received Monastic Consecration the following year. They were ordained deacons in the summer of 1997 and priests of the Byzantine (Ukrainian) Rite in fall of 1998.

To support the life of their community, the monks began picking wild berries and making jam in the spring of 1984. From humble beginnings the Jampot has grown into a much-frequented attraction for visitors to the Keweenaw Peninsula. With baked goods now accounting for about half of its sales, the business draws several thousand customers to its doors each year and serves hundreds of others by mail. Also begun in 1984, the monks' quarterly newsletter, *Magnificat*, now reaches some 29,000 households around the country.

The monks completed a new church and a major addition to their monastery in 2003. On August 24 of that year, Bishop Richard Seminack, Ukrainian Catholic Eparch of St. Nicholas, consecrated the new church. Bishop James Garland of the Diocese of Marquette participated in the service and concelebrated the Divine Liturgy with Bishop Seminack, the priest-monks of the monastery and priests from both the Diocese of Marquette and the Eparchy of St. Nicholas.

Ecclesial Lay Movements

ECCLESIAL LAY MOVEMENTS

Lay men and women are taking on new and expanding roles of apostolate in the Catholic Church. All of these individuals serve in a wide variety of ministries. Organizations, such as those whose histories are detailed below, are among the movements that foster this growth and participation. Additional ecclesial movements active in the Diocese of Marquette at the beginning of the 21st century include Blue Army, Catholic Foresters, Charismatic Renewal, Companions of Christ the Lamb, Cursillo, Koinonia, Lifeteen, Marriage Encounter, Neo Catechumenate, Perpetual Adoration, Third Order of Carmelites, White Army, Yahweh's Yoopers and Youth Encounter Christ.

DAUGHTERS OF ISABELLA. The first circle of the order of the Daughters of Isabella was formed in New Haven, Conn., in 1897 as an auxiliary of the Knights of Columbus. The first group chartered in this diocese was in the city of Marquette on April 16, 1925. The purpose of the organization is to unite all Catholic women into a fraternal order for spiritual benefits and to promote higher ideals within society. Local circles select charitable, spiritual, civic and social programs to sponsor in their area.

KNIGHTS OF COLUMBUS. The Knights of Columbus was founded by Father Michael J. McGivney of Waterbury, Conn., in 1882. Father McGivney envisioned a men's organization to foster the spiritual and family lives of members. The first U.P. council of the Knights of Columbus was established in Escanaba just 20 years later, in 1902. The organization encourages men to be a part of Christian family life by participating in social and fraternal programs of service to the church, the community and youth.

LEGION OF MARY. The Legion of Mary was started in 1921 in Dublin, Ireland. The first Curia in the Diocese of Marquette, Our Lady of the North in the city of Marquette, was formed June 4, 1960. The thrust of the organization is for the personal, spiritual growth of its members through understanding and living a practical love of neighbor. First and foremost the organization is devoted to the Blessed Virgin Mary. Active members are men and women over the age of 18 who spend at least two hours a week performing an active duty assigned by the praesidium, such as visiting the sick, elderly and home-bound, new parish members and inactive Catholics. Other works include assisting with CCD and Catholic school programs, helping at parishes and through other volunteer organizations. Junior members are boys and girls under 18 who perform one hour of active work per week. Auxiliary members recite the rosary and Legion of Mary prayers daily, offering them for the intentions of Our Blessed Lady.

MARQUETTE DIOCESAN COUNCIL OF CATHOLIC WOMEN. The Marquette Diocesan Council of Catholic Women was formed in 1948 as a way of uniting the efforts of many parish women's organizations. The MDCCW is an affiliate of the National Council of Catholic Women, started in 1920. The organization supports, empowers and educates all Catholic women in spirituality, leadership and service with programs that respond with Gospel values to the needs of the church and society in the modern world. This mission is carried out through the work of six commissions: church, community concerns, family concerns, international concerns, legislation and organization. The MDCCW organizes diocesan events to help women gain a deeper understanding of the teachings of the church and to call them to action in living and proclaiming the good news of the Gospel. Membership in the MDCCW is open to Catholic women as individuals or as parish women's groups that support the NCCW Mission.

SECULAR FRANCISCAN ORDER. The Secular Franciscans is a community of men and women who make a solemn promise to pattern their lives after Christ in the spirit of St. Francis. St. Francis of Assisi founded the international order in 1209.

Catholics in the Upper Peninsula first began making the solemn promise in the 1920s. As many as five fraternities have existed in the diocese—in Iron Mountain, Calumet, Chassell, Marquette and Escanaba.

Secular Franciscans are active in their parishes and with various community ministries. Some of their work in the Diocese of Marquette is through the St. Vincent de Paul Society, Pregnancy Services, Natural Family Planning and faith formation programs. Secular Franciscans are also active in prison ministry, eucharistic adoration and liturgical ministries. The secular order formation program consists of a minimum three-year period of both discernment and formation. The process of becoming a professed Secular Franciscan is a journey that involves three separate stages and culminates in a lifelong commitment to live the Gospel following the example of St. Francis of Assisi.

SERRA CLUB. Serra International is an organization designed to foster vocations and to affirm and support those who have chosen the ordained ministries and religious lifestyles. The organization began in Seattle in 1935 and is now thriving in 32 countries. The first Serra Club in the Diocese of Marquette was chartered in Escanaba in May 1969. Members pray for church vocations daily, hold regular Masses for vocations and attempt to develop an awareness of the need for vocations. Regular activities are held to show support and appreciation for priests and religious. The work the group does also fosters the spiritual growth of its members.

ST. VINCENT DE PAUL SOCIETY. Since the 1940s the Society of St. Vincent de Paul has been helping the poor, sick and less fortunate through the distribution of food, clothing, medicine and assistance with payments of rent, utilities and heating bills.

The Society was founded by Frederic Ozanam in Paris, France, in 1833 and named after St Vincent de Paul, the patron saint of the poor. As a law student, Ozanam was challenged with the question: "What is your church doing to help the poor today?" That is the question that inspires Vincentians to this day.

One man in the Upper Peninsula, Jack DesJardins, made a promise that ignited the spread of the society throughout the Diocese of Marquette. His daughter was struck with a serious illness, and if she survived he vowed to dedicate himself to furthering the organization. He started in Marquette by opening a store and activating conferences. His work spread across the Upper Peninsula and at the time of his death in 1980 there were 36 conferences and nine stores. In 2005 there were 38 conferences and 20 stores.

TEKAKWITHA CIRCLES. Blessed Kateri Tekakwitha was born in 1656 in Auriesville, New York. She is revered for her extraordinary practices of all virtues and her devotion to teaching prayers to children and helping the sick and aged. In 1939 the national Tekakwitha Conference was started for the evangelization of Native American Catholics and for promoting the canonization of Blessed Kateri Tekakwitha. The first Tekakwitha Circle in the Diocese of Marquette was started in the city of Marquette in 1987. The group strives to empower Native American Catholics to live in harmony with both Catholic and native spirituality and to pray for Blessed Kateri Tekakwitha's canonization, to share the story of her life and to follow her example of holiness. Members are encouraged to participate in the Michigan Tekakwitha Conference and the National Tekakwitha Conference.

Diocesan Sponsored Services

DIOCESAN CURIA

The bishop's residence was constructed in 1932 and served as the Chancery Office building. Years later, an addition was made to the residence to house the expanding offices. As more departments evolved over the years, the offices were forced to function from different locations. The original expansion to the bishop's residence was called the Pastoral Office and was located at 444 S. Fourth St. The building housed the Office of the Bishop, the Department of Administration and Finance and the Department of Ministry Personnel.

A block away, at 347 Rock St., a building constructed in 1955 as a convent for the Sisters of St. Joseph became a diocesan-owned office building in 1981. In early 2005 it housed the departments of Faith Formation and Education, Communication and Catholic Social Services, as well as offices for the Diocesan Archives and the Bishop Baraga Association. For a time prior to 1981, CSS and the education department were housed in the former Holy Family Orphans Home and *The U.P. Catholic* newspaper had offices in a small building behind the orphanage.

All offices from both locations, except for Diocesan Archives and Bishop Baraga Association and CSS, were relocated to 117 W. Washington St., Marquette, in July 2005. The Pastoral Office was converted into priest apartments in 2006.

THE OFFICE OF THE BISHOP. The diocesan bishop shepherds the diocese through the threefold ministries of teaching, sanctifying and governing. The bishop oversees the five diocesan departments and governs the diocese with assistance from seven vicars, the vicar general and the judicial vicar. The bishop's primary consulting bodies for the spiritual ministry of the diocese are the Presbyteral Council, Diocesan Pastoral Council and Diocesan Finance Council.

The chancellor, in service to the bishop, handles canonical matters and ensures that the acts of the diocesan curia are drawn up, dispatched and archived. In service to the parishes, the Office of the Chancellor answers inquiries regarding church matters.

The ministry of the Marriage Tribunal to separated and divorced persons is to uphold and preserve the integrity of the Sacrament of Matrimony.

COMMUNICATION. Bishop Francis Magner began using the mass media to proclaim Catholic truth in the 1940s. Father David Spelgatti was named editor of the official diocesan paper, *The Northern Michigan Edition of Our Sunday Visitor*, first published Jan. 6, 1946. On July 9, 1971, the weekly newspaper became a locally produced product and was renamed *The U.P. Catholic*. As a means of evangelization, *The U.P. Catholic* became a full coverage newspaper in 1999 and has since been mailed to every registered Catholic home.

From the start of Upper Michigan's first radio station in 1929, broadcasting of the Mass and other special programs, such as "Northern Michigan Catholic Hour," started in 1944, have played an important role in bringing the word of God to people throughout the U.P. The diocese appointed a director of radio and television in 1967 and became an affiliate of the Catholic Telecommunications Network of America in 1988. A full-time Office of Communications was established in 1979. Today the office distributes news releases and produces radio and television spots on diocesan programs and events. The office also offers assistance to church leaders in the field of communication.

FAITH FORMATION AND EDUCATION. The Diocese of Marquette's first organized department was that of education. The first superintendent of Catholic schools was Monsignor O'Neil D'Amour, 1953-1968. Father Aloysius Hasenberg began serving as assistant superintendent in 1957.

Under the direction of Monsignor D'Amour's successor, Father Lawrence Gauthier—appointed superintendent of schools in 1968—a centralization of services began to take shape. In order to unite the Catholic schools in meeting the challenges they were facing, and to better fulfill the diocesan mission of providing total Catholic education, the Office of Education and its divisions were established July 1, 1971. The divisions were Elementary and Secondary Education, Religious Education, Adult and Continuing Education, Campus Ministry, Personnel and Vocations. Over the next several years this structure was continually adapted to meet the changing needs of the times.

The Diocese of Marquette's education leaders were at the forefront of national efforts to cope with the changing times for Catholic schools in the United States. Father Gauthier produced the first diocesan-wide study for Catholic school education and a booklet on parish boards of education and their relationship to parish councils. Both were widely used throughout the country.

In order to sustain a total education in the most recent times, the Department of Faith Formation and Education continues to oversee the Catholic schools of the diocese. The department also works directly with parish leadership to promote lifelong personal growth and faith formation. The department assists parishes with youth ministry, the Rite of Christian Initiation of Adults, and social justice and evangelization ministries. It also oversees the Ecclesial Ministry Institute, originally called the Lay Ministry Leadership School, and a theology-ministry graduate program. Diocesan Study Days are offered routinely. The Marquette Diocesan Resource Library maintains a collection of videos and books.

FINANCE AND ADMINISTRATION. In 1983, the diocese, as required by the Code of Canon Law, established the Diocesan Finance Council and appointed a finance officer. Prior to that time a Diocesan Planning Commission, Finance Commission and Building Commission acted as advisories to the bishop on matters of property, money and building issues. The first full-time Director of Administration and Finance was appointed in 1985.

The Department of Administration and Finance is responsible for all the temporalities of the diocese including the annual operating budget, investments, insurance and benefit programs, legal matters, building matters, diocesan and parish real estate transactions, parish planning, clergy retirement program and diocesan cemetery administration.

The Upper Peninsula Catholic Services Appeal was started in 1968 under the direction of Bishop Charles Salatka. Each member of the diocese is urged to provide financial support for parish services, ministries, activities and programs of the diocese. In 2005 the UPCSA goal was about $1.59 million.

The Development Office was started in 2000 to secure gifts for Legacy of Faith, a campaign to seed the Endowment Foundation of the diocese. The foundation was begun in 1999 to provide continuous support to Catholic schools, religious education, Catholic Social Services and funds for special ministries. The Development Office manages the Legacy of Faith grant-making program, supports the Catholic school endowments, works to address parish capital needs and assists with offertory campaigns. The office also promotes planned giving.

MINISTRY PERSONNEL. In 1991, the Department of Ministry Personnel was started to focus on the promotion, recruitment, encouragement and support of the priesthood. The offices of Vocations, Priest Personnel and Continuing Education of the Clergy aid in accomplishing these goals.

The Office of the Permanent Diaconate provides for the recruitment, formation and support of the permanent deacons of the diocese. The director for women religious serves as a part of this department, offering support and formation opportunities for the religious sisters of the diocese.

The Department of Ministry Personnel oversees the Campus ministry, prison ministry, Native American ministry, hospital ministry, outreach ministry to the poor, scouting and the Marquette Diocesan Council of Catholic Women.

The Bishop Baraga Association was established in 1930 to promote the cause for canonization of Bishop Frederic Baraga. The association publishes a 16-page quarterly newsletter entitled The Baraga Bulletin. The diocese's archival collection contains nearly 2000 letters of Frederic Baraga's correspondence, several artifacts that belonged to Baraga and volumes of church related material and resources pertaining to the local history.

Catholic Social Services

In 1946 the diocese started a Social Work Office within the Holy Family Orphans Home in Marquette. The purpose of the office was to develop a program for finding the orphans adoptive parents and foster parents. In 1952 Catholic Social Services (CSS) was incorporated as a separate entity. The orphanage closed in 1965. In order to foster positive family units and reduce the incidents of child neglect, CSS began offering social services to families, children and individuals throughout the local community.

The foster home program was phased out in 1967 and the adoption program ended temporarily in 1969 after the Michigan Children's Aid Society took the responsibility to place children in homes in the U.P. CSS then concentrated its efforts on family and individual counseling.

In 1973 CSS was again licensed as a child welfare agency offering a full range of child welfare services, including foster care and adoption.

The founding dates of the six U.P. offices are: Escanaba, 1954; Houghton, 1956; Sault Ste. Marie, 1958; Marquette, 1962; Iron Mountain, 1966 and Ironwood, 1989.

The full extent of CSS services at the start of the 21st century includes counseling for individuals, married couples and families, pregnancy counseling, post-abortion counseling and problem gambling counseling, as well as services to various groups including women and shoplifters. Additional services include adoption and foster care placement and birth child or parent search.

The Family Life Office coordinates programs and services to minister to families in all stages of development. Training, resources and support for marriage preparation and enrichment are provided, as well as support for Natural Family Planning, Respect Life and Project Rachel. The office assists and supports peer ministries, such as New Dawn for the divorced and separated and Engaged Encounter.

CEMETERIES

HOLY CROSS CEMETERY, ESCANABA

Holy Cross Cemetery in Escanaba was created as the result of a merger on June 1, 1947 between St. Joseph's and St. Anne's church cemeteries.

In the late 1800s, both the St. Joseph and St. Anne churches purchased separate but adjoining land for use by their members. In the early 1900s, St. Patrick's also acquired land near the existing cemeteries. Bishop Francis Magner arranged for the reorganization of the separate cemeteries into one operated by the diocese.

Through donations from Catherine Bonifas, a cemetery chapel was dedicated Sept. 6, 1948. Located to the right of the main entrance, the chapel measures 25 feet by 36 feet and has accommodations for about 100 people.

In 1950 Babyland was established at the cemetery. A statue of the Guardian Angel marks the place where babies are buried. In July 1995 the Knights of Columbus of the area joined forces to erect a tomb for unborn children, victims of abortion. Parishioners of the former St. Peter the Fisherman Church in Fayette donated a statue of the Blessed Virgin Mary for Babyland.

On Memorial Day, June 2, 1963 Bishop Thomas L. Noa dedicated a five-foot bronze statue, which stands at the head of a newly-expanded area that provided 1,400 new gravesites.

In the spring of 1983 the Holy Cross Mausoleum Chapel was built.

HOLY CROSS CEMETERY, MARQUETTE

The Diocese of Marquette first purchased land for Holy Cross Cemetery along Wright Street in Marquette in 1891. This new cemetery would take the place of the one located along Pioneer Road and Marquette County Road 553 in South Marquette. (The Pioneer Road cemetery operated from 1861 to 1900. The last of the stones from that facility were relocated to Holy Cross in 1994.) The first 10 acres of the 38-acre Holy Cross Cemetery were cleared for use in 1892. A caretaker's house was erected at the cemetery entrance in 1932. An irrigation system was first installed in the cemetery in 1953.

On Nov. 9, 1945 The Rt. Rev. Joseph G. Pinten became the first person entombed in the Holy Cross Chapel Mausoleum Crypt.

The original cemetery chapel was replaced in 1965. The first Mass in the new facility was offered on Nov. 2, All Souls Day. The chapel still functions today with mostly special services, such as those for Memorial Day.

Holy Cross first allowed cremains to be buried in the cemetery June 18, 1977. In the spring of 1983 the Holy Cross Mausoleum Chapel Columbarium Niches was built. The first entombment was placed within the mausoleum walls that spring.

The Stations of the Cross from the former St. John the Baptist Church in Marquette were erected at Holy Cross Cemetery in 1987. (The parish had been closed the previous year.) The Stations were encased and placed along the cemetery roads. The Burch Cross—named for its donor—has graced the cemetery entrance since 1988. The cross was moved to the new main entrance in 1995.

On May 8, 1994 Bishop James H. Garland dedicated the Tomb of the Unborn. The monument, donated by the Knights of Columbus of the diocese, features a drawing of the Holy Family.

Improvements made to the cemetery in 1997 include the installation of a garden area known as the Rosary Garden, widening and paving of the road system, and the construction of 50 double and six single lawn crypts. An additional expantion in 2004 brought the total number of lawn crypts at the cemetery to about 260.

ORPHANAGES

ST. JOSEPH HOME, ASSININS

Father Gerhard Terhorst built the first home for orphans on the grounds of Holy Name of Jesus Catholic Mission in Assinins in 1881. Orphaned boys and girls, formerly housed at the diocesan-operated Aemilianum facility in Marquette, were transferred to Assinins in 1902. Sisters of St. Agnes from Fond du Lac, Wis., ran the facility for 50 years, from 1906 to 1956. Prior to that time the Sisters of St. Joseph of Carondelet staffed the school and home.

In 1928 a modern facility, dedicated as the St. Joseph Home, replaced the original at Assinins. The people of the Copper Country now had the home under their wing and provided regular financial support. Vegetables and meat came from the orphanage's own cattle and gardens.

In 1946 the diocese started a social services program at Holy Family Orphans Home in Marquette. In 1952 Catholic Social Services was incorporated as an entity separate from the orphanage. The organization began working to find private homes for the orphans and to provide counseling for families in need throughout the Upper Peninsula.

Changing trends in social services and mounting operational costs led to the amalgamation of the Assinins and Marquette orphanages in the late 1950s. It was determined that modernization efforts would be too costly at Assinins. Therefore, in the summer of 1956, St. Joseph Home was closed and residents were moved to Holy Family in Marquette. At the time, it was projected that about 100 young people would be living at the Marquette facility.

Orphanage directors included Fathers Melchior Faust (dates of service not available), Casper Douenburg, 1928-1936; Anthony Waechter, 1936-1941; Casimir Adasiewicz, 1941-1953, and Edward Wenzel, 1953-1956.

Upon the closure of the orphanage, the Assinins building was purchased by the Capuchin Province of St. Joseph and made into a novitiate.

In 1971 the Capuchins deeded the building to the Keweenaw Bay Indian Community (KBIC). That group operated the facility as a tribal center, housing the tribal court and offices, among other services. In August 1995, a political dispute led a group of disenfranchised tribal members to take over the tribal center. Shortly thereafter, the group found refuge at The Most Holy Name of Jesus Church. The people occupied the center and surrounding grounds for more than a year. The dispute eventually led to the demise of the 1928 orphanage building. The KBIC had the building demolished Feb. 17, 1997.

HOLY FAMILY ORPHANS HOME, MARQUETTE

Holy Family Orphans Home in Marquette was dedicated in October 1915. Prior to that time, the diocese had run the Aemilianum, a facility on Rock and Fifth Streets in Marquette, from the 1870s to 1902, when boys and girls were moved to the St. Joseph Home in Assinins.

Plans for the new facility in Marquette began in 1903. The four-story structure on Fisher and Altamont streets was expanded in 1922. The building consisted of a large kitchen, dining room and chapel on the first floor. The second floor had classrooms and a recreation room. Dormitories and living space made up the third and fourth floors.

The orphanage used the farm of Father Joseph G. Pinten to grow vegetables. Cows, pigs and chickens were kept for milk, eggs and meat. The farm, located on County Road 492, operated into the late 1950s.

Sisters of St. Agnes from Fond du Lac, Wis. were in charge of the daily operation of Holy Family. A resident priest served as director. The local community and parishes throughout the diocese offered financial support. Some parents were able to provide a monthly boarding fee.

The institution housed up to 200 boys and girls at one time. Life at the orphanage was strictly regimented. Daily Mass was followed by breakfast, chores and a full day of classes. The children had dinner, playtime and said the rosary every night before bed. A playground outside the facility had basketball courts and a football field in the summer and a toboggan hill or ski runs in the winter. The kids were taken on hikes and picnics at Presque Isle and every summer on a two-week campout at Camp Miniyata, located west of Ishpeming.

Holidays were fun times at Holy Family. Halloween parties were held and on Christmas Eve a band was brought in to accompany caroling. Everyone received gifts.

Father Emil Beyer formed Catholic Social Services in 1946. The organization, housed in the orphanage, aimed to place the orphans in foster homes or with adoptive families. The social services program was expanded in 1953 to include child welfare, and unmarried mothers' and family services. By 1965 the orphanage was no longer necessary and Holy Family was closed.

In the early 1960s the former orphanage building was used to house Cuban boys placed there through a Catholic Welfare Bureau program called Pedro Pan. The building was also used as a convent and for diocesan offices. Other organizations rented space until the facility was closed and permanently vacated. In 1986 the diocese sold the orphanage building to a group of investors.

Orphanage directors were Fr. Joseph G. Pinten, 1915-1921; Msgr. Henry Buchholtz, 1921-1923; Msgr. George Dingfelder, 1923-1935; Msgr. Martin Melican, 1935; Fr. Emil Beyer, 1945-1951, and Fr. Wilbur Gibbs 1951-1963.

Retreat Centers

Marygrove Retreat Center, Garden

The original vision for the Marygrove Retreat Center in Garden was to provide a place for women to experience a spiritual getaway. The men of the diocese had been enjoying a three-day annual retreat at Camp Plagens near Watersmeet, but facilities there were said to be too rustic for the ladies.

In 1948 the late Catherine Bonifas of Escanaba, wanting to do something for the church in Garden, purchased the former LaMotte Cancer Center and gave the building and 21 acres of land to the diocese.

On June 29, 1948, Bishop Thomas L. Noa dedicated the retreat center to the Immaculate Heart of Mary. The women of Garden, Cooks, Fayette and Nahma made the first retreat beginning July 9. The original facilities could accommodate about 36 people. At that time the diocese was one of very few in the country to run a retreat center. Most retreats were offered by religious orders.

Women weren't the only ones attending retreats at Marygrove. Sessions were also held from the beginning for men, high school-aged boys and girls, married couples and Catholic school teachers. In 1953, priests of the diocese began using the center for their annual retreats.

In order to assure continued maintenance and future development of the property, women of the diocese began to raise money for Marygrove by opening a re-sale shop and lending library in Escanaba.

The retreat center thrived and the need for increased facilities was evident. In April 1961 Bishop Noa announced the new Diocesan Development Fund's first project would be an addition to Marygrove. Construction of a building containing 6,600 square feet was completed in the spring of 1962. A new chapel, eight bedrooms and dining and kitchen facilities were added to bring the total capacity of the facility up to about 75 people.

Men's and women's Cursillo weekends were first held at Marygrove in 1974. Youth Encounter retreats began in 1979. The 1980s saw the start of non-Roman Cursillo weekends, family retreats, parish pilgrimages and St. Vincent de Paul Society retreats. Among the other specialized retreats are programs for lay ministers and First Knights of Columbus.

In 1992 a handicap accessible entrance with an elevator and a director's residence were completed. On the grounds at Marygrove is a monument honoring the diocese's deceased bishops, priests and deacons. Inside the center is a work of art listing all of the Orders of Women Religious to have served the diocese.

Former retreat center directors include Fathers Arnold Thompson, James Schaeffer, Msgr. Ronald Bassett, Joseph Callari, James Donnelly, William Richards, Matthew Nyman, Msgr. Timothy Desrochers and James Ziminski.

Camp Plagens, Watersmeet

For more than 30 years the Diocese of Marquette provided a children's summer camp, Camp Plagens. Situated on Moon Lake along Highway 45, south of Watersmeet, the facility was originally a Civilian Conservation Camp in the 1930s.

The U.P. Laymen's Retreat Association was organized in 1943. The group acquired the former CCC camp and held retreats at the site until 1953 when facilities were turned into a Catholic Youth Camp. Father David Spelgatti was the UPLRA chaplain and was instrumental in organizing the camp. He remained at the core of the group for 25 years. Camp Plagens was named to honor Bishop Joseph C. Plagens, the sixth bishop of the diocese (1936-1940).

In 1958 St. John's Chapel, the original Watersmeet church built in 1880, was moved eight miles to Camp Plagens. The chapel was used for worship services for the camp participants and also on weekends for residents of the area.

Camp facilities included barracks halls with accommodations for as many as 95 campers and a main hall with dining facilities.

Former campers say the experience of 10- to 12-day stays at the camp left an impression that has remained with them. Sessions for boys and girls ages 8-11 and 12-15 brought young people a variety of activities including horseback riding, archery, arts and crafts, hiking, baseball, volleyball, movie showings, swimming and more. Daily Mass and recitation of the rosary were part of the routine.

Girls' sessions were staffed by high school- and college-age girls, and the boys' sessions were led by high schoolers and college seminarians. Many future priests of the diocese were moved to test the waters of a vocation due in part to their experience at Camp Plagens.

Father Samuel Bottoni of Immaculate Heart of Mary Parish in Watersmeet served as the camp director for 30 years.

Decreased camp attendance in the 1970s and 1980s and the inability to cover the cost of much-needed improvements to the facilities led to the eventual demise of Camp Plagens. The final sessions were held in the summer of 1987. The Upper Peninsula Laymen's Retreat Association also held its last retreat at the camp in 1987 before the group disbanded the following year.

Father Bottoni continued to offer services at St. John Chapel in the summertime. In 1994 a group of parishioners eagerly renovated the interior and exterior of the historic church.

In 1996 the camp facilities were sold to the Lac Vieux Desert Band of Lake Superior Chippewa Indians. The former St. John Chapel is now the Watersmeet Historical Society Museum.

INSTITUTIONS

Catholic High Schools

Sacred Heart Central High School, Calumet

The first high school courses were added to the Sacred Heart Grade School curriculum in 1893. The first graduating class consisted of four boys and four girls.

The high school itself was built in 1902. Students were admitted on a tuition basis. Although Sacred Heart Parish built the school, Catholics from other area parishes also attended on an equal basis. A wing was added onto the school in 1913 to accommodate a library and science labs, in addition to satisfying other needs. The auditorium was later remodeled into a gymnasium.

Music became a main focus of the school in 1917, thanks to Sister M. Rose de Lima who started a high school orchestra, mandolin group and the Faber Band.

The school also became the place where many of the church's social organizations gathered. The basement facilities were equipped with bowling alleys, a swimming pool and billiard tables.

After 58 years, the end of an era came when Sacred Heart graduated its last class in 1960. The facilities were no longer considered adequate and with declining enrollment a continuing trend, it was decided not to build a new school. The former landmark of the original grade school and the high school were torn down and the lots were sold in 1967. The Sacred Heart Grade School continued until 1982.

Holy Name High School, Escanaba

A modern, central high school was opened in Escanaba in the fall of 1954. First year enrollment numbers were double that of the former St. Joseph High School. The number of students totaled some 700 in the late 1960s.

The new building, located at 409 S. 22nd St., was made possible largely through a bequest by Catherine Bonifas for a central high school. The half-million dollar pledge from Mrs. Bonifas was nearly doubled by a community fund-drive that netted almost $500,000.

Throughout much of the history of the school, boys and girls were separated for most classes. The girls' classes were taught by School Sisters of Notre Dame from Milwaukee, Wis., Franciscan Sisters of Christian Charity and Dominican Sisters of Adrian, Mich. The boys' classes were taught by Christian Brothers from St. Paul, Minn. A diocesan priest served as school administrator.

In addition to all of the Escanaba parishes, the centralized school system was supported by parishes in Gladstone, Flat Rock, Schaffer, Perronville, Bark River and Rapid River. Students from as far away as Northland and Hermansville also attended the school.

Holy Name had an outstanding drama department that offered students from rural communities opportunities that they would not have otherwise experienced. A men's booster club, credited with building the school's football field, supported Holy Name's top-notch athletic department. After much perseverance, the school was finally admitted into the Great Northern Athletic Conference.

By 1971 the school was forced to close mostly because of financial constraints. News of the closure was announced in February. The last class graduated that spring. The seniors held a Commemoration Weekend May 29-30. An open house, dinner and dance and a Mass and picnic were held to pay tribute to the tradition of the school.

Former students came together again when an all-school reunion was held July 10-11, 1998 at the Ruth Butler Building on the U.P. State Fairgrounds. Nearly 1,000 people attended the festivities, which included a celebration Mass, dinner and dancing, as well as a golf outing and open house of the current Holy Name Grade School. Many of the high school's graduates continue supporting the grade school system.

ST. JOSEPH HIGH SCHOOL, ESCANABA

St. Joseph High School in Escanaba served as that city's only source for secondary Catholic education for 70 years, from 1884 to 1954. Too small to accommodate all of the prospective students from across Delta County, the school closed to make way for a consolidated Holy Name High School.

From the beginning, Sisters of Notre Dame from Milwaukee, Wis., staffed St. Joseph's. The Franciscan priests serving the parish taught religion and performed other functions at the school.

St. Joseph's saw its first graduating class in 1888. That year 11 women received diplomas. Boys and girls from all of the Escanaba parishes were enrolled at the school, but space limitations forced many to attend public schools.

On Dec. 17, 1914, an overheated stove caused a fire that destroyed the old Green School. A new school was constructed with zeal and dedicated on Dec. 12, 1915. The William Bonifas Auditorium and Gymnasium was built in 1937.

The student council was introduced in 1928 and the student spiritual leadership council in 1939. Extracurricular activities included sports, such as basketball and football, and an orchestra and glee club, forensics and debate. A school annual, *The Purple and Gold,* was published for many years. In the school's heyday a school paper, *The Trojan*, was published bi-monthly.

Final commencement exercises at St. Joseph High School were held June 5, 1954. Bishop Thomas L. Noa addressed the class at the ceremony. That fall students attended the new Holy Name High School.

St. Ambrose/Ironwood Catholic High School

In 1892 Father Martin Kehoe, influenced by Bishop Frederic Baraga, established the first parochial school in Ironwood. Father Kehoe enlisted the help of the timbermen and miners to build the school, to be located on five lots on East Ayer Street, just a short distance from the "downtown" area and up the street from St. Ambrose Church. The Ancient Order of Hibernians (an Irish fraternal society) was instrumental in organizing construction. Franciscan Sisters of Christian Charity of Manitowoc, Wis., came to staff the school. Ninety percent of the students were Irish; thus St. Ambrose School got the name "Fighting Irish."

The high school department was added in 1894 and saw its first two graduates in 1897.

In 1901 and 1904 additional room was added to the school to meet the increasing population of students. In 1913 the high school was accredited through the University of Michigan and the Catholic University of America, the first high school in the western Upper Peninsula to attain the honor.

In the mid-1920s the elementary and middle school students were moved out of the high school building. Athletics became a part of the high school between 1910 and 1927. Football and basketball were the main offerings. The name of the team at that time was the Ironwood Ramblers.

In the ensuing years, the high school curriculum was expanded. Students were offered a variety of academic and "commercial" courses, including advanced mathematics, biology, chemistry, public speaking, chorus, orchestra, home economics, art, history, ethics and Latin.

In 1951 two sisters on staff at the high school luckily discovered a fire that could have destroyed the building. Instead only minor damage was incurred.

A new convent was built for the sisters in 1961.

In 1965, with the mines starting to close and the population declining, the Gogebic Range area moved to assure a quality Catholic education would continue. The three local parishes joined together to support the high school. The name of the high school was changed to Ironwood Catholic High School.

In 1970 the high school, St. Ambrose Grade School and St. Michael-Holy Trinity Grade School merged into one school system, Ironwood Catholic Grade School. With the high school building deteriorating and the student population falling, a decision was made to move all the grade school students into the St. Michael-Holy Trinity School building on Arch Street, leaving the school building at 106 S. Marquette St. available for use as a high school. The 75 year-old structure on Ayer Street was still used for some classes.

A gymnasium to allow for physical education classes and sporting events was ready for use at the high school for the 1968-1969 basketball season. In 1970 all classes were moved to the Marquette Street School. Several additional classrooms were needed during this time, so a portion of the church basement was converted into two classrooms.

With the population continuing to decline and the school being forced to hire lay teachers, the Home and School Association took on fund-raising efforts, such as an annual spaghetti feed, bingo and a calendar club raffle. An endowment fund was also established.

Inevitably, Ironwood Catholic High School, the last of the diocese's remaining high schools, was forced to close after the 1985 school year.

BISHOP BARAGA HIGH SCHOOL, MARQUETTE

The Ursuline Sisters opened Marquette's first Catholic School in 1867. In 1872 the Sisters of St. Joseph, of Carondelet, Mo., purchased the school from the Ursulines and named it St. Joseph Academy. In 1903 Bishop Baraga School was built to replace the St. Joseph Academy, which had been destroyed by fire earlier that year.

In a grand ceremony attended by much of the diocesan community, Bishop Frederick Eis laid the cornerstone on Nov. 1, 1903. The first class graduated from Bishop Baraga High in 1906.

Until 1957 the building housed both grade school and high school classes. High school classes were held on the second floor and younger grades on the first. Eventually, increased enrollment led to the building becoming exclusively high school.

Bishop Baraga High School contained the city's largest auditorium. A seating capacity of 1,000 allowed it to be used for countless school and community events. In the 1940s Werner Library was completed. A new gymnasium wing was added in the 1960s.

The success of the school's business education department was well recognized throughout the Upper Peninsula and employees sought its graduates. Oratory was a popular extra-curricular activity at the high school. Bishop Baraga's boys' basketball team won the State Class C Championship in 1969.

The last class to graduate from Bishop Baraga High was in June 1969. The school was forced to close due to a lack of financial support, the inability to improve facilities and the loss of the religious teaching staff.

Upon the closure of the school, the city of Marquette rented the facilities for a variety of community events. In 1975 the city bought the property. The school was later razed to make room for a new city hall.

In July 1995, about 1,200 people returned to Marquette for the first Bishop Baraga High School all-class reunion. Graduates representing classes from 1920 through the 1960s attended a July 8 dinner held at Lakeview Arena. The day consisted of a commemorative Mass concelebrated by Bishop James Garland and former priests of the school. A dinner, formal program and dancing were also part of the festivities.

St. Paul High School, Negaunee

The first class to graduate from Negaunee's St. Paul High School did so on June 12, 1938. The parish continued to support the school until it closed in 1966.

Father Frederick Eis planted the seed for the parochial school system in Negaunee when he started the parish's first school in 1882. Sisters of St. Joseph, of Carondelet, Mo., arrived in Negaunee that year starting 93 years of continued service. The original four-room building saw the addition of three more classrooms by the turn of the century.

In 1932, a new grade school, high school and convent were built. The grade school opened that year and the high school followed two years later. In the fall of 1934 there were only freshmen. A new class was added each successive year. Nineteen boys and girls made up the first graduating class.

In 1955 the school saw the expansion of the science, business and library departments. In 1959 a physical education program was started. Extra curricular programs included sports, drama and forensics. The school was a charter member of the Upper Peninsula Division of the Junior Classical League.

In 1966 the high school was closed. Declining enrollment and financial constraints were among the reasons for its demise.

Sixty years after the first class graduated from St. Paul High School, the first all-school reunion saw the return of some 600 former pupils to the Negaunee Ice Arena July 11, 1998. A commemorative Mass, dinner and dance were held to honor the heritage of the school.

Loretto Catholic High School, Sault Ste. Marie

Loretto Catholic Central High School in Sault Ste. Marie started as Loretto Academy, a finishing school for girls, in 1899. Sisters of the Institute of the Blessed Virgin Mary, or Loretto Sisters, came to Sault Ste. Marie and staffed the school. A diocesan priest carried out the school administration. The academy's first facility was located on Armory Place and was enlarged in the early 1900s. Loretto became coeducational in 1944 with its first graduates in 1948.

Despite many updates over the years, by the 1960s the original building was no longer suitable to the changing needs of the school. A new building was constructed at the south end of Minneapolis Street. Groundbreaking ceremonies were held July 26, 1964. The new structure incorporated the most modern concepts in school buildings, including movable walls and carpeted floors to cut down on noise. The curriculum too, was planned to meet future needs.

Classes began in the new school Nov. 8, 1965. Voluntary pledges toward construction of the modern facility totaled more than $400,000. The original facility was razed in 1966.

The school continued to operate until 1971 when financial constraints forced its closure. At that time the facilities were sold to the public school system.

URSULINE ACADEMY, ST. IGNACE

At the request of Bishop John Vertin, Ursuline Sisters from Chatham, Ontario, came to open a school for girls in St. Ignace in 1897. The sisters helped with the religious education of young people there until 1984.

Upon first arriving in June 1897 the Ursulines held a bazaar to raise money for a new convent. Over the years the school fund-raiser became a highly anticipated, annual event in the community.

From the opening of the school Sept. 8, 1897, until the following January, a private residence on the corner of McCann and Church streets was used as a combination school and convent. Five sisters taught 60 high-school aged girls the first year. Classes were held in the most primitive conditions. Instead of desks, most of the pupils sat around the dining room table or used other furniture.

A new building—a two-story school—dormitory and convent, was blessed Jan. 2, 1898. The facility was formally incorporated as the Ursuline Academy of Our Lady of the Straits in 1905. Renovations to the building that year added more dormitories. Facilities expanded again in the ensuing years as the community was growing and the school attendance was continually increasing. A second building was constructed in 1914 and a house nearby was purchased in order to double the overall capacity of the academy.

In 1951 the status of the school changed from a private high school for girls to a parochial, coeducational, elementary school. St. Ignatius Loyola Parish began paying rent, the teachers' stipends, providing bussing and covering other expenses. Financial burdens were among the reasons that led to the closure of St. Ignatius School in 1972. A parish religious education program took its place.

HOME FOR THE AGING

THE BISHOP NOA HOME, ESCANABA

Among a small group of Sisters of St. Paul de Chartres who came to the United States in the summer of 1963 were three sisters from Ireland who worked to transform the historic Delta Hotel on Ludington Street in downtown Escanaba into a state-approved home for the care of the elderly. The Bishop Noa Home was the vision of Bishop Thomas L. Noa, who wanted to see his diocese move into the new phase of providing care for the aging. Bishop Noa presided over the dedication ceremony at the facility's opening in October 1963. The Bishop Noa Home is the only Catholic-sponsored nursing home in the Upper Peninsula.

The diocese continued to own and operate The Bishop Noa Home from 1963 to 1988 when it was sold to the Sisters of St. Paul. Women from the order had served as nurses, administrators and social workers from the time of its opening. Full sponsorship was transferred to the Sisters of St. Paul on July 1, 1988.

By the end of 1989 the Sisters of St. Paul were seeking donations toward a new complex. The antiquated, six-story hotel could not provide the home-like atmosphere the sisters sought to offer. After receiving contributions of nearly $800,000, The Bishop Noa Home took out loans totaling $5 million.

Groundbreaking ceremonies for the new facility were held at 2900 Third Ave. South on Aug. 23, 1990. Sister Anne-Marie Audet, Superior General of the Sisters of St. Paul, came from Rome to attend the ceremony.

Residents moved into the new home in April 1992. The facility is a single floor complex measuring 65,000 square feet with 12 apartments, 81 nursing home beds and 28 beds for the aged. The facility also has a dining room, chapel, activities room, gift shop, salon and lounge areas. Catholic Mass and the rosary are offered daily.

The facility was expanded again with the completion of 17 additional apartments in January 1999, bringing the number of apartments to 29. The addition allowed for four levels of care to be offered, a service no other U.P. facility could provide. The four levels are independent apartments for active senior citizens; assisted living apartments for those who need some assistance with daily tasks; home for the aged for those needing a fair amount of assistance with daily tasks; and nursing home services for those needing health care, as well as assistance with daily tasks. Residents can move from one level to the next without much disruption to their routine.

The Bishop Noa Home has been recognized for its family-like atmosphere and exceptional service. Among the honors it has received are the 1998 Governors Award for Excellence in Care and the 1999 Facility of the Year Award from the Health Care Association of Michigan.

HOSPITALS

ST. FRANCIS HOSPITAL, ESCANABA

The history of St. Francis Hospital dates back to 1883 when Father Eugene Butterman, OFM, pastor of St. Joseph Church, was asked to obtain women religious for the Delta County Hospital's nursing staff. In an agreement signed Feb. 12, 1884, Sisters of the Third Order of St. Francis, from East Peoria, Ill., would conduct the hospital and be paid as nurses by the city of Escanaba.

The sisters' daily routine at the Delta County Hospital was very strenuous. Rising at 5 a.m. to pray and work, the sisters cared for the patients in the sick room, did all of the housecleaning and maintenance duties for the hospital and even took on the responsibility of milking cows, tending to the chickens and pigs and caring for the vegetable garden that provided patients' food.

At that time, the average daily charge per patient for all of these services was 75 cents. The sisters also provided an early outreach program, visiting the area lumber camps to offer health care to the lumbermen. A horse and buggy transported the women as far as the roads permitted, but they trekked the final miles to the lumber camps on foot while carrying their supplies.

In 1913 the sisters purchased the Delta County Hospital, and renamed it St. Francis Hospital. In 1926 fire struck the facility for the second time, damaging even further that which had been burned in 1889. The people of Escanaba came to the sisters' aid to help build a new facility located on South 14th Street. The new hospital included two wings, with an addition of needed patient rooms and a convent for the sisters. The 1927 dedication Mass saw 3,000 people gather to acclaim the new building one of the finest in the Upper Peninsula.

In 1957 and 1958 the hospital conducted a community fund-raising campaign to construct the wing built in 1959. Cost of this construction was $1.4 million. Further additions and improvements were made over the years, including improvements to the Special Care Unit in 1973 and the addition of a mammography X-ray unit in 1975.

The current hospital building, located on U.S. Highway 2 and 41, was constructed in 1986 at a cost of about $17 million. On July 24 more than 2,000 people gathered in the parking lot for an outdoor Mass dedicating the facility. When the new hospital was completed, the 14th Street facility was torn down and the property was sold.

In its first 10 years of operation many improvements were made to the new, non-profit health care facility. Equipment was upgraded and the hospital saw the addition of new services and procedures including Home Health and Hospice Care, neurology services, laser surgery, cardiac rehabilitative services and a sports medicine program.

In 1995 a 44,000 square-foot medical office building was attached to the southwest side of the hospital. The facility also houses the St. Francis Women's Center and St. Francis Home Health Care, along with several outpatient services, such as EEG testing, occupational therapy and lab testing.

In observance of such progress, Bishop James Garland celebrated a commemorative Mass outside the medical office building Aug. 4, 1996. A health fair and hospital tours were also held that day.

In 2000 St. Francis Hospital added an 11-station dialysis center.

St. Joseph Hospital, Hancock

On June 6, 1899 the Sisters of St. Joseph, of Carondelet, Mo., at the request of Bishop Frederick Eis, took on the work of administering the hospital in Hancock. The sisters purchased the existing St. Mary's Hospital from the Sisters of St. Francis. St. Mary's had been run out of Bishop John Vertin's former home on Hancock Street. After the sale the name of the facility was changed to St. Joseph Hospital. The accommodations were small for a community hospital, allowing only three small rooms for patients. After the first year, one story was added, but conditions remained unsuitable.

Ground was broken for a new hospital building on Water Street in August 1903. The following summer the new facility was completed. The original St. Mary's was torn down in 1919. The Water Street building was a five-story sandstone and brick structure of Renaissance style. The hospital included 50 beds, two operating rooms, an X-ray room and laboratory. The hospital was expanded in 1931 when a chapel and nurses' residences were completed.

The cornerstone for yet another new facility was laid on Oct. 22, 1950. The nine-story brick structure was built along Michigan Avenue at a cost of more than $2.5 million. Bishop Thomas L. Noa dedicated the new hospital July 29, 1951. Upon completion the facility had a capacity of 170 patients. New departments included outpatient services, a surgery and recovery room and emergency room.

In addition to the services offered at St. Joseph Hospital, the sisters also organized St. Joseph Hospital School of Nursing in 1920. Its first graduating class, consisting of four women, held commencement exercises Nov. 12, 1924. During World War II the school was approved by the U.S. Public Heath Service for participation in the Cadet Nurse Corps. Some 56 of the school's 62 students were enrolled in the program.

In 1951 the former Water Street hospital building was made into a residence hall for the nursing students. The old dormitory building became St. Joseph Convent. The school was fully accredited in 1959. The first male graduated from the school in 1972. By the time the last class graduated from St. Joseph School of Nursing in May 1974, the school had graduated nearly 700 nurses.

Management of St. Joseph Hospital began to change in 1972 when the first lay people joined the hospital board of directors. That year the name of the hospital was changed to St. Joseph Community Hospital.

In 1976 the hospital was transferred to the local Board of Trustees and the Sisters of St. Joseph withdrew sponsorship. The name was changed to Portage View Hospital. A program to recognize the sisters' years of service was held in the Memorial Union Ballroom at Michigan Technological University June 2.

In March 2000 the new Portage Health System opened a new hospital located on Quincy Hill.

ST. MARY'S HOSPITAL, MARQUETTE

At the request of Bishop John Vertin, Sisters of the Third Order of St. Francis, of Peoria, Ill., came to Marquette to operate a community hospital in September 1890. The sisters immediately began treating loggers and early settlers, many of whom were suffering from typhoid fever. The sisters operated in a makeshift hospital facility they created in an apartment house located at the corner of Fourth and Rock streets. Construction of the first hospital began in May 1891 on property located at the corner of Fisher and Fifth streets. St. Mary's was dedicated that October. A north wing was added to the original hospital in 1906.

After much anticipation, a "new" St. Mary's Hospital opened in 1955. A federal grant and matching funds from the sisters' motherhouse, along with $200,000 in community donations, funded a modernized facility. The new building offered 58 medical and surgical beds, 16 maternity beds and eight pediatric beds. Specialized services included obstetrics, surgery, X-ray, laboratory, dietary services and administration. A new chapel was built within the hospital for use by ambulatory patients, employees and visitors. Also at that time, the original hospital was converted into a convent with accommodations for 24 sisters. Bishop Thomas L. Noa dedicated the new facilities Oct. 16, 1955.

In April 1963 the original hospital was razed to make room for another expansion. The Upper Peninsula's first psychiatric wing was dedicated on May 6, 1965. In 1966 a long-term care unit was added.

On July 1, 1973, after 82 years of service, the Sisters of the Third Order of St. Francis relinquished ownership of the hospital, selling it to the new Marquette General Hospital Inc.

For a few years St. Mary's facilities were known as Marquette General South. Services such as rehab, oncology and psychiatric care were offered from there. Later, ownership of the building was transferred to the State of Michigan and the former St. Mary's Hospital became the D.J. Jacobetti Home for Veterans.

St. Joseph's-Lloyd Hospital, Menominee

In 1889 the Sisters of the Third Order of St. Francis from Peoria, Ill., took charge of the Bay Shore Providence Hospital Association's facilities in Menominee. The original organization disbanded and the sisters purchased the hospital in August 1893.

Working in every department from billing to surgery, the sisters overcame difficulties and the success of the hospital grew, allowing for expansions in 1900, 1906 and 1911. The 1911 remodeling increased the capacity to 78 patient beds and included construction of a new chapel and living quarters for the sisters.

To the best of the sisters' abilities, hospital services and facilities continued to be updated through the first half of the 20th century. A nursing school operated in 1918, but many difficulties kept it from continuing into the next year.

In 1937 the Lloyd Foundation was started in the name of a Menominee businessman, Marshall B. Lloyd, who wished to modernize the county's health care industry. Plans were completed for a new Lloyd section of the hospital in 1949. Extensive modernization of both the interior and exterior of the St. Joseph section also took place at this time. The total bed capacity was increased to 130. The new facility was named the St. Joseph's-Lloyd Hospital.

The era of the sisters' hospital administration ended May 31, 1974 when the women of the order relinquished ownership of the facility. The reason for the move is said to have been lack of funds needed to make state and federally mandated upgrades.

The County Hospital Authority took over operations and renamed the facility Menominee County Lloyd Hospital.

In 1985 Menominee County Lloyd and Marinette General Hospital in Marinette, Wis., consolidated to form Bay Area Medical Center.

Divine Infant of Prague Hospital, Wakefield

On Sept. 1, 1946, Sisters of St. Joseph of the Third Order of St. Francis, of Stevens Point, Wis., assumed responsibility for the administration of Wakefield Hospital. The facility, formerly operated by the Pickands-Mather Mining Co., was placed under the patronage of the Divine Infant of Prague.

The original 16-bed facility was immediately enlarged and improved upon. In the first year and a half the anesthetic and X-ray departments were expanded and a laboratory was added. By 1949 a new convent with a temporary chapel and staff room was also constructed.

On May 23, 1954, Bishop Thomas L. Noa laid the cornerstone for a $700,000-expansion project.

Upon completion of the modern hospital in July 1955, the facility had all the latest medical and surgical capabilities. Patient beds increased to 60 and services in surgical, medical, obstetrical, orthopedic and pediatric care were said to be the most up-to-date.

An addition to the sisters' home was built in 1960 that included a garage. In the two years that followed, further crowding forced additional construction in the way of more storage space and larger departments within the hospital. Later the bed capacity increased to 70.

However, a decline in the number of patients and the excessive number of available hospital beds in the Wakefield and Ironwood areas led to the eventual closure of Divine Infant Hospital. The Sisters of St. Joseph closed the facility June 30, 1978. The property was sold the following year.

SEMINARIES

SACRED HEART NOVITIATE, ASSININS

On Aug. 24, 1956, the former St. Joseph's Orphans Home in Assinins was founded as a friary for the Capuchin Franciscans of the St. Joseph (or Calvary) Province. In 1957, it was formally dedicated as a novitiate, initially for those desiring to become priests, and later for those entering the order as lay brothers.

The novices were gradually introduced to the Capuchin Franciscan way of life. Their schedule consisted mainly of prayer and meditation, work and recreation. Lay brothers were also trained in various trades, which they would use in service to the order. Besides the kitchen where the novices learned culinary skills, the friary also housed various workshops, such as a carpentry shop, a bookbindery, a cobbler shop and a tailor shop.

On June 25, 1959, the novitiate for the cleric novices moved to Huntington, Ind. In 1968 the Assinins novitiate was closed. In July of 1971, the land and the buildings of Sacred Heart Friary were deeded over to the United States Government in trust for the Keweenaw Bay Indian Community.

DIVINE WORD SEMINARY, MARENISCO

On Aug. 18, 1955, Bishop Thomas L. Noa blessed the St. Thomas Seminary of the Society of the Divine Word, located at Lake Gogebic in Marenisco. The facility opened as a juniorate for brothers in their second year of training. Initially there were 29 seminarians from a dozen different states in training. Four fathers and three brothers led the program.

The main building of the seminary was the former Northern Holiday resort, the summer home of William Bonifas.

Divine Word Missionaries were founded in 1875. The Marenisco seminary was the ninth established in the United States since 1909.

Information obtained from the province archives indicates the seminary likely did not continue past that first year, but that the order continued using the Lake Gogebic facilities from 1957 to 1969 for summer recreation.

JORDAN SEMINARY, MENOMINEE

The Society of the Divine Savior, or the Salvatorians, opened Jordan College in Menominee in September 1932. The co-educational, liberal arts college was named after the founder of the order, Father Francis Jordan. The campus on which the college began was built in 1907 by Menominee County, as an agricultural school which continued until 1929. The Michigan Military Academy conducted operations at the facility for one year in 1930.

Financial problems forced the closure of Jordan College in 1939, but determined efforts saw revitalization of the facility as Jordan Seminary from 1940 to 1943 when a one-year accelerated program to prepare "late" vocations for the college seminary was started.

Then in 1946, the Novitiate of the USA Province of the Society of the Divine Savior was moved to Jordan. In 1947 the United States Provincial Residence of the Society of the Divine Savior relocated to Menominee.

A few years later, in the spring of 1949, the seminary was reopened. In 1951 the seminary program was expanded to include the first two years of college. The number of students grew from 10 or 15 in the late 1940s to more than 100 in the late 1950s. By then the program outgrew its facilities. The students were moved to a college-seminary near Waukesha, Wis., in 1962. The novitiate and the seminary operated simultaneously until 1955 when the novices transferred out of the facility to Colfax, Iowa.

In addition to the college, Salvatorians also ran a summer camp for boys on Pelican Lake in Rhinelander, Wis. Camp St. Francis operated from 1955 to 1962. The facility consisted of 80 acres of land and had recreation and dining halls, a chapel and dormitory units.

From 1962 to 1965 Salvatorian brother candidates occupied the Jordan complex. They then moved to specialized schools and colleges in the Washington D.C. area. The property was sold to the Menominee-Marinette YMCA in1968.

CENTENNIAL MASS—In commemoration of the 100th anniversary of the Diocese of Marquette being named a vicariate apostolic, more than 5,000 people took part in a Centennial Mass held Aug. 30, 1953 at Memorial Field in Marquette. (Superior View photos)

BARAGA DAYS—Participants in the 1943 Baraga Days events gather in front of Sacred Heart Church in L'Anse. The Bishop Baraga Association has sponsored Baraga Days annually since 1948. The event is the primary fundraiser for the organization. As part of the annual meeting, association members are also given an account of the progress of the Cause of Bishop Baraga. (Diocese of Marquette Archives photo)

BISHOP BARAGA BICENTENNIAL—A polka night at St. Louis the King Church in Harvey, June 27, 1997, was part of the Diocese of Marquette's bicentennial celebration of the birth of Bishop Frederic Baraga. Other commemorative events held between June 22 and 29 included a slide-show presentation of Baraga's life and a Slovenian Mass. Baraga was the first bishop of the diocese.

VARSITY BASKETBALL—Three U.P. basketball players attending St. Lawrence Seminary High School are (from left) Mark Crowley of Marquette and Tom Gardipee and Terry Alexander of Norway. Over the years, many young men from the Diocese of Marquette have attended the Mt. Calvary, Wis., seminary, which is run by the Detroit-based Capuchin Province of St. Joseph.

CATHOLIC SCHOOLS AWARENESS—Bishop James Garland visits Father Marquette Elementary School in Marquette during Catholic Schools Week 2002. Starting on the last Sunday in January, the program aims to build support and recognition for Catholic schools across the nation. Catholic Schools Week, begun in the 1970s, is a program of the National Catholic Educational Association and the U.S. Conference of Catholic Bishops.

ALL-SCHOOL REUNION—(Top) More than 1,200 former students of Bishop Baraga High School gathered at Lakeview Arena in Marquette for the first all-school reunion July 7, 1995. The last class graduated from Bishop Baraga High in 1969. The Father Marquette Catholic Central School System continues to serve preschool through eighth grade (Joe Sullivan photo). (Left) More than 1,000 former students of Holy Name High School in Escanaba gathered for an all-school reunion held July 11, 1998, in the Ruth Butler Building of the U.P. State Fairgrounds. Holy Name High School closed in 1971. Holy Name Central Grade School continues to operate grades preschool-8.

BARAGA TOMB—A group of young people from Sacred Heart School in L'Anse, led by Diocesan Archivist Elizabeth Delene, (right) tours the tomb of Bishop Frederic Baraga, located in the crypt at St. Peter Cathedral, Marquette. Bishop Baraga died Jan. 19, 1868.

RCIA—Candidates for the Rite of Christian Initiation of Adults take part in a Rite of Election at St. Peter Cathedral. Being the cathedral church for the diocese, St. Peter's hosts many liturgical functions that are celebrated by the faithful of the entire Upper Peninsula, such as the Chrism Mass, ordination ceremonies, investiture ceremonies, commissioning rites and other special events.

BLESSING OF THE FLEET—Bishop Thomas L. Noa leads the Blessing of the Fleet celebration at Fayette State Park on the Garden peninsula in 1963. The ceremony was first held there in 1948 and continues today.

KNIGHTS OF COLUMBUS—The Knights of Columbus held the 1993 state convention at the Grand Hotel on Mackinac Island. The Fourth Degree Color Guard formed a living rosary led by Father Vincent Ouellette, state chaplain and pastor of St. Joseph Parish in Ishpeming.

MDCCW—Some 220 members of the Marquette Diocesan Council of Catholic Women gathered at St. Mary and St. Joseph Parish hall in Iron Mountain Sept. 22, 1979. Bishop Mark Schmitt was also at the gathering. The growing need for lay ministries was among the topics discussed.

ST. VINCENT DE PAUL—A dedication ceremony for the new St. Vincent de Paul Store in Gwinn was held April 20, 1980. The store was dedicated to Jack DesJardins, the pioneer of the St. Vincent de Paul organization in the Upper Peninsula. In 2005 there were 38 conferences and 20 thrift stores across the diocese.

HOME FOR THE AGING—The Bishop Noa Home in Escanaba was the vision of Bishop Thomas L. Noa. He presided over the dedication ceremony at its opening in October 1963. The diocese continued to own and operate The Bishop Noa Home until 1988. The facility was then sold to the Sisters of St. Paul de Chartres, who have operated it since it was started.

HOSPITAL BREAKS GROUND—St. Francis Hospital in Escanaba held a groundbreaking ceremony in 1985 to mark the start of construction on a new building. The Sisters of the Third Order of St. Francis from East Peoria, Ill., who own and operate the hospital, had come to the diocese to begin staffing a county-owned hospital in 1884, more than 100 years prior to the completion of this new structure. (St. Francis Hospital photo.)

ST. JOSEPH HOME—Boys and girls living at the St. Joseph Home orphanage in Assinins pose outside the facility with the Sisters of St. Joseph of Carondelet around the turn of the century. Women of the order ran the facility from its opening in 1881 until 1906 when the Sisters of St. Agnes from Fond du Lac, Wis., took over. St. Joseph Home was closed in 1956. (The Catholic Diocese of Marquette Archives photo.)

HOLY FAMILY HOME—A group of young people practice music at Holy Family Orphans Home in Marquette. The Sisters of St. Agnes from Fond du Lac, Wis., were in charge of the daily operations of the orphanage from the time of its dedication in 1915 to its closure in 1965.

CAMP PLAGENS—The U.P. Laymen's Retreat Association operated Camp Plagens as a retreat center in the 1940s. Later the facilities, located on Moon Lake near Watersmeet, became a Catholic Youth Camp. Final sessions were held in the summer of 1987.

MARYGROVE RETREAT CENTER—People from across the diocese gathered at Marygrove Retreat Center in Garden to celebrate the facility's 50th anniversary Aug. 16, 1998. Retreats for men, women, teenagers, families, parishes, priests, and lay ministers are among the specialized retreats offered at Marygrove.

FRIENDS OF ST. PAUL—A group of "Friends of St. Paul" meets with the Sisters of St. Paul de Chartres at their district house chapel in Marquette several times a year to study the writings of St. Paul and other Scripture and church documents, to share faith and to pray together. (Sisters of St. Paul de Chartres photo)

RIGHT TO LIFE—On Jan. 22, 1993, in recognition of the 20th anniversary of the Roe v. Wade Supreme Court decision that legalized abortion in the United States, a march for life was held from St. Peter Cathedral to the Marquette County Courthouse in Marquette.

MEMORIAL DAY OBSERVANCE—Holy Cross Cemetery in Marquette is the site for this Memorial Day observance May 26, 1997. The diocese operates a second cemetery, Holy Cross in Escanaba.

DIOCESAN SCHOOL BOARD—The Diocesan School Board meets at the beginning of the 1978-1979 school year. The board oversees the overall Catholic educational goals of the diocese.

MUSIC WORKSHOP—The Marquette Diocesan Association of Liturgical Musicians sponsored a music workshop at St. Mary Church in Norway Oct. 8, 1988.

OUTREACH MINISTRY—Sister Johnice Borer, OSF, prepares to deliver Christmas gifts as part of the Diocese of Marquette's Adopt-A-Family Program in December 1988. Other outreach efforts coordinated by the diocese's Outreach Office include Project Backpack and Resurrection Baskets.

HOMELESSNESS AWARENESS—Sister Cathy Mills, Catholic Campus Ministry Coordinator at Northern Michigan University in Marquette, leads a homelessness awareness event on the NMU campus April 11, 1995.

LAY MINISTRY LEADERSHIP SCHOOL—The Lay Ministry Leadership School Class of 2002 met for 20 intense weekend sessions over a two year-period. The program, renamed Ecclesial Ministry Institute, was started in 1982 to train lay people to offer ministerial services to parishes.

PASTORAL OFFICE MOVES—Members of the diocesan administrative staff pose outside the Pastoral Office building on Fourth Street in Marquette just prior to the July 2005 move to the office's new location at 117 W. Washington St. Staff members are (from left, front) Mary Jeske, Judy Jason, Bishop James Garland, Pat Peterson, Wendy Negri and Chris Sandstrom; (from left, back) Father Alex Sample, Andra Bedard, Carol Parker, Father Greg Heikkala and Rick Schaefer.

JUBILEE 2000—An outdoor Mass for the Diocese of Marquette's Jubilee 2000 Eucharistic Celebration brought 2,500 people together at Mattson Park near Marquette's lower harbor Aug. 20. The Mass was concelebrated by Cardinal Edmund Szoka, of Vatican City, Bishop James Garland, retired Bishop Mark Schmitt and several priests of the diocese. Following the Mass and a picnic with live entertainment and games, hundreds of people followed the Blessed Sacrament as it was carried through the streets of Marquette to St. Peter Cathedral for benediction.

Parishes and Missions

St. Edward, Alpha

St. Edward, Alpha

A patient people and a zealous priest led to the founding of St. Edward Church in Alpha in 1940. Prior to construction of the church, visiting priests from Crystal Falls served the people on an irregular basis. Upon Father Joseph Gondek's arrival, an old engine house from the Baltic Mine was turned into a church and a 50-year faith tradition was begun in Alpha.

FOUNDING. Priests from Guardian Angels Parish in Crystal Falls began visiting Alpha as soon as the village was incorporated, around 1913. Father Joseph Kunes was the first to serve the area.

The women of the community organized a Catholic Ladies Aid Society with hopes of raising money for an eventual church. A strong effort in 1926 had people's enthusiasm for the goal running high. The Judson Mining Company donated a former boarding house for use as a church, but the economic depression that ensued kept the dream from being realized. The Judson building was sold in 1934.

The people's faith was once again uplifted in 1939 when Guardian Angels Parish received its first assistant pastor, Father Anthony Schloss. Father Schloss' top priority was to serve the missions of Alpha and Amasa, and so Mass was now offered twice per month instead of on an irregular basis.

PARISH LIFE. In 1940 Father Joseph A. Gondek of Iron River began assisting with service to the missions. He ordered a census of Alpha and was convinced a church there was long overdue. Community support for a new church at that time was lacking, however, because the people were experiencing unemployment and tough financial times. But Father Gondek, not wanting the people to go any longer without a parish, borrowed the money himself.

With help from the men of the community, an old engine house from the Baltic Mine was dismantled and salvaged for use as a church. Father Gondek, with no construction experience, became his own contractor for the project. The ladies of the parish worked to raise money and a donation was obtained from the Catholic Church Extension Society. With all of this in hand, parishioners stepped up and pledged money toward the project as well.

The ground for the new church was blessed on June 10, 1942. Christmas Midnight Mass was held that same year amid bare, stone walls and construction straw. A new bell tower was completed the following week, just in time to ring in the new year, 1943.

On July 5, 1943 Bishop Francis Magner dedicated the parish to St. Edward and named Father Gondek its first resident pastor. In the next few years fundraising efforts were conducted and additional improvements made to the church.

To augment the spiritual lives of parishioners, a branch of the Confraternity of Christian Doctrine was established in Alpha and Amasa in October 1949.

Over the years, aggressive efforts were made to erase the church debt and to maintain and improve the house of worship. Money was earned through parties, bazaars and bake sales. Popular monthly pasty sales drew orders of 800 to 1,000 pasties. Profits benefited the church and the community.

In the 1950s the parish rectory had to be remodeled after it was heavily damaged by fire. In 1967 the church complex received a complete renovation. Space was made for a vestibule, baptismal font, additional restroom, classrooms and storage. In 1990 parishioners took on the enormous project of reverting the altar back to its original position. The St. Edward's Men's Club repainted and installed new paneling, carpeting and a new speaker system. While removing the old paneling, three beautiful stained glass windows were uncovered.

The faith of the young people of the parish was enhanced by a special, one-week religious education session in the summer. Classes were taught by a group of Franciscan Sisters. Sessions included a potluck dinner for the entire parish. Adult faith formation classes and the Renew program were also among the spiritual programs at St. Edward's. In November 1992 the first annual parish retreat was held at Marygrove Retreat Center in Garden. Weekly coffee socials after Sunday Mass, a Mother's and Father's Day breakfast and an annual Christmas party were among the parish social traditions.

CLOSURE. As a result of the diocese's pastoral planning initiative Fully Alive in '95, St. Edward Church was closed in 1995. The people were encouraged to join the faith community of Guardian Angels Parish in Crystal Falls.

RECORDS. Records for St. Edward Parish are located at Guardian Angels Parish in Crystal Falls.

PASTORS. Fathers Joseph A. Gondek, 1943-1950; Chester Franczek, 1950-1952; Clement J. LePine, 1952-1957; Stephen Mayrand, 1957; Wilfred Pellettier, 1957-1961; Raymond Smith, 1961; Matthew Strumski, 1961-1962; Joseph Desrochers, 1962-1964; Timothy Desrochers, 1964; Arthur Parrotta, 1964-1965; Henry Mercier, 1965-1968; James Hebein, 1968-1978; Michael Vichich, 1978-1989, and Raymond Valerio, 1989-1995.

St. Mary Mission, Amasa

St. Mary Mission, Amasa

Throughout their 85-year history the people of Amasa were devout in sustaining the life of St. Mary Mission. Despite several small fires and another that resulted in the need for extensive repairs, the same church building served the people until its eventual closure in 1995.

FOUNDING. St. Mary Church in Amasa was started as a mission of Guardian Angels Parish in Crystal Falls in 1910. Prior to construction of the church, Catholics there were served by pastors who commuted by horse drawn vehicles or by train. Mass at that time was said at the Amasa Town Hall.

The church was constructed on land donated by the Hemlock River Mining Company. The company also donated some of the building materials. The first pastor to serve St. Mary's was Father Joseph Kunes of Crystal Falls, from 1904 to 1926. In 1943 a church was constructed in Alpha and the priest there also began serving Amasa.

PARISH LIFE. In the early years, several near-catastrophes were averted when fires in the church were contained, leaving the structure unharmed. But when a neighboring barn caught fire in 1925, sparks fell onto the roof of St. Mary's Church. A considerable portion of the church roof and some of its interior were destroyed by the fire or damaged by water. Extensive repairs were made to the structure.

Summer catechism was started for the young people of the parish in 1936. Women religious, along with the laity, conducted the sessions.

The Ladies Altar Society was formed in the 1940s during Father Joseph Gondek's tenure. For 48 consecutive years the women held a Christmas bazaar to raise money for the upkeep of the church.

Stained glass windows were installed in 1972. The interior was remodeled for the final time in 1978. In 1991 an outside grotto was built by Deacon George Offerman. Many parishioners brought fieldstones to be incorporated into the project. Father James Challancin, a native son of the parish, blessed the grotto July 7, 1991. The ceremony coincided with the closing of the community's centennial celebration.

St. Mary's celebrated its diamond jubilee in 1985. Bishop Mark Schmitt presided over a Thanksgiving Mass held July 14. The Mass was followed by a dinner and dance at the Fur Rendezvous Building in Amasa.

Throughout the church's history, regular parish activities at St. Mary's included a Mother's Day breakfast, graduation Mass and breakfast, Father's Day picnic, Eucharistic days and family education with a potluck supper, Christmas party, dinner and dance, canoe trips, and parish picnics.

CLOSURE. St. Mary Church was closed in 1995, as a result of the diocese's pastoral planning initiative Fully Alive in '95. The people were encouraged to join the faith community of Guardian Angels Parish in Crystal Falls. The church was later razed.

RECORDS. Records for St. Mary Church are located at Guardian Angels Parish in Crystal Falls.

PASTORS. Fathers Joseph P. Kunes, 1904-1926; B. M. Weakland, Gerald Kenney, Nilus McAllister, CP, David Ferland, CP, A. L. Dufresne, Joseph E. Guertin, 1929-1935; Raymond Bergeron, 1935-1940; Philip DeNeri Jutras, 1940-1946; Joseph A. Gondek, 1943-1951; Chester Franczek, 1951-1952; Clement LePine, 1952-1957; William Pelletier, 1957-1961; Raymond Smith, 1961; Matthew Strumski, 1961-1962; Joseph Desrochers, 1962-1964; Emett Norden, Tim Desrochers, 1964; Arthur Parrotta, 1964-1965; Henry Mercier, 1965-1968; James Hebein, 1968-1978; Daniel Zaloga, 1978-1979; Michael T. Vichich, 1979-1990, and Raymond Valerio, 1990-1995.

THE MOST HOLY NAME OF JESUS/BLESSED KATERI TEKAKWITHA (ST. CATHERINE), ASSININS/ZEBA

The church of The Most Holy Name of Jesus-Blessed Kateri Tekakwitha in Assinins and Zeba was created in 1982. Two separate parishes were combined to form one parish. In 2004 pastors from Baraga and L'Anse began offering Mass once each weekend at both the Assinins and Zeba churches. The business of the Assinins and Zeba parish is conducted through the office of the church in Baraga.

The Most Holy Name of Jesus, Assinins

THE MOST HOLY NAME OF JESUS, ASSININS

Mass is still offered on a regular basis in Assinins, on the same land that Bishop Frederic Baraga reserved for a church more than 150 years ago. The site where Bishop Baraga once taught the Ojibwa people is no longer an operating schoolhouse, but rather a museum of local and religious history.

FOUNDING. When Bishop Baraga arrived to stay permanently at the L'Anse settlement in October 1843, the name L'Anse referred to what is presently Assinins, Zeba, Baraga and L'Anse. In the early part of 1844, then-Father Baraga had a cedar warehouse in Zeba dismantled, the logs moved across the frozen waters of Keweenaw Bay and reassembled at Assinins. This first church in the area was dedicated to the The Most Holy Name of Jesus Sept. 29, 1844. A new church and rectory were built of fieldstone in 1873.

PARISH SCHOOL AND ORPHANAGE. Father Baraga started the first school in Assinins in 1844. He taught the Native American men, women and children to read and write and he taught them the catechism. While at Assinins Father Baraga wrote a prayer book and dictionary in the natives' language.

In 1860 Father Gerhard Terhorst built the schoolhouse that still stands on the grounds today. In 1866 the Sisters of St. Joseph of Carondelet came to Assinins to staff the school. The St. Joseph Home orphanage opened in 1881. In June 1906 the Sisters of St. Agnes of Fond du Lac, Wis., replaced the Sisters of St. Joseph in the work of staffing the school and orphanage.

In November 1956, upon the closure of the St. Joseph Home, the Capuchin

Province of St. Joseph purchased the orphanage building and established the Capuchin Brothers Novitiate. In 1971 the Capuchins gave the orphanage and convent building to the Keweenaw Bay Indian Community. The KBIC used the facilities as a tribal center until it was torn down Feb. 17, 1997.

PARISH LIFE. Due to a fire, the stone church built in 1873 was dismantled in 1958. Worship services were then held in the chapel of the former orphanage building from the late 1950s until 1971, when the people moved to the stone convent building. That building was constructed in 1866 and part of its ruins remains on the property.

In 1976, under the leadership of Father John Hascall, parishioners took part in the construction of a log church. A devastating fire in 1982 claimed the church, but parishioners wasted no time in constructing a second log structure. That church continues to be the site of year-round worship services in Assinins.

In order to preserve and interpret the history of Assinins, a group of Holy Name parishioners have organized under the name Father Baraga's Historical Mission and Native Genealogy Center, Inc. The group is also known as Assinins–Baraga Center or ABC. The ABC has already restored the one-room schoolhouse and operates it as a museum. Plans are in the works to showcase the barn next to the schoolhouse and the historic cemetery on the grounds. Long-term goals also include establishing retreat facilities, a Native American craft shop and a picnic area for visitors.

PASTORS. Fathers Frederic Baraga, 1843-1852; Angelus Van Paemel, 1852-1853; Charles Lemagie, 1854; Edward Jacker, 1855-1861; Gerhard Terhorst, 1861-1901; Melchior Faust, 1901-1916; Casper Douenberg, 1916-1936; Anthony Waechter, 1936-1941; Paul Prud'homme, SJ, 1941-1949; Joseph Lawless, SJ, 1949-1958; Edward Wenzel, 1958; Bernardine Schlimgen, OFM, Cap., 1958-1963; Christopher Hafner, OFM, 1963-1970; John Hascall, OFM Cap., 1970-1986; Paul Yaroch, OFM Cap., 1986; Walter Kasuboski, OFM Cap., 1986-1987; Larry Abler, OFM Cap., 1987-1990; John Hascall, OFM Cap., 1990-1997; Paul Manderfield, 1997-2000; George Joseph Kallarackal, MCBS, 2000-2003; James Ziminski, 2003-2004; Chacko Kakaniyil, 2004-2005, and Augustin George, 2005-.

BLESSED KATERI TEKAKWITHA, ZEBA

The people living in Keweenaw Bay's Zeba and Pequaming areas were without a permanent parish of their own until 1949. However, Catholic Mass was offered there on an irregular basis for 300 years before Blessed Kateri Tekakwitha (St. Catherine's) was established.

FOUNDING. Jesuit missionary Father Rene Menard built a chapel and administered to Native Americans at Pequaming for nine months in 1660 and

1661. Not until Bishop Baraga's arrival in 1843 did another priest settle in the region. One of the places at which then-Father Baraga celebrated Mass was in the Pierre Crebassa trading post in Zeba. Between 1890 and 1937 priests serving elsewhere in the region visited Zeba occasionally to offer Mass.

PARISH LIFE. Father Paul Prud'homme of Assinins began providing more regular service to the people of Zeba in 1946. In 1947 he began offering Mass at the Foote School. In 1949 Father Prud'homme purchased the Catholic church in Pequaming and had it moved to Zeba. The Zeba church was originally dedicated to St. Catherine. The first Mass was said there Oct. 30, 1949.

Blessed Kateri Tekakwitha, Zeba

The church facilities were expanded upon over the years to include a side chapel and catechetical room from the former Lutheran church that was also moved from Pequaming. A trailer acquired by the mission and moved next to the church became a rectory in 1971. Father Elmer Stoffel, OFM Cap., took up residency in Zeba.

On Sunday, Oct. 27, 1974, the parish celebrated its silver jubilee, marking 25 years since Mass was first offered in the church. Bishop Charles A. Salatka celebrated the Mass, which was followed by a dinner in the Zeba Hall.

St. Catherine was rededicated Blessed Kateri Tekakwitha on Jan. 1, 1980. Known as the "Lily of the Mohawks," Blessed Kateri Tekakwitha is the first Native American to be beatified. The original donors of the church wished to have the name changed should she be beatified or canonized.

PASTORS. Fathers Paul Prud'homme, SJ, 1949-1950; Joseph Lawless, SJ, 1950-1958; Bernardin Schlimgen, OFM Cap., 1958-1964; Christopher Hafner, OFM, 1964-1970, and Elmer Stoffel, OFM Cap., 1970-1982.

St. Mary Star of the Sea Mission, Atlantic Mine

St. Mary Star of the Sea Mission, Atlantic Mine

From its beginnings the entire community of Atlantic Mine, not only Catholics, supported St. Mary Star of the Sea Parish. From construction of its first church, through its rebuilding after a 1921 fire and many successful fundraising drives, the whole-hearted support of its parishioners and friends saw the church through more than 125 years of service to the people of the area.

In the early decades of the 20th century, pastors serving Atlantic Mine helped to start mission churches in surrounding areas. Then, as populations declined in the region, St. Mary of the Sea was reverted to mission status itself in the 1960s. The church merged with St. Ignatius Loyola Parish in Houghton in 1996.

FOUNDING. Atlantic Mine was not assigned a resident pastor until 1902, but Catholic priests began visiting the area regularly in the 1860s. Father John Vertin, who later became the third bishop of the Diocese of Marquette, was among those who served Atlantic Mine. Mass was offered in the schoolhouse and in private homes.

The mission was under the care of St. Ignatius Church in Houghton until 1898. Thanks to substantial donations of money and labor from Catholics and non-Catholics alike, a church was constructed under the guidance of Monsignor Antoine Rezek. The completed structure was dedicated Dec. 18, 1898.

Mass continued to be offered only once a month for the first year, then every Sunday. The first resident priest, Father Adolph Schneider, arrived in April 1902.

MISSIONS. While serving St. Mary Star of the Sea, Father Frederick Richter also started the mission churches in Painesdale (1905) and South Range (1917).

PARISH LIFE. On March 12, 1921 St. Mary Star of the Sea Church suffered a devastating fire. Faulty wiring caused a blaze that leveled both the church and rectory. However, the structure and present rectory were rebuilt the same year. Again donations from Catholics and non-Catholics made the new church possible.

St. Mary Star of the Sea reverted from a parish to mission status early in

1963. Pastors from South Range served Atlantic Mine until 1969 when care of the church was assigned to St. Ignatius Parish in Houghton.

In 1963 the church acquired a sandstone building, the former community hall in Atlantic Mine. The structure was renovated and dedicated the St. Mary Parish Hall on Dec. 6, 1964. Social events, meetings and fundraisers took place there.

St. Mary's celebrated the 75th anniversary of its church Oct. 21, 1973. A commemorative Mass was followed by a dinner in the parish hall.

The church was well known for its roast beef fund-raising dinners. People from Houghton, Hancock, South Range and other surrounding areas supported the events. Money collected at the dinners helped to fund a church renovation project in 1990. The sanctuary was modified and repainted and new light fixtures and carpeting were installed. On June 20, 1990, a Mass of Thanksgiving was celebrated to commemorate the 125th anniversary of the mission and the rededication of the church.

CLOSURE. The final Mass at St. Mary Star of the Sea was held Saturday, Aug. 31, 1996. The mission was closed as a result of the diocese's Fully Alive in '95 pastoral planning process. The following day a banquet was held for parishioners at Michigan Technological University's Memorial Union Building.

A welcoming service was held for St. Mary's parishioners at St. Ignatius Loyola Parish in Houghton Sept. 7 and 8.

Shortly after the final Mass was celebrated there, the former St. Mary Church was revived as a house of worship. A small Russian Orthodox congregation purchased the structure and renamed it Sts. Sergius and Herman of Valaam.

RECORDS. Records for St. Mary Star of the Sea are located at St. Ignatius Loyola Parish in Houghton.

PASTORS. Fathers Antoine Rezek, 1898-1902; Adolph Schneider,1902-1904; Frederick Richter, 1904-1930; Herman Fadale 1930-1933; Ovid LaMothe, 1933-1934; Stanislaus Mikula, CP, 1934-1936; Gerald Harrington, 1936-1944; Gino S. Ferraro, 1944-1951; Andrew Shulek, 1951-1953; Edward Mihelich, 1953; Frederic Hofmann, 1953-1954; Casimir Marcinkevicius, 1954-1963; William Oremus, 1963-1964; Frank Hollenbach, 1964-1969; James McCarthy, 1969-1970; Edward Wenzel, 1970-1971; Msgr. Robert Chisholm, 1971-1975; Glen Weber, 1975-1986; Joseph Carne, 1986-1995, and Raymond Valerio, 1995-1996.

St. Therese of the Infant Jesus Mission, Au Train

Although the Mission Church of St. Therese of the Infant Jesus in Au Train was not built until the middle of the 20th century, Mass was offered periodically for the small number of Catholic families living in the resort town and its tourists as early as 1898. Today, St. Therese Church is a mission of Sacred Heart Parish in Munising, but in the past it has been under the care of Trenary, Rapid River and St. Mary's Hospital in Marquette.

St. Therese of the Infant Jesus Mission, Au Train

FOUNDING. As early as 1898 priests from Munising provided Mass occasionally for the people living in Au Train. Bishop Frederick Eis is among the priests from Marquette who occasionally walked to Au Train and Bay Furnace to celebrate Mass. A couple of early attempts at building a church did not come to fruition.

In the mid-1930s Father Frank Ignatz organized a ladies altar society and it was this group that finally was successful in raising the funds necessary to build a church. For 12 years the women held bake sales, card parties, bazaars and other socials to raise money for a church.

Their hard work paid off in September 1947 when a former Civilian Conservation Corps Camp was obtained from the United States government for use as a church. The building was moved to land donated by one of the residents and divided in two, creating a chapel and a parish hall. Bishop Thomas L. Noa dedicated the church to St. Therese on Dec. 14, 1947.

PARISH LIFE. On Nov. 4, 1952 the mission was assigned to the jurisdiction of St. Rita's in Trenary. Weekly services were routinely offered and two Masses were needed on weekends during the summer months to accommodate the large number of seasonal tourists.

In 1974, under the leadership of Father Gary Jacobs, the church was redecorated and the parish hall began to host regular bingo to raise funds.

RECORDS. The records for St. Therese Mission are located at Sacred Heart Parish in Munising.

PASTORS. Fathers Edward Mihelich, 1952-1953; Arnold Casanova, 1952-1953; Gervase Brewer, 1953-1958; Aloysius Hasenberg, 1958-1966;

Michael Hale, 1966-1968; Robert Haas, 1968-1970; Louis Wren, OFM Conv., 1971-1972; Terrence Donnelly, 1972-1973; Peter Minelli, 1972-1973; co-pastors Vincent Oullette, Timothy Desrochers, Raymond Moncher, N. Daniel Rupp, 1973-1981; Raymond Zeugner, 1981-1983; Robert Polcyn, OFM Cap., 1983-1985; Darryl J. Pepin, 1985-1988; Dino Silvestrini, 1989-1991; Richard Schaeffer, 1991-1993; Gregory Heikkala, 1993-1997; Sebastian Kavumkal, MST, 1997-2000; Thomas Joseph Thekkel, MST, 2000-2005; and Christopher Gardiner, 2005-.

HOLY ROSARY MISSION, BANAT

For 70 years the people of Banat supported a mission church of their own. First, priests from Stephenson and then from Daggett fulfilled the sacramental needs of the people. Never having had a resident priest, parishioners took it upon themselves to make improvements to their house of worship and meet the spiritual needs of the congregation.

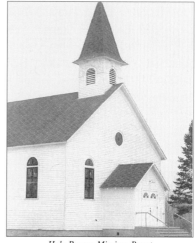

Holy Rosary Mission, Banat

FOUNDING. A colony of 37 German-Hungarian families (95 percent of whom were Catholic) established the community of Banat in 1910. At first a priest from Stephenson would offer Mass in the Gardner schoolhouse and in private homes. It is said that Father Carl Liedgens would drive a team of white horses to the mission. In 1912 the people purchased a bell that was rung three times a day to remind them of the Angelus.

PARISH LIFE. The Holy Rosary Church was constructed in 1914. Care of the mission was assigned to St. Frederick's of Daggett in September 1921.

The men of the parish did much to improve the people's house of worship. A new entrance and choir loft were among the upgrades undertaken in the late 1930s. New windows were installed in 1949 and a new roof put on in 1959.

The mission church celebrated its golden jubilee in February 1964. A memorial Mass was held to mark the milestone. Also in observance of the anniversary, parishioners again supported improvements to the church. The pews were refinished, the church interior was repainted and redecorated and the floors were sanded and refurbished.

CLOSURE. Deteriorating facilities and a lack of priests to serve in the area contributed to the decision to close Holy Rosary Church in 1984.

RECORDS. Records for Holy Rosary Mission are located at Precious Blood Parish in Stephenson.

PASTORS. Fathers Francis A. Seifert, 1921-1937; Joseph Seifert, 1937-1939; William Schick, 1939-1945; J. J. Leckman, 1945-1958; Thomas Ruppe, 1958-1963; John J. Ryan, 1963-1965; Norbert P. LaCosse, 1965-1976; Joseph Felix, 1976-1981, and John McArdle, 1981-1984.

St. Ann, Baraga

During its more than 100-year-history, St. Ann Parish has been steadily supported by the people of Baraga. From a unique project to enlarge the church in the early 1900s to the rebuilding after a devastating fire in 1918 and many subsequent upgrades and improvements, the fine church structure is an outward sign of the people's faith.

St. Ann, Baraga

FOUNDING. In 1886 Father Gerhard Terhorst of Holy Name Church in Assinins saw the need for a separate parish in the growing lumbering town of Baraga two miles away. Through the use of donated land and labor, the first church in Baraga was built at the same location as the present structure.

By the turn of the 20th century the community and the congregation grew significantly, prompting the need for a larger church. In 1902 the small church building was cut in half and a 30-foot section added in the center. The position of the church was also changed at that time. The building was turned around from a north-south position, formerly facing Ontonagon Road, to an east-west position facing the bay. But the uniquely renovated church was hit by disaster some years later. On Nov. 18, 1918, a fire of unknown origin destroyed the church.

PARISH LIFE. The parish wasted no time in rebuilding its house of worship. Bishop Frederick Eis dedicated a new brick structure on May 27, 1920.

The sanctuary was renovated in 1936. In 1947 a basement hall was added to the church, again through the use of volunteer labor by parishioners.

As the facilities were expanded, so too did the spiritual life further develop when the mission became independent from Assinins and raised to parish status. Bishop Thomas L. Noa made the declaration effective Dec. 29, 1949.

Additional improvements to the church in the early 1950s included the enlargement of the sanctuary, installation of a modern heating plant and upgrades to the hall kitchen. After many delays the parish saw completion of its first rectory in 1953. A rear entrance was added to the church in 1966. In 1992 the Knights of Columbus Father Baraga Council #2934 undertook a major repainting project within the church. The men did all of the work, including the artistic details. A barrier-free entrance was also constructed in 1992.

In 1986 the parish celebrated its 100th anniversary. A centennial Mass and dinner were held at the church Dec. 7. A commemorative booklet was also assembled in celebration of the milestone.

A parish picnic brings families together every summer for food, music and entertainment. In the fall of each year the parish raises funds through a successful Hunter's Supper that feeds hundreds of people in just a few hours. Raffle tickets and a craft and bake sale are also part of the event.

PASTORS. Fathers Gerhard Terhorst, 1886-1901; Melchior Faust, 1901-1916; Francis A. Seifert, 1916; Casper Douenburg, 1916-1936; Anthony Waechter, 1936-1949; Aloysius Ehlinger, 1949-1957; Ralph J. Sterbentz, 1957-1966; Henry Lawrence Mercier, 1965; Joseph A. Kichak, 1966-1969; William C. Oremus, 1969-1972; Gervase Brewer, 1972-1974; Clifford Nadeau, 1974-1978; Aloysius Ehlinger, 1978-1980; Peter Carli, 1980-1982; Edward Wenzel, 1982-1985; David C. Jenner, 1985-1991; Philip Naessens, OFM, 1991-1996; Paul Manderfield, 1996-2000; George Joseph Kallarackal, MCBS, 2000-2003; James Ziminski, 2003-2004; Chacko Kakaniyil, 2004-2005, and Augustin George, 2005.

Holy Family Mission, Barbeau

Located about 20 miles south of Sault Ste. Marie, the mission church of Holy Family in Barbeau is truly a church of the people. Parishioners there raised the money for construction of their house of worship and performed much of the labor. Routine maintenance and upkeep was a shared responsibility among the people.

FOUNDING. Jesuit missionaries established Holy Family Parish in Barbeau in 1883 and continued to serve there for 30 years. In 1913 priests from the Diocese of Marquette took over the work. The church had its own resident pastor until 1938. Care of the mission was then assigned to Nativity Parish in Sault Ste. Marie and later to St. Joseph Parish in Rudyard.

Holy Family Mission, Barbeau

The original 1883 church in Barbeau served as the people's house of worship until it was replaced in 1958.

PARISH LIFE. Construction of the present church began in 1957. Bishop Thomas L. Noa officially dedicated the new church Aug. 9, 1959.

Every member of the parish is said to have taken part in the raising of the structure and paying off the subsequent debt. One parishioner designed the building and other members acted as foremen during construction. Monetary donations received through the sale of greeting cards, strawberry festivals and other means were augmented by a large contribution from the Catholic Church Extension Society.

Upon completion of the church, parishioners worked to pay off the debt sooner than was thought possible by serving meals at the newly-constructed National Guard Armory. Everyone, including the pastor at the time, is said to have taken part in the project.

In 1983 Holy Family celebrated the 100th anniversary of the founding of the mission and 25 years since the construction of the present church building.

Improvements to the house of worship were made to coincide with the celebration. Carpeting was installed in the aisles and in the entryway, a new gas heater was installed and the parish hall was repainted. In 1985 the pews were refinished.

An unusual occurrence involving a dropped host brought a lot of attention to

Holy Family Mission in 1996. Some speculated that a dime-sized red blotch, which had formed on a Communion host, which was to be discarded because it had been dropped, was a miraculous sign from God. Bishop James Garland deemed the red stain to be a fungus.

PASTORS. Father Joseph Ling, S. M. Barrette, William J. Remillard, 1918-1936; William F. Schick, Raymond Przybylski, 1938; Frank Ignatz, 1940; Elmer Bares, 1946; Kenneth G. Bretl, 1965-1970; Joseph R. Callari, 1970-1975; Allan J. Mayotte, 1975-1980; Robert Polcyn, OFM Cap., 1980-1983; Paul J. Nomellini, 1983-1986; Thomas Bain, SJ, 1986; John Longbucco, 1992-1995; Mark McQuesten, 1995-1996; Francis DeGroot, 1996-1998, and John Hascall, OFM, Cap., 1998-.

ST. ELIZABETH ANN SETON, BARK RIVER/PERRONVILLE

St. Elizabeth Ann Seton, Bark River   St. Elizabeth Ann Seton, Perronville

A new parish, born from the merging of three smaller churches, Elizabeth Ann Seton boasts an active parish family. Youth groups, prayer groups and family-centered activities bring members together for faith and fellowship.

FOUNDING. As a result of the diocese's Fully Alive in '95 pastoral planning initiative, St. Elizabeth Ann Seton Parish was formed through the merger of three churches: Sacred Heart in Schaffer, St. Michael in Perronville and St. George in Bark River.

The first Mass of the combined congregation was offered at the Bark River Senior Center July 1, 1995. More than 500 members gathered for the first time to worship as one community. Bishop James Garland concelebrated with a number of priests who had formerly served in the region.

PARISH LIFE. At the time of the parish consolidation, Mass continued to be held at all three buildings. In December 1996, the Sacred Heart building in Schaffer was closed. Masses continued to be celebrated in the Perronville and Bark River church buildings. In 1998 Bishop Garland approved the building of a new facility. Early in 2006 parishioners were looking forward to the August groundbreaking for a new, larger building. Members of the parish will finally be united under one roof. The church will be located in Bark River. The former Bark River building will become the parish hall. The church in Perronville was sold.

St. Elizabeth Ann Seton Parish has an active choir, pastoral council and finance council. Prayer groups meet weekly and Eucharistic Adoration is held all day one day each week. An active youth group, annual parish retreat to Marygrove and an annual picnic at the Perronville grounds keep the parish alive. A St. Patrick's Day dinner and YMCA Sunday are among the additional activities enjoyed by members of the new congregation.

PASTORS. Fathers Jeffrey Kurtz, 1995-1996; Emmett Norden, 1996-1999; Christopher Gardiner, 1999-2004; Michael Vichich, 2004-.

St. George, Bark River

St. George, Bark River

St. George Parish in the village of Bark River, just west of Escanaba, has a proud history of loyal and hard-working parishioners. Members overcame the burden of a fire that destroyed the original church and made many sacrifices to build up their facilities and the faith of their community. In 1995, St. George's merged with neighboring churches to form St. Elizabeth Ann Seton. St. George Church became the main house of worship for the new parish.

FOUNDING. Prior to 1888 early settlers of the Bark River and Hannahville areas were served sporadically by missionary priests who celebrated Mass in private homes and then in the schoolhouse. Farming replaced logging as the principal means of earning a living, causing the community to grow. The people worked to build a church.

A parcel of land located next to the school was offered for the construction site and parishioners donated lumber and labor to the effort. In June 1889 construction was complete and Bishop John Vertin dedicated the church to St. George. The name was chosen to honor a zealous citizen, George Douglas, who spearheaded efforts leading to the birth of the church.

During the five years that followed the building of the structure, the priest of St. Francis Xavier Parish in Spalding served the parish. In 1894, Father Francis Sperlein was assigned as St. George's first resident pastor. A rectory was built shortly after Father Sperlein's arrival. From 1894 to 1905 the pastor of St. George also cared for Sacred Heart Church in Schaffer.

On March 9, 1931, in the midst of the Great Depression, the church was destroyed by fire. Sparks from the chimney were believed to have ignited the blaze. Sacred vessels and some furniture from the rectory are all that were saved. Through the deep loyalty of the people, however, plans for a new church began immediately. The cornerstone for the new church, of English-Gothic style, was laid Sunday, Nov. 8, 1931. Some 900 people attended the ceremony. During construction, Mass was said at the vacated Frechette store. Construction was complete and the new church was dedicated July 31, 1932.

PARISH LIFE. Records show a major increase in the church's population between 1911 and 1914 when a significant number of Polish families came to Bark River to farm. Founding members of the parish were mostly French Canadian, Irish and Potawatomi Indian. A "misunderstanding," as accounts refer to it, led many of the Polish members to separate from the church in the mid-1930s to form a Polish National church in Harris. Years later some people returned to St. George's and others joined different churches.

In 1952 the parish began an extensive, 10-year program of improvements and repairs. Funds came from the generosity and hard work of the parishioners.

The early 1950s also marked the beginning of faith formation efforts for parishioners of all ages. The Sisters of Dominic from St. Thomas the Apostle Parish in Escanaba administered the program. Young people attended classes during the school year and vacation Bible school in the summer months. Various adult lessons were also offered. Many high schoolers began attending Holy Name School in Escanaba when it opened in 1954.

CLOSURE. In July 1995, St. George's parishioners joined in the merger of its neighboring churches to form St. Elizabeth Ann Seton Parish. The merger of St. Michael in Perronville, Sacred Heart in Schaffer and St. George was part of the Fully Alive in '95 reorganization plan. The first Mass of the newly formed congregation was held at the Senior Center in Bark River July 1, 1995. St. George remains the main house of worship for the parish.

RECORDS. The parish records for St. George are located at St. Elizabeth Ann Seton Parish in Bark River.

PASTORS. Fathers Francis Sperlein, 1894; John Burns, Paul Datin, Mathias Jodcy, James Corcoran, 1900-1905; William B. Stahl, 1905-1917; Augustus W. Geers, 1917-1923; Diendonne J. Breault, 1923-1940; Neil B. Stehlin, 1940-1952; Joseph J. Dunleavy, 1952-1965; Thomas P. Dunleavy, 1965-1970; Robert J. Cordy, 1970-1978; Matthew G. Nyman, 1978-1983; Paul A. Schiska, 1983-1990; Paul J. Nomellini, 1990-1993; Alexander K. Sample, 1993-1994, and Jeffrey A. Kurtz, 1994-1995.

Blessed Kateri Tekakwitha Mission (St. Catherine), Bay Mills

Jesuit priests serving the Sault Ste. Marie area established the St. Catherine mission at Bay Mills around 1900 and continued serving there for most of the 20th century. The church community overcame a devastating fire at Christmas in 1966 and rebuilt its house of worship, proving the community commitment to the faith. In 1980 the name of the mission was changed to Blessed Kateri Tekakwitha.

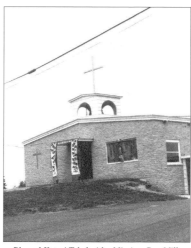

Blessed Kateri Tekakwitha Mission, Bay Mills

FOUNDING. Jesuit priests began serving the Bawating area, including present-day Bay Mills, in 1641.

It was Father William Gagnieur, SJ, who in 1904 arrived at Bay Mills and established the St. Catherine Church. Sometime after a 1909 fire at a mill on Bay Mills Point Road, Father Gagnieur obtained the mill's former laundry building for use as a church and had it moved to Bay Mills, where most of the Ojibwa people were living. That building was used until 1939.

During construction of the new church, Father Paul Prud'homme offered Mass in private homes. A sacristy where the priest stayed and parish hall were added to the church in 1963.

PARISH LIFE. Father Joseph C. Lawless served the areas from St. Ignace to Sault Ste. Marie to Drummond Island, a span of at least 200 miles, starting in 1946. He established religious education programs at Bay Mills and elsewhere and other programs for young people, both spiritual and social. Father Lawless even served as the bus driver for the programs, transporting young people himself.

On Dec. 21, 1966 a fire destroyed St. Catherine's Church. Also consumed in the blaze was a shipment of Christmas gifts that had been collected for poor families of the mission. Disheartened but not discouraged, the members of the church were determined to rebuild, despite their lack of means to do so.

News of the fire that devastated the poor community spread quickly throughout the state and the country. Along with $4,500 in donations from St. Catherine parishioners, cash donations poured in, many in small denominations. People also donated labor and materials to rebuild the church.

On Jan. 8, 1967 services began at Bay Mills Community Building. In just five months a new church was completed. Bishop Thomas L. Noa blessed the new structure Sept. 24, 1967.

On Jan. 1, 1980 the name of the mission was changed from St. Catherine to Blessed Kateri Tekakwitha, in honor of the Christian Mohawk girl declared Blessed by Pope John Paul II. In 2005, the mission was linked with St. Mary's in Sault Ste. Marie, St. Francis Xavier Parish in Brimley and Sacred Heart Mission on Sugar Island.

PASTORS.   William Gagnieur, SJ, 1904-1937; Paul Prud'homme, SJ, 1937-1970; Joseph Lawless, SJ, 1946-1993; James D. Birney, SJ, 1953-1959; John Longbucco, 1992-1995; Jeff Johnson, 1995-2001; Peter H. Fosu, 2001-2005, and Theodore Brodeur 2005-.

HOLY TRINITY MISSION, BEACON HILL

Holy Trinity Mission, Beacon Hill

From the turn of the 20th century through most of the 1960s, the people of Beacon Hill and Freda locations in Houghton County embraced the mission church of Holy Trinity. The small Beacon Hill church was not only the people's house of worship, but also a community center where parishioners gathered for fellowship, fund-raising events and regular weekend enjoyment. For most of its history, Beacon Hill was without a resident priest, so parishioners stepped up to support and maintain the church. Upon the closure of Holy Trinity, the people joined in the faith communities in Atlantic Mine and later Houghton.

FOUNDING. Around 1900 Father Frederick Richter of Atlantic Mine began traveling to Beacon Hill once a month to offer Mass in private homes. By 1908 the people of the Stanton Township communities of Beacon Hill, Freda and Redridge had completed work on the basement of an eventual church. The church was located on the county road between Beacon Hill and Freda, across from the public school. Services were held in the basement structure for four years while the church itself was constructed. The entire church was built through donated labor. Construction was completed and the first Mass said at Holy Trinity Church at midnight on Dec. 25, 1911.

A priest's living quarters consisting of a downstairs kitchen, dining room and bedroom, and an upstairs parlor, office and sacristy were later added onto the church. Only Fathers Herman Gagne and Stetz, who served prior to 1912, resided permanently at Beacon Hill. Most of the furnishings were removed from the rectory by 1921. During the rest of its history the mission was cared for by the priest serving as chaplain to St. Joseph Hospital in Hancock, assistant pastors at St. Joseph and St. Patrick Parish in Hancock, and priests at Dollar Bay and St. Ignatius Loyola Parish in Houghton.

PARISH LIFE. Prior to World War I, as many as 50 families from the Beacon Hill and Freda locations were members of Holy Trinity. The church was not only the people's house of worship, but also the place for weekly social hours and weekend parties. Card parties, plays and other entertainment were offered to parishioners and the general public.

From 1933 to 1937 Holy Trinity had attached to it a mission at Redridge. In those years, weekend Mass was offered alternately between Beacon Hill and St. Ann's chapel, the former Redridge schoolhouse. However, a 1937 fire that devastated the Redridge community also claimed the church. The people were then incorporated into Holy Trinity.

On Sunday, Aug. 23, 1959, to commemorate the church's 50th anniversary, a well-attended picnic and reunion were held on the lawn of the old Koepel residence at Beacon Hill.

Throughout its history, the young people of Holy Trinity Church were taught catechism after Sunday Mass by the priest with assistance from some lay women. In the summer months the sisters serving in Houghton and Hancock held religion classes for the children in Beacon Hill.

CLOSURE. The last recorded baptism that took place at Holy Trinity was in June 1968. Upon the closure of the mission church, the people were encouraged to attend St. Mary Star of the Sea in Atlantic Mine. Since 1996 the people of the Beacon Hill and Freda locations have attended St. Ignatius Loyola Church in Houghton. In 1973 the remainder of the Holy Trinity Church structure was purchased by a private party and materials salvaged for reuse.

RECORDS. Records for Holy Trinity Mission are located at St. Ignatius Loyola Parish in Houghton.

PASTORS. Fathers Joseph Boss, - - - Stetz, Herman Gagne, Melchior Faust, John T. Holland, Vincent Kreis, Carnell Hopkins, CP, James Schaefer, Michael Nivard, Michael Tuomey, John Leckman, Raymond Garin, Jerome Larsen, Chester Franczek, Paul Savageau, Thomas A. Drengacz, and James McCarthy.

St. Ann Mission, Bergland

St. Ann Mission in Bergland has never had a pastor of its own, but parishioners and community members have continued to maintain the individual identity of the church.

FOUNDING. Priests from Ewen first traveled to Bergland to offer Mass in the school gymnasium. In 1934 Father Gerald Harrington began offering Mass in a private home. In 1947 a grant was secured from the Catholic Church Extension Society to renovate the house into a chapel. Parishioners also contributed toward the venture. Pastors from Ewen held services there once a month.

St. Ann Mission, Bergland

PARISH LIFE. In 1962 responsibility for the care of St. Ann's was transferred from Ewen to White Pine. Mass was offered every Sunday for the first time in the history of the mission.

That same year construction began on a new church. Grant money was received, again from the Catholic Church Extension Society, and from the American Board for Catholic Missions. A solemn dedication of the new house of worship was held Oct. 6, 1963.

Improvements made to St. Ann Church in the early 1980s included a new roof, sanctuary remodeling and the installation of new carpeting throughout much of the church. Parishioners took part in fund-raising endeavors, such as bake sales, pasty sales and breakfasts to help pay for the cost of the upgrades. Parishioner donations paid for the installation of a new bell system in 1998.

The pastor of St. Catherine Church in Marenisco served St. Ann's from 1967 to 1973. Responsibility was transferred back to White Pine from 1973 to 2004. St. Ann's has since been linked to Sacred Heart Parish in Ewen. Joint ventures with the White Pine Church throughout the years benefited both parishes. Shared catechism classes at times, dual fund-raising ventures and even a combined parish council dot the history of the Catholic community there.

PASTORS. Fathers George Pernaski, 1961-1967; John McArdle, 1967-1969; Norbert Landreville, 1969-1971; David Jenner, 1971-1973; Glen Weber, 1973-1975; Wayne Marcotte, 1975-1980; Allan Mayotte, 1980-1985; Edward Wenzel, 1985-1991; John Longbucco, 1992; Michael Woempner, 1992-2002, and Thomas Ettolil, 2002.

ST. SEBASTIAN, BESSEMER

The start of the 20th century began a new era for St. Sebastian Church in Bessemer. Father Charles Swoboda arrived in 1902 and stayed for 50 years. He led the parish in adding on to its house of worship and started a grade school. The parish saw the construction of a new church building in 1979. Until 2004 the people supported their own parochial school.

St. Sebastian, Bessemer

FOUNDING. In 1886, just two years after the founding of the city of Bessemer, Father John Hennessy was sent to look after Catholics settling in the community. He held services in a hall above a store, but also purchased two lots, at the corner of Iron and Case streets.

Father Hennessy's successor, Father Edward Bordas, oversaw construction of the first church. A steeple was soon added. Upon completion of the building, Bishop John Vertin dedicated the new church to St. Sebastian on Feb. 3, 1889. A rectory was also built in 1889.

Membership and support of the parish plunged as the mining industry hit a decline in the 1890s, causing a long list of priests to serve short stints at St. Sebastian over the next 10 years. But a new era was ushered in in 1902 with the arrival of Father Charles J. Swoboda, who would serve the next 50 years.

PARISH LIFE. Immediately upon Father Swoboda's arrival, the parish supported an addition to the church. The economy of the area had improved and the congregation had grown. Another lot was purchased directly behind the existing church and a 44-foot addition was built. The entire structure was brick-veneered, stained glass windows were added and new pews and an altar were purchased. Bishop Frederick Eis blessed the renovated church May 13, 1906.

Active participation in parish organizations since the early days fostered the people's spiritual lives and benefited the church financially. Parish dinners and other activities both brought the people together for fellowship, and raised money for needed improvements to the church and school. Groups for men, women and youth have had membership of 100 percent of parishioners.

Beginning in the early 1930s the busy parish required an assistant pastor. Father Swoboda served the people of Bessemer faithfully until his death Feb. 15, 1952. He was buried in the city's Hillcrest Cemetery.

The original St. Sebastian Church was razed in 1978 to make room for a new house of worship. Bequests and money raised by parishioners made the project possible. Regular bingo games and pasty sales were among the fundraisers. In 1979 a new church was completed and dedicated.

PARISH SCHOOL. Father Swoboda started St. Sebastian grade school by purchasing the former Puritan Hotel in May 1918. The facility was moved to Iron Street, just east of the church, and renovated. Hotel rooms were made into classrooms and living quarters were created for the school staff.

The work was completed in October 1919 and the School Sisters of Notre Dame from Milwaukee arrived to start the school. On Oct. 26, 1919, Bishop Eis dedicated the facility.

A new school was erected and opened to students in September 1959. The debt was liquidated in 1963, and three years later a new parish hall and gymnasium were dedicated.

In the 1980s, the availability of sisters to staff the school declined and lay teachers began joining the staff. The year 1985 saw the school open for kindergarten through sixth grades with 100 percent lay teachers and administrators.

Declining enrollment of the schools in Gogebic County led to the April 2004 decision to combine St. Sebastian School and Our Lady of Peace in Ironwood. All Saints Academy opened in the former Our Lady of Peace School building on Aug. 31, 2004. The St. Sebastian School building was closed.

MISSIONS. From the time of its founding, the pastor of St. Sebastian Church has been responsible for serving missions in Wakefield, Mikado, Ramsay and Marenisco. From 1934 to 1952 a priest from St. Sebastian Parish offered Mass in the Anvil School gymnasium. This practice ceased when Anvil parishioners began attending Christ the King Church in Ramsay.

PASTORS. Fathers John Hennessy, 1886; Edward Bordas, 1886-1887; John Henn, 1887; Fabian Pawlar, 1887-1889; Joseph Kunes, 1889-1893; J. B. McGowan, 1893; William Joisten, 1893; Philip Erlach, 1893-1894; Martin Kehoe, 1894; Fredrick Eis, 1894; Joseph Haas, 1894-1895; Antoine Rezek 1895; Anthony Hodnick, 1895-1897; Adam J. Doser, 1897-1898; Henry Buchholtz, 1898; William Joisten, 1898-1899; Joseph Kraker, 1899-1901; Adolph Schneider, 1901-1902; Alexander Smietana, 1902; Charles Swoboda, 1902-1952; Robert Monroe, 1952-1953; Francis Krystyniak, 1953-1962; Chester Franczek, 1962-1974; Louis P. Bracket, 1974-1995; Joseph Carne, 1995-2002; James Roetzer, 2002-.

ST. MARY MISSION, BIG BAY

The founding of St. Mary Church in Big Bay followed the logging industry. It was a layman who, looking for regular Mass and instruction for his family, fueled the fire for a church and regular visits from a Marquette priest. The women of the parish are credited with raising the money for construction of the church, and later a basement for gathering space.

After nearly a century, St. Mary's continues to serve the needs of Catholics living in the small community located along Lake Superior north of the city of Marquette. The dedicated work of its parishioners keeps the church thriving.

St. Mary Mission, Big Bay

FOUNDING. Begun as the Mission of Birch on July 17, 1906, St. Mary's was set up to serve the many Catholics working in the logging industries in the communities of Birch and Big Bay.

In 1912, Bishop Frederick Eis gave care of the mission to St. Peter Cathedral in Marquette. The 50 or so Catholic families living in the area were visited only infrequently until a layman, Phil Aird, Sr., or "Grandpa Aird" as he is referred to in parish records, moved to Big Bay from Wisconsin to run the Independence Lumber Company Store. By that time, the community of Birch had disbanded following the closure of the mill, and the people moved to Big Bay.

Grandpa Aird traveled to Marquette and enticed Monsignor Mathias Jodocy of St. John Church to send a priest to the people once per month. Mass was held in the dance hall above the company store, in the schoolhouse and in the town hall.

PARISH LIFE. The women of the mission took on the task of raising money for a church. Card parties, bazaars and socials were held and, by the spring of 1919, enough money was collected to cover the cost of building the exterior of the church. The Lake Independence Lumber Company donated the site. Special collections were taken up and parishioners gave the money to finish the inside of the church. The Marquette Branch Prison donated the altar, St. Mary's Hospital in Marquette a statue, and others provided additional statues and the bell. The Stations of the Cross came from Sacred Heart Church in Munising.

Father Joseph L. Zryd was the first priest to serve the parish with weekly

Mass, beginning in 1930. Prior to that time, the people gathered every two weeks. It was through Father Zryd's "persistence," records say, that a basement was dug under the church and a parish hall with kitchen facilities and restrooms was constructed. Again, it was the women of the mission, led by Mrs. Phil Aird, Sr. who raised the money for the work.

In the 1940s the people once again banded together to bear the financial burden of renovating the church. St. Mary's became a parish Oct. 21, 1948 with the Blessed Sacrament reserved in the church for the first time. Father David Spelgatti was named the first pastor.

As work in the logging industry declined, membership in the church dwindled from 65 families in 1949 to 38 in 1950. But the people remaining in the parish stepped up to fill the void. "The material progress of the parish is almost beyond understanding. How so few people could accomplish so much is known only to the God whom they serve and love," said an article in the 1953 diocesan centennial issue of *The Northern Michigan Edition of Our Sunday Visitor*.

Bay Cliff Health Camp became a regular stop for pastors of the church. Under the leadership of Father Lawrence Gauthier, who served from 1971 to 1981, the parish council, ladies guild and liturgy committee were formed. Children's liturgies and Bible study for pre-schoolers and school-aged children plays a big role in parish life.

The parish celebrated its diamond jubilee in the summer of 1981 with special Masses, gatherings and a blessing of the fleet in the Big Bay Harbor.

St. Mary's reverted to mission status in 1991 under the care of the pastor of St. Michael Parish, Marquette. It has been served by priests of St. Peter Cathedral since July 1, 1999.

PASTORS. Fathers Joseph A. Sauriol, 1906; Jeremiah B. Moriarity, 1908; Msgr. Mathias Jodocy, 1912; Casper Douenberg, 1913; Paul Manderfield, 1913; Peter Bleeker, 1913-1914; J. Alderic Paquet, 1914-1917; Francis Seifert, 1915; Joseph Korb, 1918-1921; Edward J. Testevin, 1920; Frank Ignatz, 1921-1922; Joseph Guertin, 1921; Anthony J. Waechter, 1921-1923; Herman N. Gagne, 1923-1926; A. L. Dufresne 1927-1930; Joseph L. Zryd, 1930-1947; Martin Melican, 1930-1931; T. Stout, CP, 1933-1935; Neil Stehlin, 1936; Frank Ignatz, 1936-1937; Oliver O'Callaghan, 1942-1947; Ambrose Matejik, 1947-1948; David Spelgatti, 1948-1958; Glen Weber, 1958-1965; Charles Strelick 1965-1966; David LeLievre, 1967-1969; Timothy Desrochers, 1969-1971; Lawrence Gauthier, 1971-1981; John Shiverski, 1981-1983; Darryl Pepin, 1983-1985; James Challancin, 1985-1990; Richard Schaeffer, 1990-1991; John J. Shiverski, 1991-1995; Msgr. John E. Patrick, 1995-1999, and Msgr. Louis Cappo, 1999-.

St. Francis Xavier, Brimley

Partnerships between St. Francis Xavier and other churches in the region have resulted in joint councils and faith formation programs that provide for the needs of all Catholics in the region.

St. Francis Xavier, Brimley

FOUNDING. Jesuit priests from Sault Ste. Marie began offering Mass in private homes in 1887. Father John F. Chambon, SJ, led the parish in constructing the original church prior to the 20th century. In 1906 a larger church was constructed. In 1909 Brimley was assigned a mission of St. Joseph Parish in Rudyard.

PARISH LIFE. In April 1926, an out-of-control grass fire destroyed both the Brimley church and rectory. The present church was built and dedicated in 1929. Remodeling was undertaken in the mid-1960s and a summer parish festival was suggested to raise funds for a parish hall. Work began on the multi-purpose center in 1976. A mobile home was purchased for use as a rectory.

From 1976 to 1991, St. Francis was attached to Our Lady of Victory in Paradise. The pastor of Brimley was then given responsibility for the care of Holy Family in Barbeau and Blessed Kateri Tekakwitha in Bay Mills. A combined faith formation program was started.

Volunteers have been making and selling pasties to raise money for the church for more than 20 years. The group gathers in the parish hall regularly to prepare about 500 pasties. A $250,000 restoration project, including a new roof, bell tower repairs, new steps and sidewalks, flooring throughout the church, and new windows, including stained glass, was partially funded by pasty sales.

PASTORS. Fathers John F. Chambon, SJ, 1881-1895; J. Dulude, SJ, 1900-1907; Timothy Malone, 1907-1911; Bernard Eiling, 1911-1917; Anthony Oehlerer, 1917-1939; Peter Bleeker, 1939-1941; Robert J. Cordy, 1942-1946; James J. Schaefer, 1947-1948; Edward Malloy, 1948-1954; Francis Gimski, 1955-1965; Kenneth Bretl, 1965-1967; James Menapace, 1968-1971; William McGee, 1971-1972; Terry Villaire, 1972-1975; Joseph Francis Rausch, OFM Cap., 1978-1985; Raymond Mulhern, 1985-1989; Robert Paruleski, 1989-1991; Paul Manderfield, 1991-1992; John Longbucco, 1992-1995; Jeff Johnson, 1995-2001; Peter Fosu, 2001-2005, and Theodore Brodeur, 2005-.

Sacred Heart, Calumet

Since its founding in the late 1860s, Sacred Heart Church in Calumet has undergone many changes. Franciscan Fathers from Cincinnati, Ohio have led the parish through the highs and lows for more than a century, beginning in 1890. Economic high times for the community brought prosperous conditions to the church, allowing for many material improvements, including a new church, a grade school and a high school.

But as the copper industry declined, the people slowly moved away and the schools were eventually closed. A devastating fire in 1982 destroyed the 86-year-old church, but the spirits of parishioners were not dampened. A new Sacred Heart Church stands at the center of the Catholic community just as the original did 130 years ago.

Sacred Heart, Calumet

FOUNDING. Father Edward Jacker of Hancock began making regular visits to Calumet in 1865. Frequent trips to serve the needs of Catholics in that community between 1865 and 1868 led to his taking up permanent residency there in the spring of 1868. Not long after his arrival a modest church was erected in the Hecla Location. In 1875 the first rectory was added.

In 1890 a century of service to Sacred Heart began for the Franciscan Fathers of the St. John the Baptist Province of Cincinnati, Ohio.

PARISH LIFE. In 1897 it was decided to replace the original wooden church with a larger edifice. A new sandstone structure was erected at the site of the original church. A winter chapel, rectory and parish hall were also built within the complex. On Oct. 16, 1897 Bishop John Vertin dedicated the new church.

By 1904 Sacred Heart had withstood the separation of many of its members into five other national churches.

The Sacred Heart sanctuary was enlarged in the 1930s. In 1941 the rectory was enlarged and in 1952 the first floor was remodeled. In 1946 the church basement was excavated. Deterioration forced the removal of the church steeple in 1953. The structure was replaced by a stainless steel dome and cross. Parishioners helped to restore the old Sacred Heart Cemetery grounds in 1958.

Redecorating the church interior was among the major improvements made in the 1960s in preparation for the parish's 1968 centennial celebration. In 1990 the parish celebrated 100 years of dedicated service by the Franciscans.

PARISH SCHOOL. Sacred Heart Grade School was started in 1891. The first year, Sisters of Notre Dame from Milwaukee instructed 375 students in first through eighth grades. In 1893 a high school course was added. A new convent was built for the sisters in 1906.

Many fund-raising projects were carried out to provide financial assistance to the school. Annual picnics and bazaars were among the efforts.

The original grade school, located on Lake Linden Avenue, was deemed insufficient in 1953. Thus started a three-year fund-raising effort to construct a new building. A structure to serve students of all Calumet area parishes was erected on Calumet Avenue in Calumet. The new Sacred Heart Central Grade School opened its doors in the fall of 1957.

The last high school class graduated from Sacred Heart in 1960. The facilities were no longer considered adequate and with declining enrollment being a continuing trend, it was decided not to build a new school. The grade school continued, however, adding a pre-school program in 1970.

In 1982, after 91 years of continuous operation, Sacred Heart Central School was closed permanently. Low enrollment was the main factor behind the closure.

The parish was devastated when fire swept through the church and rectory, quickly destroying the 86-year-old landmark on Aug. 13, 1983. Following the fire, Mass was held at St. Paul's church and then at the CKL Center (Calumet-Laurium-Keweenaw) Center. The parish held a dedication ceremony for its new church on May 4, 1986.

PASTORS. Fathers Edward Jacker, 1868-1873; Gerhard Terhorst, 1873; co-pastors Henry Thiele and A. L. David 1873; Frederick Eis, 1873-1874; John Brown, 1874-1875; Fabian Pawler, 1875-1878; John Burns, 1878-1880; Luke Mozina, 1880; Peter Menard, 1880-1881; Fabian Pawler, 1881-1882; John Chebul, 1882; Theodore Aloysius Majerus, 1882-1883; Augustus William Geers, 1883-1885; John Chebul, 1885-1886; Melchior Faust, 1886-1888; Philip Erlach, 1888-1889; Ignatius Otis, 1889-1890; Peter Welling, 1890-1891; Hilary Hoelscher, 1891-1892; Pax Winterheld, 1892-1894; Lawrence Long, 1894; Angelus Hafertape, 1894-1895; Peter Welling, 1895-1899; Sigismund Pirron, 1899-1907; Casimir Dietrich, 1907-1909; Herculan Zeug, 1909-1911; Bede Oldegeering, 1911-1913; Basil Henze, 1913-1920; Julius Henze, 1920-1927; Luke Bertsch, 1927-1929; Humbert Wehr, 1929-1932; Ethelbert Harrington, OFM, 1932-1951; James Fitzpatrick, OFM, 1951-1957; Jerome Kircher, IOS, 1957-1960; Bennet Rothan, 1960-1964; Gerald Held, OFM, 1964-1970; Louis Rohr, 1970-1975; Jordan Telles, OFM, 1975-1981; Casper Genseler, 1981-1986; Robert Weakley, OFM, 1986-1992; Marian Douglas, 1992-2001; Paul Manderfield, 2001-2003, and Abraham Mupparathara, MCBS, 2003-.

St. Anne, Calumet

French members of Sacred Heart Church in Calumet left to start St. Anne Parish in 1884. The people built a grand church, but as the population of the area dwindled, economic struggles forced the closure of the parish. In 1966 four national churches merged into the new parish of St. Paul the Apostle.

St. Anne, Calumet

FOUNDING. About 100 families of French descent left Sacred Heart Church in Calumet to form a parish of their own. The vacated St. Patrick's Society Hall was remodeled into a church and dedicated to St. Louis of France on Aug. 1, 1886.

PARISH LIFE. In less than 20 years the church had become too small to accommodate the increasing membership. The original church was moved to a vacant lot and continued to be used until the new church was completed.

Excavation began in the summer of 1900 and by June of the following year a grand, $50,000 structure made of Portage Entry sandstone was complete. Bishop Frederick Eis blessed the new edifice, renamed St. Anne, June 19, 1901. In just three years the parish managed to pay off the entire debt of the new church.

Prior to the 1913 copper strike, parish membership exceeded 900 families. Overcrowding led to people standing in the streets to hear the Sunday Mass.

As the copper industry declined, the remaining parishioners struggled to support the church. Despite the economic hard times, necessary repairs continued to be made to the structure. In 1921 a pipe organ was purchased. A new roof was put on in 1928. In 1938 Father Albert J. Treilles built a grotto of Lourdes in the winter chapel.

CLOSURE. Following the 1966 merger of the four Calumet national churches into the new parish of St. Paul the Apostle, the St. Anne structure was converted into the St. Anne's Heritage Center museum.

RECORDS. St. Anne Parish records are located at St. Paul the Apostle.

PASTORS. Fathers Antoine Vermare, 1884-1889; Fabian Marceau, 1889-1895; Louis Archille Poulin, 1895-1897; Michael Letellier, 1897-1898; Joseph R. Boissonnault, 1898; James Aldric Paquet, Albert J. Treilles, 1938-1940; Joseph Beauchene, 1940-1950; Gerard LaMothe, 1950-1951; Roland Dion, 1951-1963, and Wilfrid Pelletier, 1963-1966.

St. John the Baptist, Calumet

St. John the Baptist was able to remain an independent parish for more than 50 years, despite economic hardships, then the blow of a fire that leveled the church in 1925. The people worked hard and made many sacrifices to maintain the parish facilities. Later parishioners helped support Sacred Heart parochial school. But in 1966 the church was closed and parishioners merged to form the new Calumet faith community of St. Paul the Apostle.

St. John the Baptist, Calumet

FOUNDING. At the turn of the 20th century the membership of St. Joseph Parish in Calumet was so large that something had to be done to accommodate all of the Slovenian and Croatian parishioners. Given that space was not available to add on to the church, a separation was agreed upon.

Effective in the spring of 1901, the Croatians left to form a new congregation, St. John the Baptist. Father Joseph Polic, the former assistant at St. Joseph's, became leader of the new parish.

As was customary, the Calumet & Hecla Mining Company donated land and made a monetary contribution to the new parish. During construction of the new church, services were held at St. Mary's (Italian) Church. Bishop Frederick Eis dedicated the completed structure on June 21, 1903.

On April 27, 1925, after having survived the area's economic turmoil, St. John's suffered a devastating blow. The church was destroyed by fire. Struggling financially, the parish was unable to rebuild its grand house of worship. Instead, the basement of the original structure was remodeled for use as the new church.

PARISH LIFE. Father Victor Rogulji, the first Franciscan to lead St. John Parish, was assigned its pastor in 1939. Shortly after his arrival the parish decided to build a new church. The basement facility had been deemed unfit for services. Work on a new structure began in August and just four months later, on Dec. 8, 1940, Bishop Joseph C. Plagens dedicated the new church. Parishioners and friends of the parish donated generously toward the project.

In 1941 St. John's commemorated the 40th anniversary of its founding. The celebration coincided with the 13th century jubilee of Catholicity in Croatia, which was being celebrated worldwide. A Mass of Thanksgiving was held June

29, 1941. That year the parish also published an anniversary booklet.

MISSION. In the late 1920s, St. John's pastor, Father Fortunate Ciupka, helped the people of Ahmeek and surrounding areas organize a parish of their own, Sacred Heart Mission.

CLOSURE. St. John Church was closed in 1966 when the four national churches of the city merged into the new parish of St. Paul the Apostle.

RECORDS. Records for St. John the Baptist Parish are located at St. Paul Church in Calumet.

PASTORS. Fathers Joseph Polic, 1901-1905; Henry Bontempo, SJ, 1905-1906; Alexander Wollny, 1906-1907; Anton Zuvic, 1907-1909; Michael Gattin, SJ, Msgr. Martin Krmpotic, Francis Rancinger, 1911; Joseph Medin, 1911-1921; Michael Hudack, 1921-1922; John Kovalsky, 1922-1924; Fortunatus Ciupka, SDS, 1924-1938; John Leckman, 1938-1939; Victor Rogulj, 1939-1951; Vladimir Vlahovic, 1951, and John McArdle, 1966.

St. Joseph, Calumet

St. Joseph Parish in Calumet led a prosperous independence from the time the Slovenians separated from Sacred Heart Church until the 1966 amalgamation forming the new St. Paul the Apostle Parish. The grandeur of the church structure gives witness to this prosperity. The church became the home of St. Paul Parish and was named a Michigan Historic Site in 1987.

St. Joseph, Calumet

FOUNDING. In May 1889 Father Joseph Zalokar began serving as pastor to the Slovenian and Croatian settlers in Calumet. At first services were held in the Sacred Heart Church. But by Nov. 29, 1889, Bishop John Vertin dedicated a new church to St. Joseph.

The Slovenians' church was erected on land leased from the Calumet & Hecla Mining Company, and was located on the corner of Oak and Eighth streets. A rectory was attached to the church at the time of construction. The interior of the church was lavishly decorated in 1897. In 1901 the Croatians formed a congregation of their own.

The Slovenians were in the process of planning for a parish school when their times of prosperity came to a halt. On Dec. 9, 1902, a disastrous fire destroyed the church. In just two hours the structure was leveled. All of the parish records were destroyed and it has been written that the priest barely escaped with his life. While plans got under way for the construction of a new church, St. Joseph parishioners held services at St. Mary's Italian church.

PARISH LIFE. The members of the parish, 350 families and 400 single men at the time, agreed that the new church would be rebuilt using sandstone. The cornerstone was laid Aug. 18, 1903. Young women of the parish held concerts, plays and other fundraisers to purchase the main altar. The young men followed suit and worked to raise money for an organ.

Just prior to the start of Lent in 1904 the basement of the eventual church was finished and ready for services. Bishop Frederick Eis blessed the bells May 28, 1905. Three years later, on June 18, 1908, Bishop Eis dedicated the new church. In those early days the parish was well known for having "the best church choir" in the Copper Country.

Polish Catholics in Calumet had seen the dedication of St. Anthony of Padua

Parish Nov. 5, 1882. Following the copper strike in 1913, when many residents were forced to leave the area to find work, St. Anthony closed its doors and members joined St. Joseph Church. The people of St. Anthony's presented St. Joseph's with a statue of their patron saint. The records for St. Anthony's are now located at St. Paul the Apostle in Calumet.

In 1928 St. Joseph's constructed a new rectory. Restoration of the church was undertaken in 1945, and was financed in part by church bazaars and other parish activities. A new roof was put on in 1948. Improvements to the church in the 1950s included the construction of a kitchen in the parish hall.

In the mid-1950s a Catholic Youth Organization was started at St. Joseph's. In 1957 the parish was among the five Calumet churches that banded together to form the common Sacred Heart Central Grade School.

In commemoration of the church's 75th anniversary in 1965, parishioners again contributed financially to restoring the original beauty of the church and adding some modern touches. A new tile floor, modern lighting, roof insulation and cleaning of the church hall were all part of the improvements. A diamond jubilee booklet was also published in 1965.

CLOSURE. The historic St. Joseph building was chosen for the new home of St. Paul the Apostle Parish, formed in 1966 by the merger of the city's four national churches.

RECORDS. The records for St. Joseph Parish are located at St. Paul Church in Calumet.

PASTORS. Fathers Joseph Zalokar, 1889-1892; Marcus Pakiz, 1892-1904; Lucas Klopcic, 1904-1932; Peter Sprajcar, 1932-1954, and Joseph A. Kichak, 1954-1966.

ST. MARY, CALUMET

The Italian members of Sacred Heart Parish in Calumet separated to form a parish of their own in 1897. The Assumption of the Blessed Virgin, or St. Mary's, operated as an independent parish until it merged with other national churches of the city to form St. Paul the Apostle Church in Calumet in 1966.

St. Mary, Calumet

FOUNDING. As people of the same nationality were separating from Calumet's mother church of Sacred Heart to form independent parishes, the Italians also sought a house of worship of their own. Between 1893 and 1897 several attempts were made to raise the needed money for a church and secure the land. Finally, on Oct. 12, 1897, Bishop John Vertin dedicated a new church to the Assumption of the Blessed Virgin, St. Mary's.

The pastor lived on the second floor of the sacristy until 1934 when a house next to the church was purchased for use as a rectory. Parishioners contributed financially to a remodeling of the church that took place in 1950.

CLOSURE. Following the 1966 merger of the four Calumet national churches into the new parish of St. Paul the Apostle, St. Mary's Church building was eventually sold.

RECORDS. Records for St. Mary Parish are located at St. Paul Church in Calumet.

PASTORS. Fathers Anthony Molinari, 1897-1907; Anchetto Silvioni, 1907-1911; Wenceslaus Parenti, 1911-1912; Felix Mancini, 1912-1913; Simmi, 1913-1914; Felix Mancini, 1914-1919; Francis Geynet, 1920; Francis Greco, 1920-1933; Herman Fadale, 1933-1950; Stephen Savinshek, OFM Cap., 1950-1951; Steven Wloszczynski, 1951, and Arthur Parrotta 1965-1966.

St. Paul the Apostle, Calumet

St. Paul the Apostle Church in Calumet was formed in 1966 as the result of the merger of four national churches. Parish traditions, activities and active lay ministries have united the people into one harmonious community.

St. Paul the Apostle, Calumet

FOUNDING. Until 1966, separate entities existed for the French people of Calumet at St. Anne's Church, the Croatians at St. John the Baptist, Slovenians and later the Polish at St. Joseph's and the Italians at St. Mary's. It was Bishop Thomas L. Noa who recommended the people of these struggling parishes come together into one viable unit. Low parish membership and economic constraints were among the reasons for the suggested merger.

PARISH LIFE. The historic St. Joseph building was chosen for the new St. Paul the Apostle Parish's house of worship. The structure was constructed in 1908 and named a Michigan Historic Site in 1987. The original organ dedicated in St. Joseph Church on May 31, 1908 is still in use at St. Paul's today.

Parishioners struggled with the closure of their separate churches, but Father Ephraem Sitko is said to have been instrumental in easing the unification process.

A Fall Festival started in 1975 allowed each of the ethnic groups represented in the parish to have booths displaying their best wares. The festival, along with a bingo fund-raiser, has continued for more than 25 years. Summer picnics and regular coffee and doughnut socials after Sunday Mass are among additional fellowship activities at St. Paul's. Many people also participate in lay church ministries. In 1988 the people of the parish sewed 185 stoles for priests of the diocese and vestments for the bishop—a project they take great pride in. In 1990 the parish produced a pictorial directory of its membership.

St. Paul parishioners continued supporting the Sacred Heart Central Grade School. From 1957 when the central school opened, through its closure in 1982, the people of all of the Calumet parishes made the parochial education possible.

PASTORS. Father Ephraem Sitko, 1966-1968; John McArdle, 1968-1975; Donald Shiroda, 1975-1980; Wayne Marcotte, 1980-1991; David Jenner, 1991; Cyprian Berens, OFM, 1991-2001, and Sebastian Ettolil, MCBS, 2001-.

St. Cecilia, Caspian

The history of St. Cecilia Parish in Caspian proves good things are worth waiting for. The people began gathering as a community of worshipers around 1913, but it wasn't until 1955 that the dream of having a proper church structure was realized. Some 50 years later, the faith community continues to thrive in spirituality and fellowship. The community was under the guidance of the pastor of the Gaastra parish for the first 50 years, but that relationship was reversed in 1950. When the Gaastra parish closed in the late 1980s, many of its members joined St. Cecilia.

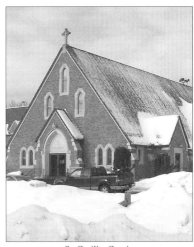

St. Cecilia, Caspian

FOUNDING. Although St. Cecilia wasn't named an independent parish until 1951, Catholics living in Caspian began worshiping as a united group around the turn of the 20th century. Priests from Iron River were the first to offer Mass regularly. In 1913, the region became a mission of St. Mary Parish in Gaastra. Private homes, the public grade school and the Duke di Abruzzi Lodge were all places where Mass was celebrated.

Unfortunate circumstances dampened many early attempts at building a church in Caspian. But the people remained eager for a parish of their own and in 1921, were able to entice the priest serving in Gaastra to take up residency in Caspian.

The Verona Mining Company donated a house for Father Albert Treilles. While living in Caspian he purchased a number of lots along Brady Avenue and formed a building committee for an eventual church. Funds were raised and the men of the parish donated labor toward a basement church. In 1923 Bishop Frederick Eis blessed the new structure. The Great Depression and the war that followed, however, kept the upstairs of the church from ever being raised. In the meantime, a rectory was built in Gaastra and the priest serving both regions moved back to that community. In October 1929 a recreational center was completed in Caspian and used for all parish activities.

PARISH LIFE. For four decades the people of Caspian remained enthusiastic in their faith despite the frustration of not having a church building. Regular religious instruction was offered during the school year and women from various religious orders gave vacation religious school in the summers. A

Catholic Youth Organization was formed and parishioners entered the Third Order of Mount Carmel.

By about 1950 records show that there were three times as many parishioners in Caspian as in Gaastra and so the newly appointed Father Herman Fadale was assigned to St. Cecilia Church with St. Mary Parish in Gaastra reverting to mission status. Father Fadale's main charge was to build a church and a rectory in Caspian. Father Joseph Schaul became pastor on June 26, 1951. The rectory was completed on April 20, 1952. The next step was to build the church.

Parishioners gathered March 14, 1954 to hear a message of encouragement from Bishop Thomas L. Noa. Then they went door-to-door to raise funds for the church. By the end of the day, more than $13,500 in cash and $40,500 in pledges had been received. The church of English Tudor style was completed and the first Mass said there April 3, 1955, Palm Sunday. Bishop Noa dedicated the new church on July 17.

When St. Mary Parish in Gaastra closed in 1988, many of its parishioners joined St. Cecilia Church. Active ministries include the St. Anne Society, Holy Name Society, choir, and St. Vincent de Paul Society.

PASTORS. Fathers John J. Stenglein, 1913-1914; William J. Remillard, 1914-1915; Hilarious Marcucci, 1915; Nickolas H. Nosbish, 1917; John Neuhaus, 1917-1921; Albert C. Pelissier, 1921; Albert C. Treilles, 1921-1938; Fortunatus Ciupka, 1938; James Alderic Paquet, 1938; Adrein Somers, 1938; Joseph J. Seifert, 1939-1940; Thomas P. Dunleavy, 1940-1942; Charles Daniel, 1942-1950; Herman Fadale, 1950-1972; Louis Brackett, 1972-1974; Chester Franczek, 1974-1978; Donald Hartman, 1978-1981; Otto Sartorelli, 1981-2001, and Norman Clisch 2001-.

SACRED HEART MISSION, CEDAR RIVER

The history of the Sacred Heart Mission at Cedar River spans almost a century. Served by priests from Precious Blood Parish in Stephenson, the Sacred Heart Mission was whole-heartedly supported and kept up by its parishioners. In 1983 the people had to bear the burden of seeing their church close.

Sacred Heart Mission, Cedar River

FOUNDING. Father Martin Fox was the first to visit the sawmilling town of Cedar River, located on the shore of Green Bay in Menominee County.

Throughout its existence, the church was served as a mission of Precious Blood in Stephenson. In 1887 Father F. X. De Langie pushed for the construction of a church at the Cedar River site.

At the time of construction, Cedar River residents gave generously, so much so that when the humble structure was completed, $50 remained in the building fund. The women of the parish then held picnics and other socials to raise the money needed for pews, church furnishings and a bell. Bishop John Vertin blessed the mission and dedicated it Sacred Heart in September 1888.

CLOSURE. After serving the people of Cedar River for more than 100 years, Sacred Heart Church was closed in 1983. The bell from the Sacred Heart Mission was donated to the Cedar River community chapel in 1990.

RECORDS. Records for the Sacred Heart Mission are located at Precious Blood Parish in Stephenson.

PRIESTS. Fathers Francis X. Becker, 1883-1884; F. X. Weninger, 1884; Mathias Orth, 1884; F. X. De Langie, 1884-1888; Prosper Girard, 1888; John Burns, 1888-1889; Anatole O. Pelisson, 1889; Michael Weis, 1889-1890; Peter P. Mazuret, 1890; Alberico Vitali, 1890; Joseph Hoeber, 1890-1891; Joseph A. Sauriol, 1891; Paul Datin, 1892-1893; William Joisten, 1893; Fidelis Sutter, 1894; John Henn, 1894-1895; Thomas V. Dassylva, 1895; Francis X. Barth, 1895-1911; Carl B. Liedgens, 1911-1924; Joseph Dufort, 1924-1931; Joseph Beauchene, 1931-1940; Philip de Neri Jutras, 1940; Albert J. Treilles, 1940-1952; Aloysius Hasenberg, 1952; Monsignor Glen Sandord, 1952-1968; John V. Suhr, 1968-1971; Conrad E. Suda, 1971-1978; John McArdle, 1978-1985, and Raymond Zeugner, 1985-1983.

Sacred Heart, Champion

Despite having to hoe a somewhat rocky road at times, the people of Champion have continued to pave the way for Catholics in western Marquette County. Started in 1873, Sacred Heart and its mission in Michigamme are among the earliest churches in the Diocese of Marquette.

Sacred Heart, Champion

FOUNDING. Catholic pioneers of the iron mining town of Champion, mostly French-Canadian, were first visited at irregular intervals by priests from Negaunee. Then in 1871, Father Francois Berbue of Clarksburg began serving regularly. Mass was initially said in private homes and later in the school house. Father Berbue took up residence and built Champion's first church in 1873. In 1882 a rectory was built separate from the church.

On July 16, 1919, the church was struck by lightning and burned to the ground. Father Alexander W. Hasenberg quickly rallied the people to replace the church. An abandoned school building some 500 feet from the foundation of the original church was purchased, moved and remodeled. For $13,000, the people had a new church transformed in Roman style. The facility was ready by Thanksgiving Day the same year.

PARISH LIFE. In 1938 the men of the parish made many improvements to the church. A landscaping project consisted of leveling a considerable amount of property toward the rear of the church and rectory. Some 60 spruce and balsam trees were planted in a semi-circle to serve as the background for a future Sacred Heart Shrine. In 1994, 1,000 Scotch pines were planted on a parcel of land owned by the church.

The early Altar/Rosary Society was well-known for its card parties with plenty of prizes and refreshments. The society also sponsored bingo to raise funds for the church.

The people again displayed much enthusiasm for building up the church in the late 1950s and early 1960s when a basement hall was dug underneath the existing building and a new heating plant installed. In the mid-1960s the church was updated to meet the changes brought about by Vatican II. New furnishings and new pews were purchased. In the 1980s the stained glass windows were refurbished and repaired.

In the early 1980s, two women religious stationed at St. Augustine Parish in Republic began serving as pastoral coordinators for Sacred Heart and St. Agnes Mission in Michigamme. Pastoral Coordinators were Sisters Maureen Freeman, CSJ, and Paul Bernadette Bounk, CSJ, 1984-1993; Margey Schmelzle, OSF, 1994-; Charlotte Ann Wagner, 1994-1997, and Lois Risch, OSF, 1999-.

The church again received a facelift in August, 1998 when a 20-foot by 40-foot addition to the north side was added and extensive interior and exterior renovations were undertaken. The construction provided a new gathering space, a Blessed Sacrament Chapel and a new vesting area. While renovations were being made, worship services took place at St. Agnes Church in Michigamme.

MERGER. St. Agnes in Michigamme was closed March 28, 1999. But unofficially, Catholics in the Champion and Michigamme area had begun thinking of themselves as one parish with two churches long before that time. In 1978 the parish councils were combined and in 1993 the finances. The social committees were also combined in the early 1980s and sponsored countless events that held the community together.

In order to recognize the blending of Sacred Heart and St. Agnes churches, several items from St. Agnes Church were incorporated into the renovated Sacred Heart Church. Five windows, the church bell, statues, a large cross from the church and a baptismal font were incorporated. The new space was blessed on May 23, 1999.

PASTORS. Fathers Joseph F. Berube, 1873-1876; Anatole Pelisson, 1876; Martin A Fox, 1876-1878; Joseph A. Hubly, 1878-1879; Daniel Swagers, 1879; Joseph Niebling, 1879-1882; Thomas J. Atfield, 1882-1885; Fabian Pawlar, 1885-1887; Francis X. Becker, 1887-1889; M. J. Van Stratten, 1889; Alberico Vitali, 1889; Edward P. Bordas, 1889-1892; John H. Reynaert, 1892-1894; John Henn, 1894; Prosper Girard, 1894-1905; Fabian Marceau, 1905-1906; Alexander Hasenberg, 1906-1921; John Nuerenberg, 1921-1922; Peter Bleeker, 1922-1924; Peter J. Dapper, 1924-1938; Thomas Anderson, 1938-1940; Bernard A. Karol, 1940-1947; Oliver J. O'Callaghan, 1947-1952; George A. Stuntebeck, 1952-1958; John H. Ryan, 1958-1963; Donald Hartman, 1963-1965; Charles J. Strelick, 1965-1969; Paul A Schiska, 1969-1971; Louis Wren, OFM, 1971; Wayne Marcotte, 1971-1975; John Shiverski, 1975-1976; Anthony J. Polawski, 1976-1977; Henry C. Gelun, SJ, 1977-1978; David C. Jenner, 1978-1979; Robert F. Polcyn, 1979-1980; James W. Genovesi, 1980-1984; and canonical pastors Peter Carli, 1984-1985; William Richards, 1985-1988; Peter Oberto, 1988-1993; James Scharinger, 1993-1994; Gilles Brault, 1994-1999; sacramental minister Edward Wenzel, 1999-2000, and canonical pastor Msgr. Peter Oberto 2000-.

St. Rose, Channing

Throughout its 60-year history, the people of St. Rose Parish in Channing have given generously in support of the spiritual and material good of the church. Now linked with Foster City, the church has also been responsible for missions in Northland and Sagola. When St. Margaret of Sagola was closed in 1982, the people were welcomed into the church of their neighboring community. Donations of labor and money for a complete remodeling of the church in the 1990s was an outward sign of the people's pride in their parish.

St. Rose, Channing

FOUNDING. Prior to the construction of a church in Channing, residents attended Mass in private homes and in two different school buildings that had been purchased for use as places of worship. Beginning in 1894 priests from St. Augustine Parish in Republic would travel the 20 miles to Channing once a month. Early and late Mass times alternated between Channing and St. Margaret Church in nearby Sagola. Father William Stahl, who served from 1917-1940, commuted in an old touring car in the summers and on the train in winters. He also went to Channing on Saturdays to hear confessions and to teach catechism.

In 1941 the people of Channing received permission to erect a church. Excavation started that fall and by Christmas Eve the building was close enough to completion that Midnight Mass was held there.

PARISH LIFE. A July 26, 1942 dedication ceremony marked the first visit by Bishop Francis J. Magner to the small parish. The bishop blessed the cornerstone of the church, offered a dedication service followed by a High Mass and then confirmed 65 young people and adults. Father Glen F. Sanford was appointed the church's first pastor. At this time, the parish also acquired a house one block away from the new church to serve as a rectory. In 1966 a new rectory was built next to the church.

From 1950 to 1963, Sisters of St. Dominic taught summer religious education classes and confirmation classes, and held missions for the young people of the parish. The women's altar society hosted a fall festival, monthly card parties, bake sales and other activities to raise money for the parish.

Under the pastorate of Father Christopher Gardiner, 1984-1991, parishioners gave generously to support a complete remodeling of the church. A spacious new addition to the front of the church replaced a small foyer. The basement was renovated into a parish hall. The main body of the church was repainted, and new carpeting, a new sound system and new lighting were installed.

In 1994 St. Rose became a mission of Guardian Angels Parish in Crystal Falls, but a year later was rejoined to St. Joseph Mission in Foster City.

MISSIONS. At the time of St. Rose's dedication in 1942, the parish was given responsibility for St. Margaret Mission in Sagola. St. Margaret's was founded in 1895. Priests from Channing continued to care for the mission until its closure in 1982. St. Rose then took over responsibility for St. Joseph Church in Northland. Care of the Northland church was given to St. Anthony of Gwinn in 1991.

PASTORS. Fathers Fabian Pawlar, 1894; Fidelis Sutter 1895; Augustus Geers, 1898-1905; Owen J. Bennett, 1906-1907; Joseph L. Hollinger, 1907-1916; George J. Dingfelder, 1916-1917; William B. Stahl, 1917-1940; Glen Sanford, 1940-1945; Philip Longlean, 1945-1946; James McCarthy, 1946-1951; Jerome Larsen, 1952-1960; George Pernaski, 1960-1961; Joseph Felix, 1961-1966; Dennis O'Leary, 1966-1970; Gino Ferraro, 1970-1972; Raymond Valerio, 1972-1983; Raymond Zeugner, 1983-1984; Christopher Gardiner, 1984-1991; Robert Paruleski, 1991-1994; Norman Clisch, 1994-1995; Michael Steber, 1995-1998; Hubby Mathew, MST, 1998-2000; George Kuppayil, MST, 2000-2005, and Peter Fosu, 2005-.

St. Anne, Chassell

St. Anne, Chassell

Since its construction more than 100 years ago, the people of St. Anne Parish in Chassell have worked hard to maintain and make improvements to their house of worship. As in many small communities, the church also serves as the site of social activities. Countless fund-raising efforts through the years have been a source of fellowship for the people, bringing in the funds necessary to enhance the church.

FOUNDING. Prior to 1890, priests serving in Houghton would travel to the Chassell area to offer Mass to Catholic farmers and lumber mill workers. Mass was offered every two weeks in the summer and once a month in the winter in the Chassell schoolhouse.

Father R. Regis, an associate pastor in Houghton, took steps to erect the first church in Chassell. He became St. Anne's first pastor in July 1890. By 1894 Father Regis' successor, Father Prosper Girard, had finished the church and overseen construction of the rectory. The St. Anne Society raised much of the money needed for the construction of the church and rectory. Card parties, dinners and a string of successful plays brought in a large sum of money.

PARISH LIFE. After two decades of continued growth, the parish saw the need for an enlarged structure. In 1917 the church and rectory received much-needed improvements. The sacristy was moved back and additional space was built into the middle of the church. A vestibule and porch, stained glass windows and a wood-burning furnace were also added. In 1953 construction of the parish's basement hall was completed. Parishioners planned and saved for the hall for five years.

The parish held a five-day celebration of its 50th anniversary in July 1937. A centennial celebration began with Christmas Eve Midnight Mass in December 1986 and continued through the year 1987. A parish pictorial directory was published, along with a centennial booklet including the parish history. The main celebration took place during the weekend of July 25-26 in observance of the Feast of St Anne. Festivities included a street dance, historic displays in the church hall, a Centennial Mass led by Bishop Mark Schmitt and a banquet at Suomi College.

In 1989 a handicapped entrance was completed on the north side of the church. A carport and a new vestibule with restrooms, an elevator and a new stairway to the parish hall were also added. A new parking lot was constructed at this time.

Upon the completion of the significant renovation project, St. Anne's parish held a rededication ceremony June 1, 1991. Improvements to the church at that time included repainting and redecorating the church interior, installing of a new sound system, heating and air conditioning system, new piano and organ, new flooring and a new freestanding lectern and baptismal font. A small Eucharistic chapel was added to the rear of the altar and, at the rear of the church, a cry room was constructed. In the mid-1990s the rectory was renovated and a new parish office was built connecting the rectory with the church.

Continuing parish activities at St. Anne's include frequent breakfasts after Sunday Mass, prepared by the men of the parish, and special holiday celebrations. Parishioners regularly participate in the community's Strawberry Festival and the Adopt-a-Highway program, cleaning U.S. Highway 41 in the community.

As a result of the diocese's pastoral planning initiative Fully Alive in '95, St. Anne Parish and Holy Family Church in South Range began sharing a pastor.

PASTORS. Fathers R. Regis, 1887-1891; Prosper Girard, 1891-1894; Joseph Hoeber, 1894; Paul Datin, 1894-1896; Thomas Dassylva, 1896-1898; Fabian Marceau, 1898-1902; Anthony Vermare, 1902-1917; John T. Holland, 1917-1919; Thomas Kennedy, 1919-1920; J. M. Morin, 1920; Joseph Dufort, 1920-1924; William Gagnieur, 1924; Albert C. Pelissier, 1924-1930; Cletus Manon, CP, 1930-1938; George Stuntebeck, 1938-1943; Frederick Hofmann, 1943-1948; Francis J. Gimski, 1948-1954; Frederick Hofmann, 1954-1963; Howard V. Drolet, 1955; William McGee, 1963-1964; Raymond Garin, 1964-1965; Claude Pulvermacher, OFM Cap., 1965; John H. Ryan, 1965-1970; Marius Noe, OFM, Cap., 1970; Dennis O'Leary, 1970-1971; Wilfred Pelletier, 1971-1973; Allen J. Mayotte, 1973-1975; William P. Russell, 1975; Thomas Weier, OFM Cap., 1975-1980; Glen Weber, 1980; William Callari, 1980-1993; Bede Louzon, OFM Cap., 1993-2000; Sebastian Ettolil, MCBS, 2000-2001, and Larry Van Damme 2001-.

St. Mary Magdalene, Cooks

St. Mary Magdalene Parish in Cooks had been a mission church under the administration of another of the Garden area parishes for much of its history. Then, in 1991, the church was raised to parish status and teamed up with Nahma and Garden to share resources, including one priest.

St. Mary Magdalene, Cooks

FOUNDING. Lumberjacks from Canada began the community of Cooks near the end of the 19th century. After the forests of the town—originally named Durham—were all leveled, these early settlers began farming the land. The first Catholics in Cooks were visited occasionally by priests from Rapid River, Manistique and Garden. Then, in 1890, parishioners banded together to build a church. The structure was completed and dedicated to St. Mary Magdalene.

The parish's first priest was Father George LaForest of Manistique who began offering services in the Cooks church regularly. Priests from Nahma also served the church in the first decade of the 20th century.

PARISH LIFE. In 1910 Cooks received its first resident priest, Father Vincent C. Savageau, O. Praem. Father Savageau was appointed to care for the missions of Cooks, Thompson, Isabella, St. Jacques and Nahma. In 1916 a rectory was built in Cooks.

Despite having all six of these churches to care for – Mass was said in Cooks only once a month – Father Savageau is said to have succeeded in "keeping the spiritual fabric of the churches intact."

Catechism classes were held regularly for the young people of the parishes. St. Mary Magdalene Altar Society was formed and the men gathered to form the Holy Name Society in 1924.

In the early 1940s Father Nolan B. McKevitt received the first assistant pastor. This allowed for Mass to be offered twice each month at each mission. A Catholic Youth Organization was also formed at this time.

In 1943 the old rectory was sold and the profits used to build a basement hall for the parish.

In 1947 the Dominican Sisters of Adrian, Mich., staffed a religious summer vacation school for the young people of the Garden area. That same year St.

Andrew's Church in Nahma was raised to the status of individual parish, leaving only Cooks and Fayette as missions of Garden. Mass began to be offered weekly at St. Mary Magdalene for the first time.

Improvements to the parish plant from the mid-1940s to mid-1950s included a kitchen in the basement hall, extensive remodeling of the interior of the church and new pews. The exterior was also painted.

In 1953 responsibility for administration of St. Mary Magdalene was transferred to St. Andrew's in Nahma. A tri-parish council was formed with an equal number of representatives from Cooks, Nahma and Garden.

A change of status for the church in 1991 raised it to an independent parish. A shortage of priests in the diocese led to Cooks, Nahma and Garden combining parish councils and sharing a priest who resides in Garden.

PASTORS. Fathers George LaForest, A. A. Vissers, O. Praem; Vincent Savageau, 1910-1940; Nolan McKevitt, 1940-1945; Glen Sanford, 1945; Wilfred Pelletier, 1945; Arnold Thompson, 1946-1948; James Schaefer, 1948; Ronald Bassett, 1949-1953; John H. Ryan, 1953-1958; Michael F. Hale, 1958-1962; Frank Hollenbach, 1962-1967; James Hebein, 1967-1968; Donald Hartman, 1968-1969; Ephraem Sitko, 1969-1978; Frank M. Lenz, 1978-1982; Peter A. Minelli, 1982-1984; Ronald Skufca, 1984-1986; John E. Martignon, 1986-1988; Ronald K. Timock, 1988-1990; Peter Petroske, 1990-1991; George S. Maki, 1991-1993; David W. Sedlock, 1993-1996; John Martignon, 1996-2002, and Thomas Varickamackal 2002-.

GUARDIAN ANGELS, CRYSTAL FALLS

Through economic and social ups and downs, the parish of Guardian Angels in Crystal Falls has stood as a symbol of hope in the community. The people were patient for more than 30 years, waiting for the right time to construct a magnificent house of worship. In the decades that followed the 1954 completion of the building project, the people's enthusiasm for spiritual and educational opportunities multiplied.

Guardian Angels, Crystal Falls

FOUNDING. The people of Crystal Falls mining camps were first visited by Father Melchior Faust of Quinnesec in the fall of 1883. Father Faust said Mass on an irregular basis in Doucet's Hall and later in a skating rink that was destroyed by fire just after the priest's belongings were removed. Then pastors of Iron River cared for the mission, two of whom are credited with building the first church. Father J. E. Struif purchased building materials and planned for the church, and his successor, Father Joseph Haas, completed the construction.

On May 8, 1887, the parish received its first resident pastor, Father Edward Chapuis. Father Chapuis built a residence onto the rear of the church. Bishop John Vertin dedicated Guardian Angels on Oct. 23, 1887.

PARISH LIFE. In 1904 Father Joseph P. Kunes arrived, and stayed at Guardian Angels for 22 years. With the community having survived the economic depression of the earlier decade, the priest and parishioners went to work making much needed improvements to the church. A 30-foot addition was put on the structure, the church was completely redecorated and new pews and stained glass windows were installed. The changes were so extensive that Bishop Frederick Eis rededicated the parish on Oct. 28, 1906.

By the late 1920s the basic church structure was deteriorating and plans were put in place for a new basement structure. After 50 years, the final Mass was said at the original church Oct. 31, 1931. Upon the church's demolition, the sacristy was preserved and used to house the Blessed Sacrament and for weekday Mass. Sunday services were offered at city hall and CCD was often held outside on the parish grounds.

The new basement church was finished for Christmas Midnight Mass in

1931. Parish activities led by the Altar Society garnered money for much of the project. A new entrance to the church to be used for weddings and funerals was added in 1936 and a series of interior and exterior improvements carried out in the mid-1940s did much to enhance the facility.

By the spring of 1953 construction of today's Guardian Angels superstructure had begun. Parishioners raised $12,000 in 10 days to pay for the veneer stone for the exterior. Additional fundraisers and parish donations helped pay for the construction and for stained glass windows.

Bishop Thomas L. Noa dedicated the new church April 4, 1954. Of modern Gothic style, the church has a seating capacity of 450. The basement structure, having served as the church for 31 years, became a social hall. A new bell system was installed in 1958. A new rectory was completed in 1962. The church interior was again updated to meet the changes of Vatican II.

The late 1970s and early 1980s saw a spiritual revival in the parish. Many new programs were implemented to enhance the spiritual, social and educational experience of the people. Greater focus was placed on parish retreats, evangelization and youth CCD programs. The tradition of the Iron County ecumenical service began at Guardian Angels in 1972.

Guardian Angels celebrated the 100th anniversary of its founding with a yearlong centennial celebration that began on Oct. 4, 1987. Highlights included a Mass of Thanksgiving and banquet, the sealing of a centennial capsule in June 1988, a Polka Mass in August, and a closing Mass and breakfast Sept. 25.

In 1993 the church acquired a former grocery store building on North 5th Street. The building was converted into an educational center. In 2000 the church interior was repainted, new carpeting installed, lighting updated, restrooms remodeled and new furniture purchased for the sanctuary.

MISSIONS. Father Joseph Kunes started a mission church in Amasa in 1910. In 1943 Father Joseph Gondek, also of Guardian Angels, started the St. Edward Parish in Alpha. Both the Amasa and Alpha churches were closed in 1995 and the people were encouraged to join the Crystal Falls church.

PASTORS. Fathers Edward Chapuis, 1887-1888; F. X. DeLangie, 1888-1889; John Chebul, 1889; Joseph Sauriol, 1889-1890; John H. Reynaert, 1890-1891; John Burns, 1891; Fidelis Sutter, 1891-1892; Antoine Rezek, 1892-1894; Fabian Pawler, 1894-1895; Frederick Eis, 1895-1899; John Kraker, 1899; John Keul, 1899-1901; William Gagnieur, SJ, 1901; Francis X. Becker, 1901-1904; Joseph P. Kunes, 1904-1926; B. M. Weakland, Gerald Kenney, Nilus McAllister, David Ferland, A. L. Dufresne, Joseph Guertin, 1929-1935; Raymond Bergeron, 1935-1940; Philip DeNeri Jutras, 1940-1946; Joseph Seifert, 1946-1948; Carl Petranek, 1948-1968; Donald Shiroda, 1968; Joseph Gondek, 1968-1991; Norman Clisch, 1991-1997; Raymond Zeugner, 1997-2003, and Dino Silvestrini 2003-.

St. Frederick, Daggett

The people of Daggett built St. Frederick Church from the ground up and continued making donations to improve the building throughout the life of the church. The church had the responsibility of caring for the Holy Rosary Mission in Banat for more than 60 years.

In 1981 St. Frederick's began sharing a priest with Precious Blood Parish in Stephenson. In 1995 the Daggett church closed and the people joined in the faith communities of neighboring parishes.

St. Frederick, Daggett

FOUNDING. After repeated petitions, Daggett residents attending Precious Blood Church in Stephenson were finally granted a parish of their own in the early 1920s.

A campaign by Father Francis Seifert to "buy a brick for the new St. Frederick's church" along with the $25 donations from each of the parish's 80 families was successful in raising money for construction of the new structure. In fact, accounts say the response to Father Seifert's campaign was so great that the Daggett Post Office was upgraded to third class because of the increase in mail.

Bishop Frederick Eis officially established St. Frederick Parish Sept. 16, 1921. One of the parishioners donated the land for the new church. During construction Mass was held in the village hall and the pastor lived in a hotel.

PARISH LIFE. Throughout its history, the people of St. Frederick's continued to make generous donations toward the betterment of the church. In the 1940s the original stucco exterior was replaced with gray asbestos shingles. The interior of the rectory and the sanctuary were redecorated, including the addition of a new altar and new Stations of the Cross. The basement was enlarged and a stoker-fed heating plant installed. The 1960s also saw many church improvements, including the complete renovation of the rectory.

In 1962, after the parish hall was damaged by a fire at the nearby Voelker Garage, St. Frederick's purchased the former village hall for use as a parish center. Shortly thereafter, parishioners purchased memorial plaques to raise money for major improvements to the new hall.

St. Frederick's observed its 50th anniversary Sept. 19, 1971. Bishop Charles A. Salatka was the principal celebrant at the Mass marking the milestone. A dinner and night of dancing followed the Mass.

St. Frederick's is proud of the many men and women from the parish who have pursued religious vocations, becoming priests and sisters.

MISSION. Upon the dedication of St. Frederick Church, the parish was also given the responsibility of caring for the Holy Rosary Mission in Banat.

CLOSURE. After more than 70 years of devotion, Daggett was without a resident pastor as of July 1, 1994. Assignment changes by Bishop James H. Garland meant parishioners there would have to attend Mass in Stephenson or Nadeau. Although Sunday Mass would no longer be offered, the doors of St. Frederick's were left open for funerals and weddings for another year.

As a result of the diocese's Fully Alive in '95 pastoral planning process, St. Frederick's Parish was officially closed on July 1, 1995. The church building was eventually sold to a private party.

RECORDS. Records for St. Frederick Parish are located at Precious Blood Church in Stephenson.

PASTORS. Fathers Frank A. Seifert, 1921-1937; Joseph Seifert, 1937-1939; William Schick, 1939-1945; John J. Leckman, 1945-1958; Thomas Ruppe, 1958-1963; John J. Ryan, 1963-1965; Norbert P. LaCosse, 1965-1976; Joseph Felix, 1976-1981; John McArdle, 1981-1985, and Raymond Zeugner, 1985-1995.

Sacred Heart, DeTour

When Father Theodore Bateski arrived at DeTour early in the 20th century, he was the first priest to stay longer than one year. In fact, he served the church and the surrounding community for more than 50 years. The foundation laid by Father Bateski continues to be built upon in the 21st century as the people of Sacred Heart Parish, and the women religious who serve as pastoral coordinators there, lead by example and create a prosperous parish out of a small number of members and limited resources.

Sacred Heart, DeTour

FOUNDING. Jesuit fathers from Sault Ste. Marie were the first to serve Catholics in DeTour. Bishop John Vertin dedicated the first church Sacred Heart Sept. 1, 1884. The first resident priest, Edward Jacker, volunteered for the post in 1886. He only stayed from spring to the start of winter that year. Because of the small parish's inability to provide for the sustenance of the pastor at that time, priests were given assignments of just one year in DeTour.

In 1897 the pastor of Sacred Heart was also given the responsibility to care for the newly established mission in Goetzville, St. Stanislaus Kostka, which was declared independent in 1922.

After a long period of many itinerant pastors, Father Theodore Bateski arrived in DeTour in July 1904. Sacred Heart was Father Bateski's first priestly assignment and he stayed there more than 50 years.

PARISH LIFE. During the first 20 years of the 1900s, parishioners, led by their pastor, did the brunt of the work and helped raise the necessary funds for a new church. Father Bateski gathered logs every day for two summers. He and the men and boys of the parish made the 200,000 bricks needed for construction. Father Bateski even went into the wholesale construction business, earning a large sum for the parish's building fund.

Finally, after two decades of hard work and sacrifice, Bishop Paul J. Nussbaum dedicated the finished structure Aug. 5, 1923. After the service a huge barbeque was held with an ox roasted for dinner.

The exquisite interior of the church in no way reflects the modest means by which the church came to be. Of Gothic modern style, the church has vaulted ceilings and stunted pillars with lights hanging from the ends. When construction was complete, the congregation with very limited means had incurred no debt, but rather remarkably had $2,000 remaining in the building fund.

Father Bateski's ambitious efforts didn't stop with construction of the church. For his involvement in civic and political efforts in DeTour he came to be known as "the fighting priest of the northland." From 1932 to 1938 he served three consecutive terms as the president of the village of DeTour. Among other endeavors, he started the Chamber of Commerce, and promoted the building of the Mackinac Bridge, an airport and new roads.

The church saw many improvements over the years. A parish hall was constructed in 1946. Kitchen equipment was purchased in 1953.

The 1960s saw upgrades to the rectory and masonry and roofing repairs to the church and rectory, while the church also was resided and re-painted, and a Blessed Sacrament shrine was constructed.

From 1983 to 1986, Sacred Heart was a mission of St. Stanislaus Kostka Parish in Goetzville. Then Sacred Heart was again elevated to parish status with St. Florence of Drummond Island as a mission. The pastor of Goetzville serves as sacramental minister for both Sacred Heart and Drummond Island. In the mid-1980s, Franciscan Sisters of Christian Charity from Manitowoc, Wis., began serving as pastoral coordinators at DeTour and Drummond Island. Pastoral coordinators were Sisters Margey Schmelzle, 1986-1994; Karen Neuser, 1986-1989; Colleen Sweeting 1989-1999, and Lois Risch, 1994-1999. With the arrival of these devoted servants came a new religious education program for the youth of the parish and a revitalization of parish life.

In 1985 Sacred Heart received a $20,000 loan from the Catholic Church Extension Society to carry out a three-year plan to renovate the church edifice.

MISSION. The pastor of Sacred Heart has been responsible for the care of St. Florence Church of Drummond Island since 1960.

PASTORS. Fathers Edward Jacker, 1886; John F. Chambon, SJ, Fidelis Sutter, 1888; Anatole O. Pellisson, 1888-1889; Adam J. Doser, 1891; Joseph Neumair, 1891-1892; Joseph G. Pinten, 1892-1893; Edward P. Bordas, 1893-1894; Prosper Girard, 1894; John F. Chambon, 1894-1895; Joseph Wallace, 1895; W. Anselm Mlynarczyk, 1896-1898; J. S. Hawelka, 1900; Theodore Bateski, 1904-1960; Raymond Smith, 1960-1963; William Russell, 1963-1964; Dennis O'Leary, 1964-1966; Robert Haas, 1966-1969; Henry Mercier, 1969-1970; Aloysius Ehlinger, 1970-1975; C. Michael Rhoades, 1975; Henry C. Gelin, SJ, 1978-1983; Frank M. Lenz, 1983-1985; Richard C. Schaeffer, 1985-1988; George Gustafson, 1988-1989; John M. Maloney, 1989-1990; Michael Steber, 1990-1995; Larry Van Damme, 1995-1997; Benedetto Paris, 1997-2000; Jacek Wtyklo, 2000-2003, and Sebastian Kavumkal, MST, 2003-.

St. Francis of Assisi Mission, Dollar Bay

Responsibility for the care of St. Francis of Assisi Mission in Dollar Bay has changed many times in the last century, but the people of the small mission have remained fervent in their faith and active in parish life.

St. Francis of Assisi Mission, Dollar Bay

FOUNDING. Prior to the 1892 construction of the Dollar Bay church, people living in the copper milling town walked to Mass in either Houghton or Hancock. As Dollar Bay's population increased, the Hancock priest began offering Mass in the Dollar Bay schoolhouse.

Father Joseph Hoeber initiated fundraising efforts for the Dollar Bay church. On Nov. 6, 1892, Bishop John Vertin dedicated St. Francis of Assisi Mission.

PARISH LIFE. In 1901, to accommodate a growing parish population, improvements were made to the church, including a 30-foot addition and construction of a confessional. The pastor of St. Francis of Assisi also began serving a small chapel constructed a few miles away at Grosse Pointe. Mass was offered there twice per month until the 1920s.

The last resident priest to serve Dollar Bay was Father Jerome Larsen in 1950. The mission was then cared for by Our Lady of Mount Carmel in Franklin Mine, 1948-1967; St. Cecilia Parish in Hubbell, 1967-1981; Sacred Heart in Calumet, 1981-1986, and St. Cecilia in Hubbell, 1986-1996. Since 1996 St. Francis has been under the care of Church of the Resurrection in Hancock.

In 1991 new siding was put on the church and rectory. The parish celebrated its centennial with a commemorative Mass and banquet held June 27, 1992.

PASTORS. Fathers Joseph Dupasquier, 1892; Adam Doser 1892; Hubert Zimmermann, 1895-1899; James Miller, 1899-1922; Michael Nivard, James Schaefer, John J. Leckman, Raymond J. Garin, Jerome Larsen, 1950-1951; Chester Francek, 1948-1950; John Noel Arneth, Michael Hale, 1954-1955; Conrad J. Dishaw, 1956-1959; S. Patrick Wisneske, 1959-1963; Robert Haas, 1963-1966; Louis C. Cappo, 1967-1968; Michael Hale, 1968-1975; John McArdle, 1975-1978; James Hebein, 1978-1981; Jordan Telles, OFM, 1981-1986; Ronald Timock, 1986-1988; James Genovesi, 1988-1996, and Wayne Marcotte, 1996-.

Immaculate Heart of Mary Mission, Donken

The Immaculate Heart of Mary Mission in Donken saw regular support from parishioners, seasonal residents and the entire community.

FOUNDING. A large number of Catholics were among those who followed the Vulcan Corporation to Donken in the 1940s. In 1948 Father Norbert Freiburger, pastor at Painesdale about 10 miles away, led the people in erecting a church of their own. Bishop Thomas L. Noa dedicated the house of worship Oct. 24, 1948.

Immaculate Heart of Mary Mission, Donken

The church was served as a mission of Painesdale until 1967, when care was transferred to South Range. In 1971 Donken became a mission of Rockland.

PARISH LIFE. To coincide with the 10th anniversary of the mission, an outdoor shrine to the Immaculate Heart of Mary was erected in 1958.

The church altar society held an annual fund-raising bazaar to support improvements to the church, such as sanctuary renovations in 1966 and the construction of a confessional in 1978.

The parish observed its 25th anniversary in 1973. A commemorative Mass was held Oct. 21. The parish also produced a booklet of its history at that time.

Summer attendance at the church was often triple that of the rest of the year. As the population of Donken declined, the mission became a seasonal church.

CLOSURE. The doors to Immaculate Heart of Mary were closed permanently following the diocese's pastoral planning initiative Fully Alive in '95. The final Mass was said Sept. 24, 1996.

RECORDS. Records for Immaculate Heart of Mary Mission are located at St. Ignatius Parish in Houghton.

PASTORS. Fathers Norbert Freiburger, 1948-1951; John Belot, 1951-1957; William McGee, 1957-1958; John Suhr, 1958-1963; Howard Drolet, 1963-1964; Wilfred Pelletier, 1964-1965; Thomas Coleman, 1965; James Hebein, 1965-1967; Frank Hollenbach, 1967-1970; Raymond Hoefgen, 1970-1973; David Jenner, 1973-1975; Aloysius Ehlinger, 1975-1978; Joseph Carne, 1978-1986; Eric Olson, 1986-1992; Bede Louzon, OFM, Cap., 1992-1993, and Ronald Timock, 1993-1995.

St. Florence Mission, Drummond Island

Jesuit missionaries began serving Catholics on Drummond Island in the 1800s. The current church was constructed in 1942 and then enlarged to meet the needs of the congregation in the 1970s. Since the 1960s diocesan priests at DeTour have ministered to the people of St. Florence Mission. Women religious have played a large role in supporting the church, first through religious education programs and, since the 1980s, by serving as pastoral coordinators.

St. Florence Mission, Drummond Island

FOUNDING. Prior to the 1941 establishment of St. Florence Church, Jesuit missionaries offered Mass at irregular intervals in the private homes of Drummond Island residents. Father Joseph F. Chambon, SJ, is known to have built a church on Drummond Island around 1890.

Father Paul Prud'homme, SJ, was the first to visit the mission on a regular basis. He led construction of the current St. Florence Church, dedicated by Bishop Francis J. Magner on June 28, 1942. Jesuits continued serving the mission until 1960 when diocesan priests took over permanently and the church was assigned a mission of DeTour.

PARISH LIFE. The St. Florence church was constructed of logs cut and sawed on the island. Bazaars and later a hunter's dinner were held to raise money for improvements to the house of worship. The parish's first rectory was purchased in 1950.

In 1977 it was stated that the church was only half the size it needed to be to serve the people. "From the opening of the fishing season in May through deer hunting season in November, there are as many people outside as in," the pastor said while requesting an addition to the structure. The original church, with seating for about 30, is now a wing of the current structure. In 1987 the sanctuary was again renovated.

On Aug. 1, 1992 the mission church celebrated its golden anniversary with a commemorative Mass and rededication. A dinner followed in the Drummond Township Hall.

In 1966, Ursuline Sisters from St. Ignace began traveling to Drummond

Island by boat in the summer months to help the priest with religious summer education programs. In 1986, Franciscan Sisters of Christian Charity from Manitowoc, Wis., began serving as pastoral coordinators at DeTour and Drummond Island. The pastor of Goetzville serves as sacramental minister for both Sacred Heart and DeTour. Pastoral Coordinators include Sisters Karen Neuser, 1986-1989; Margey Schmelzle, 1986-1994; Colleen Sweeting 1989-1999, and Lois Risch, 1994-1999.

PASTORS. Fathers Paul M. Prud'homme, SJ, Joseph C. Lawless, SJ, James D. Birney, SJ, Hank Gelin, SJ, Theodore G. Bateski 1904-1960; Raymond Smith, 1960-1963; William Russell, 1963-1964; Dennis O'Leary, 1964-1966; Robert Haas, 1966-1969; Henry Mercier, 1969-1970; Aloysius Ehlinger, 1970-1975; C. Michael Rhoades, 1975-1978; Henry C. Gelin, SJ, 1978-1983; Frank M. Lenz, 1983-1985; Richard C. Schaeffer, 1985-1988; George C. Gustafson, 1988-1989; John M. Maloney, 1989-1990; Michael J. Steber, 1990-1995; Larry P. Van Damme, 1995-1997; Benedetto J. Paris, 1997-2000; Jacek Wtyklo, 2000-2003, and Sebastian Kavumkal, MST, 2003-.

ENGADINE CATHOLIC MISSIONS

From 1967 to 1995 the conglomerate commonly called Engadine Catholic Missions consisted of Our Lady of Lourdes Parish in Engadine, St. Stephen Mission in Naubinway and St. Timothy Mission in Curtis. From 1995 to 2004 the churches in the grouping were Engadine, Naubinway and Gulliver. On Dec. 1, 2004, Our Lady of Lourdes was linked with Naubinway, Germfask and Curtis.

PASTORS   Fathers Paul Schiska, 1967-1969; Donald P. Hartman, 1969-1970; Daniel J. Sparapani, 1970-1973; Arthur J. Parrotta, 1973; David H. Rocheleau, 1973-1980; Walter Sheedlo, 1980-1987; Michael J. Capyak, 1987-1992; Jeffrey A. Kurtz, 1992-1994; Mieczyslaw T. Oniskiewicz, 1994-1997; Jan Szczkowski, 1997-1998; Mariusz Makowski, 1998-1999, and Timothy W. Hruska 1999-.

ST. TIMOTHY MISSION, CURTIS

St. Timothy in Curtis was established as a mission of Engadine in 1942 when Father Wilfred Pelletier built the first church there. Prior to that time services were held in the Curtis Township Hall. Although St. Timothy was at first a seasonal mission only, summer tourism was so high that three Sunday Masses were held. The church was closed for the winter after the deer hunting season.

St. Timothy Mission, Curtis

St. Timothy became a year-round mission in 1968.

From 1967 to 1995, Curtis saw many improvements made to its facilities. On Nov. 7, 1976 St. Timothy's dedicated a new multi-purpose room. The addition includes a kitchen area and restrooms. The multi-purpose room is the site of religious education classes, socials, conferences and other activities. In the winter, the facility doubles as a chapel. The project was completed thanks to the full cooperation of the Catholic community, visitors and a grant from the Catholic Church Extension Society.

In the late 1970s the bell from the former St. Joseph Church in Gould City was installed at St. Timothy's. The bell was rededicated Oct. 22, 1978.

The interior and exterior of St. Timothy's has been remodeled and renovated over the years. The grounds have been landscaped and additional parking space has been added.

From 1995 to 2004, St. Timothy was assigned a mission of Holy Rosary Parish in Grand Marais, about 50 miles away. As a result the laity in Curtis took on even greater responsibility for the church. St. Timothy's first pastoral council was formed during this time.

In 2006 plans were being made to construct a new, larger church.

OUR LADY OF LOURDES, ENGADINE

Prior to the 1913 construction of Our Lady of Lourdes Parish in Engadine, Catholics living in the area attended Mass at St. Mary Church in Rappinville, a small chapel constructed in 1907 on the Peter Proton farm. Mass was still occasionally celebrated at the old St. Mary Church until about 1935.

Originally, the pastor serving Engadine was also responsible for missions in Germfask, Moran, Carp River, Trout Lake, Rexton, Gilchrest and Garnet.

In the fall of 1957, the original Engadine Church was torn down and the congregation was without a church for about seven years. A new church was built and dedicated in 1964. The present rectory was purchased around 1956 and has since been remodeled several times.

Our Lady of Lourdes, Engadine

Some of the parish traditions include fish fries, bingo and a hunters dinner.

In 1981 the entryway of the church was enclosed to provide an extra classroom for faith formation.

In 1967 one centralized CCD program was started and one parish council was formed for the Engadine Catholic Missions.

PASTORS   Fathers John Manning, 1898; Joseph A. Sauriol, 1898; John Chebul, 1898; Joseph H. Beauchaine, 1910-1912; Joseph Dufort, 1912-1915; William J. Remillard, 1915-1916; Bernard LeFebre, 1916-1917; Herman N. Gagne, 1917; Francis Geynet, 1918; Joseph Tastevin, 1918; Peter Bleeker, 1918-1922; Peter Dapper, 1921; Francis A. Seifert, 1921; Joseph Guertin, 1922-1923; Charles Fox, 1923-1931; Raymond Bergeron, 1931-1935; Joseph Seifert, 1935-1937; Thomas P. Dunleavy, 1937-1939; James J. Schaefer, 1939-1943; Wilfred Pelletier, 1943-1945; Clifford Nadeau, 1945-1948; Conrad Dishaw, 1948; Joseph Kichak, 1948-1954;, Ralph Sterbentz, 1954-1957; Clement LePine, 1957; Stephen Mayrand, 1957-1960; Arthur J. Parrotta, 1960-1964; August Franczek, 1964; Ephraem Sitko, 1964-1965, and Paul Schiska, 1965-1967.

St. Stephen Mission, Naubinway

In 1887, Father John Manning of Newberry built the first church in Naubinway. The first resident pastor, Father Edward Bordas, was assigned there in July 1894. Father Bordas added a sacristy, pews and a confessional to the church, and he finished the rectory that Father Manning had started.

St. Joseph Mission church was built in Gould City in 1894. The pastor serving St. Stephen served Gould City as well until the St. Joseph mission closed in 1967. The church building was dismantled in the 1970s.

From 1906 to 1915, responsibility for the care of the Naubinway Mission was with St. Francis de Sales Parish in Manistique. Our Lady of Lourdes has cared for Naubinway since 1915. The original church and rectory in Naubinway stood until about 1952 when a new edifice was constructed under the direction of Father Joseph Kichak. No new rectory was built. The present church includes a basement hall and kitchen facilities.

St. Stephen Mission, Naubinway

PASTORS. Fathers John Manning, 1887-1889; Edward Bordas, 1894; John Manning, Joseph Sauriol, A. Hasenberg, James Corcoran, 1906-1908; Bernard J. Schevers, OP, 1908-1915.

St. Anne, Escanaba

Despite its modest start and the challenge of rebuilding after two devastating fires, St. Anne Parish has stood as a cornerstone to Catholics in Escanaba for more than 100 years. Loyal parishioners built their own school, and a tremendous modern church facility, and formed many successful programs. The people's willingness to serve others is carried out in countless outreach programs to the local community and even extends worldwide.

St. Anne, Escanaba

FOUNDING. Wanting to preserve their own language and customs, the French-Canadian members of St. Joseph Church, many of whom worked in the lumber industry, received permission to form their own church in 1887. The modest structure built of wood was dedicated to St. Anne Sept. 30, 1888. Father Joseph Martel was appointed its first pastor. In the subsequent five years, many improvements were made to the church, including construction of a rectory.

Worn out by the demands of his work, Father Martel lived only a few years after arriving in Escanaba. His remains were buried under the church, but were removed and relocated to Holy Cross Cemetery in the 1940s during further plant renovations.

PARISH SCHOOL. In 1901, after construction of St. Anne's first church, the parish started its own grade school. The Sisters of St. Joseph of Concordia, Kan., staffed the school for 20 years. Improvements were constantly made to the school, and in 1907 a convent was built to house the sisters.

In 1922 the Franciscan Sisters of Christian Charity took up the ministry of teaching at the school. Extensive renovations to modernize the school were carried out in 1947.

In 1963, 10 years after St. Anne's church was relocated, the dream of having a new school on the same grounds was realized. However, in 1971 the parish elementary school closed and the five Escanaba parishes consolidated into Holy Name Central Grade School. St. Anne's building was then used to house kindergarten through third grades. In 1982 these grades were transferred to the main building and St. Anne's began leasing its facilities to the Intermediate School District. The building is also used for St. Anne's faith formation classes.

PARISH LIFE. In April 1919, the church suffered extensive damage in a fire believed to have been caused by defective wiring. But the people took up the work of renovating and making improvements to the church. Money was raised through a subscription drive. Among the improvements made at this time was the addition of a chapel and sacristy.

Nearly 30 years later, at the same time extensive upgrades were being made to the parish school, the church was again devastated by fire. On July 15, 1947, a blaze of undetermined origin destroyed the church. Despite the massive setback, the people continued to rally for their church. A temporary chapel was set up in the parish hall in the basement of the school.

After the 1947 fire St. Anne's was moved from its original location to the southwest area of the growing city. The massive undertaking came to fruition six years later. On April 26, 1953 the modern facility was dedicated. In 1962, following major parish improvements, plans were made for a new school, rectory and convent, all of which were dedicated in September 1963.

At this new facility, successful programs flourished. The Catholic Youth Organization thrived from the 1940s through the 1950s. The famed St. Anne Adult Choir was started in 1961 by Father Stephen Mayrand. Faith formation programs were established for youth and adults in the 1970s, as were parish missions and retreats.

In September 1987, St. Anne's began celebrating its 100-year anniversary. A Mass and dinner were held at the Ruth Butler Exhibition Building at the Upper Peninsula State Fair Grounds. One year later a second celebration to close out the anniversary year was held at the same location.

In the early 1990s St. Anne's established a life memorial for the unborn. Two headstones on the parish grounds serve as a grieving place to remember those who died through abortion. Prayer vigils for life are held regularly.

Also in the 1990s, St. Anne's began to sponsor Operation Honduras. Teams of volunteers, supported by parishioners and community members, take annual mission trips to offer aid in the poor Central American country.

PASTORS. Fathers Joseph Martel, 1888-1893; Peter Menard, 1893-1912; Fabian Marceau, 1912-1916; Raymond Jacques, 1916-1935; Joseph E. Guertin, 1935-1945; George LaForest, 1945-1946; Sebastian Maier, 1946-1948; Clifford Nadeau, 1948-1960; Stephen Mayrand, 1960-1969; Louis Cappo, 1969-1971; Glen Weber, 1971-1972; Conrad Dishaw, 1972-1986; Peter A. Minelli, 1986-1998, and Michael J. Steber 1998-.

St. Joseph, Escanaba

The Catholic foundation of Delta County began with the formation of St. Joseph Church in Escanaba in 1865. St. Joseph's School offered the only Catholic educational institution until St. Anne's School was formed in 1901, and the only Catholic High School until Holy Name High School was started in 1954.

In 1883, Franciscan Fathers began a century of ministering at the church. With the merger of St. Joseph and St. Patrick parishes in 1997, the families whose ancestors once separated themselves came together again to continue the long-standing legacy of growth in faith and service as one parish community.

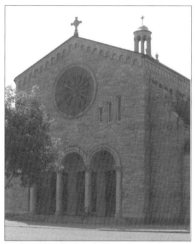

St. Joseph, Escanaba

FOUNDING. Bishop Baraga sent Father Sebastian Duroc to organize a parish in Delta County in the spring of 1865. Nelson Ludington, a pioneer in the sawmill industry, donated the lots. Money was collected from the first parishioners and from the community, and a framed church was built.

The early territory served by the pastors of St. Joseph's included all of Delta County to Fayette and Garden on the east, Metropolitan to the west, as far as Lathrop to the north, and to Stephenson on the south.

In just 10 years Escanaba's population nearly doubled and the increase in parishioners led to the need for a larger church. A new structure was dedicated Dec. 8, 1873. In 1887, the French members of St. Joseph's left to form their own church, St. Anne's. Irish members separated themselves in 1901, forming St. Patrick Parish.

In 1883 Bishop John Vertin invited the Franciscan Fathers of St. John the Baptist Province in Cincinnati, Ohio, to take over administration of St. Joseph Parish. The Franciscans served faithfully in Delta County until 1992.

PARISH SCHOOL. St. Joseph School was opened Sept. 8, 1884 under the School Sisters of Notre Dame of Milwaukee. Comprising both grade school and high school, the first facility was referred to as "the Old Green School." The sisters lived in the schoolrooms until a convent was built in 1889.

On Dec. 17, 1914 the school was destroyed by fire when a stove in the basement overheated, but the congregation immediately began construction of a new and better facility. Work started in June 1915 and the three-story, yellow brick structure was dedicated Dec. 12 of the same year.

Enrollment in the beginning was said to be one-third of the city's young people. In 1930, with more than 800 students, the school began renting a house across the street for use as classrooms. That building was condemned two years later. As a result, the school was forced to dismiss almost one-third of its students. Those belonging to other parishes were forced to attend public schools.

Dedication of the William Bonifas Auditorium and Gymnasium complex took place on April 24, 1938. The facility, named for the church's greatest benefactor, was located on land directly opposite the church. The complex provided for additional classrooms and expanded facilities.

The School Sisters of Notre Dame served the school throughout its entire 87-year history. In June 1971, all parish schools in the city consolidated to form one central grade school, Holy Name. Following the consolidation, the former St. Joseph School building was razed and the site is now a parking lot.

PARISH LIFE. Beginning May 4, 1938, Mass was held in the new gym while the old church and rectory were razed in preparation for another new building—St. Joseph's third at the original site. A large hall and kitchen were constructed under the church. The new facility was dedicated Aug. 6, 1939.

In 1983, the parish celebrated 100 years of service by the Franciscan Friars. In a commemorative booklet, Father Gabriel Buescher reflected: "Our parish records give corroborating evidence and indicate a consistent pattern of growth and development which reflects both the internal spiritual, as well as the external material growth of the parish of which we are all rightfully proud."

MERGER. In July 1997, as a result of the diocesan initiative Fully Alive in '95, the Escanaba parishes of St. Joseph and St. Patrick merged to form St. Joseph and St. Patrick Parish. Both facilities remained open with one combined parish council and shared administrative services. Father Ronald Skufca was named the first pastor of the new parish.

PASTORS. Fathers Sebastian Duroc, 1865-1869; Charles Langner, 1869-1881; Theodore Majerus, 1881-1882; Joseph Neibling, 1882-1883; Bishop Ignatius Mrak, 1883; Eugene Buttermann, OSF, 1883-1890; Francis Lings, OSF, 1890-1893; William Gausepohl, OSF, 1893-1895; Bede Oldegeering, OFM, 1895-1901; Eusebius Wagner, OFM, 1901-1906; Julius Henze, OFM, 1906-1918; Francis X. Buschle, OFM 1918-1920; Erasmus Dooley, OFM, 1920-1922; Bertrand Labinski, OFM, 1922-1931; Edward Leary, OFM, 1931-1942; Alphonse Wilberding, OFM, 1942-1948; Patrick McArron, OFM, 1948-1951; Stephen Schneider, OFM, 1951-1957; Dominic Calme, OFM, 1957-1960; Jerome Kircher, OFM, 1960-1961; Jordan Telles, OFM, 1961-1969; Fabian Gerstle, OFM, 1969-1975; Gabriel Buescher, OFM, 1975-1985; Marian Douglas, OFM, 1985-1990; Miles Pfalzer, OFM, 1990-1992, and Walter Sheedlo, 1992-1997.

ST. JOSEPH AND ST. PATRICK, ESCANABA

In 1997, two Escanaba churches, St. Joseph and St. Patrick—each with more than 100 years as separate entities—came together to form one parish. Since the merger St. Patrick's church building has been closed. Now united under one roof, the members continue supporting a city-wide parochial school and are working together to keep old traditions alive and start new customs.

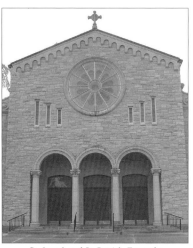

St. Joseph and St. Patrick, Escanaba

FOUNDING. The two south-side Escanaba parishes, St. Joseph Church and St. Patrick Church, were combined in 1997 through the diocese's Fully Alive in '95 pastoral planning process, an initiative to provide viable parish ministry with fewer priests. After nearly a year of study, representatives from all five Escanaba parishes deemed the merger of St. Joseph and St. Patrick the best way to meet the needs of the people of the region with only four priests.

PARISH LIFE. Father Ronald Skufca, the pastor of St. Patrick Parish, was assigned to lead the new parish. A combined parish council, along with a consolidated office staff, served the needs of both buildings. For the first five years, regular Masses continued to be held at both churches. However, in June 2002 the difficult decision was made to close the doors of the century-old St. Patrick Church building. A closing Mass was held July 28. The complex was sold shortly after.

The parish is working together to host an annual harvest dinner. Monthly breakfasts and summer picnics are a way for parishioners to interact.

St. Joseph and St. Patrick Parish continues to support Holy Name Catholic Grade School along with St. Anne, St. Thomas and St. Anthony.

PASTORS. Fathers Ronald Skufca, 1997-1999; Joseph Nagaroor, 1999-2002; Francis Dobrzenski, 2002-2004, and Richard Schaeffer 2004-.

St. Patrick, Escanaba

Parishioners of St. Patrick Parish in Escanaba built a church and a faith tradition that spanned nearly a century. St. Patrick's Brigade, a successful parish school and generations of spirited people, are among its legacies. With new parish programs and church renovations the people banded together to overcome many challenges. In 1997 the parish merged with St. Joseph Church to form the new St. Joseph and St. Patrick Parish.

St. Patrick, Escanaba

FOUNDING. The Irish members of St. Joseph Church petitioned Bishop Frederick Eis for permission to organize a separate church. Formal division was confirmed on July 26, 1901.

Services were held at St. Anne Church until St. Patrick's was erected. Land was purchased on the corner of Twelfth Street and Second Avenue South, and a structure of Romanesque design was selected. The Lady Hibernians raised much of the money for the church by holding weekly parties charging fifty cents admission. Eight-dollar church bonds were also sold to raise money. On Feb. 15, 1903 Bishop Frederick Eis dedicated the church to St. Patrick.

PARISH LIFE. On Feb. 12, 1911 Father Francis Barth organized the nationally-known St. Patrick's Brigade. The original purpose of the Brigade was to foster a movement that would interest boys; however, the idea was so successful that the organization grew until it included every member of the parish. National and church authorities recognized the brigade as a model organization of its kind in the country.

Church maintenance and repairs became a top priority in 1970. A new roof was installed, stained glass windows were restored, the interior was redecorated and the front steps and foyer were upgraded. Labor and money were donated to the project through the Ladies Guild and a parish restoration drive.

In July 1973, the large steeple on the church was hit and severely damaged by lightning. Fortunately, the church itself was not affected and the steeple was torn down and rebuilt.

Father Arnold J. Grambow, appointed pastor in 1980, led St. Patrick's in a spirit of renewal. The parish initiated several new programs including Renew, Rite of Christian Initiation of Adults, Little Church, Vacation Bible School and the annual parish retreat.

Father Ronald J. Skufca led an effort to keep the school building, vacant for nearly 20 years, open for faith formation classes. Extra rooms in the school building were rented to community organizations.

PARISH SCHOOL. In 1945 the Dominican Sisters of Adrian, Mich., were engaged to do catechetical work with the children of the parish.

On Sept. 26, 1950 ground was broken for the construction of a school on the corner of Thirteenth Street and Second Avenue South. St. Patrick School opened for the fall term on Sept. 5, 1951 admitting four grades. Three years later the school was completed with eight grades. At that time, the sisters moved to their new convent on the corner of Twelfth Street and First Avenue South.

The parish was greatly saddened on June 3, 1971 when St. Patrick School was forced to close. The church joined with the other parishes in Escanaba, however, to provide a Catholic education for children through the eighth grade by consolidating to form Holy Name Central Grade School.

MERGER. In 1996, as a result of the diocese's pastoral planning initiative, it was decided that St. Patrick and St. Joseph churches should merge to form one parish. The merger took effect July 1, 1997. The new parish was named St. Joseph and St. Patrick. With Father Skufca as pastor, both church facilities remained open and Mass was held regularly in both churches.

Father Joseph Nagaroor was appointed pastor of St. Joseph and St. Patrick Parish in July 1999. With perseverance and dedication, Father Joe took up the challenge of meeting the needs of his parishioners. He led the new parish by devout example and encouraged people to accept the change as a positive experience. In 2000 Father Nagaroor visited his homeland of India and returned with five priests, including Father Paul Karottekunnel, who became his associate.

CLOSURE. Operating with a deficit budget for five years meant St. Joseph and St. Patrick Parish could not make the necessary capital improvements to St. Patrick's building and the church was forced to close. A final Mass was held July 28, 2002. The building was sold to a private party.

RECORDS. The records for St. Patrick Parish are located at St. Joseph and St. Patrick Church.

PASTORS. Fathers Joseph M. Langan, 1901-1911; Francis X. Barth, 1911-1922; Msgr. Jeremiah Moriarity, 1922; John Mockler, 1923-1933; Thomas A. Kennedy, 1934-1945; Msgr. Martin B. Melican, 1945-1968; Charles J. Carmody, 1968-1970; Kenneth G. Bretl, 1970-1980; Arnold J. Grambow, 1980-1988; James A. Pepin, 1988-1989, and Ronald J. Skufca, 1989-1999.

St. Thomas the Apostle, Escanaba

St. Thomas the Apostle Parish in Escanaba has made great strides since its inception more than 50 years ago. The prosperity of parish life has been illustrated by construction of a modern parish plant, support of a parish grade school, and the people's outreach efforts.

FOUNDING. In the summer of 1948, Bishop Thomas L. Noa approved a petition for a church on the north side of Escanaba. More than 300 people signed the plea. The new church, being the first established by Bishop Noa, was named after his patron saint.

St. Thomas, Escanaba

The first Masses were offered in the Webster School gymnasium and later in the Exhibition Building at the Upper Peninsula State Fairgrounds. A small temporary chapel was set up on a sandy lot, home to a baseball diamond, on Ninth Avenue North. Measuring just 75 feet by 24 feet, the church soon became too small for the growing parish so the Knights of Columbus lent a portion of its clubhouse for use as a side chapel.

PARISH SCHOOL. The Sisters of St. Dominic began offering catechism classes in 1949. In 1952 the sisters moved from St. Patrick's Convent to a house rented by St. Thomas Parish. Bishop Noa presided over groundbreaking ceremonies for a parish grade school in the fall of 1950. The building was dedicated June 10, 1951 and served first as a temporary church. The grade school was opened two years later when construction of a new church was completed. The school grew grade by grade over the next six years. The Sisters of St. Dominic continued to teach the young people there until 1971 when Holy Name Central Grade School was opened to serve people from all of the Escanaba parishes.

PARISH LIFE. The 1960s saw the establishment of many parish organizations, including the first parish council and the St. Vincent de Paul Society. In the 1980s the church was totally remodeled. The area that once served as classrooms became the parish hall.

In November 1998, the parish celebrated its golden jubilee with a commemorative Mass, celebrated by Bishop James Garland, and a special dinner.

PASTORS. Fathers Arnold Thompson, 1948-1972; Henry Mercier, 1972-1983; Joseph Callari, 1984-1986; Emmett Norden, 1986-1996; David Sedlock, 1996-1997; Joseph Nagaroor, 1997-1999, and Rick Courier 1999-.

SACRED HEART, EWEN

Sacred Heart Parish in Ewen has thrived for more than 100 years, thanks to the continued support of its parishioners. In addition to regular maintenance of the church plant, the people take part in parish organizations and opportunities for continuing faith formation. The parish has cared for several missions throughout the 20th century. St. Francis Xavier Mission in Sidnaw remains under the care of the pastor of Ewen.

Sacred Heart, Ewen

FOUNDING. Sacred Heart Church was founded in 1892. One year later the saw-milling town was devastated by fire. The church survived, but the rectory and parish records were destroyed. From that point until 1903, the church was served as a mission of Michigamme. Parish records for Sacred Heart from 1893 to 1903 are located at the Sacred Heart Church in Champion.

Ewen's first resident pastor, Father Bernard Eiling, arrived Aug. 13, 1903. For many years the pastor serving Ewen also cared for missions in Kenton, Trout Creek, Watersmeet, Bergland and Sidnaw.

PARISH LIFE. A winter chapel was added to the church in 1910. The interior decoration of the church was finished between 1912 and 1917, including the lining of the walls with painted, stamped tin, installation of a hardwood flooring and the erection of two side altars.

In 1928 a new rectory was completed. Continuing upgrades to the church over the years have kept it in good repair. Major improvements to the physical plant include the replacement of clear glass windows with leaded glass in 1947 and the construction of a basement hall in 1949. In the early 1980s an altar and ambo were built, the old confessional was refashioned into an alcove for the tabernacle and the stained glass windows moved to become part of the alcove. In 1988, the east entrance of the church was enlarged to provide barrier-free access.

On June 2, 1967 Sacred Heart celebrated its diamond jubilee. A historical booklet was published at that time.

The parish observed its centennial in 1992. Bishop James Garland celebrated a commemorative Mass June 28 and several other activities were held throughout the year. A centennial booklet was published.

Parish organizations for adults and youth of Sacred Heart have kept parish life in the church thriving. Catechism classes for school-age parishioners and adult education programs provide for spiritual growth. An annual fund-raising bazaar began in Kostelnik's warehouse in 1905 and continued into the 1990s.

MISSIONS. Father Anthony Oehlerer of Sacred Heart had a church built in Trout Creek in 1912. The St. Anthony Mission remained the responsibility of the Ewen parish until its closure in 1980.

Six families in Trout Creek held parties and other fundraisers to support the construction of the church. Donated labor and materials were also contributed. At first, services were held once a month; then the Ewen pastor increased his visits to the second and third Sundays of each month.

Upon the 1980 closure of St. Anthony the stained glass windows were given to the Assembly of God Church. The old reed organ was donated to Sacred Heart in Ewen, and the St. Francis Xavier Mission in Sidnaw received vestments and some furniture.

RECORDS The records for the St. Anthony Mission are located at Sacred Heart in Ewen.

PASTORS. Fathers Renatus Becker, 1892-1893; William H. Joisten, 1893; Hubert Zimmermannn, 1893; Joseph Dupasquier, 1893-1894; John Burns, 1894-1895; James Lenhart, 1895-1898; Alexander Hasenberg, 1899-1903; Bernard Eiling, 1903-1908; Charles Diedgens, 1908-1911; Edward Feldhaus, 1911-1912; Anthony Oehlerer, 1912-1917; Joseph Ling, 1917-1934; Gerald Harrington, 1934-1936; Thomas Anderson, 1936-1938; Eugene Hennelly, 1938-1939; Vincent Savageau, O'Praem, 1940-1965; William Richards, 1965-1970; August Franczek, 1970; David Rocheleau, 1970; Donald Hartman, 1970-1971; Raymond Valerio, 1971-1972; Louis Wren, OFM, 1972-1976; Arnold Grambow, 1976-1978; Gary A. Jacobs, 1978-1984; Francis Dobrzenski, 1984-1999; Thomas Valayathil, 1999-2003; George Joseph Kallarackal, MCBS, 2003-2004, and Thomas Ettolil, 2004-.

St. Mary Mission, Faithorn

The St. Mary Mission in Faithorn was built by the eager hands of its parishioners. First a mission of St. Barbara Parish in Vulcan and then of St. Stephen in Loretto, St. Mary's only offered Sunday Mass for a two-year period, otherwise on a monthly basis. But this lack of regular service didn't dampen the spirit of its members. For nearly a century, until its closure in 1996, the small parish continued to keep a Catholic presence in the remote community.

St. Mary Mission, Faithorn

FOUNDING. Priests from Vulcan first visited Catholics living in the logging community of Faithorn in 1906. Father Raphael Cavicci would take a horse and buggy to offer Mass in private homes. Then, in 1909, a parcel of land was donated and work began on construction of a church.

PARISH LIFE. Lumber for the church was donated and the men of the parish did all of the work. The first Mass was said and the church dedicated to St. Mary on Dec. 1, 1909. In 1918 St. Mary's was assigned as a mission of St. Stephen Parish in Loretto.

During the 18 years of service by Father George Stuntebeck, many improvements were made to the church. In 1928 a bell tower was erected and the church was raised so that a basement could be built for use as a parish hall. Annual harvest dinners and other parish gatherings took place there.

A grand celebration was held in October 1930 to celebrate the purchase of a new church bell. At the dedication ceremony, a procession was held with the bell hanging decoratively on a horse-drawn wagon surrounded by girls dressed in white angel costumes.

More improvements took place at the church beginning in the late 1940s and continuing throughout the 1950s. Many new statues were given to the church at that time. The sanctuary was renovated and new vestments and furnishings were purchased. A new entrance was built leading into the basement hall, the exterior of the church was painted, and new concrete steps and a sidewalk were poured. On Oct. 20, 1959, the parish celebrated its 50th anniversary with a jubilee Mass and commemorative dinner.

St. Mary's of Faithorn remained under the care of the Loretto church until St.

Stephen's suffered a disastrous fire in 1971. The parish of St. Mary's in Hermansville cared for the Faithorn mission from 1971 to 1986 when St. Barbara's in Vulcan again took responsibility for the Faithorn church.

CLOSURE. St. Mary's closed in 1995 as a result of the diocese's Fully Alive in '95 pastoral planning process. The last Mass at the Faithorn church was said on the final Sunday in June 1996. In April 1997 the church building was sold to a private party.

To help preserve the memory of St. Mary Church, its bell and steeple were erected at the Faithorn Riverside Cemetery June 28, 1998.

RECORDS. The records for the St. Mary Mission in Faithorn are located at St. Barbara Parish in Vulcan.

PASTORS. Fathers Raphael Cavicci, 1906; John Stenglein, 1906-1909; George Stuntebeck, 1919-1937; Raphael Gherna, 1938-1943; Lester Bourgeois, 1943-1945; Edward J. Lulewicz, 1945-1950; Frederick Hofmann, 1950-1951; John McLaughlin, 1951-1957; Thomas Andary, 1957-1959; August Franczek, 1959-1963; Joseph Gouin, 1972; Edward Wenzel, 1972-1980; David Rocheleau, 1980-1984; Raymond Valerio, 1984-1986; James Hebein, 1986-1994; Jerome Nowacki, 1994-1995, and Arnold Grambow, 1995-1996.

ST. PETER THE FISHERMAN MISSION, FAYETTE

By the beginning of the 20th century, the status of the first church on the Garden Peninsula, St. Peter the Fisherman of Fayette, had been reduced from an independent parish to a mission church. But throughout the decades and beyond the closure of St. Peter's, the people of the community have assured that the ritual of the Blessing of the Fleet and other spiritual traditions started there are carried on.

St. Peter the Fisherman Mission, Fayette

FOUNDING. In the mid-1860s the Jackson Iron Co. located blast furnaces on the east shore of Big Bay de Noc, starting Fayette, the first settlement on the Garden Peninsula. Beginning in 1865, Father Sebastian Duroc of Escanaba offered Mass periodically in one of the Jackson Company's buildings. Father Duroc's successor, Father Charles Langer, also traveled aboard ore boats heading from Escanaba to Fayette to cater to the spiritual needs of residents there.

Father Martin Fox was assigned to serve the area in 1875. He offered consistent spiritual service and set plans in motion for a church and rectory.

Bishop Ignatius Mrak assigned Father Hilary J. Rosseau as the first resident pastor of Fayette in 1876. During his three-year pastorate the church was built and dedicated to St. Peter. At the same time another church was being built in the farming community of Garden, about nine miles north of Fayette.

In the last days of Father Rosseau's pastorate the church was destroyed by fire. The people had their house of worship quickly rebuilt. But the decline in the iron industry in Fayette and the growth in population of Garden led to a reversal in status near the turn of the 20th century. St. John the Baptist Church in Garden was named an independent parish with Fayette as its mission.

PARISH LIFE. St. Peter's Altar Society was formed in 1945. The women of the parish had previously served as the Goodwill Society. Organized in 1915, the women were responsible for much charitable work in the community. A Holy Name Society for the men was established in 1948.

The church in Fayette was home to many commercial fishermen. For this reason, priests of St. Peter's decided to hold an annual event to pray for their safety and for the souls of those who had perished in the waters. This "Blessing of the Fleet" was begun in 1948 and has spanned more than 50 years continuing to the present day. Bishop Thomas L. Noa officiated over the first such celebration. A grotto dedicated to Our Lady of Fatima was built near St. Peter Church. The shrine was the setting for the Field Masses held prior to the annual Blessing of the Fleet.

In 1971 the parish purchased the former Mud Lake School. The intent was to use the building for a parish hall. However, on Jan. 18, 1972, the church building was consumed by fire. The structure had served the parish for nearly 100 years. A faulty furnace was blamed for starting the blaze. All that was left was a crumbled foundation.

The land the church had been built on was leased, and so it was decided not to rebuild. Instead, an addition was put on to the school-turned-parish hall and services were held there beginning on Christmas Eve 1974.

CLOSURE. The St. Peter Mission was closed Jan. 31, 1991. The closure was the result of a parish planning study conducted among five area parishes forced to share one priest. The Mission of St. Ann in Isabella was also closed.

RECORDS. Records for the Mission Church of St. Peter are located at St. John the Baptist in Garden.

PASTORS. Fathers Sebastian Duroc, 1865; Charles Langer, 1869; Martin Fox, 1875; Hilary J. Rosseau, 1876; Luke Mozina, 1876-1880; Edward Jacker, 1880; A. Paganini, 1880-1882; Edward P. Bordas, 1882-1886; Francis Xavier Becker, 1886-1887; Fabian Marceau, 1887; Anacletus O. Pelisson, 1887-1888; Fidelis Sutter, 1888-1889; Prosper Girard, 1890; Michael Weis, 1890; Joseph A. Sauriol, 1890-1891; Paul Datin, Louis Archille Poulin, John Henn, John Chebul, 1898; Anthony Zagar, 1900; Msgr. Mathias Jodocy, 1901; Thomas V. Dassylva, 1903; Paul Fillion, 1905; Paul LeGolvan, 1905; Joseph Dufort, 1917; Joseph Morin, 1922-1926; Vincent Savageau, 1926-1940; Nolan McKevitt, 1940-1945; Glen Sanford, 1945; Wilfred Pelletier, 1945; Arnold Thompson, 1946-1948; James Schaefer, 1948; Ronald Bassett, 1949-1955; Conrad Dishaw, 1955-1960; James Donnelley, Joseph Callari, Lesli Perino 1970-1972; co-pastors Timothy Desrochers and Lesli Perino, 1970-1976; James Pepin, 1976-1978; C. Michael Rhoades, 1978-1981; Thomas L. Poisson, 1981-1984; Ronald Timock, 1984-1986, and Peter Petroske, 1986-1991.

HOLY FAMILY, FLAT ROCK

Holy Family, Flat Rock

From the time a group of men from the Flat Rock area banded together, rehearsed their plea, and headed to Marquette to petition the bishop for a church in Flat Rock, through the generations that followed, members of Holy Family Church have proven that the size of a community doesn't determine the depth of the people's spirituality and devotion to their faith community.

FOUNDING. Prior to the founding of Holy Family Parish in 1905, Catholics living around Flat Rock went to great lengths to attend Mass in Escanaba, Gladstone and Schaffer. The people, devout in their practice of the faith, took an entire day in the summer and three whole days in the winter to complete the journey to a neighboring church. But on Oct. 7, 1905, a group of fervent men traveled to Marquette to plead with Bishop Frederick Eis for a church of their own. The men said they feared the hardship of attending a neighboring church would cause young families to lose their connection to the faith. Bishop Eis granted permission to start Holy Family Parish. Boundaries were set to include the settlements of Flat Rock, Danforth, Hendricks, Cornell, Boney Falls and Chandler.

Land was quickly donated for a church and a cemetery. Construction began in April 1906. Holy Family was modeled after St. Anne's in Escanaba, but in order to prove to their neighbors that they were capable of starting their own church, parishioners made Holy Family one foot longer. The first pastor, Adrien Deschamp, arrived Oct. 1 of that year. Mass was first said in the church Oct. 7, 1906.

Sadly, the first church was destroyed by fire. Not even the pastor's personal belongings could be saved. But with $20,000 of insurance money and the zeal of the church's people, a drive was soon initiated to rebuild. Mass was held in the Township Hall until construction of the current church-rectory complex was completed Dec. 15, 1940.

PARISH LIFE. By 1946, the people had retired the debt from construction of the new church and managed to save a good amount of money for decorating the interior of their new house of worship. New Stations of the Cross, an organ and rubber tile flooring were among the improvements made at the time.

Father Roland Dion designed and made the solid oak woodwork inside the parish. He also made the frames for the stations, which were oil paintings on copper plate.

It is recorded that parishioners took great pride in the beauty of the church. Contributions from "self-sacrificing" and "devout" members made the dreams of a parish family a reality, records say.

In September 1956, the parish celebrated its golden jubilee. A Solemn High Mass, presided over by Bishop Thomas L. Noa, and an anniversary dinner were among the festivities.

From within the parish have come several vocations to the priesthood and religious life. Many young adults of the parish attended St. Joseph High School in Escanaba and many lay people are members of the Secular Franciscan Order.

PASTORS. Fathers Adrien Deschamp, 1906-1909; A. A. Vissers, O.Praem, Bernard Eiling, 1909; Paul Fillion, 1909-1910; Joseph Dufort, 1910-1912; Joseph H. Beauchene, 1912-1916; Edward J. Testevin, 1916-1918; Francis Geynet, 1918-1919; William DeHaan, 1919-1920; Francis Geynet, 1920-1927; George LaForest, 1927-1938; Peter Bleeker, 1938-1939; Mathias LaViolette, 1939-1946; Roland L. Dion, 1946-1951; Gerard F. LaMothe, 1951-1959; Thomas Andary, 1959-1967; Raymond Przybylski, 1967-1973; Mathias LaViolette, 1973-1980; Kenneth G. Bretl, 1980-1986; Arnold Grambow, 1986; Conrad Dishaw, 1986-1992; Christopher Gardiner, 1992-1998; Raymond Cotter, 1998-2000, and Frank Lenz, 2000-.

St. Joseph Mission, Foster City

St. Joseph Parish in Foster City has thrived through economic downturns, a disastrous fire that destroyed the church building, and the lack of a resident priest for most of its existence. Despite these struggles, the people living in Foster City, Hardwood, Felch and surrounding areas have stayed the course and kept sturdy the foundation of their faith.

St. Joseph Mission, Foster City

FOUNDING. The downfall of the mining industry around Metropolitan and the subsequent migration to the lumbering town of Foster City, where a new sawmill was thriving, led to the birth of St. Joseph Church in Foster City.

Prior to the building of the church, priests from Escanaba offered occasional Masses for the people living in Hardwood, Felch and Foster City. After 1894, these communities and logging camps were served by priests from the Bark River and Schaffer churches.

In 1906 Foster City's first church was built on land owned by the Morgan Lumber and Cedar Co. The company donated all of the lumber for the church. Windows and doors also were given to the church, allowing the structure to go up without the parish incurring any debt. In 1915 the Morgan company deeded the land to the parish.

The first resident pastor of St. Joseph Parish, Father John Nuerenberg, was appointed in 1920. A rectory was built and the bell, statues and vestments from Metropolitan's St. Lawrence Parish (closed in 1906) were given to the Foster City church.

PARISH LIFE. Within two years of the 1923 sawmill closure, St. Joseph's parish membership dropped from 60 families to 10. The pastor at the time, Father Thomas Drengacz, moved his residence to St. Michael's in Perronville, for which he had also been responsible. St. Joseph's then became a mission of St. Michael's. Mass was still celebrated in Foster City every week until 1936. At that time the mission of Northland was also added to Perronville. From then until 1949 Sunday Mass alternated between Foster City and Northland. Regular services at all three churches resumed under the leadership of Father Gabriel Waraxa beginning in October 1949.

The parish was devastated June 29, 1950, when the bell tower was struck by lightning causing the church to burn to the ground. Only newly purchased pews, the organ and vestments were saved.

Plans began almost immediately for construction of a new house of worship. A church built of cement block with stone exterior and plastered interior was dedicated March 4, 1951. Within a couple of years work on a rectory was started, but never finished. The parish has been without a resident priest since 1925. It celebrated its golden jubilee Oct. 7, 1956.

Improvements to the parish complex over the years included the addition of a bell tower and an outdoor statue of St. Joseph in 1973. Since the 1960s the parish had hosted a picnic either at Norway Lake or the town hall in Hardwood. In 1978, a new pavilion was erected on the church grounds. The event continues to be a successful fundraiser for the parish.

The longstanding link between St. Joseph's and St. Michael's ended in 1995 when responsibility of the mission was handed over to St. Rose of Channing. For a time in the mid-1990s St. Joseph Mission was served by priests from Iron Mountain.

The church was completely renovated in 1993. Among the highlights of the project are a new altar, baptismal font and pulpit, Blessed Sacrament Chapel, reconciliation room and sacristy.

PASTORS.   Fathers William Stahl, 1906-1917; Augustus Geers, 1917-1920; John Nuerenberg, 1920-1921; John F. Kulczyk, 1921-1922; Edward J. Testevin, 1922; Thomas Drengacz, 1923-1936; Francis Krystyniak, 1936-1940; Raymond Przybylski, 1940-1947; Francis Gimski, 1947-1948; Gabriel Waraxa, 1948-1951; Conrad Suda, 1951-1963; Raymond J. Smith, 1963-1968; August Franczek, 1968-1970; Emmett M. Norden, 1970-1973; Raymond J. Hoefgen, 1973-1976; Raymond Zeugner, 1976-1981; Donald Hartman, 1981-1984; N. Daniel Rupp, 1984-1989; Paul J. Nomellini, 1989-1990; Michael Vichich, 1990-1991; Robert Paruleski, 1991-1994; Patrick Murphy, 1994-1995; Michael Steber, 1995-1998; Hubby Mathew, MST, 1998-2000; George Kuppayil, MST, 2000-2005, and Peter Fosu, 2005-.

Our Lady of Mount Carmel Mission, Franklin Mine

Humble accommodations but enthusiastic spirits outline the history of Our Lady of Mount Carmel Mission in Franklin Mine. The congregation, formerly located in what is known as the Quincy Hill area, succeeded in obtaining a pastor of its own, but plans to erect a church proper never came to fruition. Instead, a small but devoted group of families weathered many economic storms and remained zealous in their faith while worshiping for 70 years in a basement church. The church closed in 1981.

Our Lady of Mount Carmel Mission, Franklin Mine

FOUNDING. Priests from Hancock began serving the needs of the Catholic people in Franklin Mine in 1910. At that time a Norwegian church located just behind the Quincy Mine office was used for services.

In 1911 the people considered their numbers, about 135 families, large enough to warrant a parish of their own. They petitioned Bishop Frederick Eis to assign a permanent pastor. On Oct. 21, 1911, in response to their request, the bishop sent Father Henry Kron.

The following autumn, thanks to many successful fund-raising efforts and generous donations, a basement church was completed. The dedication of the new facility to Our Lady of Mount Carmel took place Sept. 29, 1912. A parish rectory was constructed in 1916.

PARISH LIFE. In the years that followed, economic hardships fell on the community. The number of parishioners declined with the loss of jobs in the area. As a result, the proposed church edifice was never constructed. The small parish weathered many financial storms and made do with a humble house of worship.

Members of Our Lady of Mount Carmel organized into social societies almost immediately after the founding of the parish.

Donated labor and money supported improvements over the years, such as the rebuilding of the roof, which was originally intended to be temporary. This work, along with extensive interior renovations, took place in the early 1960s. Just prior to Our Lady of Mount Carmel's golden jubilee celebration the church vestibule was completely remodeled.

Bishop Thomas L. Noa presided over the parish's 50th Anniversary Mass held July 16, 1961. A coffee social followed in the Quincy Fire Hall. A complete parish history was also published at the time.

In 1963 a priest shortage and a steady decline in membership led to declaration of the church as a mission of St. Joseph and St. Patrick in Hancock. From 1968 to 1981, retired priest Father Casimir Adasiewicz took up residency in Franklin Mine and offered daily and Sunday Mass until his death.

CLOSURE. Our Lady of Mount Carmel was closed in 1981. The final Mass was offered May 3. The rectory was used for awhile by two Felician Sisters who taught catechism in Hancock. Then the church was given to the St. Vincent de Paul Society.

RECORDS. Records for Our Lady of Mount Carmel are located at Resurrection Parish in Hancock.

PASTORS. Fathers Henry Kron, 1911-1924; Peter Bleeker, 1924-1935; Msgr. George Dingfelder, 1935; Eugene Hennelly, 1935-1938; William F. Schick, 1938-1939; Thomas P. Dunleavy, 1939-1940; Francis X. Ronkowski, 1940-1942; Gino S. Ferraro, 1942-1944; Arnold E. Thompson, 1944-1946; Aloysius E. Ehlinger, 1946-1949; Noel Arneth, 1949-1954; Michael F. Hale, 1954-1956; Conrad Dishaw, 1956-1959; S. Patrick Wisneske, 1959-1963; Robert Haas, 1963-1966; Charles Reinhart, 1966-1976, and Casimir Adasiewicz, 1968-1981.

St. Mary, Gaastra

Catholics living in Gaastra worshiped in their home parish for nearly 80 years until finally, the declining economy of the area and a priest shortage in the diocese led to the closure of the church in 1988. But the parishioners, whose forefathers sacrificed so much to build and maintain the house of worship, were successful in keeping the church structure intact in the nearby community of Caspian. The people of Gaastra now worship in Caspian or Iron River and the heritage of their beautiful church is preserved in the Caspian museum site.

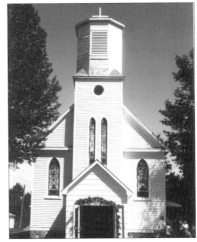

St. Mary, Gaastra

FOUNDING. Priests from St. Agnes Parish in Iron River first served Catholic immigrants working in the mines of western Iron County around the turn of the 20th century. Clergy from as far away as Iron Mountain were also asked to visit the people in the mission areas of Palatka, Caspian, Pentoga and Stambaugh. Mass was offered in private homes, the school and the town hall.

In 1911, Father James Lenhart of Iron River led eager parishioners in the building of St. Mary Parish. Douwe Gaastra donated four lots and the parishioners donated their time and talent to erect the wooden church. Originally it was named St. Mary of Palatka. The community was renamed Gaastra in 1919 when it was incorporated as a village. Bishop Frederick Eis dedicated the church in August 1912.

MISSIONS. In 1913 Father John J. Stenglein was named St. Mary's first pastor. He also was put in charge of the missions of Caspian to the west and Pentoga to the east. Parishioners often drove the priest to the missions in horse-drawn, covered wagons or sleighs. In June 1951, Caspian became independent and the mission of Pentoga ceased to exist, as people were able to easily attend church elsewhere.

In 1981 St. Mary's of Gaastra was named a mission of St. Cecilia Parish in Caspian.

PARISH LIFE. When Father Albert J. Treilles arrived in 1921, he did much to improve the quality of parish life at St. Mary's. Most noteworthy in parish records is the construction of a grotto along the south side of the parish. The people of Gaastra built a structure of wood, stone and mortar measuring 48 feet long and 18 to 20 feet high. With a statue of Our Blessed Lady at the center of the garden, a circulating fountain stocked with goldfish and an altar facing the church, the grotto became a tourist attraction and a landmark for the community. Parishioners fondly remember celebrations there, such as that of the Feast of the Assumption. The grotto was removed in 1965.

Also in 1921, a stone foundation was built under the church and St. Mary's first rectory was constructed. Prior to the building of the rectory, the priest either stayed at parishioners' homes or, for a short time, lived in Caspian. During Father Treilles' tenure, many social clubs and other parish organizations were formed. An impressive choir was started and members of St. Mary's and St. Cecilia's banded together to perform plays all over, including Marquette, Ishpeming and Negaunee.

In the mid-1950s the church's interior underwent significant remodeling. A new main altar was installed and above it was affixed a seven-foot-tall crucifix. New pews, floor tiles, walnut-paneled wall coverings and acoustical ceiling tiles were also put in place. Additional changes were made to the church and rectory in 1965 and again in the late 1970s.

An anniversary booklet titled *75 Years of Worship* tells how proud the parish was to welcome Father Otto Sartorelli as its pastor in 1981. Father Sartorelli is a native of Gaastra. He was ordained by Bishop Thomas L. Noa in 1950 and 30 years later returned to his home parish to serve as pastor.

The parish celebrated its diamond jubilee in August 1987, marking 75 years since the date of its dedication.

CLOSURE. St. Mary's Parish closed in 1988 and the church building was moved to the grounds of the Caspian museum. Former parishioners organized "St. Mary's-on-the-Move," a group to preserve the church of their forefathers and impressive memorials to early parishioners, such as stained glass windows and the structure itself. The building now serves as the center for summer workshops and art classes. The basement houses the Bernhardt Art Gallery.

RECORDS. Records for St. Mary Parish in Gaastra are kept at St. Cecilia Parish in Caspian.

PASTORS. Fathers John J. Stenglein, 1913-1914; William J. Remillard, 1914-1915; Hilarious Marcucci, 1915; Nickolas H. Nosbisch, 1917; John Neuhaus, 1917-1921; Albert C. Pelissier, 1921; Albert J. Treilles, 1921-1938; Fortunatus Ciupka, 1938; James A. Paquet, 1938; Adrein Somers, 1938; Joseph J. Seifert, 1939-1940; Thomas P. Dunleavy, 1940-1942; Charles Daniel, 1942-1950; Herman Fadale, 1951; Joseph F. Schaul, 1951-1952; Frank J. Ignatz, 1952-1963; Conrad Dishaw, 1963-1968; William F. Schick, 1968-1981, and Otto Sartorelli, 1981-1988.

ST. JOHN THE BAPTIST, GARDEN

Responsibility for St. John the Baptist Parish in Garden has changed throughout the years, yet a stable foundation has always remained. Parishioners are dedicated to providing youth a solid Catholic education, as well as opportunities for participating in the faith. The population of the Garden Peninsula has declined steadily since the beginning of the 20th century, but the church traditions are still alive.

St. John the Baptist, Garden

FOUNDING. In the late 1870s Bishop Ignatius Mrak granted permission for churches at Fayette and Garden Bay. Prior to construction of St. John the Baptist, the Fayette priest would travel to Garden to offer Mass in the Richard Boarding House and later in the Antoine Deloria General Store. Finally a church and rectory were constructed in Garden. Bishop John Vertin dedicated the church in 1884.

With the arrival of Father Anthony Zagar in 1900, parish organizations were started for men, women and young people and a spiritual revival began. It was at this time that the rectory in Fayette was sold and responsibility for care of St. Peter's Church was given permanently to the Garden Parish.

PARISH LIFE. In the years preceding The Great Depression continuing efforts were made to improve the parish property. Card parties, dinners, dances and bazaars were held to raise the needed money. The church was enlarged and a sacristy was built, as was a large new rectory.

From 1892 until about 1933, the Societe de Saint Jean Baptiste served as a tremendous asset to the parish. The group built its own meeting hall in the middle of the village and sponsored an annual picnic there. The work of the fraternal group was later taken up by the Holy Name Society. The St. Anne Altar Society is the only organization to have spanned the entire life of the church, from 1886 to the present.

In 1926 care for the Garden and Fayette parishes was given to Father Vincent C. Savageau, of the Premonstratention Order, serving at Cooks. For 14 years Father Savageau, due to a priest shortage in the diocese, was responsible for churches at Cooks, Nahma, Isabella, St. Jacques, Fayette and Garden. Mass was offered at each site only infrequently.

Garden was named the mother parish of all six churches in 1940. The first assistant priest was assigned to St. John the Baptist at this time. Mass was offered at each mission twice a month. In 1947 St. Jacques was closed and Nahma became an independent parish with Isabella as its mission.

In the summer of 1941 three School Sisters of Notre Dame arrived to teach religious vacation school. A permanent catechetical center was started in 1946 by the Dominican Sisters of Adrian, Mich.

St. John and St. Peter established their first parish council on Oct. 24, 1971. Several commissions were formed to take care of the various needs of the parish.

In January 1991, the missions of Fayette and Isabella were permanently closed. Garden, Cooks and Nahma began functioning with one pastor. The three churches also named one parish council. Each parish functions independently on a financial basis in every way except that all three share financial responsibility equally for the pastor and his residence in Garden. All three parishes combine efforts for common events, such as the annual Blessing of the Fleet and a sacramental camp for young people.

In June 2000 the Garden parish dedicated a new parish hall. The center, constructed adjacent to the church, was built without incurring any debt thanks to the generosity of St. John parishioners. Members donated all of the money for the project. The 2,300-square foot facility is handicapped accessible and has a kitchen and storage facilities. Church improvements at this time included renovations to the choir loft and new carpeting and light fixtures. Rectory renovations have also taken place.

PASTORS. Fathers Sebastian Duroc, 1865; Charles Langer, 1869; Martin Fox, 1875; Hilary J. Rosseau, 1876; Luke Mozina, 1876-1880; Edward Jacker, 1880; A. Paganini, 1880-1882; Edward Bordas, 1882-1886; Francis X. Becker, 1886-1887; Fabian Marceau, 1887; Anacletus O. Pelisson, 1887-1888; Fidelis Sutter, 1888-1889; Prosper Girard, 1890; Michael Weis, 1890; Joseph A. Sauriol, 1890-1891; Paul Datin, Louis Archille Poulin, John Henn, John Chebul, 1898; Anthony Zagar, 1900; Msgr. Mathias Jodocy, 1901; Thomas V. Dassylva, 1903; Paul Fillion, 1905; Paul LeGolvan, 1905; Joseph DuFort, 1917; Joseph Morin, 1922-1926; Vincent Savageau, 1926-1940; Nolan McKevitt, 1940-1945; Glen Sanford, 1945; Wilfred Pelletier, 1945; Arnold Thompson, 1946-1948; James Schaefer, 1950-1951; Ronald Bassett, 1951-1955; Conrad Dishaw, 1959-1963; James Donnelley, Joseph Callari, Lesli Perino, 1970-1972; co-pastors Timothy Desrochers and Lesli Perino, 1970-1976; James Pepin, 1976-1978, C. Michael Rhoades, 1978-1981; Thomas L. Poisson, 1981-1984; Ronald Timock, 1984-1986; Peter Petroske, 1986-1991; George S. Maki, 1991-1993; David W. Sedlock, 1993-1996; John Martignon, 1996-2002, and Thomas Varickamackal, 2002-.

St. Therese Mission, Germfask

Early attempts to establish a permanent Catholic Church in Germfask were quite intermittent. St. James was the first church, built in 1908. Regular services started with the founding of St. Therese Mission in 1932. Responsibility for the care of St. Therese changed from one parish to the next until Holy Rosary in Grand Marais held responsibility for the mission from 1941 to 2005. The unique cobblestone church was destroyed by fire in 1974. With a new, modern facility the people of Germfask continue supporting their church and providing a stable atmosphere for worship.

St. Therese Mission, Germfask

FOUNDING. Prior to the founding of the first church in Germfask in 1908, Catholics there were visited one or two times each year by Father Augustus Geers of Newberry. Father Geers would take a train to Seney, then travel by handcar to Germfask. Mass was offered in Morrison Hall.

In 1908 St. James Church was built in Germfask. Responsibility for administration of the church was given to Father Bernard Schevers of Manistique. Mass was only offered once or twice each year. Father Schevers traveled to Germfask by horse and buggy. The original church was eventually overcome by disrepair and so Mass ceased to be offered.

PARISH LIFE. Finally, in 1932, Germfask's population had increased and the people banded together to build a permanent house of worship.

St. Therese Church was built of cobblestone gathered from the shores of Lake Superior and hauled to the building site by horse and wagons. Local Seney and Germfask residents donated all the labor. On Sept. 18, 1932, Father Schevers dedicated the church. People from all over the world are said to have visited the beautiful cobblestone church.

Upon completion of St. Therese Church, members of the former Mission Chapel in Seney began attending services in Germfask. Mission Chapel was built in 1894. Since 1925 priests from Marquette or Newberry administered to the Seney mission. Prior to that time the priest serving Newberry had visited Mission Chapel monthly. The church was eventually sold and razed.

In 1933 care for St. Therese Mission was transferred to the pastor serving

Engadine. Mass was offered once a month.

Responsibility for the mission again changed hands in 1941. The priest serving Holy Rosary Parish in Grand Marais also began serving St. Therese. In 1943 a rectory was purchased for the priest's use while in Germfask.

The St. Therese Guild, formed in 1943, and the men's Booster Club, started in 1953, worked diligently to support improvements to the church. From 1957 to 1967 a parish picnic, complete with a horse-pulling competition, drew more than 2,000 people annually.

Tragedy struck St. Therese on Jan. 30, 1974 when fire demolished the cobblestone landmark. The blaze was the result of a furnace room explosion.

Before the construction of a new house of worship, Mass was held at the churches of other denominations in the area. Father Theodore Brodeur accepted the generous offers of other churches so that the people would get to know their neighbors better.

The dream of a new church was realized in December 1974. The first Mass held in the present structure was offered on Christmas Eve. Monetary contributions and donated labor from parishioners and others in the community and surrounding areas helped cut down tremendously on costs. Various improvements to the church building and grounds have since been made.

Picnics, parish retreats and other socials bring the people of St. Therese together. The parish celebrated its 75th anniversary July 8-10, 1983. Festivities culminated with a diamond jubilee Mass celebrated by Bishop Mark Schmitt.

In 2005 Germfask was linked to the church in Engadine.

PASTORS. Fathers Bernard Schevers, 1908-1933; Raymond Bergeron, 1933-1935; Joseph Seifert, 1935-1937; Thomas P. Dunleavy, 1937-1939; James Schaefer, 1939-1941; Roland Dion, 1941-1943; Gerald LaMothe, 1943-1946; Thomas Andary, 1946-1948; John Belot, 1948-1951; Casimir Marcinkevicius, 1951-1954; George Pernaski, 1954-1956; Louis P. Bracket, 1956-1957; B. Neil Smith, 1957-1965; Terrence F. Donnelly, 1966-1967; Raymond Valerio, 1967-1971; Theodore J. Brodeur, 1971-1976; James Williams, 1976-1981; N. Daniel Rupp, 1981-1983; Matthew Nyman, 1983-1987; Patrick E. Murphy, 1987-1992; Pawel J. Mecwel, 1992- 1997; Joseph Plappallil, 1997-2000; Glenn Theoret, 2000-2002; Joy Joseph Adimakkeel, 2002-2004, and Timothy W. Hruska, 2004-.

ALL SAINTS, GLADSTONE

All Saints Parish in Gladstone was formed by its members more than 100 years ago. Rebuilding and improving upon the structure of the church and parish school over the years is a testament of parishioners' continued growth and dedication to their faith.

All Saints, Gladstone

FOUNDING. Franciscan Friars from St. Joseph Church in Escanaba first served Catholic immigrants in Gladstone following the construction of the Soo Line Railroad in 1880. But the people wanted their own priest so badly that in 1889 they took it upon themselves to build a church. The structure was a small frame building said to fit only a few people. In 1890 a rectory was built. In response to the people, Bishop John Vertin appointed Father Fidelis Sutter the first pastor. On May 4 of that year the church was dedicated to St. Fidelis.

Continued growth of the community led to the need for a larger facility. On Nov. 6, 1898 a new church was dedicated and the name was changed to All Saints.

This second church served the parish well until it was destroyed by fire March 4, 1920. A meeting was set to take place that evening to discuss building a larger, more permanent facility. That decision became inevitable when the stove lit to heat the place for the meeting overheated and the structure burned to the ground. On May 25, 1920, the parish sold the original rectory and bought a home on the corner of Seventh Street and Wisconsin Avenue. It served as the parish rectory until 1976.

Following the 1920 fire, Mass was celebrated in the Lyric Theater while reconstruction got under way. Within the same year, the basement of the present church was constructed and Masses were held there. The new, third church was dedicated Sept. 4, 1921.

The church is built of brick and cut stone. The stained glass windows, most of which were purchased by parishioners in memory of loved ones, were imported from Germany. The designs depict the mysteries of the rosary.

PARISH SCHOOL. The tradition of All Saints Grade School began in 1912, when the parish purchased the Hawarden Inn for use as a school and convent. The Sisters of St. Joseph of Concordia, Kan., taught students in third through eighth grades.

Monsignor Matt LaViolette, during 27 years of faithful pastoral leadership, guided the spiritual lives of the people of All Saints from 1946 to 1973. Under Msgr. Matt's guidance, the parish built a new school and convent. The old school, the famous Hawarden Inn, was demolished in 1958. A brand new school and convent complex was constructed the same year. The complex consisted of 10 schoolrooms, a multi-purpose room and living quarters for the sisters. The new All Saints School was dedicated Oct. 27, 1958. The facility served the children of the parish until 1972. The decision was made to close the school due to declining enrollment and increased difficulty in securing religious faculty.

PARISH LIFE. In 1973 All Saints sold the school building to the Gladstone Public Schools for use as a middle school. At the same time, the convent was renovated to serve as a six-classroom CCD center with an apartment for the sisters. In 1976 the parish rectory was constructed next to the church.

All Saints has striven for total parish involvement by offering countless opportunities for parish and community service, liturgical involvement and volunteering. The annual parish appreciation and harvest dinners, summer picnic and Bible camps bring parishioners and others together to grow in faith and fellowship.

In 1989 All Saints celebrated its 100th anniversary as an organized parish. Extensive remodeling to the inside of the church helped commemorate the anniversary. Additional improvements, such as extending the altar 14 feet into the congregation, took place in recent years.

PASTORS. Fathers Fidelis Sutter, 1889-1890; Joseph Haas, 1890-1891; Antoine Rezek, 1891-1892; Thomas Dassylva, 1892-1893; Alexius Centner, OFM, 1893; Francis X. Becker, 1893-1894; Joseph Pinten, 1894; John Manning, 1894-1896; Joseph E. Neumair, 1896-1898; Frederic Glaser, 1898-1899; Joseph Hollinger, 1899-1902; Dennis Sullivan, 1902-1903; Henry Reis, 1903-1904; Adam Doser, 1904-1907; Owen J. Bennett, 1907-1923; Sebastian Maier, 1923-1938; Joseph Schaul, 1938-1946; Mathias H. LaViolette, 1946-1973; John Noel Arneth, 1973-1984; John E. Patrick, 1984-1995; N. Daniel Rupp, 1995-1996, and Arnold Grambow, 1996-.

St. Stanislaus Kostka, Goetzville

The community of Goetzville has remained somewhat isolated, located in the far eastern tip of the Upper Peninsula. But the Catholic tradition in the area started out strong in the mid-1880s and continues to be a driving force in the people's lives. From construction of its first parish, to rebuilding after a devastating fire and continued maintenance and upgrades throughout the years, the people have pooled their resources to keep their house of worship a strong foundation in the community. St. Stanislaus celebrated its centennial in 1997, its church structure is nearly as old and the people keep nurturing the traditions and values it represents.

St. Stanislaus Kostka, Goetzville

FOUNDING. Jesuit missionaries and diocesan priests from Sault Ste. Marie served early settlers of the Goetzville area. In 1880 the Goetz family erected a small log church there.

An increase in population in the 1890s has been attributed to Father Anselm Mlynarczyk of Sacred Heart Parish in DeTour. Father Mlynarczyk encouraged several Polish and a few Slovak families from Pennsylvania and New Jersey to come to Goetzville.

Bishop Frederick Eis dedicated St. Stanislaus Kostka Parish on May 12, 1905. Just 18 months later the church burned to the ground. Circumstances around the fire are said to have been questionable. Religious intolerance and bigotry were cited. Work was taken up immediately on the present structure. Labor, materials and money were donated to the project. The Goetzes led the way toward the purchase of a 500-pound bell and each person bought a chair for the new church. The completed structure was dedicated Oct. 13, 1907.

Until 1922 the pastor from DeTour continued to care for the mission at Goetzville. That year, Father Romanus Klafkowski became Goetzville's first resident pastor. Again from 1926 to 1929 Sacred Heart's pastor took over at Goetzville. But the church has been an independent parish ever since.

MISSIONS. St. Stanislaus' pastor began serving Our Lady of Snows Mission in Hessel and Holy Cross Mission in Cedarville in 1929. The two churches were officially attached as missions in 1936. In 1957 Cedarville was closed. At present Our Lady of the Snows remains a mission of St. Stanislaus.

PARISH LIFE   In the 1930s, parishioners were successful in saving the church from burning a second time. Sadly, the large beautiful rectory was consumed by fire. But members of the parish are said to have been on the roof of the church putting out any sparks that landed there.

The rectory was rebuilt between 1937 and 1940. Many improvements were made to the church and rectory in the mid-1940s. Also during this time, the church basement was excavated for use as a recreation hall. Additional improvements to the church and rectory, as well as the cemetery, were made in the ensuing years. A major refurbishing of the parish hall and re-siding of the church exterior took place in 1973 to coincide with the parish's diamond jubilee celebration. A year-long celebration commemorating the 75th anniversary of the founding of the parish began with Mass in a snow-and-ice chapel built in February of that year. The annual Fourth of July celebration had an anniversary flair and a jubilee Mass in August was said in Polish to honor the founding members. Parishioners dressed in period garb and walked to the celebration. Also that year a historic tribute to the parish was published in the booklet *Lest We Forget*.

On June 15, 1997, St. Stanislaus Kostka Parish celebrated its centennial with a Mass of Thanksgiving, followed by a banquet at the Raber Hall.

Well-known traditions at St. Stanislaus include a Fourth of July picnic started in the 1940s, and a Hunters' Dinner during the firearm deer season in November. A full turkey dinner is served complete with homemade sauerkraut.

PASTORS.   Fathers W. Anselm Mlynarczyk, 1897-1898; John F. Chambon, SJ, 1898-1904; Theodore G. Bateski, 1904-1922; Romanus Klafkowski, 1922-1924; John Kovalsky, 1924-1926; John Kraker, 1929-1937; Frank J. Ignatz, 1937-1940; Casimir Adasiewicz, 1940-1941; Edward Lulewicz, 1941-1945; Walter J. Franczek, 1945-1952; Chester M. Franczek, 1952-1962; Edward Wenzel, 1962-1970; Anthony J. Polakowski, 1970-1976; Theodore J. Brodeur, 1976-1981; David C. Jenner, 1981-1982; Frank M. Lenz, 1982-1985; Richard C. Schaeffer, 1985-1988; George C. Gustafson, 1988-1989; John M. Maloney, 1989-1990; Michael J. Steber, 1990-1995; Larry P. Van Damme, 1995-1997; Benedetto J. Paris, 1997-2000; Jacek Wtyklo, 2000-2003, and Sebastian Kavumkal, MST, 2003-.

HOLY ROSARY, GRAND MARAIS

The presence of the Catholic Church in Grand Marais dates back to the 1600s when Jesuit missionaries first visited the harbor. Holy Rosary Parish was established in 1895.

The only Catholic church within a 50-mile radius, Holy Rosary remains one of the diocese's most isolated churches. Depending largely on their own resources, the people of the parish and their pastors have sacrificed a great deal to support continued growth in the faith.

Holy Rosary, Grand Marais

FOUNDING. The first permanent settlement at Grand Marais followed the establishment of a sawmill around 1880. As the population increased, Father John F. Chambon, a Jesuit serving in Sault Ste. Marie, began serving the community somewhat regularly. Father Chambon would arrive a few times each year by boat or train, and in the winter either by dog sled or snowshoes. Mass was said in private homes.

Property for a church was purchased in 1889. About three years later a small frame building was erected and served initially as both the church and rectory.

Finally in 1895, Holy Rosary Parish was established. The first resident pastor arrived in August and began construction of a new church and rectory.

PARISH LIFE. A rapid succession of priests kept the church and rectory from being completed until 1901. By the turn of the century the busy lumbering and commercial fishing community had an active and growing Catholic church. Two Masses were offered every Sunday.

Then, a rapid decline in population, from 2,000 people in 1900 to just 300 in 1913 following the end of pine logging, led to the church being placed in mission status. From 1917 to 1941 the church was served from Newberry, Munising or Marquette. Services were offered only monthly until the mid-1920s when Highway M-77 was built. By the late 1930s weekly Mass was again offered.

On Sunday, March 3, 1935, the church and rectory were destroyed by fire. Parishioners got right to work planning to rebuild their house of worship. Mass was held in the James Thompson grocery store, then in the school gymnasium.

Using donated labor, a new church was up and enclosed that summer. For the first two years, Mass was held in the basement while the church was being completed. Due to a shortage of funds during the Depression and a lack of materials during World War II, the interior remained unfinished for the next 15 years.

In 1941, after being a mission for nearly 25 years, Holy Rosary received another resident priest. A small house was rented for use as a rectory and the exterior of the church was sided. Father Roland Dion also took it upon himself to put his woodworking skills to use improving the interior of the church. It is recorded that parishioners entering the church for Sunday Mass would often have to make their way around Father Dion's table saw in the vestibule.

Members of religious orders, including the School Sisters of Notre Dame from Bessemer, came for many years to conduct a two-week summer school for young people of the parish.

In 1956 a new rectory was built. In the late 1970s stained glass windows and the steeple chimes were installed.

A major church renovation was begun in 1995 to coincide with the parish's centennial. This included a new front entrance to both the church and the basement hall, with stair-lifts for easier accessibility. A new greeting and gathering area was provided at the church entry, which also allowed for additional pews and enlargement of the choir loft. The basement hall and church sanctuary were also renovated. All improvements were barrier-free. In 1998 additional property was purchased for a parking lot and storage building. Major improvements were made to the 1955 rectory in 2002. Many dinners, bingos and barbeques are held to raise funds to support the church.

MISSIONS. Beginning in 1941, Holy Rosary's pastor was also responsible for the care of St. Therese Mission in Germfask. In 1948 responsibility for serving the mission of Blaney Park was added. In 2005 Grand Marais was linked with St. Gregory in Newberry and Our Lady of Victory Mission in Paradise.

PASTORS. Fathers W. Anselm Mlynarczyk, 1895; Fidelis Sutter, 1896; John Chebul, 1897; Frederic Glaser, 1898; John Mockler, 1899-1901; Adam Doser, 1901-1903; Adolph Schneider, 1903-1904; Fabian Marceau, 1904-1905; Prosper Girard, 1905-1911; Joseph Tastevin, 1911-1913; Herman N. Gagne, 1914-1917; Peter Manderfield, 1915-1935; Bernard Eiling, 1917-1936; Theodore Stout, Thomas Drengacz, Anthony Schloss, 1937-1939; Joseph Gondek, 1939-1940; Frederick Hofmann, 1940-1941; Roland Dion, 1941-1943; Gerald LaMothe, 1943-1946; John F. Belot, 1948-1951; Casimir Marcinkevicius, 1951-1954; George Pernaski, 1954-1956; Louis P. Brackett, 1956-1957; B. Neil Smith, 1957-1965; Terrence Donnelly, 1966-1967; Raymond Valerio, 1967-1971; Theodore Brodeur, 1971-1976; James Williams, 1976-1981; N. Daniel Rupp, 1981-1983; Matthew Nyman, 1983-1987; Patrick Murphy, 1987-1992; Pawel J. Mecwel, 1992- 1997; Joseph Plappallil, 1997-2000; Glenn Theoret, 2000-2002; Joy Joseph Adimakkeel, 2002-2004, and Paul Karottekunnel, MST, 2004-.

SAINTS PETER AND PAUL MISSION, GREENLAND

In its 135-year history, the church of Ss. Peter and Paul in Greenland held the status of independent parish for about 20 years. But the people who supported the church did so whole-heartedly up to the time of its closure in 1995. A new church in the early 1930s was constructed without incurring debt, and the people supported necessary improvements to their house of worship throughout the years.

Saints Peter and Paul Mission, Greenland

FOUNDING. Father Martin Fox of St. Mary Church in Rockland took it upon himself to build a church in Greenland, or Maple Grove as the area was called at the time. The church was completed in 1859 and dedicated to Saints Peter and Paul.

The church was served as a mission of Rockland for nearly its first 50 years. Then, in 1905, a rectory was built. The first pastor to occupy the rectory was Father Eisele in 1908.

PARISH LIFE. By 1922 the copper mines had ceased to be successful and people left the area in droves. From that time on, Saints Peter and Paul Church was a mission of Rockland.

After years of fund-raising and anticipation, a new church was erected in Greenland in 1932. Members of the small church began raising money for the effort in 1913 by holding tea and card parties, dinners and other activities. Parishioner pledges allowed the structure to go up without incurring debt.

The new church was built on the site of the original. The first Mass was said there on Dec. 13, 1932.

Significant improvements were made to the church in 1978. A new roof was installed, as was a steeple cross and new front doors. A confessional was added and the sanctuary and basement were renovated. Eleven stained glass windows were installed at the church in 1988. The entryway was again renovated in 1993.

CLOSURE. Saints Peter and Paul Mission was closed in July 1995 as a result of the diocese's pastoral planning process Fully Alive in '95.

RECORDS. Records for Saints Peter and Paul Mission are located at St. Mary Parish in Rockland.

PASTORS. Fathers Martin Fox, 1858-1868; Henry Thiele, 1868-1871;

Edward Jacker, 1871-1872; Oliver Comtois, 1872-1873; Anthony Hubly, 1874-1878; William Dwyer, 1878-1882; Charles Dries, 1882-1883; Charles Langner, 1883-1884; Anacletus Pelison, 1884-1885; Joseph Haas, 1885; John Burns, 1885-1887; Michael Weis, 1887-1889; John Henn, Augustus Geers, 1890; John Reichenbach, 1890-1891; Joseph Haas, 1891-1892; Renatus Becker, 1893-1894; James Lenhart, 1894-1895; Fidelis Sutter, 1895-1896; Edward Bordas, 1896-1897; Renatus Becker, 1897-1900; Frederick Sperlein, 1900-1902; Peter Manderfield, 1902-1908; - - - Eisele, 1908-1909; Anthony Waechter, 1909; Joseph Lamotte, Edward J. Testevins, 1920-1922; Bernard Linnemann, 1922-1945; Edward Malloy, 1945-1948; Frederick Hofmann, 1948-1950; John McLaughlin, 1950-1951; Thomas Ruppe, 1951-1958; Frank Hollenbach, 1958-1961; George Pernaski, 1961-1962; Robert Haas, 1962-1963; Norbert LaCosse, 1963-1965; Donald LaLonde, 1965-1967; Raymond Moncher, 1967-1969; Joseph Polakowski, 1969; Lesli Perino, 1969-1970; Raymond Hoefgen, 1970-1973; David Jenner, 1973-1975; Aloysius Ehlinger, 1975-1978; Joseph Carne, 1978-1986; Eric Olson, 1986-1992; Bede Louzon, OFM, Cap., 1992-1993, and Ronald Timock, 1993-1995.

DIVINE INFANT OF PRAGUE MISSION, GULLIVER

Divine Infant of Prague Church in Gulliver celebrated its 25th anniverary in 1984, a significant milestone for parishioners. The people of Gulliver have shown great pride in their parish, donating to its construction in 1959 and to many improvements since.

FOUNDING. Bishop Thomas L. Noa established the Divine Infant Mission in Gulliver in 1949. Father Francis M. Scheringer, pastor of St. Francis de Sales Parish in Manistique, led the people of the Gulliver and Blaney-Green School areas in organizing the congregation.

Divine Infant of Prague Mission, Gulliver

Mass was first offered in the Mueller Township Hall using a homemade altar and wooden benches. Later Mass was held in the Blaney-Green School and then in the community building.

PARISH LIFE. Finally in 1958, years of fund-raising efforts culminated with construction of a church. A site was chosen on donated land located midway between Gulliver and Blaney-Green School. In addition to parishioners' pledges, various fundraising efforts included weekly coffee socials, rummage sales and an annual harvest supper. The first Mass was said in the new church May 17, 1959. That July Bishop Noa dedicated the house of worship to the Divine Infant of Prague.

Improvements to the church over the years include renovations to the sanctuary and installation of a chair lift in 1984.

The parish celebrated its 25th anniversary in the fall of 1984. Bishop Mark Schmitt celebrated a commemorative Mass of thanksgiving.

Responsibility for the care of Divine Infant remained with Manistique until 1995 when it was reassigned as one of the three churches making up what is commonly referred to as the Engadine Catholic Missions. On Dec. 31, 2004, the Gulliver church was again linked to Manistique.

PASTORS. Francis M. Scheringer, 1950-1973; Norbert Frieburger, 1973-1979; James Menapace, 1979-1995; co-pastor C. Michael Rhoades, 1981-1982; Mieczyslaw T. Oniskiewicz, 1995-1997; Jan Szczkowski, 1997-1998; Mariusz Makowski, 1998-1999; Timothy W. Hruska, 1999-2004, and Glenn Theoret 2004-.

St. Anthony, Gwinn

St. Anthony, Gwinn

Priests from the Diocese of Marquette began reaching out to Catholics settling in the Gwinn area shortly after mining companies began building the "model town" in 1902. It has been recorded that St. Anthony Church and its missions saw ups and downs, which followed the pattern of the mining industry's good and lean years. Although mining operations ceased in the region in 1946, the tradition of the church is still going strong.

FOUNDING. Prior to completion of the first church in Gwinn, an assistant pastor from Negaunee traveled to the area by train offering Mass and catechism in private homes, schoolhouses and the Odd Fellows Hall. He would visit Princeton, Gwinn, Little Lake, Forsyth, Turin (McFarland) and Lathrop on a three-week rotation.

Work began on the foundation of the church in 1911. The first Mass was said in the basement in 1912. The following year the church received its first pastor, Father Anthony Waechter. He oversaw construction of the present rectory.

In the spring of 1917 Father Sebastian Maier was assigned to the pastorate and began the task of completing the church structure. Under his leadership, material progress was coupled with a spiritual revival, according to an article in the Centennial Issue of *The Northern Michigan Edition of Our Sunday Visitor* published in 1953. Bazaars, picnics and dinners were held to raise money for improvements to the church.

PARISH LIFE. With the growth of K.I. Sawyer Air Force Base, the original church proved to be too small. Fund drives were held and in June 1969, a new church with a capacity of 350 was dedicated. The "church in the round" design is believed to have been one of the first in the area.

An educational wing was added in 1978. Religious education classes had previously been held at the Gilbert Elementary School. The inside of the church was completely refurbished in the 1990s.

The parish boasts of its active parish council, parishioners' lively participation in service organizations, and the extraordinary success of Eucharistic Adoration, resulting in increased spirituality and increased opportunities to practice the faith.

MISSIONS. Turin (McFarland) was settled in 1863. Mass there was offered in a private home until 1902, when enough money was raised to build a chapel. The church was dedicated to St. Charles Borromeo. Some of the early records are found at Perkins and Gladstone. That church burned in 1929 and a schoolhouse was purchased for use as a church in 1937. Services continued there through 1968.

The Little Lake area was also settled in 1863 and at one time was a center for lumbering. Mass was offered there only as often as a priest could come, which sometimes meant not for months. But once Gwinn received a resident pastor, a church dedicated to St. Henry was erected in 1922. St. Henry Mission also continued through 1968.

St. Anthony's has cared for the mission of St. Joseph of Northland since 1991.

PASTORS. Fathers Anthony Waechter, 1913-1917; Sebastian Maier, 1917-1923; Joseph Lamotte, 1923-1927; Francois E. Bonny, 1927-1931; Carl J. Petranek 1931-1932, Neil Stehlin 1932-1940, James A. Paquet 1940-1942, Frederick Hofmann, 1942-1943, George Stuntebeck 1943-1952, Charles Reinhart 1952-1966, George Pernaski 1966-1991, David Jenner 1991-1998, Ronald K. Timock 1998-

CHURCH OF THE RESURRECTION, HANCOCK

Church of the Resurrection, Hancock

Resurrection Parish in Hancock was the result of a rebirth of the former St. Joseph and St. Patrick Parish in 1976. The roots of Catholicism there date back to the mid-1800s. Through separation and then reunification came the modern church whose people raised a new house of worship in a new location with a new name. Members of the former Our Lady of Mount Carmel Mission in Franklin Mine joined the parish in 1981.

FOUNDING. The people of St. Joseph and St. Patrick Parish in Hancock worked devotedly from November 1972 to October 1976 to see the construction of a new church complex.

Ground was broken at the site of the former Catholic cemetery on Quincy Street on Aug. 24, 1975. During the next two months a fund-raising campaign netted more than $200,000. Construction progressed quickly and plans were made for the celebration of the first Mass. But before that could happen, Father Charles Reinhart, who had led the parish through the construction process, died of cancer, and never saw completion of the project.

The people agreed with Bishop Charles Salatka to name the parish Church of the Resurrection. A dedication ceremony took place Oct. 10, 1976.

In recognition of Father Reinhart's service to the parish (1966-1976) and in honor of his leadership in the construction of the new church, the new social hall was named after him.

PARISH LIFE. In the 1980s additions were made to the parish grounds, including a monument to Father Edward Jacker, a memorial stone commemorating all who are buried in the former cemetery and a tower with St. Joseph's bell.

The parish worked hard through bake sales, bingo, bazaars and other efforts to help pay off the debt of the parish hall in 1983.

Regular Bible studies, youth and adult faith formation, coffee socials after Sunday Mass and an annual appreciation dinner are among the parish activities.

PASTORS. Fathers Paul Schiska, 1976-1977; Emmett Norden; 1977-1983; Henry Mercier, 1983-1991, and Wayne Marcotte, 1991-.

ST. JOSEPH AND ST. PATRICK, HANCOCK

St. Joseph and St. Patrick, Hancock

Hancock's first Catholic Church, St. Anne's, was started at the insistence of Bishop Frederic Baraga. He assigned Father Edward Jacker, of Houghton, to also take on responsibility for a new Hancock church. A dedication ceremony took place on Aug. 4, 1861.

A growing parish community with diverse nationalities led to a parish split in 1885. The Germans and French-Canadians had a new church constructed, St. Joseph's. The Irish decided to stay with the existing church, but renamed the parish St. Patrick's.

After a fire at the St. Patrick Church in 1937 and given the declining population of the region, the two parishes reunited under the name St. Joseph and St. Patrick in 1953.

ST. JOSEPH PARISH

St. Joseph Parish was dedicated in October 1885 and Father Joseph Langner was named the first pastor of the congregation.

In 1908 the parish took on the financial burden of enlarging both the school and church. A wing added onto each side of the church nearly doubled its seating capacity. The church was redecorated in 1929. The school was modernized and the church again redecorated in the 1940s.

PASTORS.   Fathers Charles Langner, 1885-1888; E. Chapuis, 1888-1898; Joseph Zalokar, 1889; Thomas Dassylva, 1889; Julius Baron Von Gumpenberg, 1889-1990; John Kossbiel, 1890; Joseph Boissonault, 1890; Francis Schafer, OFM, 1890-1891; Joseph Hoeber, 1891-1892; Fidelis Sutter, 1892-1893; Frederick Eis, 1893; Anthony C. Keller, 1893-1901; Augustus W. Geers, 1901-1907; Anthony Waechter, 1907-1908; Frederic Glaser, 1908-1920; Alexander Wollny, 1921-1935; Michael Nivard, 1935-1936; Caspar Douenberg, 1936-1940; Dieudonne J. Breault, 1940-1951, and Edmund Mihelich, 1951.

ST. PATRICK PARISH

Prior to the splitting of the parish in 1885, it was evident to all that the St. Anne church building no longer met the needs of the growing parish. On March

17, 1889 a new structure was completed. The Irish saw the dedication of their church under a new name on the Feast of St. Patrick 1889.

The 1913 copper strike and the closing of the Quincy Mine in 1929 started a population decline that continued through the 1950s.

Nonetheless, parishioners funded a major church renovation project in 1930. The walls were reinforced with steel, the steeple was lowered, a copper roof was laid, the church interior was renovated and upgrades were made to the rectory.

After all of this was completed, the parish was devastated when a fire broke out on May 6, 1937, destroying the church, school and rectory. The church was only insured for one-tenth of its value. After the fire, the property was cleared and plans to erect a new church began.

But plans for a new church did not come to fruition due to financial constraints. Instead, the parish began using the St. Joseph facilities. St. Patrick's retained its separate identity, and for about one year, its pastor. When Father Erasmus Dooley was transferred in 1938, the pastor of St. Joseph's began to serve St. Patrick's congregation as well.

PASTORS. Fathers Thomas J. Atfield, 1889-1919; James Corcoran, 1919-1937, and Erasmus Dooley, 1937-1938.

MERGER. At the request of trustees representing people from both parishes, a merger began in 1940. Bishop Thomas L. Noa officially unified the two entities into the new parish of St. Joseph and St. Patrick effective Jan. 1, 1953. In 1976 the parish was "reborn" into the new Resurrection Church. A new church in a new location with a new name started a new era for Catholics in Hancock.

PARISH SCHOOL. The united St. Joseph and St. Patrick Parish banded together to construct a new school and convent in the 1950s. Groundbreaking ceremonies for the structure, located in West Hancock, were held April 25, 1958. The new edifice was completed and the first classes commenced Jan. 5, 1959. Sisters of St. Joseph of Carondelet, from St. Louis, Mo., staffed the school.

It was a joyous day Dec. 6, 1964 when the parish paid off the final debt for the new building and held a mortgage-burning celebration.

A shortage of religious teachers and the cost to maintain and operate the school forced its closure in 1972. It was sold to the Copper Country Intermediate School District. Catechism classes continued to be held at the school building until the new Resurrection complex was completed in 1976.

ST. JOSEPH AND ST. PATRICK PASTORS. Thomas Lester Bourgeois, 1952-1966, and Charles Reinhart 1966-1976.

St. Louis the King, Harvey

In 40 short years St. Louis the King Parish in Harvey, located just south of the city of Marquette, has more than tripled in the number of registered families. Both the size and beauty of its church complex have also grown immensely.

The people's enthusiasm for the faith is evident in the continually high numbers for the Rite of Christian Initiation of Adults, religious education programs, youth ministries and the church's annual community summer festival.

St. Louis the King, Harvey

FOUNDING. Parish history reveals that Catholics living in the Chocolay Township area as early as the mid-1870s were served by priests from the French church in Marquette, St. John the Baptist. But it wasn't until the 1950s that plans were made to build for the people a church of their own.

Finally, on June 30, 1954, Bishop Thomas L. Noa announced the formation of a new parish, St. Louis the King. Boundaries would include Harvey, Lakewood, Hiawatha Shores, Sand River, Beaver Grove, Green Garden, Mangum, West Branch, Skandia, Dukes and Sands. Father David T. Harris was appointed the parish's first administrator. He presided over the first Mass, held July 18, 1954, in the Chocolay Township Hall.

Groundbreaking ceremonies for the church were held July 20, 1955. Members of the parish helped contractors complete the basement by the time of the first Mass and dedication, Dec. 4. The basement church served as the site for worship services for the next four years.

In November 1957 a private home was purchased for use as a rectory. Construction of the church began in July 1959, and the first Mass was said in the new structure on Dec. 25. Bishop Noa dedicated the church on Feb. 28, 1960. At the time about 120 families were registered.

PARISH LIFE. Over the years additional land was purchased and upgrades made to the St. Louis the King facilities. In 1972 a new rectory was attached to the church. In 1988 a gazebo project was completed with money and labor being donated by members of the parish.

In 1999, when the population of the parish had swelled to 660 families, members took on a $2.4 million project to build a new complex. A groundbreaking ceremony, led by Bishop James Garland, took place March 14.

The rectory and garage were separated from the church and relocated on the property. A new gathering space, which leads to a new church, went up in its place. The seating in the sanctuary was increased from 250 to 450. Office space and a basement for religious education facilities and meeting rooms were added. The existing church building became the church hall for social gatherings, and a new kitchen was built behind it. During construction, parish offices were moved to the Knights of Columbus building across the street from the church.

A dedication ceremony for the new structure, in which Bishop Garland led parishioners from the old parish to the new, took place May 13, 2000. Concelebrating were Pastor Father Guy Thoren, founding pastor Father David Harris, former pastor Lawrence Gauthier and retired Bishop Mark Schmitt.

The social flair of St. Louis the King parishioners has been particularly displayed in a community festival, now the Annual Chocolay Summerfest, beginning in 1988. The parish celebrated the 30th anniversary of its founding in 1990 with a commemorative Mass in the gazebo.

In the early 1990s St. Louis the King had the largest number of people of any parish in the diocese to complete the Rite of Christian Initiation of Adults and receive the Easter sacraments. The parish also has a hearty participation in parish retreats held at Marygrove Retreat Center.

PARISH SCHOOL. St. Louis the King was among the six Marquette area parishes to jointly operate the Bishop Baraga Central High School and grade school and it continues to contribute to the Father Marquette Catholic Central School system.

PASTORS. Fathers David T. Harris, 1954-1971; Charles J. Strelick, 1971-1975; Joseph R. Callari, 1975-1983; Lawrence Gauthier, 1983-1994; Guy S. Thoren, 1994-2002, and Benedetto Paris, 2002-.

St. Mary, Hermansville

St. Mary, Hermansville

Catholics living in Hermansville first banded together to raise money for the construction of a church. Through the years, the people have made donations to maintain and improve upon their house of worship.

A fire in the late 1940s that destroyed the interior of the church did nothing to put out the spirit of the people. With donated labor and money, the church was rebuilt in a matter of months.

When the history of an era for St. Mary's ended in 1995, parishioners gracefully merged with those of St. Francis Xavier in Spalding to form the new parish of St. John Neumann. The people of Hermansville continue to support and strengthen the Christian faith of the community.

FOUNDING. Hermansville was a mission of Father Martin Fox's when he began serving the Menominee area in the 1870s. A priest visited the village once each month, offering Mass in the old school house.

In 1900 a committee began canvassing the community asking for donations for a church. Families were asked to donate $1 and single men 50 cents per month. Construction was completed and, on Sunday, Dec. 19, 1902, the church was blessed. The first resident pastor was Father Anthony Waechter, who served the parish from 1906 to 1907. A rectory was built in 1908. In 1910 a steeple was added to the church.

PARISH LIFE. Many improvements were made to the church and rectory in the mid-1940s, including the addition of a garage and sun porch onto the rectory and landscaping of the church grounds. The parish hall was also updated.

Within a few years a devastating fire struck, destroying the interior of the church. The March 15, 1949 blaze was started during morning Mass when wind blew through an open door, causing a candle to ignite velvet altar drapes.

The people of the parish came together, and in just four months renovation of the damaged building was completed. Through the donations of money and labor, the church was rededicated by Bishop Thomas L. Noa on July 26, 1949. While renovations were under way, services were held at the Croatian Society Hall. A new marble altar and bronze tabernacle under a marble and gold cross was the center figure of the new sanctuary. A new organ was also purchased.

The parish celebrated its diamond jubilee in 1975. The celebration of 75 years as a parish family commenced with an anniversary Mass and confirmation ceremony Sept. 21. Bishop Charles A. Salatka presided over the celebration. A dinner followed the Mass.

Also in 1975, a wooded parcel of land next to the church was purchased for use as a much-needed parking lot.

The church underwent major renovations in 1989, thanks to the generous donations of parishioners. An $800,000 transformation was undertaken in part to comply with the changes brought about by the Second Vatican Council. Improvements included reinforcing the foundation of the church, changing the wall structure, installing a new handicapped entrance, enlarging the parish hall and adding restrooms. The interior of the sanctuary was also completely redone.

On Sunday, Aug. 6, 2000, Bishop James Garland celebrated a centennial Mass at the church. A reception, guided tours of the new building and a banquet were also part of the anniversary celebration.

MERGER. In July 1995 St. Mary Parish was merged with St. Francis Xavier in Spalding to form the new St. John Neumann Parish. The move was a result of the Fully Alive in '95 pastoral planning process. Both parish complexes remain in full use. The parish has one pastor, one finance council and one parish council.

PASTORS. Fathers Frederick Glaser, 1900-1906; Anthony Waechter, 1906-1907; Joseph Dittman, 1907-1908; John Crocker, 1908-1919; John Henn, 1920; George Stuntebeck, 1920; Herman N. Gagne, 1920-1923; Joseph Hollinger, 1923-1943; John Belot, 1943; Eugene Hennelly, 1943-1946; Alderic Paquet, 1946-1950; Charles Daniel, 1950-1951; Steve Avinshek, OFM, 1951-1952; Fredrick Hofmann, 1952-1953; Thomas Anderson, 1953-1961; Gerald LaMothe, 1961-1964; Patrick Frankard, 1964-1965; Gervase Brewer, 1965-1971; Joseph Gouin, 1972; Edward Wenzel, 1972-1980; David Rocheleau, 1980-1984; Raymond Valerio, 1984-1990, and Michael Vichich, 1990-1995.

Our Lady of the Snows Mission, Hessel

Just like the Jesuits who founded Our Lady of the Snows Mission in Hessel, parishioners today continue to illustrate what a small group of faith-filled people can do to enlighten their community. From maintaining a Catholic presence in an isolated region despite having no resident priest, to continually upgrading worship facilities, parishioners strive to touch the lives of the entire community and the many tourists to the area.

A prayer garden overlooking beautiful Hessel Bay with outdoor Stations of the Cross is the most recent enhancement to the spiritual lives of the people there.

Our Lady of the Snows Mission, Hessel

FOUNDING. A Catholic mission was established in Hessel in 1850. The first church there was erected in 1891 and dedicated to St. Anaclete.

In 1906 the original church was replaced by a white frame structure, dedicated Our Lady of the Snows. This second church was built on a hill overlooking the Hessel Harbor.

In 1936 Our Lady of the Snows, along with Holy Cross Mission in Cedarville, was attached to the St. Stanislaus Kostka Parish in Goetzville. In 1957 the church at Cedarville was closed and the missions combined to form one mission church.

PARISH LIFE. The tourism industry in Hessel was on the rise and by 1962 the need for a larger church was obvious. By the end of 1964 pledges for the new church totaled $58,000. The new building was constructed using local resources of limestone for the stonework and cedar for the woodwork. The design of the church included several square peaks to reflect the tepee homes of the original Native parishioners.

During construction, the white frame church was moved farther back on the grounds and remained in use. The final Mass there was offered Wednesday, March 27, 1968. That building was later sold. Services in the current church began on Passion Sunday, March 31, 1968. A dedication ceremony led by Bishop Charles A. Salatka took place Aug. 5 of that year.

While in Hessel, the priest from Goetzville would stay in the homes of Hessel and Cedarville residents or in the basement of the church. Finally, in

1991, the parish's first rectory was purchased. Through contributions from the people, the rectory was paid for in full that year. The women's Altar Society helped furnish the house.

In 1993 the parish celebrated the 25th anniversary of the present church building.

Starting in the early 1990s, catechism classes began taking an annual fall trip on a hay wagon into a local pumpkin patch to select their own pumpkins and gourds. A quilt show is also held regularly at the church.

In 1995 a library of religious books and videos for loan to parishioners and visitors was established at Our Lady of the Snows.

During the summer tourism season, an additional 50 or so Catholic families join the 120 year-round families for Sunday Mass. Coffee and doughnut socials on the porch outside after Mass provide time for fellowship.

The church basement is the site of religious education classes, parish potluck dinners and other activities, such as wedding receptions and anniversary parties. Summer Bible study is held for the youth of the mission church.

In 2001 a Smiling Madonna and Child Jesus statue was donated to the church and a prayer garden was established. In 2005 the garden was expanded to include outdoor Stations of the Cross. Bishop James Garland blessed the stations Oct. 9.

PASTORS. Fathers John F. Chambon, SJ, 1891-1895; William Gagnieur, SJ; John Kraker, Frank Ignatz, 1937-1940; Casimir Adasiewicz, 1940-1941; Edward Lulewicz, 1941-1945; Walter Franczek, 1945-1952; Chester Franczek, 1952-1962; Edward J. Wenzel, 1962-1970; Anthony J. Polakowski, 1970-1976; Theodore Brodeur, 1976-1981; David C. Jenner, 1981-1982; Frank M. Lenz, 1982-1985; Richard C. Schaeffer, 1985-1988; George C. Gustafson, 1988-1989; John M. Maloney, 1989-1990; Michael J. Steber, 1990-1995; Larry P. Van Damme, 1995-1997; Benedetto J. Paris, 1997-2000; Jacek Wtyklo, 2000-2003, and Sebastian Kavumkal, MST, 2003-.

St. Albert the Great, Houghton

Established in 1963, St. Albert the Great Parish at Michigan Technological University in Houghton originated as a Newman Club in May 1946. The club grew into a center and eventually into an independent parish serving mostly college students. As the population at Michigan Tech University has increased, so has the parish and its many ministries and opportunities for faith formation, spiritual growth and Christian service.

FOUNDING. Father Arnold E. Thompson, while serving Our Lady of Mount Carmel Parish in Franklin Mine, started a Newman Club for the students of the Michigan College of Mining and Technology. Newman Clubs are named after Cardinal John Henry Newman of England (1801-1890), who believed in educating the whole person intellectually, physically and spiritually.

St. Albert the Great, Houghton

In December 1946, Father George LaForest, pastor of St. Ignatius Parish in Houghton, was named Newman chaplain. In May 1950, as Father LaForest was nearing the end of his pastorate at St. Ignatius Parish, he announced the purchase of the former Myers home at 1301 Ruby Ave. in Houghton. The "Newman House," as it was called, was to provide a place for college students to live in a Catholic Christian atmosphere.

The family continued to grow, and by 1954, the Newman House became the Newman Center. The first Mass at the Newman Center was celebrated on Sept. 28, 1958. The center was also home to the Aquinas Club for married students.

PARISH LIFE. As attendance at the Newman Center's daily Mass, meetings, lectures, socials, and discussions grew, so did the need for a larger complex. In June 1959 a Newman Foundation was established to raise funds to purchase property and build a student chapel. Many Michigan Tech students, faculty, staff and local community members prayerfully worked in innovative ways with Father William McGee and area clergy to raise money for the project. Land was procured on the south side of Michigan Tech's campus, next to the Good Will Farm. In April 1963 bids were awarded for construction of the new complex. The center would be named after St. Albert the Great (1206-1280), patron saint of natural scientists.

On May 5, 1963, groundbreaking ceremonies took place. The cornerstone was laid on October 6. The first Mass was offered by Monsignor Thomas Drengacz on Jan. 6, 1964. Bishop Thomas L. Noa dedicated the church on May 3, 1964 and St. Albert the Great was established as a student parish on Oct. 2 of that year. On Nov. 15, the Feast of St. Albert the Great, Father William McGee was named its first pastor.

As the student population grew at Michigan Tech University, so did the parish and its many ministries and opportunities for faith formation, spiritual growth and Christian service. In 1968 Father Donald Shiroda became a co-pastor with Father McGee and eventually succeeded him as pastor. During the pastorate of Father William Callari (1984-1997), the parish offices were enlarged and a meeting room and new apartment for the student residents was built. In 2000 the parish numbered nearly 1,000 members, 930 of them Michigan Tech students. A number of Michigan Tech alumni have gone on to become ordained priests.

PASTORS   Fathers William McGee, 1964-1971; Donald Shiroda, 1968-1971; co-pastors Terry Villaire and George Wallner, 1971-1972; Donald Zanon, 1972-1974; Thomas Wantland, 1974-1984; William Callari, 1984-1997, and Larry Van Damme, 1997-.

St. Ignatius Loyola, Houghton

St. Ignatius Loyola, Houghton

St. Ignatius Loyola Parish in Houghton is among those started by Bishop Frederic Baraga. Although the original building is no longer standing, pride in their current house of worship has prompted parishioners to take up the work of maintaining and improving the church. In 1987 the church was named to the National Register of Historic Places. Parish retreats and regular missions are among the opportunities offered to help St. Ignatius members to grow spiritually.

FOUNDING. Bishop Frederic Baraga was the first to offer Mass to the miners and other early settlers of the Portage Lake area. Then-Father Baraga traveled by foot from L'Anse to Houghton, offering Mass in private homes. His successor in L'Anse, Father Edward Jacker, continued to make occasional visits to the mission.

When Bishop Baraga returned to Houghton Sept. 5, 1858, he administered the Sacrament of Confirmation for the first time in the region, and he spearheaded efforts for the construction of Houghton's first church. Ground was broken in the spring of 1859, and on July 31 of that year Bishop Baraga returned to dedicate the completed structure to St. Ignatius Loyola.

PARISH LIFE. After a long list of priests who stayed just a year or two, St. Ignatius was blessed to receive the services of Father—later Monsignor—Antoine Rezek. Father Rezek's tenure with the parish spanned 51 years, from 1895 to 1946.

Father Rezek first organized the parish to build a larger church. Parishioners and non-Catholics alike donated toward the project. The women of the church worked to raise much of the needed funds.

The last Mass was said in the original church Oct. 8, 1899. Bishop Frederick Eis dedicated the new edifice Aug. 10, 1902. Over time the interior of the new church was decorated, again thanks to the efforts of parishioners. The people helped fund three Gothic-style altars and beautiful stained glass windows.

The original church built by Bishop Baraga was razed in 1951 and a garage for use by the parish was put up in its place.

While serving the parish Father Rezek also authored the two-volume *History of the Diocese of Sault Ste. Marie and Marquette*, published in 1907. The historical account of the founding of Catholicism in the Upper Peninsula through 1900 earned him an honorary Doctorate of Law degree from the University of Wisconsin-Milwaukee in 1911.

In preparation for the observance of the parish's centennial in 1959, many improvements were made to the parish plant. Additional parking was added and an east entrance to the church was constructed. The basement hall was enlarged and renovated and a kitchen added. The hall was named Monsignor Rezek Hall.

The three-day centennial celebration was held July 30, 31 and Aug. 1, 1959. Festivities included a parish picnic with games, entertainment and a bonfire, a Mass of Thanksgiving, and a centennial banquet held at the Memorial Union Building on the campus of Michigan Technological University.

PARISH SCHOOL. Father Thomas Atfield is credited with organizing Houghton's first parochial school. St. Ignatius Loyola opened in September 1887 under the direction of the Sisters of St. Agnes of Fond du Lac, Wis.

The school struggled for support until 1896 when Father Rezek abolished the tuition fees, making it the first free school in the diocese. By 1906 the enrollment had nearly doubled and the need for a larger school soon became evident. A new school opened in 1913.

With the closure of many copper mines over the years, the number of students attending the school declined. By 1970 the school was forced to close. The last sisters left the parish in 1971 after 86 years of continuous service.

Major plant improvements in the late 1980s included the addition of a 30-seat chapel and interior church renovations, such as repainting and the installation of new pews. A new pipe organ was also purchased. Bishop Mark Schmitt rededicated the church July 30, 1988. In 1991-1992 a new building was added onto the existing structure. The first floor houses church offices and the second floor serves as the rectory. The parish hall was again enlarged in 1993.

MISSIONS. In addition to missions at Atlantic Mine and Beacon Hill, St. Ignatius pastors also cared for St. Rachael on Isle Royale. From 1957 through the 1960s, Mass was offered in a recreation hall at Rock Harbor on the island.

PASTORS. Fathers Dennis O'Neil, 1859-1860; Edward Jacker, 1860-1864; Aloysius Kopleter, 1864-1865; John Powers, 1865-1867; co-pastor John Burns, 1865-1866; John Vertin, 1867-1871; Anatole Pellisson, 1872-1875; William Roy, 1875-1877; Fabian Pawlar, 1877-1880; James Kelly, 1880-1886; Thomas Atfield, 1886-1888; Charles Langer, 1888-1890; Francis Becker, 1890; John Manning, 1892-1894; Augustus William Geers, 1894-1895; Antoine Rezek, 1895-1946; George LaForest, 1946-1951; Thomas Drengacz, 1951-1966; James McCarthy, 1966-1970; Edward Wenzel, 1970-1971; Robert Chisholm, 1971-1975; Glen Weber, 1975-1986; Joseph D. Carne, 1986-1995; Raymond Valerio, 1995-1997; Thomas L. Poisson, 1997-2002, and John Martignon, 2002-.

ST. CECILIA, HUBBELL

St. Cecilia, Hubbell

From the time of its founding through the celebration of its 100th anniversary in 1993, the humble St. Cecilia Parish in Hubbell has remained a cornerstone in the community. The people continue to worship in the original church structure built in 1893. Despite their modest surroundings, nearly 50 young people from the parish have been touched by the Holy Spirit to pursue religious vocations.

FOUNDING. The first settlers of Hubbell were mostly employees of Calumet and Hecla Smelting Works who moved from Lake Linden to be closer to their work. But for years the men and their families continued to walk the two miles to Sunday Mass at St. Joseph Church in Lake Linden.

On Aug. 24, 1893 Father Joseph A. Sauriol arrived to establish a new church in Hubbell. The first Mass was said in a skating rink. Remarkably, however, the cornerstone to a new church was laid just one month later. On Nov. 1 of the same year, Bishop John Vertin dedicated the completed structure to St. Cecilia. A rectory was built the following year.

PARISH LIFE. In 1899 St. Cecilia Parish welcomed a new pastor, Father Hubert Zimmermann, whose tenure in Hubbell spanned 37 years. Father Zimmermannn is credited with starting the St. Cecilia Grade School in 1903. He later led parishioners in enlarging the church to accommodate the growing membership. The church was cut in half just outside the altar rail and the sanctuary section moved some 30 feet to make room for an addition.

While other churches in the diocese saw many divisions to meet the needs of various nationalities, Father Zimmermann kept his people united by saying Sunday Mass in three languages: French, German and English.

The people so loved their pastor that in 1910, when he planned a vacation to his homeland of Bavaria, parishioners surprised him by purchasing a round-trip ticket. This was their way of assuring that he'd return to Hubbell. The people welcomed him back with a parade in which the Silver Cornet Band played and Monsignor Antoine Rezek gave a welcome-home speech. In the *St. Cecilia Parish Diamond Jubilee Booklet* of 1968, Father Lawrence Monville, SJ, wrote:

"When on March 5, 1936 the church bell tolled for the death of Father Hubert

Zimmermann, it was as though the heart of Hubbell had ceased to beat."

At one time membership in parish organizations is reported to have been nearly 100 percent. June roast beef dinners and fall festivals every year continue to bring in much-needed funds for parish maintenance.

Between 1958 and 1965 the design of the church sanctuary was modernized to comply with Vatican II standards. A new roof in 1988 was damaged by a lightning strike and was replaced a second time in 1991.

The parish began a year-long celebration of its 100th anniversary at Christmas in 1992. Every month offered a different theme and a unique celebration. Bishop James Garland presided over the Jubilee Mass June 26, 1993. A banquet and reunion followed. Also in commemoration of the anniversary, a complete parish history was published.

The parish boasts of the many young men from St. Cecilia's who went on to pursue priestly vocations. More than 40 women from the parish joined religious orders.

PARISH SCHOOL. In 1903 the School Sisters of St. Francis in Milwaukee arrived to staff a parochial school in Hubbell. St. Cecilia School opened to about 350 students in first through eighth grades.

Children from all faith backgrounds studied piano and violin at St. Cecilia's. The school is also well remembered for the plays and skits it performed, especially the "Passion Play," which toured the Kerredge Theater in Hancock and the Calumet Theater.

Beginning in the 1930s, financial constraints resulting from the decline in the copper industry made it difficult for the parish to continue supporting the school. From September 1936 to June 1952, the local public school leased the facilities. The services of the Sisters of St. Francis were retained, however. The women dressed in plain clothes and continued teaching the children.

A slight economic upswing in the area in the 1950s allowed the parish to again take over administration of the school. Considerable renovation and modernization took place. However, as a result of declining enrollment, the schools of St. Joseph and Holy Rosary in Lake Linden and St. Cecilia in Hubbell were combined into the Torch Lake Central School in 1969. Two years later the school was closed permanently.

PASTORS. Fathers Joseph A. Sauriol, 1893-1894; Raphael Cavicchi, 1894-1899; James Miller, 1899; Hubert Zimmermann, 1899-1936; Bernard Eiling, 1936-1957; Edward J. Wenzel, 1955-1956; Joseph Desrochers, 1957-1958; Gervaise Brewer, 1958-1965; Louis Cappo, 1965-1968; Michael Hale, 1968-1975; John McArdle, 1975-1978; James Hebein, 1978-1986; Ronald Timock, 1986-1988; James Genovesi, 1988-1996; Eric Olson, 1996-2004, and Francis G. Dobrzenski, 2004-.

IMMACULATE CONCEPTION, IRON MOUNTAIN

Getting off to a "royal" start, thanks to the efforts of an Italian count who became a priest, Immaculate Conception Parish in Iron Mountain has been held in high esteem throughout its 110-year history. The structure itself is listed on both the National and Michigan registers of historic places. But it is the dedication and commitment of parishioners that binds the church family.

Immaculate Conception, Iron Mountain

FOUNDING. Italians living in Iron Mountain first attended St. Joseph Church downtown, but in 1890 permission was granted to start a church of their own. A frame structure, dedicated as Holy Rosary Church, was erected in the neighborhood of Lake Antoine. That structure was destroyed by fire Nov. 2, 1893. However, work quickly commenced to rebuild the church on the original foundation.

PARISH LIFE. A great renewal of faith occurred in the region when, in April 1902, Father Pietro Sinopoli came to the church from Sicily. Born of noble parents, Father Sinopoli renounced his title as count to become a priest and dedicated his life to serving Italian immigrants in America.

"Every night he preached, sang and gave benedictions," according to the church's historical accounts. "Every night the church was crowded and was too small for everyone to sit." The tremendous "reawakening of faith" led Father Sinopoli to push for construction of a new church, which is still standing.

The priest began digging the foundation for the new church himself. He drew the design for the building and on July 6, just three months after arriving in the city, laid the cornerstone for a new structure. Parishioners gave significant amounts of money to the project and donated labor. Miners quarried and hauled sandstone with horse and wagon for the walls.

Father Sinopoli also led the decoration of the interior of the church. With much pageantry, the church was dedicated Jan. 1, 1903 under the title Immaculate Conception. Father Sinopoli remained in Iron Mountain only one year, but left a lasting impression on the people.

In 1923, the current rectory was built. Many improvements were made to the church in subsequent years, including significant upgrades in the 1960s. From

1980 to 1990, repairs were made to the exterior stone of the church and the stained glass windows. The organ was replaced and handicapped accessible restrooms were installed.

In December 1952 the parish celebrated the 50th anniversary of the blessing of its current church. The booklet *Golden Jubilee of the Blessing of the Church of Immaculate Conception 1902-1952* was published.

Events were held all year long to celebrate the parish's centennial in 1990. Several fund-raising activities took place to support the effort. Commemoration festivities ranged from a rededication of the church to printing of a historic souvenir calendar and book, as well as "Festa Italiana" dinner and dance. A grand centennial celebration was held Aug. 12, with Bishop Mark Schmitt, former pastors and sisters joining parishioners in salute of the church.

The unique design and history of Immaculate Conception led to its being declared a Michigan Historic Site in 1979. In 1990 the church was included on the National Park Service's National Register of Historic Places.

PARISH SCHOOL. In 1942 the Missionary Sisters, Servants of the Holy Ghost from Techny, Ill., arrived to teach summer catechism classes to the youth of the parish. The program later evolved into year-round classes.

In September 1955, doors to the parish school opened to first through third grades. Each year another grade was added until instruction was given for youngsters through eighth grade. The school also served as a parish recreation center when the old Swedish Lutheran Hall was destroyed by fire in 1955. From 1961 to 1971 the Sisters of St. Joseph of Stevens Point, Wis., staffed the school.

In 1971, the Immaculate Conception School and that of St. Mary and St. Joseph consolidated to form Dickinson Area Catholic School. From 1970 to 1989 Immaculate Conception housed first through third grades and the older students were taught in the downtown facilities. Since 1989 all classes have been held at the St. Mary and St. Joseph facility. The former Immaculate Conception school building was leased to the Iron Mountain Public School with the gymnasium still used for parish functions.

PASTORS. Fathers Raphael Cavicchi, 1890-1894; Joseph Pinten, 1894-1898; Benjamino Berto, 1898-1902; Peter Sinopoli, ISCB, 1902-1903; Aloysius Lango, ISCB, 1903-1911; Victor E. Cangiano, ISCB, 1911-1912; John Ferrara, ISCB, 1912-1913; Cherubim Messardri, OFM, 1914-1917; Ugolino Bifarini, OFM, 1917-1919; Peter Jani, 1920-1943; Stephen Wloszczynski, 1943-1945; Glen E. Sanford, 1945-1948; Joseph H. Seifert, 1948-1951; James M. McCarthy, 1951-1966; Gino S. Ferraro, 1966-1970; James M. McCarthy, 1970-1980; Donald L. Shiroda, 1980-1985; Gary A. Jacobs, 1985-1988; Darryl J. Pepin, 1989-1998, and Msgr. James A. Kaczmarek, 1998-.

St. Joseph, Iron Mountain

With the discovery of iron ore and the founding of the famed Chapin Mine in Iron Mountain in 1880 came a huge influx of Catholics who settled in the area. The population of the city is said to have increased by 1,000 annually for the first 11 years. It was not long before priests from the diocese began to minister to the needs of these early settlers. St. Joseph Church, built in 1884, was the first to serve the Iron Mountain area.

The church withstood the separation of the Italians, then of the non-French members near the turn of the century. But two devastating fires led to financial struggles. Wanting to provide a Catholic education for its young people and needing to be a stronger, more unified faith community, St. Joseph's merged with St. Mary's Parish in 1942 to form St. Mary and St. Joseph Parish.

St. Joseph, Iron Mountain

FOUNDING. In 1884, Father Melchior Faust, pastor of the church in Quinnesec, arranged for construction of Iron Mountain's first Catholic Church, a structure measuring just 105 by 50 feet. The church included a sanctuary and living quarters for the priest.

In 1889 the Italian members of the parish left to form Immaculate Conception Parish (originally dedicated as Holy Rosary). The Austrians, Germans and Irish members did the same a year later, starting St. Mary Parish.

Prior to the founding of St. Mary's, however, tragedy struck St. Joseph's. The church was destroyed by fire on Christmas Day 1890. The blaze started from a defective flue in the chimney.

PARISH LIFE. St. Joseph's was rebuilt on the south half of the original property. The new church was dedicated June 1, 1899. This second church was much larger. In subsequent years art glass windows, bell chimes, a hand-carved altar and Stations of the Cross were added.

But the church was again leveled by fire on April 16, 1930. Immediately, plans began for a third church. For three years, while reconstruction took place, Mass was held in the Bijou Theater. The altar was on the stage and parishioners sat in the theater seats. In fact, when the church was complete, the seats from the theater were installed in the church.

Parishioners made many sacrifices to complete the church. The men labored through the winter without heat. The pastor, Father Joseph H. Dufort, led the efforts. He, too, was among those who worked all through the nights. The new church was dedicated in 1933.

MERGER. St. Joseph's was greatly in debt from the construction of the new church in 1938 when St. Mary's was destroyed by fire. With one parish in need of a church, the other in debt and both longing for a Catholic school, a merger of the two was proposed.

For the next three years, many of the people rejected the idea of merging and the parishes functioned as two separate entities under Father Albert C. Pelissier. St. Joseph's building was used for services and Father Pelissier lived in St. Mary's rectory. The two parishes had separate finances, operated with two choirs, dual sets of altar servers and the like. But the separation was detrimental to the longing for a Catholic school.

On May 5, 1942 Bishop Francis Magner enacted a formal proclamation combining the two churches. At the same time another decree abolished the nationalism of all Iron Mountain parishes and set up territorial boundaries.

RECORDS. Records from St. Joseph Parish are kept at St. Mary and St. Joseph Parish in Iron Mountain.

PASTORS. Fathers Melchior Faust, 1884-1886; A. T. Schuettlehoeffer, 1886-1887; Don Vento, 1887; John H. Reynaert, 1887-1888; John A. Keuhl, 1888-1890; Honoratus Bourion, 1890-1893; Thomas V. Dassylva, 1893-1895; Michael Letellier, 1895-1897; Louis Archille Poulin, 1897-1900; L. Z. Huet, 1900-1901; Thomas V. Dassylva, 1901-1905; Raymond Jacques, 1905; George LaForest, 1912-1915; Joseph Beauchene, 1915-1931; Joseph H. Dufort, 1931-1938, and Albert C. Pelissier, 1939-1942.

ST. MARY, IRON MOUNTAIN

The non-French members of St. Joseph Church in Iron Mountain left to form their own parish, St. Mary's, following a fire in 1890. St. Mary's held its own for about 50 years, but after the church was destroyed by fire in 1938 the people realized their attempts to remain separate would not be fruitful. A 1942 merger united members of St. Mary's and St. Joseph's into one church community.

St. Mary, Iron Mountain

FOUNDING. Germans, Poles, Austrians and Slovenians were among those making up the population of the Church of the Assumption of the Blessed Virgin Mary, or St. Mary's as it came to be known. The parish acquired land for its church on the same block as St. Joseph's, when that building was destroyed by fire in 1890. As part of the separation agreement, St. Joseph's gave the north half of its property to St. Mary's for a new church. In 1900 a home was purchased for use as the first rectory.

St. Mary's thrived for nearly 50 years. But on Armistice Day, Nov. 11, 1938, fire destroyed the church. The cause of the fire is not known. The Blessed Sacrament, sacred vessels, vestments and other items were removed. But the church was gone for good, never to rise again.

Another church relic that was saved from the blaze was the church bell. Metal was recovered from the ruins and recast for use at the new St. Mary and St. Joseph Church. St. Mary's had acquired the bell from St. Joseph's first church.

MERGER. A 1939 merger agreement was the result of the loss of St. Mary's church, St. Joseph's lingering debt, and the longing of both parishes for a Catholic school. But it would be a few years before the people were truly united. They did share a priest and a church building, but functioned as two separate entities with dual purposes until 1942 when Bishop Francis Magner decreed the two would be come one under the name St. Mary and St. Joseph Church.

RECORDS. St. Mary records are at St. Mary and St. Joseph Parish.

PASTORS. Fathers Francis Xavier Becker, 1893; John Chebul, 1893; Joseph P. Kunes, 1893-1897; Anthony Hodnik, 1897; Adam J. Doser, 1897-1898; Nickolas H. Nosbisch, 1898-1901; John Kraker, 1901-1904; Nickolas H. Nosbisch, 1904; James Corcoran, John Mockler, Paul N. Fillion, Francis Seifert, and Albert C. Pelissier, 1939-1942.

St. Mary and St. Joseph, Iron Mountain

St. Mary and St. Joseph, Iron Mountain

Two separate Iron Mountain churches, St. Mary's and St. Joseph's, merged to form one combined parish in 1939. Although uniting didn't come easy at first, the two church families had both suffered fires that destroyed their church buildings and both faced financial burdens.

It took a couple of years, but the people eventually put aside their pride in their national origins and their prejudices and became one family in Christ. This united community focused on providing a Catholic education for the youth of the parish and other ventures, such as caring for the Carmelite Monastery and the Veterans Administration Hospital in Iron Mountain.

A devastating fire in January 2003 caused millions of dollars in damage to St. Mary and St. Joseph Church. Through the efforts of many, the landmark has been renovated and restored.

FOUNDING. The loss of St. Mary's church to a fire in 1938 and St. Joseph's lingering debt from rebuilding after a fire in 1930, as well as the longing both parishes had for a Catholic school, led to a merger agreement in 1942.

But it would take about three years before the people truly became one parish. St. Joseph's building was the people's house of worship and the pastor lived in St. Mary's rectory. The two parishes had separate finances, operated with two choirs, dual sets of altar servers and the like.

PARISH SCHOOL. The Sisters of St. Dominic of Adrian, Mich., conducted summer vacation school for the children of the parish from 1940 to 1943 when a year-round catechetical school was opened.

Then, after decades of anticipation, the combined efforts of the new parish led to the erection of a parish school. St. Mary and St. Joseph School opened with six grades in September 1954. The following year saw the addition of a seventh grade and in 1956, eighth grade.

The school operated under the parish until 1970 when it merged with that of Immaculate Conception School to form the Dickinson Area Catholic School. From 1970 to 1989 Immaculate Conception housed first through third grades and the older students were taught in the St. Mary and St. Joseph facilities. Since

1989, in order to save money, all classes have been held at the former St. Mary and St. Joseph School.

PARISH LIFE. During his 27 years as pastor of St. Mary and St. Joseph Parish, Monsignor Albert Pelissier led the parish through the processes of merging to form one united community. He is also credited with the formation of the parochial school and was instrumental in getting the Monastery of the Holy Cross located in Iron Mountain. For all of these works, and for his contributions to the city, he was named Iron Mountain-Dickinson Citizen of the Year in 1964. In the early 1970s the parish erected a memorial in his honor.

Material improvements to the church over the years included a major exterior renovation in 1968. At that time the two wooden steeples atop the towers were deemed unsafe and were removed. In 1975 the sanctuary was renovated. A new rectory was built across the street from the Catholic school in 1988. In 1998 new steeples were erected atop the church towers.

In October 1999 a three-year fundraising campaign got under way for the construction of a two-level addition to the parish plant. The project included a secondary vestibule, restrooms, an elevator, ramped corridor and a new stairway.

Then, on Jan. 5, 2003, fire ravaged St. Mary and St. Joseph Church. Damages, including those caused by smoke and water, totaled about $3 million. Faulty wiring caused the fire. Much of the interior of the church was gutted by the blaze.

Upon completion of the renovation, the pews, the altar, the floors, the windows, and the new addition to the church were restored. The choir loft and vestibule were enlarged. The church hall and kitchen on the lower level were extensively remodeled. All new equipment was installed in the kitchen. New windows, ceilings, lighting, woodwork and a sound system were included in the restoration.

Surviving the fire was the large crucifix above the altar, an icon of Our Mother of Perpetual Help (that also survived the 1938 fire at St. Mary's Church), stained glass windows and the Stations of the Cross. All were incorporated into the restoration of the church. While the work was being done, other local churches and the public school system offered their facilities to St. Mary and St. Joseph Parish.

PASTORS. Fathers Albert C. Pelissier, 1939-1966; Thomas Lester Bourgeois, 1966-1970; James Donnelly, 1970-1989; George Gustafson, 1989-1996, and Daniel Zaloga, 1996-.

Assumption of the Blessed Virgin Mary, Iron River

Assumption of the Blessed Virgin Mary, Iron River

Although the church was dedicated in 1912, the people of Assumption of the Blessed Virgin Mary Church began making steps toward separation from St. Agnes in Iron River near the beginning of the 20th century. The Polish Catholics of the city and surrounding villages made great sacrifices, donating money and labor, so that one day they might have a church of their own.

The people thrived in the stately looking Gothic-style house of worship for nearly 70 years. However, in 1981, following a widespread closing of the local iron mines, the subsequent decline in the economy, and the shortage of priests in the Diocese of Marquette, the parish was forced to close its doors. The people rejoined the parishes their forefathers had once left.

FOUNDING. In 1903 the Polish members of St. Agnes parish began to separate themselves in hopes of establishing a church of their own. The people formed a fraternity under the patronage of St. Joseph.

Soon this group was made up of about 200 families. In July 1909 land was purchased in the Youngs Addition, and the following spring construction of a basement church was under way. The foundation was dug mostly by hand, using horse-drawn scrapers to haul the dirt away. The men worked hard and families made many sacrifices so that money could be donated to the project. The work on the lower level was completed in the fall of 1911, and Bishop Frederick Eis dedicated the basement church July 21, 1912.

In the fall of 1912 a rectory was built, again through donated money and labor. Members of the parish came from the communities of Iron River, Stambaugh, Gaastra and Caspian.

PARISH LIFE. Construction of the superstructure of the church began in 1920. A Gothic-style structure with a massive tower and stately buttresses was erected. The structure is said to have been a "beauty spot of the Iron River Community." Mass was first celebrated there on March 27, 1921, Easter Sunday. Bishop Eis dedicated the completed church on July 9, 1922. Construction of the church was final in 1923.

Church decoration was completed in 1949. A new organ was installed in 1956. In celebration of the golden anniversary of the parish in 1960, partial remodeling was done in the church parlors, the sanctuary was redecorated and new lighting was installed. The parish also commemorated the milestone by publishing a Golden Jubilee booklet.

Active organizations at the time of the 50th anniversary included the Holy Name Society, Ladies of Mary, Rosary Society, the Third Order of St. Francis and the Catholic Youth Organization.

The five West Iron County parishes attempted to support St. Agnes School after the loss of the Sisters of St. Dominic in 1969, but the financial strain was too great. The school closed following the 1969-1970 school year.

CLOSURE   In 1981 it was decided that Assumption of the Blessed Virgin Mary and Blessed Sacrament in Stambaugh would close. Members were encouraged to join the existing churches in the area.

The people of the former Assumption church held an annual celebration in honor of the Feast of the Assumption. On Aug. 15, 1998, Father Norman Clisch celebrated the final Mass at the church, which had been closed for 18 years. The building was then sold.

RECORDS   The records for Assumption of the Blessed Virgin Mary Church are located at St. Agnes Parish in Iron River.

PASTORS   Fathers Albert Walloch, 1909-1910; Leopold Broda, 1910; Jerome Schneider, OFM, 1910-1911; Valentine Chrobok, 1911-1919; John F. Kulczyk, 1919-1921; Fridolin Rinkowski, OFM, 1921-1928; Cyril Piontek, OFM, 1928-1933; Casimir J. Adasiewicz, 1933-1940; Francis E. Krystyniak, 1940-1951; Edward Lulewicz, 1951-1957; Stephen Wloszczynski, 1957-1963; Conrad Suda, 1963-1968; Raymond Smith, 1968-1973; Emmett Norden, 1973-1977; Anthony Polakowski, 1977-1978, and Howard Drolet, 1978-1980.

St. Agnes, Iron River

Parishioners of St. Agnes Church in Iron River have overcome hard times, including a fire that leveled their house of worship. The people have remained faithful and continued to make sacrifices to improve the parish plant. The community of believers grew after 1981 when the parishes of Blessed Sacrament in Stambaugh and Assumption of the Blessed Virgin Mary in Iron River closed. Many of the people joined St. Agnes.

St. Agnes, Iron River

FOUNDING. The first priest to visit Iron County's mining and lumbering camps was Father Melchior Faust of Iron Mountain. From 1882 to 1885 priests offered Mass in the school building and stayed in private homes. Iron River's first Catholic church was built in 1885. Three years later the first rectory was constructed.

Father James Lenhart began a 37-year pastorate at St. Agnes on Sept. 1, 1898. He quickly rallied parishioners for a larger church. The cornerstone for the new structure was laid Nov. 28, 1901. Parishioner donations and support from others allowed for the purchase of new statues and stained glass windows.

In the beginning, parishioners were Irish, French, German, Italian, Polish, Slovenian and Croatian, and traveled from the surrounding areas of Stambaugh, Sanders, Pentoga, Caspian, Gaastra and Watersmeet. In 1903 Watersmeet was detached from St. Agnes. In 1910 the Polish members of St. Agnes left to start Assumption of the Blessed Virgin Mary Church, and in 1913 the faithful in Gaastra and Caspian each formed a parish of their own.

PARISH LIFE. Havoc in the parish and in the community in the early 1930s would take years to overcome. Father Lenhart "was attacked outside the rectory and brutally murdered by an unstable man," says the *Centennial Celebration, St. Agnes Church, 1883-1983*. Around the same time, a St. Agnes parishioner willed the parish land for a school, but difficulties within the church at the time kept the school from being started.

From 1935 to 1945 parishioners worked hard to reestablish the church. In 1946 Sisters of St. Dominic of Adrian, Mich., took up residency at the parish convent and began a catechetical school for the youth. The church was redecorated, a new organ installed and the church basement redesigned into a parish hall.

St. Agnes celebrated its golden jubilee in February 1951. Bishop Thomas L. Noa presided over the ceremony.

On Dec. 8, 1954, a fire started in the kitchen area and spread quickly throughout the church, consuming the entire structure.

Immediately it was decided to rebuild the church on the same site. In the meantime, Mass was held in St. Agnes School. Two separate classrooms on the second floor were combined to create the makeshift church.

In a grand ceremony attended by several hundred people, Bishop Noa laid the cornerstone for the new church in July 1956. The completed structure was dedicated Nov. 25 the same year. A new rectory was built in 1965.

In 1981 and 1982 the St. Agnes community was enlarged when it began welcoming parishioners from the former Assumption Church in Iron River and Blessed Sacrament Parish in Stambaugh, both having closed.

Active parish organizations include the St. Agnes Senior Choir, Saturday Night Choir, CCD, Daughters of Isabella, Knights of Columbus, Boy Scouts, Altar Society and Right to Life. The parish's annual church picnic and Mass was at one time held at Sunset Lake and now takes place at the city park.

PARISH SCHOOL. A parochial grade school was built in 1948, uplifting the parish and adding to the entire Iron River community. Located on property along Third Avenue, at the rear of the church, St. Agnes School opened its doors to first through fourth grades. An upstairs addition to the building allowed for one class to be added each year through eighth grade.

In 1952, when the public school stopped offering transportation to the children, men of the parish took turns volunteering to drive a bus that St. Agnes purchased for that purpose. In 1969 the school was informed that the Dominican Sisters were withdrawing from the school. An effort was made to continue all eight grades using lay teachers and combining the resources of the five West Iron County parishes, but the financial strain proved too much to bear. The school was forced to close in June 1970.

PASTORS. Fathers Anatole O. Pelisson, 1883-1885; Charles Raphael, 1885; Fabian S. Marceau, 1886; J. E. Struif, 1886; Joseph Haas, 1885-1887; Joseph Barron, 1887; Edward Chapuis, 1887; M. J. Van Straten, 1888-1889; Philip J. Erlach, 1889; John Chebul, Alberico Vitali, Dennis Cleary, James Miller, Nickolas Nosbisch, W. Anselm Mlynarczyk, John Henn, Hubert Zimmermannn, Adam Doser, John Manning, James Lenhart, 1898-1934; Stanislaus Mikula, 1933-1935; Joseph Guertin, 1935; George Dingfelder, 1935-1946; Eugene T. Hennelly, 1946-1961; Thomas J. Anderson, 1961-1968; Aloysius Hasenberg, 1968-1997, and Norman Clisch, 1997-.

Holy Trinity, Ironwood

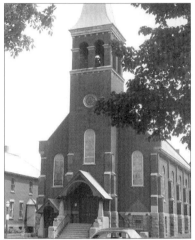

Holy Trinity, Ironwood

Shortly after Holy Trinity Parish in Ironwood was formed in 1907, membership grew to the extent that an addition had to be made to the church. In the 1960s the parish joined forces with St. Michael's of Ironwood to create a parochial school. The people worked hard to maintain their facilities and support the school. But by the 1980s the Catholic population of the city was not great enough to support three separate parishes and two schools. Holy Trinity was part of the merger that led to the creation of the unified Our Lady of Peace Parish and School.

FOUNDING. In 1907 the Slovakian, Croatian, Slovenian and Bohemian members of St. Michael Church in Ironwood petitioned Bishop Frederick Eis for a parish of their own. The group raised a good sum of money, and by January 1909, final permission for a new church was received. The first Mass was said in Holy Trinity Church on Jan. 2, 1910.

Just two years later the church sanctuary was enlarged to accommodate an increased number of parishioners. A large sacristy was also added, which was later used as a winter chapel. A parish rectory was completed in 1914. An addition enlarging the church proper was accomplished in 1916.

PARISH LIFE. Interior re-decorating of the church took place in the late 1940s. During the early 1950s the parish hall underwent major renovations and a modern kitchen was added. In the next two years the exteriors of the church and rectory were renovated.

In 1943 Father Carl Petranek established a catechetical school and enlisted the Slovak Dominican Sisters of Oxford, Mich., to serve as teachers. In 1952 parishioners purchased a home on West Ayer Street for use as a convent.

In order to provide for the increasing number of parishioners, more Masses were added and a Franciscan priest from Pulaski, Wis., offered Holy Trinity's pastor assistance with Sunday worship.

Holy Trinity celebrated its golden jubilee in 1960. Bishop Thomas L. Noa presided over a commemorative Mass on Sunday, Aug. 28. A souvenir booklet was published in connection with the anniversary. At that time the parish had a number of young men and women pursuing religious vocations.

PARISH SCHOOL. The Slovak Dominican Sisters of Oxford, Mich., who had staffed the Holy Trinity catechetical school since 1943, were later called upon to run the Holy Trinity-St. Michael Grade School, which opened its doors to first through fourth grades in 1962. One grade was added every year until there was the full complement of eight grades.

The people of Holy Trinity worked hard to maintain their facilities and support the school. But, by the 1980s, the Catholic population of the city was not great enough to support three separate parishes, two grade schools, and a high school. The grade school system was unified and renamed Ironwood Catholic Grade School. The school was housed in the Holy Trinity-St. Michael School building until 1986. The high school was closed after the 1985 school year and the grade school moved to its facilities. The former Holy Trinity-St. Michael building was sold to a private party and renovated into apartments.

MERGER. In 1986 Holy Trinity merged with St. Michael and St. Ambrose churches in Ironwood to form the new Our Lady of Peace Parish. The consolidation was the result of fewer priests to serve the area and an overall declining membership. The former St. Ambrose Church building is the parish's house of worship.

When the Holy Trinity Church did not sell, it was demolished. Many of the furnishings were given to other parishes in the diocese and elsewhere. The rectory was sold to a private owner and still stands.

RECORDS. Records for Holy Trinity Parish are located at Our Lady of Peace Church in Ironwood.

PASTORS. Fathers Stephen Ulrich, 1909-1910; Peter Sprajcar, 1910-1932; Carl J. Petranek, 1932-1948; Ambrose C. Matejik, 1948-1969; Joseph Kichak, 1969-1971; Matthew Nyman, 1971-1973; Joseph Polakowski, 1973-1985, and co-pastors Emmett Norden and Paul Manderfield, 1985-1986.

Our Lady of Peace, Ironwood

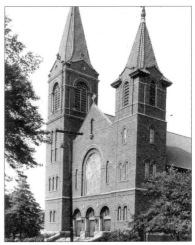

Our Lady of Peace, Ironwood

Since the founding of Our Lady of Peace Parish in 1986, parishioners have overcome the devastation of a church fire and grown into a unified faith community. The people have joined forces to make additional improvements to their house of worship and continue supporting a parochial school.

FOUNDING. On June 30, 1986, three Ironwood parishes consolidated to form one parish. St. Ambrose, St. Michael and Holy Trinity became Our Lady of Peace. The parish's new house of worship is the former St. Ambrose church building.

At the time of the consolidation all three parishes were economically sound and the buildings in relatively good condition. The merger was the result of fewer priests and a reduced overall membership resulting from a population decline in the area, since the closing of the iron ore mines there.

PARISH LIFE. Our Lady of Peace Parish celebrated its first Masses the weekend of July 5 and 6, 1986, with its new pastor, Father Norbert Landreville. At the start of the Mass three banners signifying the three original churches were carried forward in the entrance procession. During the offertory time, those three banners were retired from the sanctuary and a new banner emblazoned with the name Our Lady of Peace was carried forward and elevated in the sanctuary, signifying the oneness of the new parish.

In 1990, just four years after organizing, Our Lady of Peace parishioners were forced to cope with a terrible fire. A blaze on Friday, July 13, ripped through the sanctuary of the church. The fire destroyed the sanctuary, and smoke and soot damaged much of the rest of the church. Volunteers banded together and readied the parish gym with an altar, ambo and chairs for the weekend services. In fact, the first service held in the gym was a wedding scheduled for the next day.

Plans were made to repair, renovate and redecorate the church. It was decided that some structural changes would be made to bring the worship space into the era of the Second Vatican Council. The altar platform was to be moved forward. A Blessed Sacrament Chapel would use the space formerly occupied by the altar area, and a new reconciliation room would be added to replace the old confessionals. Almost a year later, on March 17, 1991, the church was set for occupancy and rededicated. In a grand Eucharistic liturgy concelebrated by Bishop Mark Schmitt, Father Landreville and numerous area clergy, the church and altar were blessed and dedicated.

In order to provide barrier-free access to the church facilities, studies were undertaken and it was decided to build a large, spacious addition to the south side of the church. It would contain a barrier-free entrance, handicapped restrooms, offices and meeting rooms. It would also join the church, parish rectory and school together and provide barrier-free access to both the church and school facilities. In 1996, after a successful fund-raising campaign, the St. Joseph Family Room became a reality.

In late summer of 1999 the vacant convent was renovated into the parish rectory and the former rectory became offices. Since a garage was torn down in the process of building the St. Joseph Family Room, a new garage was also built.

Most recently, additional repair work was done on the Spanish clay tile roof of the church, and the brickwork of the main bell tower was restored. Plans are being made to renovate and upgrade the parish hall.

On July 12, 1998, Our Lady of Peace Parish hosted a Mass of thanksgiving and reception honoring the Franciscan Sisters of Christian Charity from Manitowoc, Wis., who had served the educational needs of the Ironwood area for 106 consecutive years. The sisters were reassigned and left Ironwood that year.

Despite a severe drop in population over the past decade, the parish works diligently to continue the work of the church, support a Catholic elementary school—All Saints Catholic Academy—and provide outreach programs that touch many people, Catholic and non-Catholic, in the greater Ironwood area.

PARISH SCHOOL. When Our Lady of Peace Parish was founded in 1986, the former St. Ambrose and the Holy Trinity-St. Michael parish schools consolidated and were renamed Ironwood Catholic Grade School. The St. Ambrose/Ironwood Catholic High School closed in 1985. The following year the school was renamed Our Lady of Peace Catholic Grade School. A pre-kindergarten program was started in 1987 and in 1993 a pre-school was begun. Since the Franciscans sisters left the Ironwood area, lay men and women have staffed and administered the school, along with a lay Board of Education.

Declining enrollment of the schools in Gogebic County led to the April 2004 decision to combine Our Lady of Peace and St. Sebastian School in Bessemer. All Saints Academy opened in the former Our Lady of Peace School building on Aug. 31, 2004. The St. Sebastian School building was closed.

PASTORS. Fathers Norbert Landreville, 1986-1998, and Darryl Pepin, 1998-.

St. Ambrose, Ironwood

The people of Ironwood's mother church, St. Ambrose, began a tradition of Catholicism that eventually led to the erection of two additional churches in the community. Parishioners supported an elementary school and a combined high school. In the 1920s a larger church with a new rectory was constructed. Today, that church building is the house of worship for all Ironwood Catholics whose sacrifices led to the 1986 merger into Our Lady of Peace Parish.

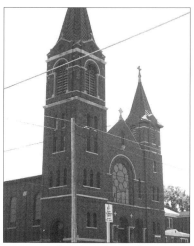

St. Ambrose, Ironwood

FOUNDING. In 1885 Father John Hennessy, an assistant priest serving Bessemer, began offering Sunday Mass in the Ironwood schoolhouse on Vaughn Street. About a year later, in the summer of 1886, the community's first Catholic Church–St. Ambrose–was erected. A parish rectory was constructed prior to the arrival of Father Martin Kehoe, the first resident pastor, in 1890.

PARISH SCHOOL. Immediately on his arrival at St. Ambrose, Father Kehoe got to work establishing a parish school. He felt that a school would bring a more solid growth to the parish. Five lots were purchased on Ayer Street just a few blocks from the church. By 1892 construction of the facility was complete. The Franciscan Sisters of Christian Charity from Manitowoc, Wis., were called on to staff the school. A high school department was added in 1894.

The success of the school in the mid- to late-1920s led to overcrowding and the need for larger facilities. The Ashland Annex Building and Frobel Buildings were purchased for this purpose. The parishes of St. Michael and Holy Trinity also established a school, so at one time there were two Catholic grade schools and a Catholic high school in Ironwood.

At the time of the 1986 consolidation of the three Ironwood parishes, grades seven through 12 had been eliminated from the school system and the two Ironwood elementary schools became one.

PARISH LIFE. St. Ambrose parishioners were blessed by the 40-year pastorate of Father Jeremiah Moriarty, from 1912 until his death in 1951.

Under Father Moriarty's leadership the people united in support of a larger church structure. However, original plans were set aside when in 1914, 191 men of the parish were called to serve in World War I. The plans received an additional setback in 1922 when Father Moriarty was transferred. He returned in the fall of 1923 with a renewed vigor and began making plans to see that a new church was built. Dedicated May 5, 1926, the new building and the accompanying new rectory were financed by parishioner donations. Fund-raisers such as dinners and bazaars were held over the years to cover the costs of construction. In 1930 a new pipe organ was installed in the church.

In 1945 Father Moriarty was honored for his zealous work and was elevated with the honor of Domestic Prelate and the title of Monsignor. The parish was extremely saddened when, on Nov. 25, 1951, Monsignor Moriarty died.

In the 1950s the church was renovated and redecorated, including the installation of stained glass windows.

Monsignor Moriarty's successor, Monsignor Joseph Seifert, oversaw building of a new convent for the sisters serving the school. Monsignor Seifert also had built the Catholic grade school, which still stands. In April 1965 Monsignor Joseph J. Dunleavy became pastor. He oversaw the demolition of the old St. Ambrose High School and the moving of classes into the St. Ambrose Grade School building. He also had a gymnasium added onto the school.

MERGER. In 1986 St. Ambrose Parish consolidated with that of St. Michael and Holy Trinity to form the new parish of Our Lady of Peace. The merger was in response to a decline in population in the community and a priest shortage in the diocese. The new parish is housed in the former St. Ambrose Church building.

RECORDS. Records for St. Ambrose Parish are located at Our Lady of Peace Church in Ironwood.

PASTORS. Fathers Martin Kehoe, 1890-1901; Nickolas H. Nosbisch, 1901-1904; Msgr. Henry A. Buchholtz, 1904-1912; Msgr. Jeremiah B. Moriarty, 1912-1922; Joseph Hollinger, 1922-1923; Jeremiah B. Moriarty, 1923-1951; Joseph H. Seifert, 1951-1965; Msgr. Joseph J. Dunleavy, 1965-1971; Thomas Ruppe, 1971-1985, and co-pastors Emmett Norden and Paul Manderfield, 1985-1986.

ST. MICHAEL, IRONWOOD

The people of St. Michael Parish in Ironwood banded together to form their church in the late 1800s and worked hard to keep their faith community thriving. Many improvements were made to St. Michael Church throughout the decades, often through donated labor. The people joined forces with the neighboring church of Holy Trinity to form a parish school in the 1960s. Then in 1986, the parishes of St. Michael, St. Ambrose and Holy Trinity were canonically suppressed and the new Ironwood parish of Our Lady of Peace was formed.

St. Michael, Ironwood

FOUNDING. St. Michael Parish was founded in 1891 by Polish, Hungarian, Slovak, Slovenian, Bohemian and Croatian members of St. Ambrose Church in the same city. Parishioners, numbering about 250 families, purchased two lots on McLeod Avenue and quickly had a wood-framed church with an adjoining rectory built. Father Anselm Mlynarczyk was named the first pastor.

In 1907, the Slovak, Hungarian and Croatian parishioners of St. Michael's left to form Holy Trinity Church. The majority of St. Michael's remaining parishioners were of Polish descent.

PARISH LIFE. From 1896 to 1925 the parish was under the leadership of Father Fabian Pawlar. During his 30-year pastorate, Father Pawlar had the church veneered in brick. He also spurred construction of the parish's first school and he repurchased the rectory building—which had been owned by a saloonkeeper and then by the Menominee Brewing Co.

The 1940s brought many improvements to the church, including new pews and hardwood flooring, a new organ, construction of the steeple and interior decoration. The Ladies Altar Society reorganized in 1945 to help support these improvements. The group is credited with rebuilding the church basement to include a modern kitchen and dining room in 1949.

In 1952 the parish's Holy Name Society and Third Order of St. Francis were started.

St. Michael's celebrated the 75th anniversary of its founding in 1966. Bishop Thomas L. Noa presided at a commemorative Mass Sept. 25.

PARISH SCHOOL. St. Michael's first parish school was constructed in 1908. Just 10 years later financial difficulties led to the closure of the school. The building was demolished in 1944 and the property sold. From 1952 to 1963 the Sisters of Mercy of the Holy Cross held regular catechism classes for the young people of the parish.

It wasn't until St. Michael joined forces with Holy Trinity Parish in the 1960s that the dream of a parish school again became a reality.

The Holy Trinity-St. Michael Grade School opened its doors to first through fourth grades in 1962. One grade was added every year.

In 1986 Holy Trinity-St. Michael School merged with St. Ambrose School to form the Ironwood Catholic Grade School. The St. Michael facility was vacated and operations began at the Marquette Street facilities.

MERGER. In 1986 St. Michael Parish merged with St. Ambrose and Holy Trinity churches in Ironwood to form the new Our Lady of Peace Parish. The consolidation was the result of fewer priests to serve the area and an overall declining parish membership, following a regional population shift. The former St. Ambrose Church building is the parish's house of worship. Attempts to sell the former St. Michael building were unsuccessful and so the church was dismantled.

RECORDS. Records for St. Michael Parish are located at Our Lady of Peace Parish in Ironwood.

PASTORS. Fathers W. Anselm Mlynarczyk, 1891-1892; Francis Jiranek, 1893; Frank Maciarcz, 1893; John C. Bienarz, 1893-1895; Stanislaus Baranowski, 1895-1896; Fabian Pawlar, 1896-1925; Francis Ignatz, 1925-1930; Charles Szygula, 1930-1942; Francis X. Ronkowski, 1942-1976; Frank Hollenbach, 1976-1984, and James Genovesi, 1984-1986.

St. John the Evangelist, Ishpeming

St. John the Evangelist Parish in Ishpeming survived the separation of its French members, who formed St. Joseph Parish in 1890. St. John then saw its mission church, St. Pius X in North Lake, flourish to become its own parish. For nearly 90 years St. John's supported an elementary school, the facilities of which are still used as a religious education center.

St. John the Evangelist, Ishpeming

FOUNDING. When St. John's first church was built in 1867, it was considered a mission of St. Paul Parish in Negaunee. In 1874, the original building was replaced by a church constructed on Main Street. The parish was dedicated to St. John the Evangelist 13 years later, on Sept. 13, 1887. The French members of the parish left to start St. Joseph Parish in 1890.

Father Henry Kron was assigned to St. John's in 1924 and he continued the fund-raising efforts already under way for a third church. In the spring of 1927 the wooden structure that had served the parish well for the previous 50 years was torn down. Bishop Paul J. Nussbaum laid the cornerstone for the new church on July 3. Dedication of the current building took place on Feb. 14, 1928.

PARISH SCHOOL. In 1884 the first classes were held at St. John School, staffed by the Sisters of St. Joseph of Carondolet, of St. Louis, Mo.

Improvements to the school first came in 1913 with major remodeling. The sisters' residence was moved and an addition to the school was built.

As Ishpeming grew and new housing sprang up north of U.S. Highway 41, St. John's purchased land near the Ishpeming Cemetery, potentially for the construction of a new school. But instead, the land was sold to St. Joseph Parish for a new church.

In 1963 construction was completed on a 42,600-square foot addition to the St. John Parish complex. A rectory, office space, a two-story 12-classroom grade school, parish hall and convent were erected. The "K-D" hall, as it came to be known, was named for Father Henry Kron and Monsignor George Dingfelder, whose pastorates spanned from 1924 to 1958.

In June 1971, just eight years after the opening of the new school, it was announced that St. John's School would close. To fill the gap of the school's closure, an intense tri-parish religious education program was started for the Ishpeming churches. In 1975, after the public school ended a lease for use of the St. John School building, it became the tri-parish CCD Center.

PARISH LIFE. St. John's Church expanded its care of the North Lake Mission in 1947. Father Louis Cappo, assistant at St. John's, was the first to offer regular Sunday Mass at the North Lake School auditorium.

In September 1958, a fire in the sacristy caused extensive damage to St. John's Church.

Disaster struck again in 1963 when the left bell tower was struck by lightning, causing major damage to the wiring of the church.

Tragedy was averted in 1974 when, at the start of the 7 p.m. Mass June 9, the congregation was terrified when one of the decorative buttresses broke loose and fell into the congregation. Several people were injured in the incident.

For nearly 10 years, St. John's was fortunate to have a vibrant recreation center. In 1967, on property that the Ford Motor Co. had deeded to the parish in 1961, buildings were erected to make a parish recreation center. The 56-acre parcel on Boston Lake was named Patmos. However, on Aug. 20, 1975, an arsonist set fire to and destroyed the Patmos installation. It was a great loss to the parish.

In 1978 the church was redecorated, floors carpeted and new glass doors installed in preparation for the 50th anniversary of the building. A new altar and pulpit were installed in 1998 and the interior of the church repainted in 2000.

On June 9, 1991, St. John's held a Parish Day of Commemoration honoring Monsignor David Spelgatti's 50th anniversary of ordination. Msgr. Spelgatti served the parish from June 1958 until his retirement in July 1991.

PASTORS. Fathers John N. Stariha, 1871; Honoratus Bourion, 1871; Sebastian Duroc, 1871; John Burns, 1871; John Vertin, 1872; Theodore A. Trottenburg, 1877; Martin A. Fox, 1878; Edward Jacker, 1879; Charles Langer, 1879; Ignatius Mrak, 1879; John Brown, 1879; Thomas J. Atfield, 1880; Luke Mozina, 1880; Theodore A. Majerus, 1881; Hilary J. Rosseau, 1881; Edward Bordas, 1881; Frederick Eis, 1881; Augustus W. Geers, 1882; Charles Dries, 1883; Francis X. Becker, 1883; Fabian Marceau, 1885; Joseph Barron, 1886; J. O'Keefe 1887; Fitzsimmons, 1887; Peter O'Connell, 1887; Joseph Langan, 1888; Thomas V. Dassylva, 1888; Honoratus Bourion, 1889; C. F. Schelhamer, 1889; C. Murphy, 1890; John Keul, 1890; Joseph Boissonnault, 1891; Joseph Langan, 1894; Henry Buchholtz, 1898; James Corcoran, 1898; Francis R. Doherty, CSP, 1901; Martin Kehoe, 1901; Renatus Becker, 1902; Henry Reis, 1903; Napoleon Raymond, 1904; Joseph Beauchene, 1908; Martin Sommers, 1919; Joseph L. Hollinger, 1922; Henry Kron, 1924; George Dingfelder, 1946; David Spelgatti, 1958-1991; Charles Strelick, 1991-1995, and Peter Oberto, 1995-.

St. Joseph, Ishpeming

Construction of the St. Joseph Church in Ishpeming began in the mid-1960s. For more than three years, Mass and other services were offered in the church hall, until construction of the church proper was complete.

As was not the case when St. Joseph's founders broke away from St. John the Evangelist Church in the late 1800s, today a close partnership exists between the two parishes. A joint religious education program is just one of the positive ventures the two parishes share.

St. Joseph, Ishpeming

FOUNDING. St. Joseph Parish was founded Aug. 28, 1890, when the French members of St. John the Evangelist Parish in Ishpeming received permission from Bishop John Vertin to form a church for themselves.

Construction of a church for the French-Canadian congregation took place just one block from St. John's on the corner of Lake and Johnson streets on land leased from the Lake Superior Iron Company.

St. Joseph's relinquished its interest in St. John's School in 1907. Parishioners paid tuition to attend the school.

In 1958, action began to reorganize the parishes of St. Joseph, St. John and St. Pius X in West Ishpeming according to geographic territories.

In 1962, fundraising began for a new St. Joseph Parish that would be located on a triangular plot of land north of U.S. Highway 41. The land was purchased from St. John's Church. The tract was once considered for a new St. John School.

Construction of a parish hall began in 1964 and, before it was complete, Mass was conducted there for the first time Dec. 20.

From the time of the closing Mass at the original church, Oct. 15, 1967, until a new church was finished three and a half years later, all services were conducted in the new church hall. The rectory and offices moved to Duncan Street Jan. 17, 1968. The first Mass in the church proper was said May 18, 1971.

Also in 1971, the Ishpeming Area Board of Education was formed to administer religious education and pastoral services to all three of the Ishpeming churches, using the St. John School building as its headquarters. Religious education classes for elementary and high school, all pre-sacramental instructional programs, adult education and other services and training are still offered through the collaborative effort.

In 1984, St. Joseph's purchased the current rectory on Prairie Avenue.

PARISH LIFE. St. Joseph's longest serving pastor was Father Paul LeGolvan who served 35 years, from August 1915 to April 1949.

The parish celebrated its centennial in 1990 with events and social gatherings, including a commemorative dinner and Mass held Sept. 9. The parishioners purchased a statue of the Holy Family to mark the milestone.

In 1996 a new main entrance connecting the church and hall and a new room for meetings and social gatherings was constructed. The addition consisted of a full basement, above ground storage and a handicapped accessible restroom.

PASTORS   Fathers Michael Letellier, 1890-1891; Joseph Boissonnault, 1891-1898; Thomas Dassylva, 1898-1901; Louis Archille Poulin, 1901-1902; Fabian Marceau, 1902-1904; E. Proulx, SJ, 1904; Paul LeGolvan, 1904-1905; Edward P. Bordas, 1905-1915; Peter Bleeker, 1915; Paul LeGolvan, 1915-1949; William Schick, 1949; Wilfrid Pelletier, 1949-1957; Clement J. LePine, 1957-1986; Vincent L. Oullette, 1986-1998; Walter Sheedlo, 1998-1999; Mieczyslaw Oniskiewicz, 1999-2000, and James Challancin, 2000-.

St. Pius X, Ishpeming

Mass for the people of Ishpeming's North Lake Location was first held in the mid-1940s in a school auditorium and later in a renovated clubhouse donated by the local mining company. The recreation facility turned church served parishioners of St. Pius X for eight years before a new church was built along U.S. Highway 41 in 1959.

After serving the people well for nearly 50 years, St. Pius X was forced to close in 1995 as a result of the diocese's pastoral planning initiative. But before disbanding, the people of the parish contributed a large sum of money to local church organizations.

St. Pius X, Ishpeming

FOUNDING. Originally founded as a mission of St. John the Evangelist Parish in Ishpeming, St. Pius X had its humble beginnings in 1946. The pastor of St. John's Church realized a need for ministry to be offered to a growing mining community, the North Lake Location, five miles west of Ishpeming.

The boundaries of the mission would be the westerly limit of St. John Church to the easterly limits of the Diorite mission, previously served by Republic.

Mass was initially held on Sunday mornings in the auditorium of the North Lake School. But in 1951 the longtime dream of the people to have their own church was realized. Cleveland Cliffs Iron Co. donated its vacant clubhouse, a former recreation center.

In just one month the building, which formerly had bowling alleys, a poolroom and a reading room, was converted into a parish with seating for more than 100 people. A residence for the priest was on the upper floor.

PARISH LIFE. On Sunday, Aug. 5, 1951, Father George J. Neault, O. Praem., who had been born and raised in North Lake, said the first Mass.

The next summer, parishioners, under the direction of a contractor, began constructing a confessional, choir space and a permanent residence. That same year, the parish boundaries were extended to include the outlying communities of Clarksburg and Humboldt as far as the junction of M-95.

The Sisters of St. Joseph from St. John Church in Ishpeming had held weekly religious education classes at the North Lake School. When the new church was organized, classes were expanded to include one weekly lesson from the sisters and a second lesson from the pastor.

Six years later, in 1957, a two-year fundraising drive began to construct a new church along U.S. Highway 41. Plans were to adapt the North Lake facilities for use as a parish hall and catechism center.

On Sunday, June 7, 1959, the new church was dedicated to St. Pius X. A dinner and reception followed.

CLOSURE. St. Pius X was closed in 1995 as a result of the diocese's "Fully Alive in '95" pastoral planning initiative. The small size of the parish and a reduction in members over the last five years were cited as reasons to close.

Upon the closure of the church, the parish had a substantial amount of money in its savings account. The members of the parish decided to donate $100,000 to local charitable organizations. The money was split three ways: $50,000 was given to the Diocesan Seminarians' Fund; $25,000 was given to the Marygrove Retreat Center in Garden; and $25,000 was given to the St. Vincent de Paul Conferences of St. Joseph Church, Ishpeming, St. John Church, Ishpeming, Our Lady of Perpetual Help, Palmer and St. Paul Parish, Negaunee.

RECORDS. Records for St. Pius X Parish are available at St. Joseph Parish, Ishpeming.

PASTORS. Fathers Robert J. Chisholm, 1951-1963; Edmund Szoka, 1962-1963; Thomas Ruppe, 1963-1966; Joseph W. Felix, 1966-1972; Milton Vanitvelt, 1972-1993, and Vincent Ouellette, 1993-1995.

KEWEENAW CATHOLIC MISSIONS

Catholicism spread to the Keweenaw Peninsula in 1847 when Father Frederic Baraga began making regular trips to mine sites there. Over the years, people gathered to worship at several different churches in the region. However, many of the churches have closed as the population of the northernmost communities of the peninsula has declined.

From 1905 to 1963 and from 1978 to 2001 members of the Franciscan Friars Minor, Province of St. John the Baptist from Cincinnati, Ohio, stationed at Sacred Heart Parish in Calumet, ministered to what is commonly referred to as the Keweenaw mission churches.

Today, the Keweenaw Catholic Missions consist of only one year-round church. A priest from Calumet visits Our Lady of Peace Parish in Ahmeek for Sunday services. Two mission churches, at Eagle Harbor and Copper Harbor, are open in the summer months. A rectory in Mohawk is available for the visiting priest.

PASTORS. Friar pastors 1905-1963: Alban Schneider, Boniface Klinger, Dunstan Leary, Gabriel Linfert, Benjamin Oehler, Bonaventure Kilfoyle, Juniper Hukenbeck, Clarence Tittel, Jordan Telles and Gerald Held. Friar pastors 1978-2001: Faran Boyle, Matthew Krempel, Camillus Hogan and Miles Pfalzer.

Diocesan priests: John McArdle, 1963-1967; Donald LaLonde, 1968-1969; John Chrobak, 1969-1970; Norman Clisch, 1970-1972; John Landreville, 1972-1977, and Father Sebastian Ettolil, MCBS, 2001-.

OUR LADY OF PEACE, AHMEEK

Our Lady of Peace Church in Ahmeek is the last of the Keweenaw Catholic Missions to hold Sunday Mass the year around. Attendance varies from 25 to 60 people, depending on the season. The parish has an active ladies club, parish council and finance council.

Our Lady of Peace, Ahmeek

The people of Ahmeek and the surrounding areas first organized to form a parish of their own in 1927. Mass at the new Sacred Heart Church was first held Dec. 18, 1927. The church was built on the foundation of the Morgan-Grierson General store. A donation from the Catholic Church Extension Society helped make the work possible. The pastor of St. John's church in Calumet assumed responsibility for serving the mission.

A Summer Festival at Gabe Chopp Park in Ahmeek became an annual fundraiser for the mission churches starting in 1970. The event was later abandoned.

After much study, it was decided to combine the Catholic communities of Ahmeek and Mohawk into one parish. Beginning July 1, 1985, Sacred Heart Church became the new home of Our Lady of Peace Parish. The Mohawk church was abandoned, but the rectory there continues to be used.

OUR LADY OF THE PINES MISSION, COPPER HARBOR

With the influx of thousands of summer tourists to Copper Harbor each year comes the seasonal opening of Our Lady of the Pines Church.

Beginning in 1941, Franciscan Fathers serving the Keweenaw from Calumet began holding regular Sunday services in Copper Harbor. Mass was offered either in the Swykert cottage, the Kirkish cottage, or in the schoolhouse.

Finally, construction of a church began in the spring of 1952. After over-

Our Lady of the Pines Mission, Copper Harbor

coming many obstacles, Our Lady of the Pines was erected in 1953. The log cabin church is built on donated land set among the pines overlooking Lake Fanny Hoe. All of the material that went into building the structure came from the Keweenaw Peninsula. The first Mass was celebrated there on June 22, before the roof was even on. As work continued throughout that summer, the faithful gathered for Mass in the roofless structure, weather permitting. To raise money for completion of the church, the parish sold bronze, white and two-toned, white and blue "Our Lady of the Pines" oval plaques. The souvenirs were molded in Lake Linden. Bingo, raffle drawings and special collections were also held to raise money.

The church was completed the following year. A dedication ceremony led by Bishop Thomas L. Noa was held Aug. 23, 1953.

Mass continues to be held there on Saturdays in the summer months.

HOLY REDEEMER MISSION, EAGLE HARBOR

From 1847 to 1853 Father Frederic Baraga traveled to the Keweenaw Peninsula twice each year visiting mine sites from Copper Harbor to Cliffton. In October 1854 Bishop Baraga appointed Father Henry L. Thiele to serve the people of the Keweenaw on a permanent basis. Before winter had settled in that year, Father Thiele had built a modest church at Eagle Harbor and dedicated it as Holy Redeemer. From Holy Redeemer Father Thiele and his successors visited the other communities of the peninsula offering Mass in private homes, school buildings and eventually in new churches as they sprang up.

A rectory separate from the church building was constructed at Eagle Harbor in 1884 and added to in 1892. Both the church and rectory remain in use in much the same original condition.

Holy Redeemer Mission, Eagle Harbor

Maintenance of the church was neglected for many years until the 1930s when some improvements could be made. A new roof was put on the church in 1934. The exterior was painted in 1936 and in 1938 the sacristy was renovated and new carpeting installed. In the mid-1960s a cabinet displaying Bishop Baraga artifacts was built in the back of the church. Holy Redeemer Church was named to the National Register of Historic Places in 1972. Renovations made to the church between 1987 and 1988 included interior repairs to the steeple, replacement of glass in the windows, rebuilding of the entrance stairs, new exterior siding, refurbishing of statues, extending the floor area around the altar and installing new carpeting. The church interior was also repainted.

Almost 150 years since its founding, Holy Redeemer is the oldest church building in continuous use in the diocese. The small number of residents and the many tourists to Eagle Harbor enjoy the setting of the church. Sunday Mass continues to be held there in the summer months. The church has also been the site of several unique weddings and other celebrations.

St. Joseph Mission, Gay

Ten years after the founding of St. Joseph Parish in Gay, the people's hard work and sacrifice resulted in the completion of a church of their own. On land

St. Joseph Mission, Gay

donated by the Mohawk Mining Company, the new structure was dedicated July 4, 1915. Prior to construction of the church, people attended Mass in the town hall.

Regular church services ceased in Gay in 1965, but the building was still used occasionally. Then, on Aug. 15, 1987, the structure was demolished.

A bell from the church was saved and is now on display at the Phoenix church museum.

St. Mary Mission, Mohawk

Prior to the founding of St. Mary Parish in Mohawk, Mass was offered in the village schoolhouse. Then, in 1909, the missions purchased a church formerly owned by Norwegian Lutherans. Franciscans Friars serving Sacred Heart Parish in Calumet traveled to the peninsula to offer regular services until 1964 when leadership of the missions was given to diocesan priests. A rectory was built in Mohawk in 1970 and diocesan priests continued to serve the Keweenaw from there until 1978.

St. Mary, Mohawk

In 1984 it was decided that the existence of churches at both Mohawk and Ahmeek—less than two miles apart—was no longer warranted. Both St. Mary's and Sacred Heart were in dire need of repair. On Feb. 1, 1985, the Mohawk church was abandoned. The separate communities of Mohawk and Ahmeek then came together as one parish with the new name of Our Lady of Peace.

The Mohawk rectory continues to be used by visiting pastors and as the central office for the Keweenaw Catholic Missions. Business, however, is conducted through St. Paul Parish in Calumet. The church building was razed Sept. 15, 1987.

Church of the Assumption Mission, Phoenix

The former Church of the Assumption in Phoenix is today a museum of local Catholic history run by the Keweenaw County Historical Society.

The first Mass was said in the re-erected house of worship at Phoenix, called Church of the Assumption, on Oct. 9, 1899. The structure itself had been built some 50 years earlier in Cliffton. St. Mary's, as it was called at the original site, saw its demise with the closure of the Cliff Mine in 1870. The church was cut in half and moved by horse and wagon to Phoenix.

Church of the Assumption celebrated the 75th anniversary of its founding in 1933. Over the next 25 years people began leaving the community to find work elsewhere. In the 1950s regular services gave way to periodic Masses. Then, in 1957, the church was closed permanently and the people began attending services at nearby Mohawk or Eagle Harbor.

The Phoenix building stood vacant for almost 30 years. Then, on June 21, 1985, the Diocese of Marquette donated the structure to the Keweenaw County Historical Society. The organization continues to maintain the church as a memorial to Catholics in the Keweenaw. The museum contains two artifacts from every church in Houghton and Keweenaw Counties. The building is still the site of weddings and other celebrations. In March 2000, the structure was named to the U.S. Department of Interior's National Register of Historic Places.

Church of the Assumption Mission, Phoenix

AMERICAN MARTYRS, KINGSFORD

Catholics living in the Kingsford area struggled in the beginning for a parish and resident priest of their own. These dreams were realized in the late 1930s, proving the people's strength and commitment. Just over 10 years after starting out as a mission church, parishioners banded together to form an independent parish, build a church and then a parochial school. Under the dedicated leadership of only five different priests in almost 70 years, the faith community embraces several active ministries and strives for continued growth in spirituality and fellowship with one another.

American Martyrs, Kingsford

FOUNDING. Ten years prior to the 1937 founding of American Martyrs Parish, efforts were made to serve the growing population of Catholics living east of Kingsford and Garden Village. In 1926, Father Erasmus Dooley offered Sunday Mass in the Garden Village School. But when he was reassigned, people living in the region were forced to attend Mass at an Iron Mountain parish.

The recently erected Ford Motor Co. plant was drawing workers to the area and Kingsford's population was quickly increasing. On Nov. 21, 1937, Bishop Joseph C. Plagens granted permission for a church. Father Frank Seifert of St. Mary Parish in Iron Mountain held a meeting of some 400 Catholic families at the old Capitol Theater. It was decided to rent the theater and remodel it for use as a church. The parish was started as a mission of St. Mary's and dedicated as the Church of the American Martyrs. The first Mass was held Christmas Day 1937.

PARISH LIFE. The first resident pastor, Father George LaForest, arrived in June 1938 but stayed just two months, due to poor health. Father John G. Hughes arrived at American Martyrs in August 1939.

With the zeal of a young pastor and a parish eager for its own church, excavation for a new building began in July 1940. Thirteen lots were obtained for the parish property at the corner of Sagola and Newton streets. Using mostly donated labor, the structure was ready for dedication in November of the same year.

A new rectory was occupied in 1943 when a home was moved closer to the church and remodeled.

Through the dedicated labor of parish organizations, all debt was liquidated in 1945 and a new fund was started for a parochial school.

PARISH SCHOOL. Six Sisters of Christian Charity started the first summer catechism program for youngsters in Kingsford in 1938. In the summer of 1942 a home was purchased for use as a convent and three Sisters of St. Joseph of Carondelet, from St. Louis, Mo., arrived to conduct catechism classes during the school year. The Sisters of St. Joseph are credited with convincing the people of the parish of the need for a Catholic education for their youngsters.

Bishop Thomas L. Noa presided over groundbreaking ceremonies for the construction of American Martyrs Parochial School in June 1948. The school opened to students in first through fourth grades in September 1949. One grade per year was added through the next four years until the first class graduated in June 1954.

The school served the needs of the children of the parish until 1970 when the increasing need to hire lay teachers became too great a burden for the parish. The building was converted into a religious education center and continued as such through the 20th century. The parish has been a member of the consolidated Dickinson Area Catholic School program since 1980.

In 1956 the exterior of American Martyrs Church was remodeled to replicate the natural materials reminiscent of the Upper Peninsula during the late 17th century, the period of the American Martyrs. The interior of the church was remodeled in 1964 to recall the patrons of the parish. The names of the eight martyrs are listed on the altar. The altar cross resembles the version of the cross worn by Jesuits and the support beams are designed to simulate the longhouse of the Iroquois Indians. The beams are painted to resemble wampum belts, bearing the colors gold and black to reflect the Jesuits. Red, the color of martyrs, is used extensively. The main altar of the church actually encases a primitive altar used by Bishop Frederic Baraga.

Active ministries include monthly exposition of the Blessed Sacrament, a regular weekday Mass and breakfast, Bible study and faith formation programs and active participation in the diocese's Cursillo and Youth Encounter movements. The parish also offers monthly support to the Rio Bravo Mission in Mexico.

PASTORS. Fathers Frank A. Seifert, 1937-1938; George LaForest, 1938; John G. Hughes, 1939-1979; Norbert LaCosse, 1979-1990, and Father Joseph Gouin, 1990-.

St. Mary Queen of Peace, Kingsford

The founding date of St. Mary Queen of Peace Parish in Kingsford coincides with Bishop Francis Magner's decreeing it a parish in 1944. But the people of Kingsford Heights had actually gathered as a united worshiping community 20 years prior. Mass was first offered in the community building and later in the pool hall. Parishioners made many sacrifices and their perseverance eventually paid off. The first church building was completed in 1945. The parish celebrated its golden jubilee in 1995.

St. Mary Queen of Peace, Kingsford

FOUNDING. The community of Kingsford sprang up around 1920 as the Ford Motor Co. plant was being built. Catholics were attending Mass in Iron Mountain, but quickly banded together for a parish.

On Jan. 1, 1940 a mission was set up under the care of Father Albert Pelissier of Iron Mountain. Dominican Sisters from Adrian, Mich., began teaching summer catechism for the youth, and the women of Kingsford Heights formed an altar guild to raise money for a church. In 1941, five lots were purchased on Marquette Boulevard for the future structure.

Services were held for two years in the local community building. Then, in 1943, an old pool hall was purchased and remodeled for use as a church. The first Mass there was held on Christmas Day.

PARISH LIFE. In 1944, anxious for a church of their own, the people bought a house for use as a rectory should they receive a resident pastor. On June 14, Bishop Magner issued a decree forming the parish and Father Gerald Harrington was assigned as the first pastor.

Funds received from the Catholic Church Extension Society helped to finance a church. Bishop Magner laid the cornerstone in a well-attended ceremony held Oct. 22, 1944. So many people attended the service that some scaffolding over the basement collapsed, causing some injuries, but no fatalities.

The bishop returned for the dedication of the new church on Aug. 12, 1945.

The church was built in an early American style using cream-colored stone and brick. In the next few years the debt was paid off, the church was decorated and stained glass windows were installed. A new rectory was completed in 1957.

Father Arnold Thompson, who would serve as pastor for 20 years, arrived in 1972. He also served as a Serra Club chaplain and spiritual director for Renew in the Diocese of Marquette. Upon Father Thompson's death in 1992, the people of the parish dedicated a special alcove in the church to his memory.

In 1984 the church was renovated to comply with changes to the liturgy brought about by the Second Vatican Council. In August of that year the parish gathered to celebrate its 40th anniversary.

In 1995 a yearlong celebration was held to commemorate the 50th anniversary of the building of the church. A golden jubilee Mass was held Aug. 12. Festivities also included monthly events, rededication of the cornerstone, a parish mission and youth retreat, holy hours, and a dedication of the flagpole and outdoor sign.

PASTORS. Fathers Gerald F. Harrington, 1944-1946; Thomas J. Anderson, 1946-1950; Joseph A. Gondek, 1950-1968; Thomas J. Anderson, 1968-1972; Arnold Thompson, 1972-1992; Jeff Johnson, 1993; Paul Nomellini, 1993-2002, and Michael A. Woempner, 2002-.

PARISHES AND MISSIONS

HOLY ROSARY, LAKE LINDEN

The large size of the parish in the 1880s drove some of the members of Lake Linden's St. Joseph Church to separate and form a second parish in the community. About 75 years later it was the opposite, a decline in population, that forced the merger of Holy Rosary and St. Joseph churches into one faith community.

Throughout its history, Holy Rosary parishioners supported a parochial school and saw the rebuilding of its facilities after a destructive fire. Upon the closure of the church in 1966, ancestors of the original church rejoined the St. Joseph community.

Holy Rosary, Lake Linden

FOUNDING. The German and Irish members left St. Joseph's to form a new church in 1888. The new congregation was first led by Father John Henn. A combination church and school structure was erected for the people on donated land near the western border of the town. On Oct. 12, 1888, Bishop John Vertin dedicated the parish as Holy Rosary.

PARISH LIFE. After witnessing short stays by several priests, the parish welcomed the arrival of Father Henry Reis to Lake Linden in 1904. Father Reis's tenure with Holy Rosary Parish spanned 50 years.

Just one year after Father Reis's arrival, he and his parishioners had to endure the aftermath of a fire that ripped through the church properties. A June 1, 1905 blaze destroyed the church, school and rectory.

Immediately, plans began for rebuilding. The new church would be located in the business section of town rather than at the original location.

During construction, Sunday Mass was held in city hall and a makeshift school was erected in two vacant store rooms. The new school was occupied in March 1906. On June 17, 1906, the new church was dedicated. Parishioners donated labor to build a new rectory in 1909. By the summer of 1915 the School Sisters of Notre Dame were relocated to a house just a few blocks from the church and school.

Holy Rosary celebrated its golden anniversary May 29, 1938 with Bishop Joseph C. Plagens officiating a commemorative Mass. In August 1963 a Mass and banquet were held in celebration of the parish's 75th anniversary. Bishop Thomas L. Noa was the chief celebrant.

PARISH SCHOOL. The same year as the founding of the church, Holy Rosary School opened in the fall of 1888. At first two laymen led the school. School Sisters of Notre Dame of Milwaukee, Wis., replaced them in 1894.

The school saw continued success with additional classrooms being added to accommodate the increasing enrollment. In 1903 a home near the school was purchased for use as a convent.

The school was renovated and an even greater focus was placed on Catholic education during the pastorate of Father William Oremus, 1951-1963. He began a hugely successful Mardi Gras event to raise money for school expenses. The annual fundraiser was a much-anticipated event for the entire community. Under Father Oremus's pastorate, CCD classes for high school students also started.

Decreasing enrollment and a shortage of teaching sisters forced the closure of Holy Rosary School in June 1957. The Sisters of Notre Dame had served the parish for 62 years.

MERGER. As a result of economic difficulties that hit the area in the 1950s and 1960s, many families moved away from Lake Linden. Eventually, the population reached the point that only one church was needed in the area. Holy Rosary Parish closed its doors permanently June 30, 1966, and the people again became part of the St. Joseph faith community.

The freestanding, modern altar from Holy Rosary was moved to St. Joseph Church at the time of the merger.

RECORDS. Records for Holy Rosary Parish are located at St. Joseph Church in Lake Linden.

PASTORS. Fathers John Henn, 1888; A. T. Schuettlehoeffer, 1888-1889; Joseph Haas, 1889-1890; Augustus W. Geers, 1890-1893; Nickolas H. Nosbisch, 1893-1895; Joseph E. Neumair, 1895-1896; Nickolas H. Nosbisch, 1896-1898; Joseph E. Neumair, 1898-1901; John Henn, 1901; Frederick Richter, 1901-1903; Adam J. Doser, 1903-1904; Henry Reis, 1904-1955; William C. Oremus, 1951-1963, and Michael F. Hale, 1963-1966.

St. Joseph, Lake Linden

St. Joseph Parish was the first church to serve the people of Lake Linden, but it wasn't to be the only one. For almost 80 years a second church, Holy Rosary, was home to many Catholics of the area. In 1967 the two parishes were reunited into one faith community.

Father Napoleon Joseph Raymond was St. Joseph's pastor through much of its history. In 57 years there he oversaw the construction of a new church, school and rectory. The parish celebrated its 100th anniversary in 1971. That same year, the community closed its parochial grade school.

St. Joseph, Lake Linden

FOUNDING. Except for the occasional services offered in the local public school building or in private homes, early settlers of Lake Linden attended Mass in Calumet. On Aug. 27, 1871, Bishop Ignatius Mrak dedicated a small church to St. Joseph Calasanz. This first church was added to and completely remodeled. On Nov. 5, 1892 it was rededicated, this time to St. Joseph, Spouse of the Blessed Mother.

In 1888, due mainly to overcrowding, German and Irish members of St. Joseph's left to form Holy Rosary Parish.

PARISH LIFE. Efforts to construct a new church for the St. Joseph Parish community were bogged down for a while by internal parish strife. Beginning in January 1902 a new basement that would become a foundation for an eventual superstructure was first used for a church. Finally, in 1912, under the leadership of Father Napoleon Raymond, the new church was completed. With a seating capacity of about 1,000, the church was built with three 20-foot high altars. The exterior consists of two 100-foot-high towers each with a cross at the top. Bishop Frederick Eis dedicated the structure Dec. 8, 1912.

In 1937 the church was redecorated. At that time 16 stained glass windows were installed. A new rectory was completed in 1952.

Father Raymond served 57 years of his 59 as a priest in Lake Linden. He died Feb. 5, 1963 and was buried in that town.

The parish marked its 100th anniversary Sunday, Aug. 22, 1971. Bishop Charles A. Salatka celebrated the commemorative Mass. A dinner and family dance followed in the parish hall.

More than 40 men and women from the parish have pursued religious vocations, becoming priests, sisters and brothers.

In 1992 the parish began a fundraising tradition that has resulted in the baking of as many as 1,500 pork pies and netted more than $60,000 over the years. During one week in November, the men, women and children of the parish gather to bake and sell the pies. The money is used to pay for church maintenance and upgrades. Most recently, restoration of the interior of the sanctuary was undertaken.

PARISH SCHOOL. The parish's first school was started in a private home in 1881. Five years later St. Anne Academy was started. At first the young people received instruction from lay teachers and women religious. Then, from 1896 to 1971, Sisters of St. Joseph, of Concordia, Kan., undertook the responsibility.

Plans for the construction of a new school and convent were set on the fast track by a fire in 1928 that destroyed the original school. Completed in 1930, the new building contained the only movie house in the community at the time. The movie theater was on the first floor, the convent on the second and the classrooms and library on the third story.

As a result of declining enrollment, St. Joseph School (supported also by the Holy Rosary Parish in Lake Linden) combined with St. Cecilia School in Hubbell to form the Torch Lake Central School in 1969. Two years later the school was closed permanently. The public school system took over use of the facilities.

MERGER. In the 1950s and 1960s, the economy of the area began to wane and the population declined. As a result, the Holy Rosary Parish in Lake Linden was closed. After operating independently for nearly 80 years, the families of Holy Rosary again joined the church from which their ancestors started out, St. Joseph's. The two have operated as one parish community since 1967. Since 1996 St. Joseph of Lake Linden and St. Cecilia in Hubbell have shared one priest.

PASTORS. Fathers Francis Heliard, 1871-1881; Peter C. Menard, 1881-1893; Michael Lettellier, 1893-1895; Fabian S. Marceau, 1895-1896; Paul Datin, 1896-1897; M. T. Dugas, CSV, 1897; Edward P. Bordas, 1897-1905; Msgr. Napoleon J. Raymond, PD, 1905-1963; Roland Dion, 1963-1966; James Donnelly, 1966-1967; Clifford Nadeau, 1967-1970; Henry Mercier, 1970-1972; Otto J. Sartorelli, 1972-1978; James A. Pepin, 1978-1988; Arnold J. Grambow, 1988-1990; Allan J. Mayotte, 1990-1992; Eric E. Olson, 1992-2004, and Francis G. Dobrzenski, 2004-.

Sacred Heart of Jesus, L'Anse

Although rebuilt after a destructive fire in 1912, Sacred Heart of Jesus Church in L'Anse was originally constructed in 1894. In addition to maintaining the house of worship, parishioners have taken great strides to overcome financial challenges and assure the continuation of the parish school.

FOUNDING. Prior to 1871, one large settlement called L'Anse consisted of the present-day L'Anse, Baraga and Assinins. Assinins was the original center of activity and the site of Bishop Frederic Baraga's mission in the area.

Sacred Heart of Jesus, L'Anse

Present day L'Anse received its first church in 1872. One of Bishop Baraga's successor priests in the region, Father Gerhard Terhorst, quickly recognized the booming economy in L'Anse and began construction of a wooden church and a three-room rectory there. This first church was dedicated to St. Joseph. From 1872-1886 Father Terhorst traveled from Assinins to L'Anse to offer Mass every Sunday. In 1886 L'Anse received its first resident pastor, Father Anatole O. Pelisson.

PARISH LIFE. Despite a rapid succession of priests in the early years, the parish membership continued to increase. A larger, stone church—the one in use today—was constructed in 1894. This structure was originally dedicated to St. Joseph, but the name was later changed to Sacred Heart.

The church had to be rebuilt in 1912. A fire Jan. 30 left only the stone walls standing. In 1925 the present church was remodeled and enlarged and a sacristy and chapel added. In the 1930s Father Albert Pelissier made alterations to the rectory. A new rectory was completed in 1967.

The first women religious to serve the parish were the Dominican Sisters from Adrian, Mich., who offered the young people a summer religious education program from 1928 to 1936.

In 1972 the parish celebrated the 100th anniversary of its founding.

Active organizations at the start of the 21st century included an organ choir and a folk choir. The ladies group of the parish holds a fall bazaar and a soup and sandwich luncheon in the spring.

PARISH SCHOOL. Looking to start a parochial school, the parish secured the aid of the Sisters of St. Joseph of Carondolet from St. Louis, Mo. In

1945 a house across the street from the church was used for a convent and the first catechetical school, which included a music department.

A fund was started for the construction of a parochial school. On June 13, 1954, ground was broken for construction of the school on Baraga Avenue overlooking Keweenaw Bay. Earlier that spring a building on Baraga Avenue was purchased and renovated for the Sacred Heart Convent.

During construction of the school, the sisters taught classes from October 1954 to the following spring in the church, sacristy, chapel and basement hall. Attendance was so high the first year that enrollment had to be temporarily capped at 142. Classes were taught for the first time in the new school March 7, 1955. At first, only second through sixth grades were taught, using just three classrooms. Bishop Thomas L. Noa dedicated the school on Sept. 18 that year.

By September 1958 the school was composed of first through eighth grades. The first lay teacher was also hired that year. In the years that followed, a shortage of teaching sisters led to an increase of lay instructors. Sacred Heart School has served only first through sixth grades since 1966.

PASTORS. Fathers Gerhard Terhorst, 1872-1886; Anatole O. Pelisson, 1886-1887; T. S. Guilmin, 1887-1888; Joseph Haas, 1888-1889; Thomas Dassylva, 1889-1890; John H. Reynaert, 1890; C. F. Schelhamer, 1890-1891; John Henn, 1891-1892; Joseph C. Wallace, 1892; Joseph Dupasquier, 1892-1893; Fidelis Sutter, 1893; William H. Joisten, 1894-1898; Joseph G. Pinten, 1898-1899; J. H. Colin, 1899-1900; co-pastors Otto Ziegler, OFM, and J. A. Reinhart, 1900; Joseph A. Sauriol, 1900-1901; John Henn, 1901-1917; George Dingfelder, 1917-1922; D. Joseph Breault, 1922-1923; James Miller, 1923-1924; Carl B. Liedgens, 1924-1930; Albert Pelissier, 1930-1940; Joseph Dufort, 1940-1942; Francis M. Scheringer, 1942-1950; Thomas J. Anderson, 1950-1953; Casimir J. Adasiewicz, 1953-1968; Louis Cappo, 1968-1969; Thomas Andary, 1969-1979; Paul Schiska, 1979; Vincent Ouellette, 1979-1985; Donald Shiroda, 1985-1986; Guy Thoren, 1986-1994; Thomas Poisson, 1994-1997; Gregory Heikkala, 1997-2004; Chacko Kakaniyil, 2004-2005, and Augustin George, 2005-.

St. Stephen, Loretto

Started as a mission of St. Barbara's in Vulcan, St. Stephen Parish in Loretto grew quickly and took on the responsibility of caring for two mission churches of its own, in Quinnesec and Faithorn. The men labored to improve the church and the women worked to raise the money for necessary improvements. After more than 60 years of worshipping in their own community, the people were saddened to lose their church in a 1971 fire. Afterward, St. Stephen parishioners joined permanently in the faith community of their neighbors in Vulcan.

St. Stephen, Loretto

FOUNDING. Catholics in the mining town of Loretto first gathered for Mass around 1900 in the town hall. Some 10 years later a church was built and dedicated to St. Stephen. The mining company donated the land for the church and the men of the parish did the construction work. The women raised money, solicited a house for use as a rectory and sought donations for furnishings.

The people's efforts were rewarded by Bishop Frederick Eis in 1918 when the parish, previously a mission of St. Barbara's in Vulcan, became a separate entity and received its first resident priest, Father Lawrence P. Stropher. A year later the parish assumed responsibility for the St. Mary Mission in Faithorn. In 1922 responsibility was added for a third church, St. Mary in Quinnesec.

PARISH LIFE. During the 18-year pastorate of Father George Stuntebeck, from 1919 to 1938, the parish saw much spiritual and material growth. Parishioners enjoyed concerts, spaghetti dinners, picnics and parties. During this time the church was redecorated and stained glass windows and a bell were installed. A rock garden and stone arch that could be seen from the highway were erected in the front of the church. Father Stuntebeck's heartfelt legacy also includes providing the people with a solid foundation in the catechism of the Catholic Church.

St. Stephen's original rectory caught fire, and it is documented that parishioners raised the money to purchase a house across the street in just one night!

The church and rectory were both refurbished in the early 1940s. Parishioners banded together in the 1950s and dug a basement hall underneath the church. In the 1960s, in preparation for celebrating the parish's golden jubilee, even greater work was taken up to improve the parish plant. A cry-room was added, the interior of the church was redecorated, and a new front entrance was completed, all thanks to donations made by parishioners.

Bishop Thomas L. Noa presided over a jubilee Mass in honor of the 50th anniversary of the founding of St. Stephen in the summer of 1960. A parade, commemorative dinner and reception were also part of the festivities.

CLOSURE. On Monday, Jan. 10, 1971, St. Stephen church was destroyed by fire. Instead of rebuilding the structure, the church was closed permanently and parishioners joined the community of St. Barbara's in Vulcan.

RECORDS. Records for St. Stephen Parish are kept at St. Barbara Parish in Vulcan.

PASTORS. Fathers Lawrence P. Stropher, 1918-1919; George Stuntebeck, 1919-1938; Raphael Gherna, 1936-1943; Thomas Lester Bourgeois, 1943-1945; Edward J. Lulewicz, 1945-1950; Frederick Hofmann, 1950-1951; John McLaughlin, 1951-1957; Thomas Andary, 1957-1959; August Franczek, 1959-1963; S. Patrick Wisneske, 1963-1966, and Thomas Ruppe, 1966-1971.

STE. ANNE DE MICHILIMACKINAC, MACKINAC ISLAND

For more than 300 years, St. Anne Parish has played a significant role in the lives of people living at and visiting Mackinac Island. Efforts to make improvements to the church have continually been supported by the seasonal population of the island and by Catholic and non-Catholic permanent residents. A church museum tells of the role St. Anne's has played in the history of Mackinac Island and the surrounding communities. Today the thriving parish is considered a core aspect of life on the island.

Ste. Anne de Michilimackinac, Mackinac Island

FOUNDING. Baptismal and marriage records for Ste. Anne de Michilimackinac Parish on Mackinac Island date back to 1695. Jesuit missionaries wintered on the island and set up a bark chapel as early as 1670.

The original St. Anne Church was built in what is now Mackinaw City in 1743. In 1780 the structure was dismantled and hauled across the ice-covered Straits of Mackinac to Mackinac Island. In 1827 the church was moved to its current location. The present church was built in 1874 and the rectory, still in use today, was built in 1881.

Although many of the early pastors served very short terms, the island has had, for the most part, a resident priest since the late 1820s.

PARISH LIFE. St. Anne Parish is said to be at the center of community life on Mackinac Island. The church is also used by members of other denominations. The interfaith tradition on the island can be documented as far back as the 1830s.

The island's many college-age workers and other seasonal employees often look to St. Anne's for weekly dinners and recreational opportunities. After the tourism season ends and the last of the one million or so Mackinac Island visitors have passed through, the approximately 100 year-round parishioners consider each other to be like family. An annual Christmas bazaar nets thousands of dollars for island charities.

In 1950 the church basement was excavated and a hall built. Bishop Thomas L. Noa dedicated an outdoor shrine to St. Anne that was built on the parish property in 1962. The central feature of the shrine, commemorating the parish as the oldest church in the United States dedicated to St. Anne, is a white Italian Carrara statue of the mother of the Blessed Virgin Mary. Behind the statue had stood an 18-foot Onaway stone wall. The area, once adorned with shrubs and flowers and an outdoor altar, has most recently been maintained as a picnic area, although the statue is still there.

In 1986 a number of small donations and parishioners' fundraising efforts made possible the rebuilding of an elaborate wooden front porch. The porch was originally added to the church in 1874. Decades of deterioration caused the porch to fall in the 1950s. At that time the steps leading to the church entrance were remade using concrete.

In the 1990s the church underwent drastic renovations totaling almost $900,000. The basement and foundation were redone, a side porch and museum were constructed and the interior was restored to its original 1890s Victorian style. Bishop James Garland blessed the restored structure Sept. 9, 1995.

In July 1996 St. Anne's celebrated its tri-centennial. A Mass of Thanksgiving, ice cream social and oral history pageant took place July 26. The 300th anniversary was delayed one year to coincide with the completion of the church renovations and of *Fishers of Men*, a book by Jesuit Brother Jim Boynton. The book recounts the parish's 300-year history.

July 1996 also saw the opening of the Church Museum of Ste. Anne de Michilimackinac, located in the parish basement. The exhibit is called "Images of Faith: The Catholic Church at Mackinac 1670 ... ." Among the artifacts on display is the original parish register from 1695. The chalice that Father Jacques Marquette used while celebrating Mass on the island more than 300 years ago can often be found on display, as well. In 1997 the museum received a certificate of commendation from the American Association for State and Local History.

PASTORS. Fathers Moise Mainville, 1872-1873; Edward Jacker, 1873-1876; William Dwyer, 1876-1878; John Brown, 1878-1879; John C. Kennedy, 1879-1881; co-pastors Kilian Haas and Isidor Handtmann, 1881-1882; Joseph Niebling, 1883; P. G. Tubin, 1883-1884; William Dwyer, 1884-1887; Peter O'Connell, 1887; Joseph Barron, 1887-1888; Alberico Vitali, 1888; Philip J. Erlach, 1890; Adam Doser, 1890-1891; James Miller, 1892-1899; William Joisten, 1900; Francis X. Becker, 1900-1901; John A. Keul, 1901-1904; Francis H. Swift, 1904; Joseph N. Raymond, 1904-1905; Martin Sommers, 1905-1919; John Keul, 1919-1922; William Teehan, 1923-1924; Thomas Kennedy, 1924-1934; Joseph Ling, 1934-1958; Wilbur Gibbs, 1958; William Schick, 1962-1968; Terrence Donnelly, 1968-1969; John Chroback, 1969; Joseph Polakowski, 1969-1973; Joseph Francis Rausch, OFM Cap., 1973-1978; Guy S. Thoren, 1978-1986; Raymond Hoefgen, 1986-1988; William Richards, 1988-1990; James Williams, 1990-2005, and Reynaldo Garcia, SJ, 2005-.

St. Francis de Sales, Manistique

The present Manistique congregation of St. Francis de Sales is the result of fruitful labors and faithful efforts dating back more than 100 years. But the beginning of Catholicism in the region goes back an additional 50 years when Father Frederic Baraga established his first Indian mission nearby at Indian Lake.

As the settlement of Manistique grew the people banded together and the church grew stronger. A rectory, convent and parish school were all added and the community supported many missions in the region.

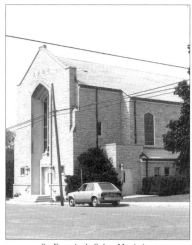

St. Francis de Sales, Manistique

FOUNDING. Father Frederic Baraga first visited Indian Lake, three miles north of Manistique, in 1833. As a result of his visit, the Chippewas living at the site are reported to have built a small chapel of logs and birch bark almost overnight. Father Baraga visited the mission three times, baptizing the people and blessing the church and cemetery.

Activity at the Indian Lake Mission declined until there was no sign of its ever having existed. Afterward, Catholics in the area were visited only occasionally by priests from Garden. Mass was offered in private homes and the town hall until 1883 when Father Theodore Aloysius Majerus was named the first pastor of St. Francis de Sales Parish. The first church was raised the following year.

An exhaustive list of pastors in the first 25 years led to a slow start for the parish. Nonetheless a rectory, convent and parish school were built. The parish also supported the missions of Gould City, Naubinway and all the stations on the Soo Line from Manistique to Trout Lake.

Finally in 1908, a new era was ushered in with the arrival of Father Bernard J. Schevers, O.P. A member of the Norbertine Fathers of West DePere, Wis., Father Schevers remained at St. Francis until his death in May 1950.

As the small village grew to a modern city, the church was enlarged twice to meet the needs of the increasing population. In the years leading up to Father Schevers' death the parish managed to save a large sum of money, about $93,000, for future building projects. Under Father Schevers' successor, diocesan priest Father Francis Scheringer, the school and convent were modernized and plans drawn up for a new church and rectory.

On the morning of April 29, 1953, a basement fire inside St. Francis de Sales

Church caused extensive damage rendering the facility unsafe for use. The flames did not get inside the church auditorium, and vestments and sacred vessels were removed. The rectory was unscathed by the blaze. The fire expedited plans already in the works for a new church on the original site. During construction, services were held in the Oak Theater and the school hall.

PARISH LIFE. Groundbreaking ceremonies for the new church were held in June 1953. A time capsule containing current church memorabilia was placed in the cornerstone when it was blessed in August of that year.

The modern Tudor-Gothic style structure was completed in 1954 and dedicated on June 15. Father Scheringer also oversaw construction of a mission church in Gulliver in 1958. Just a few years later, in 1962, a shrine to the Blessed Virgin Mary was erected at Indian Lake to mark Bishop Baraga's former mission site. A Michigan Historical Marker has also been erected.

In 1984 the parish celebrated its 100th anniversary. An anniversary booklet was printed to coincide with the centennial.

PARISH SCHOOL. In 1900 Father Joseph P. Kunes converted the former parish hall into a six-room school. The move was in answer to parishioners' pleas for a Catholic education for their children. In 1902 the first teachers arrived, Franciscan Sisters of Christian Charity from Manitowoc, Wis. At first, means were only available to teach the lower grades. In 1907 classes for the upper grades began. In 1914 Father Schevers built a two-story building on Oak and Maple streets. The facility served the school for 51 years. A convent was constructed in 1923.

The school was modernized with construction of a new complex in 1966. The structure consists of eight classrooms, a library, kitchen, conference room and multi-purpose room.

On June 4, 1977 the school celebrated its 75th anniversary. The last of the Franciscans serving the school left after the 2003-2004 school year.

PASTORS. Fathers Theodore Aloysius Majerus, 1883-1885; Augustus W. Geers, 1885-1886; John Chebul, 1886-1887; Joseph Haus, 1888; Melchior Faust, 1888; John Burns, 1889; Philip J. Erlach 1889-1890, A. O. Pelisson, 1890; Fabian Pawlar, 1890-1892; Antoine Rezek, 1892; John Henn, 1892; Frederic Sperlin, 1892-1893; Joseph Wallace, 1893-1894; John H. Reynaert, 1895-1898; Joseph P. Kunes, 1898-1904; William B. Stahl, 1904-1905; James Corcoran, 1905-1908; Bernard J. Schevers, OP, 1908-1950; Francis M. Scheringer, 1950-1973; Norbert Frieburger, 1973-1979; James Menapace, 1979-1996; co-pastor C. Michael Rhoades, 1981-1982; George C. Gustafson, 1996-1998; Peter Minelli, 1998-2002, and Glenn Theoret, 2002-.

ST. CATHERINE MISSION, MARENISCO

William Bonifas was the driving force behind the founding of St. Catherine Mission in Marenisco. In its 70-year history, the mission has been cared for by priests from Bessemer, Wakefield, Ironwood and Watersmeet.

St. Catherine Mission, Marenisco

FOUNDING. Mass was celebrated in the Marenisco Town Hall until 1932. At that time lumberman William Bonifas, who had established a sawmill at Marenisco, recognized the need for a church to serve the growing population. Mr. Bonifas underwrote the cost of construction and in time the parish repaid him. The Women's Altar Society held countless dinners and other fundraising events to help raise the money to retire the debt.

Local volunteers helped with the construction of the church. The building was dedicated on July 24, 1932. In 1934 a bell from the former Sacred Heart Church of Verona, Wis., was donated to the mission.

PARISH LIFE. Improvements to the church over the years include heating system upgrades and storm window and roof replacements in the 1950s. In the 70s a new boiler system was installed and the ceiling renovated.

St. Catherine's continued as a mission through the 1950s. Father Samuel Bottoni, pastor of Immaculate Conception Parish in Watersmeet, saw the need for a resident pastor in Marenisco and began planning for construction of a rectory there. The rectory was completed in the mid-1960s. In 1967 Father John McArdle was appointed St. Catherine's first resident pastor and was also assigned the St. Ann Mission in Bergland. In 1973 the church was again given mission status and has since been under the care of the pastor serving Immaculate Conception Parish in Wakefield. Retired priests of the diocese continue to live in the Marenisco rectory and serve the people of the mission.

PASTORS. Fathers Cronan Flynn, CP, 1932; Jeremiah Moriarty, 1932-1950; Thomas A. Drengacz, 1950-1952; Samuel Bottoni, 1952-1967; John McArdle, 1967-1969; Norbert Landreville, 1969-1971; David Jenner, 1971-1973; Joseph Kichak, 1973-1980; Edward Wenzel, 1980-1982; David Jenner, 1982-1985; Allan J. Mayotte, 1985-1990; John Maloney, 1990-1995; Allan J. Mayotte, 1995-2000; Chacko Devasia Kakaniyil, 2000-2004, and James Roetzer, 2004-.

St. Christopher, Marquette

St. Christopher Parish was started in the mid-1950s to serve about 200 Catholic families living in Marquette Township. Rapid growth in the first decade included families from the K.I. Sawyer Air Force Base located near Gwinn. The military families of various backgrounds and cultures added a unique dimension to the church atmosphere.

The Sisters of St. Paul de Chartres, who came from countries around the world, offered an additional avenue for diversity at St. Christopher's. The sisters served as Catholic school teachers and eventually as pastoral coordinators.

St. Christopher, Marquette

FOUNDING. In October 1952, anticipating the needs of the Catholic families living in Marquette Township, the diocese purchased four acres of land in Trowbridge Park for an eventual church. St. Christopher's Parish was established on June 30, 1954, and Mass was first celebrated July 18 of that year in a rented, remodeled building located on U.S. Highway 41. An altar, tabernacle, communion rail, lectern and vestments were procured from other parishes throughout the diocese. With seating for only about 100, the rented building soon proved inadequate. On June 26, 1955, ground was broken and a basement begun on the property purchased three years earlier.

The basement was completed and the building and grounds blessed by Bishop Thomas L. Noa in November 1955. Mass was held there for two years until construction of the church proper was completed in 1957. The first Mass upstairs was held Oct. 6.

In February 1956 the parish acquired the township's old Bancroft School and had it moved to the church grounds. The men of the parish converted the school to a rectory and offices. The structure, built in 1891, also served as a temporary convent.

Major renovations were made to the church, rectory and parish grounds in 1995.

PARISH SCHOOL. In October 1967, under the direction of Monsignor Edmund C. Szoka, the parish saw its dream for a parochial school come to fruition. A school board was elected two years before final plans for the structure were drawn up. The building, located across from the church and rectory, was dedicated on Oct. 28, 1967. The first enrollment was 122 students in first through sixth grades. The Sisters of St. Paul de Chartres staffed the school.

Serving families from the K.I. Sawyer Air Force Base, St. Christopher's School boasted that it was "bi-lingual, bi-racial, geographic and multicultural." The local children had the advantage of associating with children from many backgrounds who contributed much of their culture and race to the school atmosphere. The majority of school instructors were sisters from the Philippines.

The school closed in 1987 due to low enrollment and financial constraints. Since then a scholarship fund has helped parishioners finance their education. The fund is in memory of Father Howard Brown, St. Christopher's longest serving pastor who was at the church from 1978 until his death in 1993. St. Christopher's school building is still used today for religious education and for early childhood daycare and pre-school programs. The parish makes an annual contribution to Father Marquette Central School system. The amount is less than the other Marquette churches are assessed because the number of children from the parish who attend the school is much lower.

PARISH LIFE. An annual tradition of the parish "The Blessing of Automobiles" began in 1954 and carried on for years. To follow in the footsteps of century-old rituals, parishioners had their automobiles, bicycles and other modes of transportation blessed in the name of St. Christopher, originally the patron of ferrymen and in modern times of motorists.

Another local legacy of the church is pasty making. The women of the parish produce 1,000 pasties per month, nine months out of the year.

In 1974 the parish held its 20th anniversary celebration the weekend of June 29 and 30. Festivities consisted of afternoon barbecues, family games, an evening street dance and a commemorative Mass concelebrated by Bishops Charles A. Salatka and Edmund C. Szoka, then bishop of Gaylord.

Since 1994, leadership at St. Christopher's has been offered through a religious pastoral coordinator and canonical pastor-sacramental minister. Sister Mary Ann Laurin, SPC, was named the first pastoral coordinator. She was succeeded in that role by Sister Francis Mary Mortola, SPC, 1997-1999, and Sister Colleen Sweeting, OSF, 1999-.

PASTORS. Fathers Arnold Casanova, 1954-1957; Msgr. Edmund Szoka, 1958-1971; Vincent L. Ouellette, 1971; Donald Shiroda, 1971-1975; Robert J. Chisholm, 1975-1977; John Landreville, 1977-1978; Howard Brown, 1978-1993; Jeff Johnson, 1994; Peter Oberto, 1994-1995; canonical pastor and sacramental ministers George Maki and Ronald Timock, 1995-1996; Alexander K. Sample, 1996-2006.

St. John the Baptist, Marquette

The history of St. John the Baptist Church is that of a loyal and affectionate congregation. In 1906 an elaborate new church building was erected, thanks to donations of money and labor from parishioners. Until its closure in 1986, parishioners worked hard to save the historic landmark.

At the center of much of the church's history was Monsignor Mathias Jodocy, who served St. John's from 1905 to 1948.

St. John the Baptist, Marquette

FOUNDING. The French-Canadians of Marquette banded together to form St. John the Baptist Parish in 1872. They bought a log church from the Methodists and, according to records, "put clapboards on the outside and 'catholicized' the inside."

By July 1890, a new church was badly needed. Pastors and parishioners worked hard for years to raise the money for a new house of worship.

On Sept. 16, 1906, the cornerstone was laid for a church of Spanish Renaissance style. Located near the corner of Fourth and Washington Streets, the seating capacity was 770 in the church proper and another 230 in the balcony. It was first occupied on Jan. 5, 1908.

The landmark building is said to have been a fine tribute to the generosity of its members and friends. "Even the poorest cheerfully gave the 'widow's mite' often depriving themselves to do so," reports say. The excavation, the foundation and the laying of the floor were all accomplished by donated labor.

Three rectories were at different times part of the parish. The first was built in the 1870s on a lot west of the parish. Shortly after Father Jodocy's arrival in 1905, the parish bought a dwelling on north Fourth Street. It was replaced in 1965 by an administration building adjoining the bell tower. The building still stands today, along with the tower. The building is used for offices.

In 1938, the parish built a one-story building to the west, which contained two stores that were rented out. Also in 1938, an underground heating plant was installed to heat the church, rectory, the rental building and the Green and Ida Blocks, which were east of the church on the corner of 4th and Washingon streets. Two large coal-burning boilers were the source of heat.

PARISH SCHOOL. In 1911, the Ida Block next to the church was purchased and an eight-grade school started. Classes were held there and in the basement of the church. The quarters soon proved to be insufficient for handling the number of students, however. In 1928 the vacated Ely Public School located on Bluff Street was purchased for St. John's School.

Franciscan Sisters from Canada were the school's first teachers. Around 1920 the Ursulines began 25 years of serving in that capacity. In 1945 the Franciscan Sisters of Christian Charity of Manitowoc, Wis., staffed the school. A convent was also located on the Ida Block next to the school.

PARISH LIFE. Contributing much to the history of St. John's was Monsignor Mathias Jodocy, who served as pastor for 43 years, from 1905 to 1948. The diocese's centennial edition of *Our Sunday Visitor* said: "His devotion to the parish and welfare of its members was outstanding. ... His true priestly qualities contributed much to the development of a strong Catholic faith in the parish."

St. John's celebrated its centennial in 1972. Festivities June 23 and June 24, included a centennial ball with period costumes, a Mass of thanksgiving and a banquet. Local radio stations broadcast portions of the banquet program.

CLOSURE. On Jan. 19, 1986, the diocese announced St. John's would be closed permanently due to structural damage that was posing a threat to the people's safety. Since the month prior, Mass had been held in the Bishop Baraga school gym. The $250,000 necessary for repairs was deemed too expensive. In a letter to the people Bishop Mark Schmitt said, "The cost to maintain the parish becomes prohibitive when viewed from the perspective of a declining membership and the large number of older people who comprise the parish. To inflict a large debt on the next generation would be irresponsible."

Committees of parishioners attempted to raise the money to save the historical church, but were unsuccessful. Letter writing and public information campaigns were among the aggressive efforts.

The parish officially closed June 30, 1986. The building was purchased by a Marquette contractor and razed in late December 1986.

RECORDS. Records for St. John are at St. Peter Cathedral in Marquette.

PASTORS. Fathers W. T. Roy, 1872; Oliver Comtois, 1874; James F. Berube, 1875; Anatole O. Pelisson, 1876; B. Simon Marceau, 1877; Louis Paquet, 1878; Joseph Berube, 1878 Hilary J. Rosseau, 1879; Ignatius Mrak, 1879; Maurice Hens, OMC, 1879; Joseph E. Martel, 1881; Fabian S. Marceau, 1888; Antoine Vermare, 1889; Raymond G. Jacques, 1902; Msgr. Mathias Jodocy, 1905-1948; Raymond Garin, 1948; William Oremus, 1964; Charles Olivier, Dominic Zadra, 1968; Paul Schiska and Raymond Moncher, 1969; Otto Sartorelli, 1978-1981; James Von Tobel, SJ, 1981-1984, and Thomas Bain, SJ, 1984-1986.

St. Michael, Marquette

The 64-year history of St. Michael Parish in Marquette has been marked with an extremely active laity and family-oriented environment.

From its beginnings in a vacated college dormitory to its present existence as a cornerstone for parishioners and Catholic school students in the city of Marquette, St. Michael's continues to be a driving force for the faithful.

St. Michael, Marquette

FOUNDING. Toward the mid-1900s, as the city of Marquette rapidly expanded to the north, the need for another Catholic church became urgent. The announcement of a new church was made on Easter Sunday, 1942.

That spring, a former priest of the diocese, retired Bishop Joseph G. Pinten of Grand Rapids, turned over to the diocese the "dormitory property" adjacent to Northern Michigan College. He donated the property on two conditions: that the new parish would be named after St. Michael, the protector of the church, and that parishioners would build a school to be staffed by the Sisters of St. Joseph of Carondolet.

Diocese of Marquette Bishop Francis Magner commissioned Monsignor Joseph L. Zryd to organize the parish. Boundaries would be north of Park Street in the city, north of Cleveland Street in the Piqua Location and north of Moran Street in Trowbridge Park.

"Families residing in that territory who were of French origin had the option of retaining their affiliation with St. John the Baptist Parish," according to an article printed in the Centennial Edition of the diocese's *Our Sunday Visitor* in 1953. There were, indeed, mixed emotions among people hesitant to leave the St. Peter Cathedral, according to parish reports.

A group of men began organizational committees and set to work remodeling the old dormitory. Volunteer labor kept expenses down and work moved quickly. The dormitory, built in 1900, formerly housed students attending the Normal School, and had living quarters for the president of the school, Dwight B. Waldo, and his wife. It was built and owned by Longyear and Ayer, area developers. During World War I, the building was used temporarily as a barracks for a Student Army Training Corps.

In addition to the dormitory, a residence on the same tract of land was purchased. The home was used first for a convent and later for a rectory.

The formal decree establishing the new parish came Aug. 20, 1942. It is recorded that the Oct. 4, 1942, dedication of the church and blessing of the school and convent momentarily overshadowed news and restrictions of the war. Some 3,000 people were said to have been present at the ceremonies.

By the mid- to late-1950s, overcrowded Masses, deteriorating facilities and the retirement of debt on a new school building led to major development drives and, finally, the construction of a new church. Work began in the summer of 1962 and was completed on Palm Sunday, April 4, 1963. A new rectory, convent, multi-purpose room and office space were part of the new development. At that time the Campus Ministry Center was also added.

PARISH SCHOOL. On Sept. 15, 1942, an initial school opened in the dormitory building to 90 students in kindergarten through third grade. Enrollment increased rapidly with 300-plus pupils registered in 1945. By 1947 the school graduated its first eighth grade class. Modern facilities were a must.

Nearly every parishioner was contacted in the drive to raise funds for a new school. Doors to the modern facility opened in September 1949. The former dormitory classrooms were remodeled to increase the seating capacity of the church.

St. Michael's joined in support of Bishop Baraga Central High School until the school's closure in 1969.

In 1987 the Sisters of St. Joseph of Carondolet left the parish. The Sisters of St. Paul de Chartres took over serving in the area of religious education.

St. Michael's School fully consolidated with Bishop Baraga to form Father Marquette Catholic Central School in 1991. Facilities at St. Michael's house fifth through eighth grades.

PARISH LIFE. The constitution of the parish council was adopted in November 1967. At that time a 19-member executive board and 10 commissions were active in the day-to-day operation of the parish. All members aged 16 and older were urged to play a role in one of the commissions.

In the mid-1990s, St. Michael's became a tithing parish. A portion of its monthly income is distributed to those in need worldwide.

PASTORS. Msgr. Joseph L. Zryd, 1942-1951; Fathers Robert J. Cordy, 1951-1955; Msgr. Joseph L. Zryd, 1955-1960; Patrick W. Frankard, 1960-1963; Arnold L. Casanova, 1963-1971; Msgr. Joseph J. Dunleavy, 1971-1985; co-pastor Lawrence Gauthier, 1981-1983; Vincent Ouellette, 1985-1986; Paul Nomellini, 1986-1988; John J. Shiverski, 1988-1995, and John Patrick, 1995-.

St. Peter Cathedral, Marquette

St. Peter Cathedral, Marquette

Bishop Frederic Baraga chose the site of the first Catholic church in Marquette on Oct. 12, 1853. That same year the Upper Peninsula became a Vicariate Apostolic and Father Baraga was named its first bishop. The original two-story frame building was replaced by a framed Gothic-style cathedral.

St. Peter's continues to serve as the cathedral church and, as such, hosts many special Masses for the faithful of the diocese.

FOUNDING. Mass was first said in Marquette in a log cabin located on what is now Spring Street. In 1853, Bishop Baraga selected the site of the current cathedral for construction of St. Peter's church. Bishop Baraga laid the cornerstone for the cathedral and dedicated it to Saint Peter the Apostle in 1866.

PARISH LIFE. After a fire in 1879, parishioners first attended Mass at St. John Church while construction of a new church was under way. But this arrangement proved inadequate for both parishes, so Mass was held in the basement of the cathedral from Christmas Eve 1883 to July 27, 1890 when the superstructure was being completed. The present rectory was built on the west side of the cathedral in 1922.

When a second fire struck the church on Nov. 3, 1935, records say that Father Francis Scheringer and the parish custodian put on masks and tied themselves together for safety in order to fight through the smoke and retrieve the sacred vessels from the main altar. The men were successful in the attempt and escaped just prior to the collapse of the roof and floor. The auditorium of Baraga High School was used for Mass for many months until the basement of the new cathedral could be used. Restoration was completed in September 1938. Formal dedication took place in the summer 1939.

Mammoth Romanesque-style columns supported the body of the church. A marble altar and bishop's throne, stained glass windows depicting the mysteries of the Lord's life, and mosaic Stations of the Cross framed in marble were installed. All of the new statues were of colored marble. The basement was redesigned with storage facilities, a kitchen and banquet facilities for 600.

In 1947, the cathedral was redecorated and the mural depicting Christ's presentation of the keys of heaven to St. Peter was painted above the high altar. In the 1960s, alterations were made to meet changes in liturgical worship brought about by the Second Vatican Council. In 1980 the cathedral was again redecorated. The parish celebrated its centennial in 1981 to coincide with the 100th anniversary of the laying of the cornerstone of the present church.

In 2000 work was completed on a multi-million dollar, two-story annex that connects the church with the rectory and provides new gathering space, meeting rooms and barrier-free restrooms. The rectory was also renovated.

PARISH SCHOOL. Soon after his arrival in Marquette, Bishop Baraga worked to establish a school. The Ursuline Sisters from Chatham, Ontario began an academy and day school in 1867. The Sisters of St. Joseph of Carondelet, Mo., took over the work in 1872 and stayed for more than a century.

The original St. Joseph Academy was destroyed by fire on Feb. 17, 1903. Two and a half years later, the parish decided to fund the construction of the Bishop Baraga School. In 1957 the entire building became used exclusively as a high school, and Little Baraga School was started for kindergarten through fifth grades. In 1958 a new St. Peter's School replaced Little Baraga.

In 1977 St. Peter's, St. John's and St. Louis the King parishes jointly assumed operations and the school system was renamed Bishop Baraga Central Grade School. The high school closed in 1969. Father Marquette Catholic School System was developed in 1991 as a joint effort between the Marquette area parishes. The school serves students in developmental kindergarten through eighth grades.

PASTORS. Fathers Sebastian Duroc, 1857-1864; Henry L. Thiele, 1864-1866; Edward Jacker, 1866-1868; Edmond Walsh, 1868; Megnée, 1868; Martin Fox, 1868-1870; Ignatius Mrak, 1870; Frederick Eis, 1870-1873; John Brown, 1873-1874; Hugh McDevitt, 1874; Oliver Comtois, 1875; Hilary J. Rosseau, 1876; A. O. Pellisson, 1876; T. A. Trottenberg, 1876-1877; John C. Henry, 1877-1878; Hilary J. Rosseau, 1878; John C. Kenny, 1879; Bishop John Vertin, 1879-1880; - - - Maurice, OFM, 1880; Theodore Aloysius Majerus, 1880-1881; Augustus W. Geers, 1882; Charles Dries, 1882; Martin Kehoe, 1882; M. McCloy, 1882; A. Parella, 1883; Francis X. Becker, 1883; Theodore Aloysius Majerus, 1883; Kilian Haas, 1884; Joseph Barron, 1884-1885; Matthew Lyons, 1885; Fabian Marceau, 1885; F. X. Weninger, SJ, 1885; Thomas Turner, 1885-1886; Augustine Bayer, OSF, 1886; J. E. Struif, 1886; Philip Kummert, 1886; Ignatius Balluff, 1886-1887; John Keul, 1887-1888; Joseph Langan, 1885-1894; James Miller, 1894-1895; Nickolas H. Nosbisch, 1895-1896; Adam Doser, 1896-1897; Anthony Zagar 1896-1897; Joseph Sauriol 1897; Msgr. Mathias Jodocy 1897-1899; Joseph G. Pinten, 1899-1916; Henry A. Buchholtz, 1916-1945; John T. Holland, 1945-1948; Glen Sanford, 1948-1950; Nolan B. McKevitt, 1950-

Epiphany, Menominee

Epiphany, Menominee

People of German descent living in Menominee left their mother church to form a congregation of their own in the early 1890s. For 70 years the people were able to support the parish and school. However, Epiphany and the five other Menominee churches merged into three new parishes in 1972.

FOUNDING. In 1891 the German parishioners of St. John Parish became the second group in Menominee to separate and form a church. Land for Epiphany was purchased at the corner of 10th Avenue and 10th Street from the Sisters of St. Agnes of Fond du Lac, Wis. Bishop John Vertin dedicated the new church Nov. 13, 1892.

PARISH LIFE. In 1938, Epiphany became the first parish in the diocese to hold a weekly novena to Our Sorrowful Mother. When the church basement was remodeled into a modern kitchen and hall, generous parishioners had a Sorrowful Mother plaque and new Stations of the Cross installed.

On Oct. 26, 1952 the parish celebrated its 60th anniversary. High Mass was followed by dinner and a parish reunion. In 1962 significant maintenance and repair projects were undertaken to mark the milestone of another decade passing.

PARISH SCHOOL. In 1902, Epiphany purchased a school building vacated by St. John's and modernized the structure for its own use. In 1922 that building was replaced by a new structure.

Sisters of St. Agnes taught at the school until 1946. In 1948 the Ursuline Sisters took charge. A new convent was blessed Oct. 28, 1951.

In 1964 the schools of Epiphany, St. Ann and St. John consolidated. In 1965 additional classrooms were constructed.

MERGER In 1972, when the Menominee Area Catholic Planning Commission decided to merge the six area parishes into three, it was decided to retain use of Epiphany Church as the new house of worship for Holy Spirit Parish.

RECORDS. Epiphany Parish records are located at Holy Spirit Church.

PASTORS. Fathers Melchior Faust, 1891-1901; Joseph E. Neumeier, 1901-1933; Peter Manderfield, 1935-1937; Sebastian Maier, 1938-1946; Joseph Schaul, 1946-1951; James J. Schaefer, 1951-1969, and Milton Vanitvelt 1969-1972.

Holy Redeemer (Holy Trinity), Menominee

Located in Menominee's Birch Creek area, five miles north of the Menominee city limit, Holy Redeemer Parish has played a large role in the faith community of the region. As a result of a 1972 merger of Menominee's six parishes, the name of the church was changed from Holy Trinity to Holy Redeemer.

Serving the people of St. Mary Mission in Sobieski from 1980 to 1995, and extending their good fortune by way of supporting various international missions, the people of Holy Redeemer have proven that they are as dedicated to Christ today as their predecessors were in starting the church more than 100 years ago.

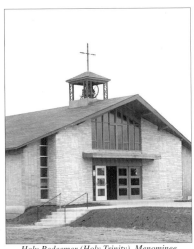
Holy Redeemer (Holy Trinity), Menominee

FOUNDING. Before the construction of Holy Trinity Church in 1884, the 13 Catholic families living in Birch Creek walked the railroad tracks to Epiphany Parish in Menominee to attend Sunday Mass. The first Holy Trinity Church was a clapboard-covered wooden structure, that had a heater in the middle aisle and seated 185 people. A Green Bay priest said the first Mass there in 1886.

The new church was equipped with a 650-pound Angelus bell that was delivered to the site by oxen. The bell was rung every day at noon.

From 1884 to 1898 Birch Creek was a mission of Epiphany. In 1898 administration of the parish was transferred to St. Adalbert Parish in Menominee and continued as such until it was elevated to parish status in 1931.

PARISH LIFE. Father Charles Fox was named Holy Trinity's first pastor. A new rectory was completed in 1932. The parish acquired a hall and picnic grounds in 1935.

The 1940s brought many improvements to the church. Redecorating included the installation of new pews and repainting the entire interior and exterior of the church.

But later efforts to keep the building in good repair seemed fruitless. In 1940, an initial attempt to raise funds for a new church was unsuccessful. Efforts were met with enthusiasm, however, in 1954. Parishioners pledged generously, and many bazaars, dinners and other events were held to raise the money needed for a new house of worship.

The final Mass was said in the original church Feb. 27, 1961. Bishop Thomas L. Noa dedicated the new structure Nov. 12 of the same year. The church is of block and brick construction with a stone front and laminated arches. The same Angelus bell first purchased by founders of the original church was added to the tower of the new church. In 1965 the parish hall was completed.

In the 1972 consolidation, Holy Trinity's name was changed to Holy Redeemer.

In 1980, Holy Redeemer took over responsibility of the St. Mary Mission in Sobieski. Priests of Holy Redeemer offered regular services there until the mission closed in 1995.

The parish purchased the former Birch Creek public school in June 1979. The building served as a religious education center and was the site of many dances.

Major renovations to the parish were made in the late 1970s. A new baptismal font, pulpit and a Holy Family statue were added. A Baldwin organ was purchased, air conditioning was installed, more parking spaces created and remodeling was done for new office space.

The Menominee parishes are unique in that they each take on different responsibilities and offer different services to all Catholics in the community.

Holy Redeemer has a tradition of supporting various missions through its annual Fun Day event. The church is also known for its Valentine and Halloween parties and for its annual chicken dinners.

The parish has supported the Menominee Catholic Central School since it was formed in 1972.

PASTORS. Fathers Michael Weis, Martin Fox, Melchior Faust, Joseph Boever, Joseph Neumeier, Anthony Keller, Philip J. Erlach, - - - Kasenberg, 1877-1898; Julius Papon, 1898-1917; Louis Kania, 1917; Victor Karch, 1917-1931; Charles Fox, 1931-1939; Anthony Oehlerer, 1939-1949; Frank Ignatz, 1949-1952; Joseph H. Schaul, 1952; William Schick, 1952-1962; Milton Vanitvelt, 1962-1969; Otto Sartorelli, 1969-1972; Joseph Felix, 1972-1974; Joseph Gouin, 1974-1990; Thomas Poisson, 1990-1991; Rick Courier, 1991-1999; Ronald Skufca, 1999-2005, and Joseph Vandannoor, MST, 2005-.

Holy Spirit, Menominee

Holy Spirit, Menominee

Holy Spirit Church was created as the result of a 1972 merger of the six Menominee area parishes into three. The parochial school system was also strengthened through a consolidation.

After the merger many improvements were made to Holy Spirit's house of worship, and action was taken to create a new identity for the unified people.

FOUNDING. In 1970 Bishop Charles A. Salatka formed a planning commission to study the greater good of the Menominee area parishes. Two representatives from each of the six Menominee churches sat on the commission. Two years later, the group recommended a consolidation. Members of Epiphany, St. John and St. Ann would come together as one parish family forming the new Holy Spirit Church, housed in the former Epiphany Church. At the same time, Resurrection Parish was born out of the merger of St. Adalbert and St. William parishes. The former Holy Trinity was renamed Holy Redeemer.

PARISH LIFE. Following the merger, all of the parishes' outstanding debts were combined and great efforts were made to reduce the obligations. Buildings and properties were sold, the school system was consolidated and other actions were taken to improve the fiscal condition of the parishes.

In the midst of all of these adjustments, Holy Spirit Parish saw many improvements to its facilities.

The church itself was completely renovated and redecorated. The hall was updated and new kitchen facilities were added. A new roof and storm windows were installed and a new vestibule was constructed. The former Epiphany School was renovated for use as catechism classrooms and for youth ministries. A new administrative building was also constructed.

To celebrate its rebirth, members of Holy Spirit banded together to commemorate the fifth, 10th and 20th anniversaries of the founding of the new parish. On July 13, 1997, the people joined with parishioners of Resurrection and Holy Redeemer parishes in a grand 25th Jubilee of the 1972 merger.

One of the traditions Holy Spirit is especially known for is its Mardi Gras chicken dinners. The custom was started at St. Ann Church in 1967 and continues at Holy Spirit.

PARISH SCHOOL   The parochial schools of Menominee were also combined in the 1970s to offer more efficient operations. Each parish assumed equal responsibility for running the schools. With the money saved in consolidating and selling off surplus properties, a foundation was created to assure the future success of the parochial school system.

From 1972 to 1978 Menominee Catholic Central North (the former St. William's School building) and Menominee Catholic Central South (the former St. Ann School building) both housed kindergarten through eighth grades. Then in 1978, kindergarten through third graders moved to Menominee Catholic Central North and fourth through eighth graders began attending Menominee Catholic Central South. Since 1997, all classes including preschool have been housed in the Menominee Catholic Central South building. The north building was sold to the Menominee County Intermediate School District.

PASTORS.   Fathers S. Patrick Wisneske, 1972-2003; Ronald Skufca, 2003-2005, and Joseph Vandannoor, MST, 2005-.

Resurrection, Menominee

Since Resurrection Parish in Menominee was founded, through the 1972 merger of St. Adalbert and St. William parishes, members have strived to create a unified identity. In 1997 Menominee's three area churches joined together to celebrate 25 years of a new era.

FOUNDING. The 1972 merger was the result of a consolidation of six Menominee parishes into three. Resurrection's house of worship is the former St. Adalbert Church. Also born out of the consolidation were Holy Spirit Parish and Holy Redeemer in Birch Creek.

Resurrection, Menominee

PARISH LIFE. One of the first goals of the three new Menominee parishes was to reduce their combined debt. Buildings and property were sold, the school system merged and other actions were taken to pay off outstanding debt and move ahead in the new era.

The people of Resurrection Parish also came together to support improvements to their church. Upgrades included a new roof and air conditioning for both the church and rectory. A new office and multi-purpose room were built in the basement and the building was made handicapped accessible. A bell tower was also constructed, using the bell from the former St. Ann Church.

Resurrection Parish has become known throughout Menominee for its Men's Club bingo and soup luncheons, annual fall festival and summer Bible programs.

On July 13, 1997, members of the parish joined with the people of Holy Spirit and Holy Redeemer to commemorate the 25th anniversary of the mergers.

PARISH SCHOOL. The parochial schools of Menominee were also combined in the 1970s. Each parish assumed equal responsibility for running the schools. With the money saved in consolidating and selling off surplus properties, a foundation was created to assure the future success of the Menominee Catholic Central School.

PASTORS. Fathers Norman Clisch, 1972-1991; co-pastor Joseph Gouin, 1972-1974; co-pastor Robert Haas, 1974-1979; Dino Silvestrini, 1991-2003; Emmett Norden, 2003, and Francis DeGroot, 2003-.

St. Adalbert, Menominee

Many unfortunate circumstances led to St. Adalbert Parish getting off to a slow start. Short stays by various priests, tension among parishioners in the early years, and outside forces drawing people away, should have dampened the future for the parish. But the people bounced back from these struggles—as well as from two terrible fires—to continue for 80 years as an independent parish.

A 1972 merger of the Menominee area parishes ended an era for St. Adalbert's, but its facilities remained intact and became the home of the new Resurrection Parish.

St. Adalbert, Menominee

FOUNDING. The Polish members of St. John the Baptist Parish in Menominee began to separate and form a church of their own in 1890. Property was purchased along 13th Avenue and 13th Street. Construction of the church began the following year, upon the arrival of the first pastor, Father Julius Papon. The church was completed on April 18, 1891.

The original structure was damaged by fire in 1897, and soon after, lightning struck the building causing further damage. The entire church was rebuilt without accumulating any debt.

PARISH LIFE. Members of St. Adalbert's struggled in the beginning to form a parish identity. A highly diversified people, eight priests in six years, and differences of opinion regarding a parochial school caused the parish roster to dwindle significantly until the arrival of a new pastor.

Father Victor A. Karch was assigned to St. Adalbert's on July 26, 1917. His pastorate spanned almost 50 years, to 1966. Father Karch first focused on unity and organization within the parish. Under his leadership the people came together and supported $50,000 worth of improvements to their house of worship.

Men of the parish did the excavation for a basement hall and the landscaping for the church yard. The church was completely remodeled and redecorated. The choir loft was rebuilt and a new pipe organ was installed. Father Karch himself designed a mural over the high altar depicting the Coronation of the Blessed Virgin as Queen of Heaven.

The parish was able to overcome periods of separation among its people. In 1931 a lumber mill fire sent about 60 families of the parish looking for work in other communities. In 1940, forty-two more families left St. Adalbert's when St. William Parish was formed.

On March 29, 1961, the place St. Adalbert parishioners called home for 70 years was destroyed by fire. The blaze started in the steeple and worked its way through the roof. The roof caved in, but the steeple and four walls were left standing. Remains of the charred structure were later razed.

On Sept. 23, 1962 Bishop Thomas L. Noa dedicated a new church on 18th Street. The modern structure with an attached rectory includes a basement hall. During construction, Mass was held at St. Ann's.

MISSIONS. Pastors of St. Adalbert were also responsible for administering to the missions of Holy Trinity in Birch Creek and St. Mary of Sobieski. Holy Trinity was named an independent parish in 1931.

MERGER. During the 1972 merger of the Menominee churches, St. Adalbert and St. William parishes were merged to form the new Resurrection Parish. The former St. Adalbert building became the house of worship for the new parish.

RECORDS. Records for St. Adalbert Parish are located at Resurrection Church in Menominee.

PASTORS. Fathers Julius V. Papon, 1891-1892; - - - Krezesniak, W. Anselm Mlynarczyk, William Joisten, Stanislaus Baranowski, John C. Bieniarz, Fabian Pawlar, Francis Maciarcz, Julius Papon, 1897-1917; Victor A. Karch, 1917-1966; Raymond Przybylski, 1966, and Walter Franczek, 1966-1972.

St. Ann, Menominee

The French people of St. John the Baptist Parish in Menominee left to form a new congregation in 1886. St. Ann's was successful in supporting a church, rectory, school and convent. Lightning struck the church steeples three times, causing the most damage the third time, in 1924. The structure was then rebuilt to prevent further ruin.

Consolidation of the parishes and schools in the city in 1972 brought the people of Menominee back into one united faith community.

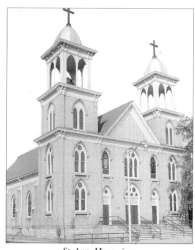

St. Ann, Menominee

FOUNDING. In October 1886, Bishop John Vertin granted permission to the 400 French members of St. John the Baptist Parish to form their own parish. The new parish received $4,000 compensation for the people's previous support of St. John's. Father Michael Letellier was named the first pastor.

Prior to the construction of St. Ann's Church, a St. Ann's Society was formed to raise money for the new structure. Services were held at St. John's until construction was completed in the fall of 1887. Ground was broken on the corner of 10th Avenue and 13th Street in the spring of 1887, and the dedication took place in September. The first rectory was also purchased that year.

PARISH LIFE. Improvements to the church in 1905 included the installation of windows in the sanctuary, the purchase of a pipe organ and the decoration of the interior of the church.

Three times the church suffered a fire when lightning struck the belfry. The most destructive was on May 5, 1924, when several thousand dollars damage was done to the interior of the church, which had recently been redecorated. The reconstruction began immediately and this time precautions were taken against lightning strikes. In 1958 the former Lemieux Funeral Home was purchased and converted into a rectory and parish offices.

PARISH SCHOOL. St. Ann School opened in 1887 in a two-story building located behind the church. The Sisters of St. Agnes of Fond du Lac, Wis., staffed the school. In 1900 a new school with living quarters for the sisters was erected on 10th Avenue. For a while, St. Ann's was exclusively a French-speaking school, but this designation caused enrollment to drop considerably and so French was discontinued. In 1907 the Little Sisters of Mary from Bay St. Paul,

Quebec replaced the Sisters of St. Agnes. In 1923 the Franciscan Sisters of Christian Charity from Silver Lake, Wis., came to staff the school.

A third school building was constructed in 1953. The next 12 years saw four additions put on the structure and the purchase of a house for use as a convent. In 1961-1962 improvements included office space, a lounge, social room, hall and gymnasium.

In 1964 St. Ann's School consolidated with St. John and Epiphany to form a more efficient and comprehensive program. The three parishes combined efforts in 1965 to have additional classrooms constructed.

MERGER. Discussions on a merger between St. Ann's and St. John's had taken place over the years, but were not well received by the members of St. Ann's. By 1972 it was decided that all six area parishes would merge to form three churches. St. John, St. Ann and Epiphany parishes became Holy Spirit and St. William and St. Adalbert became Resurrection. The name of Holy Trinity was changed to Holy Redeemer.

In 1973 the St. Ann building was sold and razed. The stained glass windows went to a California firm and the bell was transferred to Resurrection Parish.

RECORDS. Records for St. Ann Parish are located at Holy Spirit Church in Menominee.

PASTORS. Fathers Michael Letellier, 1886-1890; Hilary J. Rosseau, 1890-1891; Anatole O. Pelisson, 1891-1893; Honoratus Bourion, 1893-1902; Louis Archille Poulin, 1902-1911; Raymond G. Jacques, 1911-1916; George LaForest, 1911-1927; Francis Geynet, 1927-1959; Robert Haas, 1959; Gerard LaMothe, 1959-1960; Clifford Nadeau, 1960-1967; Thomas Andary, 1967-1969; Roland Dion, 1969-1970, and Conrad Dishaw, 1970-1972.

St. John the Baptist, Menominee

St. John the Baptist, Menominee

St. John the Baptist is considered the mother church of the city of Menominee. Four other churches got their start from St. John's. As people of different nationalities separated around the turn of the 20st century, those remaining banded together and rebuilt a landmark structure.

In 1972 St. John's was closed as a result of a city-wide parish merger that made six churches into three. The churches that started as one again united, marking a new era.

FOUNDING. The first church in Menominee was erected in 1872 when a group of Catholics decided they would no longer settle for taking a hand-operated ferry boat across the Menominee River to Marinette to attend Mass. Priests from Marinette visited Menominee to offer services from time to time in the schoolhouse, but only infrequently.

In August 1872 St. John the Baptist Church was constructed without informing Bishop Ignatius Mrak, but when the bishop learned of the move, he immediately sent Father Martin Fox to serve as the parish's first pastor. Bishop Mrak blessed and dedicated the church on June 29, 1873.

PARISH LIFE. In 1886 the French members of St. John's left to form St. Ann's. In 1891 the Germans separated to form Epiphany, and the Polish formed St. Adalbert's.

During the 44-year pastorate of Father Dennis Cleary (1892-1936) the original St. John's structure was razed and a modern church and rectory built in its place. While the new church was being constructed, parishioners attended Mass at St. Adalbert's. Bishop Frederick Eis dedicated the new edifice Oct. 22, 1922. Most of the structure was paid for by parishioner pledges. Continued parishioner support helped retire the remaining debt in five years, and eventually the interior of the church was decorated.

Extensive repairs were made to the building in 1937 and again in 1947, when parishioners contributed to significant upgrades of the facilities.

A grand celebration was held Sunday, June 20, 1948 to mark the 75th anniversary of the founding of the parish. Bishop Thomas L. Noa was present at a High Mass commemorating the milestone. A banquet followed.

PARISH SCHOOL. In 1876, the Sisters of St. Agnes of Fond du Lac,

Wis., established a school at St. John's. For the first two years about 30 students attended classes in the choir loft of the church.

In 1902 a four-room school was constructed on the corner of 12th Avenue and 9th Street. That building served young people until 1965. The Sisters of St. Joseph of Carondelet, from St. Louis, Mo., took over operation of the school in 1902. In 1937 Sisters of St. Francis of Manitowoc, Wis., replaced the Sisters of St. Joseph.

In 1964 St. John School consolidated with those of St. Ann and Epiphany to form a more efficient and comprehensive program. In 1965 new classrooms were constructed.

MERGER. After having served its people for nearly 100 years, St. John Church was closed in 1972. St. John, St. Ann and Epiphany parishes merged to form the new Holy Spirit and St. William and St. Adalbert became Resurrection. The name of Holy Trinity was changed to Holy Redeemer. The former St. John church building became the Menominee County Historical Museum. In July 1995 the structure was named to the National Register of Historic Places.

RECORDS. Records for St. John the Baptist Church are located at Holy Spirit Church in Menominee.

PASTORS. Fathers Martin Fox, 1873-1875; Oliver Comtois, 1874-1875; Ignatius Mrak, 1875; Peter Menard, 1875-1880; Frederick Eis, 1880; Bishop Ignatius Mrak, 1880-1881; Fabian Pawler, 1881; Francis Heliard, 1881-1883; Fabian Pawler, 1883-1885; Thomas Atfield, 1885-1886; Michael Letellier, 1886; Augustus W. Geers, 1886-1888; Joseph Kunes, 1888; Melchior Faust, 1889-1892; Dennis Cleary, 1892-1936; James J. Corcoran, 1937-1948; Msgr. John T. Holland, 1948-1962; Msgr. Robert J. Chisholm, 1962-1969, and Stephen Mayrand, 1969-1972.

St. William, Menominee

St. William's grew from a makeshift chapel in a living room to an independent parish with its own parochial school. Facilities were continuously upgraded thanks to the generosity of the parishioners, and the school continues serving students of Menominee Catholic Central School.

St. William, Menominee

FOUNDING. Menominee's St. William Mission was started under the care of St. Ann Parish for Catholics in the expanding northern section of the city.

In 1941, a private residence was purchased on State Street and Taylor Avenue and renovated to serve as a temporary chapel. Sunday Mass and religious education began there June 29, 1941.

PARISH LIFE. The mission grew in size very quickly and by 1942 plans were under way to erect a new church. The men of the parish and others from the community did much of the work. On Aug. 9, 1942, St. Williams became a parish and Bishop Francis Magner dedicated the new church.

During the next five years parishioners contributed financially to many church improvements, such as new furnishings, a church bell, a new garage and rectory renovations. A new organ was installed in November 1947.

In just 12 years the parish had nearly tripled in size. In 1951 a north wing was added to the church for catechism classes.

On Aug. 10, 1952 the parish family held a daylong celebration to commemorate its 10th anniversary.

PARISH SCHOOL. The parish opened its own school in 1964. The Sisters of St. Paul de Chartres from Marquette operated the facility, located on 41st Avenue. The building was overcrowded almost immediately so an addition was constructed. Classrooms were again added in 1966.

CLOSURE St. William Parish was closed in 1972 as a result of a merger of all six Menominee area parishes into three. St. William and St. Adalbert parishes combined to form the new Resurrection.

RECORDS. St. William records are located at Resurrection Church.

PASTORS. Fathers Robert J. Monroe, 1942-1952; Oliver O'Callaghan, 1952-1954; Thomas P. Dunleavy, 1954-1965; Louis Bracket, 1965-1971, and Arthur Parrotta, 1972.

St. Agnes Mission, Michigamme

St. Agnes Mission, Michigamme

From its beginning, the mission of St. Agnes in Michigamme is said to have struggled for existence. But at one time it was an independent parish responsible for the care of Sidnaw, Covington, Ewen, Kenton, Trout Creek, Bergland and Watersmeet. St. Agnes was closed in 1999 and the people encouraged to join the faith community of Sacred Heart in Champion.

FOUNDING. St. Agnes was built in 1873 by Father Joseph F. Berube of Champion's Sacred Heart Church. The original church was enhanced by the addition of a steeple in 1887, a sacristy in 1891 and interior remodeling in 1942. A rectory was constructed in 1888.

PARISH LIFE. The people's hospitality in welcoming summer visitors and others was said to be legendary, and a gift that was later brought to the Sacred Heart community. The people's deep sense of pride in their church was illustrated by the amount of volunteering they did to keep it operating. The interior of the church was kept spotless by women who cleaned the wood floor on hands and knees. The men attended to the exterior, doing the painting, lawn mowing and snowplowing.

In 1982, women religious began serving as pastoral coordinators at St. Augustine Parish in Republic, Sacred Heart in Champion and St. Agnes Mission. Pastoral Coordinators were Sisters Maureen Freeman, CSJ, and Paul Bernadette Bounk, CSJ, 1984-1993; Margey Schmelzle, OSF, 1994- ; Charlotte Ann Wagner 1994-1997; Lois Risch, OSF, 1999- .

CLOSURE. As a result of a shortage of priests, St. Agnes Church was closed and the community merged with Sacred Heart Church in Champion on Palm Sunday, March 28, 1999. Parishioners from St. Agnes and Sacred Heart gathered in Michigamme for the blessing of palms and the Gospel reading. Parishioners were then entrusted with the sacred vessels and other items, which would be used at Sacred Heart Church. A fleet of about 40 vehicles headed to the church in Champion where several parishioners were on hand to welcome all into the church. It truly was a day of sadness and some hopefulness for what this combined community would become. The St. Agnes building was donated by the Diocese of Marquette to Michigamme Township. It was reopened to the public for reading, meditation and other personal uses, and was named "The Quiet Place."

RECORDS. Sacramental records from St. Agnes Church are located at Sacred Heart Church.

PASTORS. Fathers Joseph F. Berube, 1873-1886; Fabian Marceau, 1886; J. Reding, 1886; Philip Kummert, 1886-1887; Edward Bordas, 1887; Francis Becker, 1887; Gideon Beliveau, 1887-1888; Thomas Butler, 1888; Alberico Vitale, 1888-1890; John Henn, 1890; Joseph R. Boissonnault, 1890-1891; Thomas Dassylva, 1891-1892; Joseph Sauriol, 1892; John H. Reynaert, 1892; Joseph Dupasquier, 1892-1893; John Burns, 1893-1894; James Lenhart, 1894-1898; Alexander Hasenberg, 1898-1921; John Nuerenberg, 1921-1922; Peter Bleeker, 1922-1924; Peter J. Dapper, 1924-1938; Thomas Anderson, 1938-1940; Bernard A. Karol, 1940-1947; Oliver J. O'Callaghan, 1947-1952; George A. Stuntebeck, 1952-1958; John H. Ryan, 1958-1963; Donald Hartman, 1963-1965; Charles J. Strelick, 1965-1969; Paul A Schiska, 1969-1971; Louis Wren, OFM, 1971; Wayne Marcotte, 1971-1975; John Shiverski, 1975-1976; Anthony J. Polakowski, 1976-1977; Henry C. Gelin, SJ, 1977-1978; David C. Jenner, 1978-1979; Robert F. Polcyn, 1979-1980; James W. Genovesi, 1980-1984; Canonical Pastor Peter Carli, 1984-1985; Canonical Pastor William Richards, 1985-1988; Canonical Pastor Peter Oberto, 1988-1993; James Scharinger, 1993-1994; Canonical Pastor Gilles Brault, 1994-1999; Sacramental Minister Edward Wenzel, 1999-2000, and Canonical Pastor Msgr. Peter Oberto, 1999-.

IMMACULATE CONCEPTION, MORAN

Immaculate Conception Church in Moran has only held the status of independent parish for about 60 years, not a long time considering that the Catholic faith has had a constant presence in the community since the 1880s.

The village of Moran, located in the south central region of Mackinac County, isn't big, but the territory served by the parish over the years has been large.

Since 1985, Immaculate Conception has been functioning without a resident priest, but it retains its parish status.

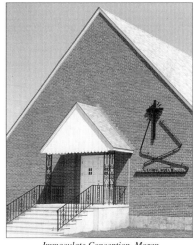

Immaculate Conception, Moran

FOUNDING. The Diocese of Marquette first acquired land for a mission in Moran on March 28, 1888. That year a church was built and dedicated to the Sacred Heart of Mary. Membership at that time totaled just five families, all of German descent.

A new church was built in 1903. Twenty years later that structure was enlarged. Until 1941 the church was a mission, served first by the pastor of St. Ignatius Parish in St. Ignace and also the chaplain of the Ursuline Academy. Later the pastor came from the church in Engadine.

PARISH LIFE. On June 20, 1941, Immaculate Conception was named an independent parish and received its first resident pastor, Father Lester Bourgeois. The territory covered by the parish and the missions assigned to it stretched from the borders of St. Ignatius Parish in St. Ignace to St. Gregory's in Newberry, a distance of 45 miles; and from the borders of St. Joseph's in Rudyard to Lake Michigan, another 35 miles. Of the communities of Trout Lake, Gros Cap, Brevort, Epoufette, Ozark and Strongs, only Trout Lake and Gros Cap had churches of their own. Sacred Heart Mission Church on Gros Cap Road was built in 1918. The church was closed in 1967. Moran was relieved of the responsibilities at Trout Lake in 1986.

The present church in Moran was erected in 1957. The cornerstone was placed on the completed structure on Sept. 22 of that year. Hunters' dinners, bazaars and bingo have been a part of parish life at the church.

Immaculate Conception has been operating without a resident priest since 1985. The pastor serving St. Ignatius Parish in St. Ignace also serves in Moran and the two congregations have a joint parish council.

In 1995 Immaculate Conception reaffirmed its parish status in the religious community of the region by holding a Founder's Day celebration July 15. Festivities included a historical photo display and presentation by parishioners. A commemorative Mass and dinner also took place.

PASTORS.   Fathers Thomas Lester Bourgeois, 1941-1943; James McCarthy, 1943-1946; Charles J. Reinhart, 1946-1949; Gervase Brewer, 1949-1951; John H. Ryan, 1951-1953; Edward Mihelich, 1953-1955; Patrick Frankard, 1955-1960; Donald Hartman, 1960-1963; Kenneth Bretl, 1963-1965; Norbert Landreville, 1965-1969; David Rocheleau, 1970-1973; John Chrobak, 1974-1981; Peter Oberto, 1981-1985; Norbert Landreville, 1985-1986; Raymond Hoefgen, 1986-1991, and C. Michael Rhoades, 1991-.

Sacred Heart, Munising

Sacred Heart, Munising

Founded at the time the community of Munising was begun in 1896, Sacred Heart Church has been an integral part of the spiritual and social life for Catholics there. Parishioners have set expectations high, kept the faith and worked hard to raise money for the upkeep of the original church, the rectory, parochial school and convent.

FOUNDING. The people of Munising welcomed the first pastor, Father Anthony Molinari, in 1896. While the church was being built, Father Molinari offered Mass at Kelly's Hall (later known as the Fraternal Hall). Various fundraising events were held, including special dinners for loggers and their families and other townspeople. The church, of wood construction, had an interior of Collegiate Gothic Style, and was dedicated in the fall of 1897 by Bishop John Vertin. Temporary living quarters in the sacristy were replaced by construction of a rectory in 1898. Later additions to the original church included a choir loft and pipe organ and a church bell imported from Belgium. In the early years quite a variety of both social and spiritual events were held, including bazaars, dances, dinners and a chartered boat outing to Marquette.

PARISH SCHOOL. Acting on the encouragement of Bishop Vertin, Father Joseph Dittman rallied parishioners to support a Catholic school. Construction of an eight-grade school was begun in 1913 and completed just over a year later. Dominican Sisters of Adrian, Mich., staffed the school for 56 years, until it closed in 1970. The sisters were lodged on the top floor of the school, and classes were originally held in the basement and first floor area. A much larger convent, originally designed to be a rectory, was made available by Father Peter Manderfield in 1924.

The number of sisters teaching varied over the years from eight in the beginning until the final years, when six or fewer were available. A decision was made to close the school in 1970, due to decreased enrollment, the need for major safety improvements and fewer sisters available to teach.

When the Catholic school program was discontinued in Munising, the convent and its adjacent property were sold to the Munising public school system. The convent was razed and a playground and bus maintenance garage were erected. The school continued to be used for religious education classes until the early 1980s, when temporary classrooms were constructed in a portion of the basement of the new Sacred Heart Church.

On the morning of April 27, 1933 a spark from the chimney set the Sacred Heart Church on fire. The Blessed Sacrament was removed from the tabernacle, but little else was saved in the blaze, except the sacristy wing, which was later removed from the site. Following the disaster, Mass was first offered in the Delft Theatre and then in the Mather High School auditorium. Excavation for church reconstruction was begun with 55 men doing the work, but the project was abandoned, and the basement of the parish school was converted into a church. Services were held there until the present church building was completed in 1950.

PARISH LIFE. The laying of the cornerstone for the present Sacred Heart Church took place on Sept. 4, 1949. Bishop Thomas L. Noa dedicated the completed structure on June 16, 1950. The new structure was erected on the corner of Elm Avenue and Jewell Street, the site of the original church. A large rose window adorns the main entrance. The inside of the church is of Romanesque design. The facility has a full basement, which is used as a parish hall. In 1966 a new rectory was built. In the 1980s a new southern entrance became a barrier-free, ramped entrance. A Mass of thanksgiving and rededication was held in June of 1980, marking 30 years of the new church.

In 1996 the parish celebrated its centennial. Opening Masses and closing Masses in the summertime drew many parishioners to the area, along with former pastors, women religious and lay teachers of Sacred Heart School. A centennial booklet with a parish history and personal pictures and vignettes was published.

Sacred Heart has enriched the spiritual lives of parishioners through adult education opportunities and had offered a family-oriented religious education program. The Polish-American Society of Munising has sponsored a "Polka Mass" for a number of years.

MISSIONS. Over the past 100 years, pastors from Sacred Heart have cared for the spiritual needs of people living in Shingleton, Cusino, Grand Marais, Au Train, Sand River and Onota. Ministry at Shingleton continued until the 1960s. In 2005 Munising and Au Train were again linked.

PASTORS. Fathers Anthony Molinari, 1896; John Burns, 1897-1898; Henry A. Buchholtz, 1898-1904; John Crocker, 1904-1908; Joseph Ditttman, 1908-1915; Peter Manderfield, 1915-1935; Ovid J. LaMothe, 1935-1946; Gerald Harrington, 1946-1963; Emil Beyer, 1963-1975; Timothy Desrochers, 1975-1977; Vincent Ouellette, 1975-1978; Raymond Moncher, 1978-1997; Dennis Borca, 1997-2004, and Christopher Gardiner, 2004-.

St. Bruno, Nadeau

St. Bruno Parish in Nadeau was established in 1887. By 1904 significant improvements to the church facilities led to its rededication. In addition to fulfilling the spiritual needs of area Catholics, the church was also the hub of recreation in the community. Two missions were started from St. Bruno's and continued until the 1940s. Upgrades to the facilities were also part of the parish's centennial year celebration in 1987.

St. Bruno, Nadeau

FOUNDING. In the spring of 1887, Bruno Nadeau, founder of the area's first sawmill, donated land and building materials for a church in Nadeau. Before 1887, priests from Escanaba, Menominee, Spalding and Stephenson offered Mass in private homes in the area.

The parish's first priest, Father Peter Mazuret, was appointed to the post Sept. 15, 1889. A rectory was built upon Father Mazuret's arrival. In the early- to mid-1890s an addition was put on the church. New pews and stained glass windows were also installed at this time.

During the start of Father Frederick Sperlein's 34-year pastorate at St. Bruno's, a large sacristy was added. The addition also included a basement clubhouse. On Nov. 16, 1904, the extensive improvements to the church were recognized with a rededication of the parish.

Early in his pastorate at St. Bruno's, Father Sperlein also started two mission churches in the rural communities of Gourley and Holmes Township—Saints Peter and Paul and St. Joseph respectively. People of the villages donated the land for the mission churches. These churches closed by the 1940s.

PARISH LIFE. In 1933 St. Bruno's purchased the old Woodman's Hall. The center was the focus of recreation for parishioners, including roller skating events and the annual harvest dinner. The Nadeau Township Schools used the hall for basketball games until the school built its own gymnasium.

Extensive renovations were done to St. Bruno Church from 1937 to 1945. The first floor of the parish hall was excavated, a new roof was put on the church and new Stations of the Cross and new lighting were installed. The late 1940s saw installation of a new heating plant, a new kitchen in the clubhouse and new siding for the church and rectory. A Hammond organ was also purchased.

In 1946 a large granite monument was erected between the church and rectory. The shrine lists the names of the 101 members of the parish enlisted in active military service in World War II.

St. Bruno's celebrated its centennial in 1987. Many improvements were made to the church itself to commemorate the anniversary. Parishioners contributed funds to re-carpet and to add new pews, a new altar and a baptismal font. Two Masses were held to mark the 100th anniversary of the founding of the church. Bishop Mark F. Schmitt presided over one of the special liturgies. The other was a Polka Mass followed by a parish picnic. A centennial booklet was also published to mark the milestone.

PASTORS. Fathers Peter Mazuret, 1889-1891; Joseph A. Sauriol, 1891; Michael Letellier, 1891-1893; Joseph Wallace, 1893; Louis Archille Poulin, 1893-1895; Fabian Pawler, 1895; Anthony Hodnick, 1895; John Burns, 1895-1896; Fabian Marceau, 1896-1898; John Henn, 1898-1901; Peter Manderfield, 1901-1902; Frederick M. Sperlein, 1902-1936; Frank Seifert, 1936; George Stuntebeck, 1936-1937; Joseph Duquette, 1937-1945; Thomas L. Bourgeois 1945-1951; Gino S. Ferraro, 1951-1966; Aloysius E. Ehlinger, 1966-1967; Ralph Sterbentz, 1967-1985; Joseph Polakowski, 1985-1986; Raymond Valerio, 1986-1988; Rick Courier, 1988-1991; Thomas Poisson, 1991-1994; Raymond Zeugner, 1994-1997; Raymond Hoefgen, 1997-2002, and Mathew Perumpally, 2002-.

St. Andrew, Nahma

An independent parish since the late 1940s, St. Andrew Church in Nahma got its start as a mission just prior to the 1900s. The parish later took on the responsibility of caring for other small chapels, including the St. Lawrence Church at Indian Point and the St. Anne Mission at Isabella. Sharing a pastor with Garden and Cooks since the 1990s has allowed St. Andrews to keep its community church. Parishioners have wholeheartedly supported major renovations to their church at the turn of the 21st century.

St. Andrew, Nahma

FOUNDING. The lumbering town of Nahma, located at the mouth of the Sturgeon River, was founded in 1848. The needs of the early settlers were met by traveling missionaries. Later, priests from Rapid River and sometimes Garden would offer Mass in the schoolhouse.

By 1905 a parcel of land was leased and the men of the parish banded together to construct a church. St. Andrew's was completed and dedicated May 16, 1906, by Bishop Frederick Eis. The church was enlarged and a sanctuary and two sacristies were added. In 1926 a rectory was added adjacent to the church.

PARISH LIFE. During World War I, St. Andrew's was a mission of St. Mary Magdalene Parish in Cooks. Then, in 1920 responsibility for the care of the Nahma parish was given to the pastor of St. John the Baptist Parish in Garden.

St. Andrew's became an independent parish in 1947. Father Jerome Larsen was named the first resident priest. On Feb. 1, 1952 the Bay de Noquet Lumber Co., which owned much of the town, deeded the church property to the Diocese of Marquette.

In the 1940s the Adrian Dominicans housed at the Marygrove Retreat Center in Garden taught weekly catechism classes in Nahma.

The first major improvements to the church since 1952 came under the pastorate of Father John Martignon (1995-2002). The church was made handicapped accessible, an addition with a larger gathering space and restroom was constructed, and the interior of the building was renovated and redecorated. A rededication was held in August 2001 upon the completion of the project.

In 1991 St. Andrew's was linked with St. Mary Magdalene of Cooks and St. John's in Garden and became known as the Garden Area Catholic Churches.

MISSIONS. St. Anne Mission at Isabella was founded in the early 1900s by Father Sebastian Maier. The mission was entrusted to the care of St. Andrew Parish in 1953. Prior to that time, priests from Rapid River, Cooks and Garden served the people of St. Anne's. The church was closed canonically in 1982, but use as a chapel continued until 1990. Official closure came in January 1991.

St. Lawrence's Indian Mission, formerly located on the shore of Ogontz Bay at Indian Point in Nahma Township, was started by Jesuit missionaries in the late 1800s. Church services were held once a month in the spring, summer and fall. The church was closed during the winter months. As many as 40 to 50 parishioners are said to have attended services offered in the Chippewa language. The Jesuits took care of the religious services at St. Lawrence for much of its existence. During the 1960s Father Michael Hale of Nahma offered Mass on Sunday afternoons. When Father Hale was transferred, services were no longer offered.

St. Andrew's had also cared for the St. James Mission at St. Jacques until the 1940s when the church ceased to exist.

PASTORS. Fathers E. Nayl, 1910-1913; Sebastian Maier, 1913-1927; Vincent Savogeau, 1916-1934; Nolan McKevitt, 1940-1944; James Donnelly, 1942-1943; Joseph Kichak, 1943-1944; Ralph Sterbentz, 1944-1947; Jerome Larsen, 1947-1949; Thomas Andary, 1951; Gervase J. Brewer, 1951-1953; John Ryan, 1953-1958; Michael Hale, 1958-1963; James Hebein, 1967-1968; Donald Hartman, 1968-1969; Ephraem Sitko, 1969-1978; Frank Lenz, 1978-1982; Peter Minelli, 1982-1984; Ronald Skufca, 1984-1986; John Martignon, 1986-1988; Ronald Timock, 1988-1990; Peter Petroske, 1990-1991; George Maki, 1991-1993; David Sedlock, 1993-1996; John Martignon, 1996-2002, and Thomas Joseph Varickamackal, 2002-.

NATIVE AMERICAN MISSIONS

Christianity was brought to Michigan in 1641 by Jesuit missionary Father Isaac Jogues. The dedicated men of the order maintained a unique relationship with the Native Americans of the Upper Peninsula throughout the 20th century.

St. James, Hannahville

Traveling an average 25,000 miles per year from one mission to the next, the Jesuits went to incredible lengths to offer the Holy Sacrifice of the Mass, instruction in the catechism and sacramental preparation to the Native Americans. The missionaries made personal visits to the natives' homes, provided Catholic literature and took other steps to encourage the people's faith in the Catholic Church.

Where churches were established the buildings were often simple. In regions where the Indians lived and there was no church, the missionaries visited when possible and encouraged them to attend parish churches in neighboring areas.

The Diocese of Marquette helped to support the work of the missionaries financially and otherwise. But the availability of priests, changing assignments for the missionaries, and ease in getting to other churches resulted in the closure of many of the Native American missions. A listing of missions for which a record exists follows:

Sacred Heart, Baie de Wasai; St. Catherine, Bay Mills (became a diocesan church); St. Catherine, Brimley (became a diocesan church); St. Florence, Drummond Island (became a diocesan church); Our Lady of the Way, Eckerman; St. James, Hannahville; St. Lawrence, Indian Point; St. Aloysius, Neebish Island; Holy Angels, Payment; St. Isaac Jogues, Sault Ste. Marie (became a diocesan church); Sacred Heart, Stonington; Sacred Heart, Sugar Island (became a diocesan church); Immaculate Conception, Watersmeet (became a diocesan church); Saints John and Ann, Wilwalk; St. Catherine, Zeba (became a diocesan church).

St. Paul, Negaunee

One distinction of St. Paul's Church in Negaunee is that four of the priests who served there later became bishops. The first consecration of a bishop in the Upper Peninsula took place at the Negaunee church, and the first priest of the diocese to be named a monsignor was a pastor serving at St. Paul's.

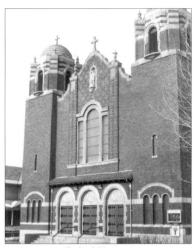

St. Paul, Negaunee

FOUNDING. Bishop Frederic Baraga founded St. Paul Church in 1861. The original church was located on the corner of Case Street and Brown Avenue. Prior to its founding, Negaunee was a mission of St. Peter Cathedral in Marquette. Priests from Sault Ste. Marie are known to have ministered to Catholics living in Negaunee as far back as 1853.

As Negaunee's mining industry saw rapid growth, a larger church was needed. Construction of a new building at the site of the current church was completed in 1871.

On April 25, 1919 a fire destroyed the church and rectory. Despite heroic efforts by the fire department and the townspeople, little could be saved. Reports say high winds caused the fire to spread and the roofs of several nearby buildings caught fire from its embers.

For two years, while plans were made to erect a new church, Mass was said at the Adelphi Roller Rink and in the Negaunee Fire Hall.

Dedication of the new church took place on Saturday, Jan. 30, 1921. The people of the parish held numerous benefits to raise money for the new church. Many pledged money for statues and windows. A large portion of the church was paid for through mineral royalty funds collected from the mining company.

PARISH SCHOOL. For nearly a century the people of St. Paul Parish also supported a parochial school.

The Sisters of St. Joseph, of Carondelet, Mo., arrived in Negaunee in 1882 and ran the school for 93 years until it closed in 1975. The first school building consisted of four classrooms.

In 1932, a new grade school, high school and convent were built. The grade school opened that year and the high school followed two years later. In the fall of 1934 there were only freshmen, and a new class was added each successive year. In 1938, St. Paul's saw its first graduates, a class of 19.

In 1966 the high school was closed. Continued declining enrollment at the elementary school and the financial burden on the parish led to its demise in 1975.

An all-school reunion saw the return of some 600 former pupils of St. Paul's to the Negaunee Ice Arena July 11, 1998. A commemorative Mass, dinner and dance were held to honor the heritage of the school.

MISSIONS. A priest from Negaunee regularly ministered in the homes of people living in Champion until a church was built there in 1871. The spiritual needs of the people in what is now Gwinn were also first met by a visiting priest from Negaunee. It is recorded that pastors from Negaunee would take a train to the settlement known as Old Swanzy, then travel by stagecoach to various locations around mines, sawmills and railroads, ministering to the people. Our Lady of Perpetual Help Mission church in Palmer is still served by Negaunee.

PARISH LIFE. Parishioners served the church through participation in many organizations. One group unique to St. Paul's was the St. Paul's Players, a dramatic society that performed many plays in the St. Paul's Auditorium during the 1930s. During World War II the group was inactive, but was revived in the 1950s and 1960s.

In observance of St. Paul's centennial in 1961, parishioners donated $30,000 for renovations to the church. Rewiring, new lighting, repainting, the addition of a mothers room off the sanctuary, and a baptistry with a font to match the altars completed the project.

In 1984, the St. Paul Concert Choir was started. The group began with 26 members, mainly people from the parish. Six of the existing members have been in every concert since its beginning. The choir now averages 65 members and has become an ecumenical group with participants coming from surrounding communities.

Many of the priests who served St. Paul's went on to become monsignors and bishops. Bishops Ignatius Mrak, John Vertin, Frederick Eis, all of the Diocese of Marquette, and Bishop John N. Starika of the Diocese of South Dakota all served as pastors or assistants at St. Paul's. Bishop Vertin was the first to be consecrated bishop in the U.P. The consecration took place in Negaunee. Father Charles Langner, who served as pastor at the Negaunee church for 22 years, was the first priest in the diocese to be named a monsignor.

PASTORS. Fathers Honoratus Burion, 1861-1871; John B. Vertin, 1871-1879; Frederick Eis, 1880-1890; Charles Langner, 1890-1912; Henry A. Buchholtz, 1912-1915; Joseph F. Dittman, 1915-1951; Joseph Zryd, 1951-1955; Robert J. Cordy, 1955-1970; Frank Hollenbach, 1970-1973; co-pastor William Russell, 1972-1973; co-pastor William Richards, 1973-1977; Charles Olivier, 1975-1995; co-pastor Peter Carli, 1977-1980, and John Shiverski, 1995-.

ST. GREGORY, NEWBERRY

For more than 100 years St. Gregory Parish has been a steady pillar in the Newberry community. Parishioners and area residents have built three churches and a parish school, and the parish has served the Newberry State Hospital and the mission church of Our Lady of Victory in Paradise. St. Gregory's was home to the Diocese of Marquette's first permanent deacon.

FOUNDING. Priests from St. Ignace first served settlers in the lumbering town of Newberry. The men would make the 55-mile journey on foot to offer Mass in the public schoolhouse.

St. Gregory, Newberry

Finally, in August 1886, Father John G. Manning arrived to build a church. This undertaking was accomplished in just five months. The first Mass was said on Christmas Day that year. However, six weeks later, just before the church was dedicated, the structure was destroyed by fire. Thanks to the firefighting efforts of the townspeople the rectory was saved. With deep determination the people completed construction of a second church just four months later. The church was to be dedicated to St. Gregory Nazianzen on June 19, 1887.

At that time the pastor of St. Gregory's was also responsible for the care of missions in Seney, Naubinway, Germfask and Rappinville.

PARISH LIFE. After several years of hard work, sacrifice and anticipation by parishioners, Bishop Thomas L. Noa blessed the cornerstone for a new church July 5, 1950. The new structure, of Gothic style, was built on the corner of Harrie and Robinson streets. On May 9, 1951, the feast of St. Gregory, the last Mass was offered at the church and dedication of a new edifice took place. The basement of the church was designed with an auditorium and stage, a kitchen area, restrooms and storage facilities. The mid-1950s and early 1960s brought renovations to the rectory and interior decoration of the church and parish hall.

St. Gregory's was responsible for the care of the Newberry State Hospital. The mission of Our Lady of Victory was built in Paradise in 1944 and since then has been attached to St. Gregory's.

Starting in 1977, teenagers from Cedarville and Manistique joined young people at St. Gregory's for Youth Enrichment Weekends.

St. Gregory's was blessed to be the home parish of the Diocese of

Marquette's first permanent deacon, Dean Hermann. Deacon Hermann was ordained June 18, 1981 by Bishop Mark Schmitt.

In 1986 St. Gregory Parish celebrated its centennial. To commemorate the anniversary, the parish published a lengthy book of church and community history.

PARISH SCHOOL. On Nov. 8, 1940, St. Gregory's Catechetical School opened under the leadership of Sisters of St. Dominic, Congregation of the Holy Rosary in Adrian, Mich. The women's service continued in Newberry for 30 years.

The success of the catechetical school illustrated the need for a parochial school, which got under way with a fund drive in 1959. A total of 177 parishioners pledged $79,000. Construction of the school was completed and dedication took place Sept. 11, 1960. After 10 years of operation, financial struggles, low enrollment and the loss of women religiousas teachers, the school was forced to close.

PASTORS. Fathers John G. Manning, 1886-1889; Joseph R. Boissonnault, 1889-1890; John Reichenbach, 1890; Fidelis Sutter, 1890-1891; Joseph Haas, 1891-1892; Philip Erlach, 1892-1893; John Chebul, 1893-1896; Joseph L. Hollinger, 1896-1899; Frederick Glaser, 1899-1901; J. S. Hawelka, 1901; Renatus Becker, 1901-1902; Martin C. Sommer, 1902-1905; Joseph F. Dittman, 1905-1907; Augustus Geers, 1907-1917; Bernard Eiling, 1917-1936; Philip de Neri Jutras, 1936-1939; Joseph Beauchene, 1939-1940; Francis Scheringer, 1940-1942; Joseph Duford, 1942-1946; Robert Cordy, 1946-1951; Emil Beyer, 1951-1963; Aloysius Ehlinger, 1963-1966; Raymond Moncher, 1966; Dominic Zadra, 1966; Wilbur M. Gibbs, 1966-1971; Paul A. Schiska, 1971-1976; Raymond Hoefgen, 1976-1984; Peter Minelli, 1984-1986; James Williams, 1986-1990; N. Daniel Rupp, 1990-1995; George Maki, 1995-2001, and Paul Karottekunnel, MST, 2001-.

St. Joseph Mission, Northland

The mission of St. Joseph in Northland has been under the administration of several parishes throughout the years. Responsibility for the small church, whose territory spans 25 miles, has gone from Flat Rock to Escanaba to Perronville, Gwinn, Channing and, since 1991, back to Gwinn. The one thing that has remained consistent, however, is the will of the people from Cornell to Rock to see their parish through the changes.

St. Joseph Mission, Northland

FOUNDING. In the beginning of the 1900s, Catholic men working in lumbering camps near Cornell and Ralph were first visited irregularly by priests from St. Joseph Parish in Escanaba, then from Bark River.

An attempt to start a church at Northland was first made in 1907 by Father A. A. Vissers. His effort, however, failed. In 1913, Father Joseph Beauchene, pastor at Flat Rock, erected a church using lumber from the previous attempt.

The parish did not want to incur debt, and so the work went along at the pace donations were collected. Since 1908 the women of the parish have banded together to raise money for the parish through socials, bake sales, and in 1910 the first picnic.

In 1915 services were moved from the village school to the new church and the parish was dedicated to St. Joseph. Pews were purchased in 1917 and the next year, a bell.

PARISH LIFE. Although the church had been completed, Mass was offered only occasionally. Since 1949 services have been offered every Sunday.

The priest from Flat Rock continued to serve until 1926 when the mission was turned over to St. Anne's Church in Escanaba. In 1937 it was joined to Foster City. From 1981 to 1991 St. Joseph's was a mission of St. Rose in Channing. Since 1991, St. Anthony of Gwinn has been responsible for St. Joseph's.

A small number of dedicated parishioners have supported regular maintenance and improvements to the church. In 1946, the entire church was raised and a basement added. In 1949, after 35 years of not being refurbished, the interior was redone using knotty pine. In 1952, with the support of parishioners to raise the necessary funds, a new heating plant and cushioned pews were installed, and the exterior of the church was sided.

In 1997, a new covered front entrance and glass doors were added. In 1998 the floors were refinished and new carpeting was installed. In 1999 the interior was completely renovated. The integrity of the style of the original church built in 1910 was preserved.

RECORDS. The records for the mission of St. Joseph, Northland are kept at St. Anthony Parish in Gwinn.

PASTORS. Fathers Arnold Vissers, 1907-1911; Joseph Beauchene, 1912-1918; Francis Geynet, 1918-1926; George LaForest, 1926-1927; Anthony Waechter, 1927-1937; Francis Krystyniak, 1937-1940; Raymond Przbylski, 1940-1947; Frank Gimski, 1947-1948; Gabriel Waraxa, 1948-1951; Conrad Suda, 1950-1963; Raymond Smith, 1963-1968; Walter Franczek, 1968-1970; Emmett Norden, 1970-1973; Raymond Hoefgen, 1973-1976; Raymond Zeugner, 1976-1978; George Pernaski, 1978-1981; Raymond Valerio, 1981-1983; Raymond Zeugner, 1983-1985; Christopher Gardiner, 1985-1991; Robert Paruleski, 1991; David Jenner, 1991-1998, and Ronald Timock, 1998-.

ST. MARY, NORWAY

St. Mary, Norway

St. Mary's Parish in Norway was started as a mission of Quinnesec in 1878. In the beginning the stability of the church and of the new community wavered on the fortunes of the mining industry. But after a permanent church was built in the late 1920s and maintained throughout the years, and a still vital parochial school started in the 1960s, parishioners had a firm foundation that has faithfully carried them into the 21st century.

FOUNDING. Operations at the Norway Mine were booming in the late 1870s and Father Hilary J. Rosseau of nearby Quinnesec had begun offering Mass in private homes in the growing new community. By May 1880 a mission church, Santa Maria Immaculata, and rectory were built on a large piece of land overlooking the town of Norway.

The first parishioners were of English, French, Belgian and Polish descent and traveled to St. Mary's from Loretto, Waucedah, Vulcan, New York Farm and Sturgeon Mill areas.

The Franciscan Sisters of Alverno, Wis., opened the first parochial school in Norway in 1888. The work was taken up by the Sisters of St. Joseph of Concordia, Kan., from 1895 to 1902, when the school closed.

In the early 1900s major improvements were made to the church, including lengthening the structure 40 feet to accommodate the growing membership. Parishioners and friends of the church donated beautiful stained glass windows, many statues and the main and side altars. Religious organizations, such as the St. Anne's Society, The Knights of Columbus and the St. John the Baptist Society, flourished in the parish during this time.

PARISH LIFE. In 1928, a new church was constructed at 401 Main St. The pews, windows and altars from the original church were among the items incorporated into the new structure. The original church, rectory and schoolhouse were sold and razed and the proceeds used for construction of the new church. The women of the parish are also credited with raising money for the endeavor. Bishop Paul J. Nussbaum dedicated the new church St. Mary in November 1929.

The large basement hall was renovated in 1949. The present rectory was built in 1952 and enlarged in 1965.

A capital campaign begun in 1998 netted the necessary funds to fully restore the exterior of the church and to make it a barrier-free structure. A new parking lot was developed, elevator installed, new sidewalks and railings created and landscaping improvements were made. Plans were then set in place to make the necessary upgrades to the interior of the church.

In 1983 the parish traditions of a spring fling and a summer outdoor Mass and picnic at Marion Park were started.

The parish boasts of the many men and women who have pursued religious vocations and become priests and sisters.

PARISH SCHOOL. In 1964, as plans were under way to start a new school, St. Mary's made history by holding the first Catholic school board election in the United States. Five board members were elected through secret ballot, making headlines across the country, including coverage through the Associated Press.

In June 1965, permission was granted to build Holy Spirit Central School, a cooperative effort of the Norway, Vulcan and Loretto parishes. A solemn dedication of the structure took place May 14, 1967. The Missionary Sisters of the Holy Spirit staffed the school through July 1988. The school has been staffed by lay people since then.

PASTORS. Fathers Hilary J. Rosseau, 1878-1881; Lucas Mozina, 1881-1882; Ignatius Mrak, 1882; Mathias Orth, 1882-1883; John Brown, 1883; Martin Kehoe, 1883-1890; John Chebul, 1890-1891; John Reynaert, 1891-1892; John Henn, 1892-1893; Augustus W. Geers, 1893-1894; Francis X. Becker, 1894-1900; William H. Joisten, 1900-1916; Joseph Hollinger, 1916-1922; Edward Feldhaus, 1922-1926; Erasmus Dooley, 1926-1937; George Stuntebeck, 1937-1938; Erasmus Dooley, 1938-1948; Sebastian Maier, 1948-1963; O'Neil C. D'Amour, 1964-1966; Elmer Bares, 1966-1981; William G. Richards, 1981-1985; Peter J. Carli, 1985-1992; Arnold Grambow, 1992-1996, and Mark McQuesten, 1996-.

Holy Family, Ontonagon

In the course of its 150-year-history, parishioners of Holy Family Parish in Ontonagon have worshiped in several different church buildings. The modern church was constructed in the late 1950s. The 25-year pastorates of three priests helped to maintain a steady faith.

Holy Family, Ontonagon

FOUNDING. Bishop Frederic Baraga sent Father Lawrence Dunne to construct a church in Ontonagon in 1854.

Upon Father Dunne's reassignment in 1858, the Ontonagon church became a mission of St. Mary Parish in Rockland. Twenty-seven years later, in 1885, Father Joseph Haas was assigned resident pastor of the Ontonagon church. It has been an independent parish ever since.

Parishioners replaced the original church with a grander structure on the south side of the city in 1894. This church was dedicated to the Holy Family. A disastrous fire swept through Ontonagon Aug. 25, 1896. The church, along with 340 other buildings, was destroyed. A third church was dedicated in 1897.

PARISH LIFE. School Sisters of Notre Dame taught a catechetical school from 1945 to 1952. Felician Sisters carried on the work until the 1990s.

A new Holy Family Church was constructed on Michigan Avenue in 1958. Stained glass windows from the old church were installed. A later update to the facility was remodeling of the entryway. In 1989 the bell was restored.

PASTORS. Fathers Lawrence Dunne, 1854-1858; Patrick Moyce, 1858; Martin Fox, 1858-1868; Henry Thiele, 1868-1871; Edward Jacker, 1871-1872; Oliver Comtois, 1872-1873; Anthony Hubly, 1874-1878; William Dwyer, 1878-1882; Charles Dries, 1882-1883; Charles Langner, 1883-1884; Anacletus Pelisson, 1884-1885; Joseph Haas, 1885-1886; Joseph Barron, 1886-1887; Gideon Beliveau, 1887-1888; John Chebul, 1888-1889; John Henn, 1889-1890; Julius Baron Von Gumpenberg, 1890; Joseph Boever, 1890-1892; Philip Erlach, 1892-1893; John Burns,1892; Joseph Neumair, 1892-1895; Renatus Becker, 1895-1898; James Corcoran, 1898-1899; William Shea, 1899-1902; Joseph Hollinger, 1902-1907; Adam Doser, 1907-1920; Joseph Lamotte, 1920-1923; Owen Bennett, 1923-1954; Charles Herbst, 1954-1971; David Harris, 1971-1995; John Longbucco, 1995-2002; Abraham Kazhunadiyil, 2002-2004; Thomas J. Thekkel, 2005, and Antony Lukose, 2005-.

SACRED HEART MISSION, PAINESDALE

Enthusiastic Catholics in Painesdale took it upon themselves to petition the bishop for a resident pastor. When the Painesdale church was destroyed by fire in 1952, the people rallied to rebuild in just three months. Upon the 1997 closure of the mission, parishioners joined in the faith community at South Range.

Sacred Heart Mission, Painesdale

FOUNDING. Sacred Heart Church was founded in 1905 and served by Father Frederick Richter of Atlantic Mine. He assisted the people in securing their own church.

PARISH LIFE. The population steadily increased and the Painesdale parishioners became restless for a priest of their own. A committee of men banded together and took a petition with 900 signatures to Bishop Frederick Eis. The first resident priest, Father Stanislaus Rogosz, arrived on Sept. 1, 1913.

On Saturday mornings, the young people of Sacred Heart received catechism instruction from the Sisters of St. Agnes serving St. Ignatius Parish in Houghton.

On March 2, 1952, the Painesdale church was leveled by fire. In just three months a new church was erected on the original foundation, and was dedicated July 13, 1952.

CLOSURE. As a result of the diocesan pastoral planning initiative in 1995, Sacred Heart Church was closed on July 1, 1997. Parishioners were encouraged to attend the Holy Family Parish in South Range.

RECORDS. Sacred Heart records are at St. Anne Church in Chassell.

PASTORS. Fathers Frederick Richter, 1905-1913; Stanislaus Rogosz, 1913-1915; Stanislaus Jaksztys, 1915-1918; Joseph Henn, 1918; Alphonse Kozlowski, 1918-1925; Paul Weissmann, OFM, 1925-1928; Edmund Krystiniak; OFM, 1928-1930; Jordan Black, CP, 1930-1932; Peter McGuire, CP, 1932-1937; Stephen Wloszcnski, 1937-1943; James J. Schaefer, 1943-1946; Norbert Freiburger, 1946-1951; John Belot, 1951-1958; John Suhr, 1958-1963; Howard Drolet, 1963-1964; Wilfrid Pelletier, 1964; Thomas Coleman, 1965-1967; James Hebein, 1965-1967; Francis Hollenbach, 1967-1976; Raymond Smith, 1976-1996, and Bede Louzon, OFM Cap., 1996-1997.

Our Lady of Perpetual Help Mission, Palmer

Our Lady of Perpetual Help in Palmer has always been a mission of St. Paul Church in Negaunee. Palmer parishioners are eager to step up and meet the challenges that come with not having a resident pastor. The people continually make their presence known by participating in diocesan endeavors, such as the role they played in the Jubilee Year 2000 celebrations held in Marquette.

Our Lady of Perpetual Help Mission, Palmer

FOUNDING. Father Charles Langner included Palmer among his outreach efforts when he was assigned to St. Paul's in 1890. Through the mid-1930s, Mass was offered in private homes and the schoolhouse once or twice per month. The Sisters of St. Joseph, of Carondelet, Mo., serving in Negaunee, also taught catechism in people's homes.

In 1936, under the direction of Father Matt LaViolette, an old barbershop was rented and remodeled for use as Our Lady of Perpetual Help's first church. The Ishpeming Knights of Columbus financed the project.

Then, in 1938, as Palmer's population was rapidly increasing, the people took up the work of building a church. A local resident donated the lot and, a member of the parish drew up the plans for the church and was put in charge of the building project. Men of the church did the excavation work by hand and on Labor Day, 1940, the first concrete was poured.

Work on the building was started in the spring of 1941. The interior was completed and an additional lot next to the church was purchased. Donations to the church included Stations of the Cross, a tabernacle, monstrance, candlesticks and a sanctuary lamp. In May 1942, the first Mass was said in the basement of the church. Bishop Francis J. Magner presided over the dedication ceremony held Oct. 25 of that year.

PARISH LIFE. Members of the parish attended their church's dedication ceremony, proud of the fact that no debt had been accumulated. All of the labor was donated. The women of the parish held bazaars and sold an estimated 20,000 pasties to raise money for the project.

In subsequent years, the people's dedication continued. New pews were purchased, the exterior of the church was painted, and the interior renovated to accommodate changes in the celebration of the liturgy brought about by the Second Vatican Council. In 1961 a new organ was purchased. Stained glass windows were installed in 1962. Since that time, many additions and alterations have occurred. Recently, new kitchen cabinets and countertops were put in place.

Due to a shortage of priests in the diocese, Our Lady of Perpetual Help has been served by a lay pastoral associate since 1984. Weekly Mass is still offered.

On Aug. 4, 1991 a yearlong, 50th anniversary celebration was begun with Mass celebrated by Bishop Mark F. Schmitt and the dedication of a new statue for the alcove.

The parish is proud of its participation in the diocese's celebration of the Jubilee Year 2000. Members of Our Lady of Perpetual Help's choir and two of its cantors took part in the diocesan-wide confirmation celebration held at the Superior Dome in Marquette. Parishioners also constructed the staging for an outdoor Mass held at Marquette's Lower Harbor Park and one of its younger members served as lector.

PASTORS. Fathers Joseph Dittman, 1915-1951; Joseph Zryd, 1951-1955; Robert Cordy, 1955-1970; Frank Hollenbach, 1970-1973; co-pastor William Russell, 1972-1973; co-pastor William Richards, 1973-1977; Charles Olivier, 1975-1995; co-pastor Peter Carli, 1977-1980, and John Shiverski, 1995-.

Our Lady of Victory Mission, Paradise

Our Lady of Victory in Paradise was founded as a mission of Newberry more than 50 years ago. Parishioners of the small, rural church continue to support its daily operation. The people succeeded in building an addition on the original structure, then later building an entirely new church following a 1994 fire. The people are steadfast in their will to keep the Catholic faith alive in the community.

Our Lady of Victory Mission, Paradise

FOUNDING. Our Lady of Victory Mission in Paradise was established in 1944. Before that time Jesuit missionaries served Catholics in the area. Father Raymond Przybylski of Sault Ste. Marie said Mass at Shelldrake, located midway between Paradise and Whitefish Point.

In the beginning, priests made the 50-mile trip from Newberry on the first and third Sundays of the month in the summer, and in the winter, only once a month. In its first years, the parish had a membership of 10 families and 20 single persons.

Paradise and Newberry area residents donated much of the funding and labor for construction of the original church. The 35-mile territory of the parish stretches from Eckerman to Whitefish Point.

PARISH LIFE. From 1944 to 1976, priests from Newberry served the mission, which is located in a grove of birches just outside the village of Paradise. In 1976, care of Our Lady of Victory was transferred to St. Francis Xavier Parish in Brimley. Newberry again took up responsibility for the mission in 1991.

Along with receiving religious education instruction from the dedicated laity of the church, young people of Our Lady of Victory also attended summer sessions with the Sisters of St. Dominic serving in Newberry, who traveled to Paradise.

Improvements made to the original church included new pews and a confessional in 1956 and a new roof in 1974. On March 12, 1994 fire destroyed an addition that had been constructed on the rear of the church. The sanctuary received significant smoke damage, but parishioners were able to restore the church proper for use until a decision could be made regarding its future.

Later that year, the people held a grand celebration commemorating the 50th anniversary of the founding of Our Lady of Victory. Bishop James Garland, along with several other priests of the diocese, concelebrated a jubilee Mass Nov. 27, 1994. A reception followed in the community center.

Finally, on Dec. 19, 1998, the mission celebrated its first Mass in a new church building. Constructed on the same grounds, the old church was not torn down until the new one was ready for use. The new structure includes a sacristy, confessional, a partition that allows for additional seating and a kitchen area. Much of the furnishings for the new church, including the pews, Stations of the Cross, tabernacle and statues, were donated by other Catholic churches in the diocese.

The Parish Council and Altar Society work hard to support the church and make necessary improvements to the building and grounds. Parish socials include an annual Christmas decorating event and participation in the local blueberry festival in August.

PASTORS. Fathers Joseph Duford, 1944-1946; Robert Cordy, 1946-1951; Emil Beyer, 1951-1963; Aloysius E. Ehlinger, 1963-1966; Raymond Moncher, 1966; Dominic Zadra, 1966; Wilbur M. Gibbs, 1966-1971; Paul A. Schiska, 1971-1976; Joseph Francis Rausch, 1978-1985; Raymond Mulhern, 1985-1989; Robert Paruleski, 1989-1991; N. Daniel Rupp, 1991-1995; George Maki, 1995-2001, and Paul Karottekunnel, MST, 2001-.

St. Joseph, Perkins

St. Joseph, Perkins

The 35-year pastorate of Father Alphonse Coignard left a lasting impact on St. Joseph parishioners in Perkins. His leadership in building a new church and his services to other missions started a tradition of service that is being carried on nearly 100 years after the birth of the parish.

FOUNDING. Between 1860 and 1880, priests from Gladstone and Escanaba visited Perkins twice each year, in the fall and in the spring, offering Mass and administering the sacraments.

In 1901 the men of the community built the first church, a wooden structure located about one mile south of Perkins. The first resident pastor arrived in 1905.

In the early 1900s, priests from St. Joseph Parish served the missions of Rock, Trombley, Osier, Brampton and St. Thomas.

In 1923 St. Joseph Parish had a new brick church constructed in the center of the town. The structure was erected without incurring any debt.

PARISH LIFE. During his 35-year pastorate, from 1916 to 1951, Father Coignard made great progress both in the spiritual and material welfare of the church. Father Coignard's knowledge of medicine benefited the people as well, especially during a flu epidemic in 1919 and 1920, when he treated people of all denominations who were unable to see a doctor.

Parish organizations, such as the Holy Name Society established in 1911, and the St. Ann's Society started in 1916, continue to be active. A Catholic Youth Organization and the Third Order of St. Francis were started in the early 1950s.

Improvements to the facilities in the 1970s included construction of a pavilion and new church entrance, renovation of the rectory and church redecorating.

PASTORS. Fathers Paul N. Fillion, 1905-1909; George LaForest, 1909-1912; Edward J. Testevin, 1912-1916; Alphonse C. Coignard, 1916-1951; Charles O'Neil D'Amour, 1951; Charles Daniel, 1951-1954; Edward Malloy, 1954-1968; Conrad Suda, 1968-1971; Wayne Marcotte, 1971; Edward Wenzel, 1971-1972; Walter Franczek, 1972-1986; Gilbert Neurohr, 1986-1987; Walter Sheedlo, 1987-1992; Allan Mayotte, 1992-1995; Joseph Nagaroor, 1995-1997; Antony Nirappel, 1997-1999; Emmett Norden, 1999-2003, and Jacek Wtyklo 2003-.

St. Michael, Perronville

St. Michael, Perronville

The founding of St. Michael Parish in Perronville goes back to 1911 when the first Polish-speaking priests began offering Mass on a regular basis. A couple of makeshift churches followed until 1921 when the people finally had their own permanent church. Through the years parishioners worked diligently to improve the church and raise funds to support it. Among their successful ventures was a 1940s drama group that performed across the country earning money for the parish.

FOUNDING. From 1911 to 1912 Father Valentine Chrobok of Iron River offered monthly Mass and religious education at the LaBranch School Hall. The first Mass in Perronville was offered in a private home in 1912. Before that time, the English settlers attended Mass in Bark River and the French in Schaffer. The nearest Polish Church was in Birch Creek.

In 1915 Menazipe Perron, for whom the village is named, donated land for a church. At first a horse barn on the property was used as a church, and then one of the cabins. Mass in the cabin church was so crowded that children sat on the steps leading to the attic. In May 1919, the first resident pastor was appointed and Perron donated land south of the Ten Mile Creek for a cemetery.

The log cabin church was replaced by a former hall owned by the Ford River Lumber Co. The hall was dismantled and the lumber brought to Perronville. A church measuring 20 feet by 40 feet, including a small sacristy, was set up. It was dedicated to St. Michael.

In September 1921, before the church was even completed, it burned to the ground. However, with the insurance money and donations from the people, the parish began work on a new structure. Parishioners donated much of the labor. They dug the basement by hand and worked through the winter to complete the project.

PARISH LIFE. When Father Thomas Drengacz arrived in Perronville in October 1923, the church was unfinished but already in use. He led efforts to finish the work. In 1926 a gasoline generating plant was installed in the basement of the church. The plant also provided electricity for the streetlights of the town.

Father Drengacz became very involved in parish and community affairs. He introduced the "Macierz Polska" (Polish Alma Mater Society). He organized troupes of players who performed throughout the country raising money for the parish, which was especially needed during the Depression; he formed baseball teams in Perronville and Foster City, and he started a successful barter market.

From 1924 to 1936, the Franciscan Sisters of Blessed Cunegunda in Chicago came to teach religion during summer vacation. The Dominican Sisters from Racine, Wis., took over teaching the children and continued to do so until 1952. In 1952 the Franciscan Sisters of Manitowoc, Wis., from St. Anne's Church in Escanaba, took over in Perronville.

From 1936 to 1953, many improvements were made to the church, thanks to the generosity and hard work of parishioners. In 1939 extensive remodeling took place. In 1949 the basement was made into a hall. Also in 1949, a farmhouse was purchased for use as the first rectory. In October 1954 the church was moved next to the rectory. A new cemetery was plotted in 1957.

In June 1944, the first raffle and picnic were held. Money collected allowed the parish to be debt-free for the first time. The tradition of the picnic carried on into the 21st century.

In August 1961, the parish celebrated 50 years of faith-filled devotion. "Old Settlers Day" consisted of a Solemn High Mass followed by a picnic and a day of games. The church was again remodeled to commemorate the anniversary and an extensive booklet of parish history was produced.

MISSIONS. Priests of St. Michael's began serving the missions of Foster City in 1923 and Northland in 1936.

MERGER. In 1995 St. Michael's merged with St. George Parish in Bark River and Sacred Heart Parish in Schaffer to form the new parish of St. Elizabeth Ann Seton. The merger was part of the diocese's Fully Alive in '95 pastoral planning initiative. The Perronville church building remains in use with regular Saturday Mass.

RECORDS. The records of St. Michael Parish are located at St. Elizabeth Ann Seton Parish in Bark River.

PASTORS. Fathers John F. Kulczyk, 1919; Valentine Chrobok, 1919-1921; Francis Ignatz, 1921-1923; Thomas Drengacz, 1923-1936; Francis Krystyniak, 1936-1940; Raymond Przybylski, 1940-1947; Frank Gimski, 1947-1948; Gabriel Waraxa, 1948-1951; Conrad Suda, 1951-1963; Raymond J. Smith, 1963-1968; August Franczek, 1968-1970; Emmett M. Norden, 1970-1973; Raymond Hoefgen, 1973-1976; Raymond Zeugner, 1976-1981; Donald Hartman, 1981-1983; N. Daniel Rupp, 1983-1988; Paul J. Nomellini, 1988-1993, and Alexander K. Sample, 1993-1995.

ST. MARY MISSION, QUINNESEC

St. Mary Mission, Quinnesec

Called the "mother church" of the Dickinson area, St. Mary's in Quinnesec was the first church in the county. However, many of the early priests who came to serve there left after a short time to minister in the new parishes of neighboring communities.

Through the decades, the mission was placed under the guidance of several different parishes. Despite many hardships and sacrifices, the people of St. Mary's persevered and remained in their parish community until the church was closed in 1995.

FOUNDING. Father Martin Fox built the modest church of St. Mary's in Quinnesec in 1877. The parish offered Mass every Sunday, but retaining a resident priest was not easy because the surrounding towns were outgrowing Quinnesec. Father John Brown became the first resident pastor in 1883. He was also charged with serving Iron Mountain, Iron River and Crystal Falls. Bishop John Vertin dedicated the parish to Mary Immaculate on May 6, 1883.

By 1884 the mines on the Menominee range were no longer prospering and many people were forced to leave to look for work elsewhere. As a result, St. Mary's in Quinnesec became a mission church of Iron Mountain. Once that change was made, Mass was only offered once each month.

Those parishioners who stayed in Quinnesec, however, remained faithful to their parish, furnishing the church and building a stately rectory.

A fire in the community on May 18, 1906 destroyed half of the buildings in the town, including the church of St. Mary. The small group of parishioners who remained in Quinnesec at the time remained dedicated to their faith despite going 10 years without a church. They met for Mass in the parish rectory.

PARISH LIFE. As a witness to their ultimate goal of building a new church, parishioners purchased a bell, which they erected on the lawn of the rectory. For a decade, women solicited donations from the communities, and held raffles and a hugely successful bazaar to raise money for the building project.

Finally on Oct. 1, 1916, a new St. Mary's was dedicated without any debt having been accumulated. The parishioners donated most of the church furnishings.

In 1922 the parish came under the direction of St. Stephen Parish in Loretto, which also served St. Mary Mission in Faithorn. All three parishes flourished spiritually and materially. The 18-year pastorate of Father George Stuntebeck, who served from 1919 to 1938, afforded the people an excellent knowledge of Catholic doctrine.

The church in Quinnesec received new pews, a new bell and remodeled the side altars in the late 1930s and early 1940s. A new foundation and basement hall for use as a parish center were built in the 1950s. The old rectory was sold and demolished at this time. Renovations included the construction of a sacristy, new roof, chimney, tower and painting. The church interior was also redecorated, including the installation of a new window depicting the Immaculate Conception with two adoring angels.

In 1966, the affiliation with Loretto came to an end and responsibility for St. Mary's was given to American Martyrs of Kingsford. On Aug. 4, 1970, St. Mary's became a mission of the church in Norway.

The parish celebrated its centennial Oct. 8, 1977, with a commemorative Mass, dinner and program.

CLOSURE. St. Mary Parish was closed July 1, 1995, as a result of the diocesan pastoral plan "Fully Alive in '95." The people of the parish were welcomed into the faith community of St. Mary Parish in Norway.

In 1996 the Menominee Range Historical Foundation purchased the Quinnesec church. The group intended to develop a museum dedicated to the display of religious goods. However, the endeavor did not develop.

RECORDS. Records for St. Mary Parish in Quinnesec are located at St. Mary's Parish in Norway.

PASTORS. Fathers Martin Fox, 1877-1878; Hilary J. Rosseau, 1878-1881; Luke Mosina, 1881-1882; Mathias Orth, 1882; John C. Kenny, 1882; John Brown, 1883; Melchior Faust, 1883-1886; A. T. Schuttelhoffer, 1886-1887; John H. Reynaert, 1887-1888; John Keul, 1888-1890; Honoratus Bourion, 1890-1893; Francis X. Becker, 1893; John Chebul, 1893; Joseph Kunes, 1893; Anthony Hodnik, 1893-1897; Adam Doser, 1897-1898; Nickolas H. Nosbisch, 1904-1910; James Corcoran, 1910-1919; John Mockler, 1919-1922; George Stuntebeck, 1922-1938; Raphael Gherna, 1938-1943; Thomas Lester Bourgeois, 1943-1945; Edward J. Lulewicz, 1945-1950; Frederick Hofmann, 1950-1951; John McLaughlin, 1951-1957; Thomas Andary, 1957-1959; August Franczek, 1959-1963; S. Patrick Wisneske, 1963-1966; John Hughes, 1966-1970; Elmer Bares, 1970-1981; William G. Richards, 1981-1985; Peter J. Carli, 1985-1992, and Arnold Grambow, 1992-1995.

CHRIST THE KING, RAMSAY

For nearly 50 years the people of Ramsay and surrounding locations supported their own independent parish. From the parish's start in 1940 in a former boarding house, to the construction of a new church in the 1950s, the people remained steadfast in their commitment to Christ the King Church. Then, in 1996, as a result of the diocese's Fully Alive in '95 pastoral planning initiative, the Ramsay church was closed.

Christ the King, Ramsay

FOUNDING. Ramsay's Christ the King Church was started in 1940 as a mission of Wakefield. The first church building was a former boarding house leased from the Castile Mining Co. The mining company's superintendent had the two-story building renovated. Pastors from churches across the Upper Peninsula made donations to the church, including the altar, vestments and a monstrance. Parishioners purchased statues, pews, the tabernacle and other furnishings. The first Mass was offered there May 5. That fall the second floor was renovated for use as a convent.

Within the parish boundaries was Verona, or Mikado, as it was called earlier. Verona had its own church, Sacred Heart, from 1903 to 1921.

PARISH LIFE. An increase in Christ the King's membership by 1948 caused Bishop Thomas L. Noa to elevate the church status to an independent parish with a resident priest.

By 1952 the people of Ramsay had collected $5,000 for the construction of a new church. The diocese matched that amount and soon plans for construction were in the works. That same year the parish grew to include the people of Anvil Location, who had formerly been served by a priest from Bessemer.

CLOSURE. Christ the King Church was closed in 1996 as a result of the diocese's pastoral planning initiative. The final Mass, a Polka Mass, was offered Sunday, June 30. A parish gathering followed.

RECORDS. Records for Christ the King Church are located at St. Sebastian Parish in Bessemer.

PASTORS. Fathers Clifford Nadeau, 1948; Thomas Andary, 1948-1951; Louis Cappo, 1952-1965, and B. Neil Smith, 1965-1996.

St. Charles Borromeo, Rapid River

St. Charles Borromeo Parish in Rapid River thrives on the long-standing tradition of building up the church and the faith of its members. Since the church got its modest start in the late 1800s, members have worked hard to raise money for improvements to the facilities.

Ministering to seasonal visitors, serving early mission churches, and selling pasties by the hundreds keep the people's faith alive.

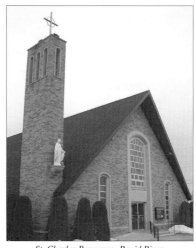

St. Charles Borromeo, Rapid River

FOUNDING. The first Catholic Church in Rapid River was begun as a mission of Gladstone in 1892. Donations were solicited from the townspeople and nearby lumber camps and a humble church was built. The church was named St. Charles Borromeo in honor of the Archbishop of Milan, Italy. There was at first no bell tower or sacristy. Benches without backs were used for pews and there were no kneeling benches. The first Mass was the wedding of three couples held Nov. 21, 1892.

Four years later, in May 1896, the first resident priest arrived, Father Joseph A. Sauriol. The following year a house and property located across from the present rectory were purchased and used for the priests' residence until 1916.

PARISH LIFE. Membership in the parish increased from just 34 families in 1896 to 140 in 1951. During those years many improvements were made to the church. Upgrades were partially funded by the Altar Society. An addition to the parish plant came when the church acquired a Civilian Conservation Corps barracks from the federal government. The building was converted into a parish hall and also served as a winter chapel for weekday Mass.

Mass was held in the "old white" church for the last time May 2, 1961. The original building was razed and construction began on a new, modern facility on the same site. The new church, dedicated July 29, 1962, is twice the size of the original. The Gothic-style structure contains windows of hammered cathedral amber glass. Many hand-carved statues and other decorations imported from Germany adorn the church. The bell tower contains the 450-pound bell from the original church, as well as a new one. Also from the old church, a lawn statue of

Our Lady of Grace was placed in a niche in the bell tower.

Father John McLaughlin, who oversaw construction of the new church, died just a few months after the project was completed. His was the first funeral held in the new church.

In 1966 a group of six women started a continuing tradition of earning money for the church by making and selling pasties. Originally making 300 to 400 per month and selling them for 65 cents each, the women raised enough money to pay off the debt of the new church and eventually of a new parish center. From 1968 to 1974, they earned $18,000 for the church. An average 2,000 pasties are sold each month. Money is used to fund educational scholarships and to buy furnishings and equipment for the church. In 1987 a new parish center was dedicated.

The parish held large celebrations to commemorate its golden jubilee in 1946, its 75th anniversary in 1971 and its centennial in 1996.

MISSIONS. St. Charles had been responsible for the mission churches at Stonington, Nahma, Isabella, Cooks and Trenary. In 2005 the Rapid River church was linked with Perkins and Trenary.

PASTORS. Fathers Joseph A. Sauriol, 1896-1897; Frederick Glaser, 1897-1898; Msgr. Mathias Jodocy, 1898; Paul Datin, 1898; Raymond Jacques, 1901-1902; Anthony Vermare, 1902; Paul LeGolvan, 1902-1904; A. Deschamps, 1904-1906; Joseph Dufort, 1906-1910; Henry Kron, 1910-1911; Peter Manderfield, 1911-1912; William Soulard, 1912-1916; Joseph Schaul, 1916-1923; Joseph Guertin, 1923-1929; Ovid LaMothe, 1929-1933; Joseph Duquette, 1933-1937; Francis M. Scheringer, 1937-1940; Thomas Anderson, 1940-1946; Anthony Schloss, 1946-1951; Thomas M. Andary, 1951-1957; John McLaughlin, 1957-1962; James Donnelly, 1962-1963; John V. Suhr, 1963-1968; Conrad Dishaw, 1968-1970; Joseph Felix, 1974-1976; Emil Beyer, 1976-1985; John McArdle, 1985-1991; Raymond Hoefgen, 1991-1996; David Sedlock, 1996-2004, and Jacek Wtyklo, 2004-.

ST. AUGUSTINE, REPUBLIC

St. Augustine, Republic

St. Augustine Parish in Republic has had four churches since its founding in the 19th century. The church grew and flourished during the high points in the community's mining industry. In recent years, since the closing of the iron ore mines, the church has had to overcome many struggles to keep a Catholic presence in the town. Other parishes have absorbed the mission communities formerly served by the Republic church. A core group of parishioners and dedicated women religious serving as pastoral coordinators keep the parish thriving.

FOUNDING. Republic was a mission of Clarksburg in the early 1870s. In 1877, as Republic grew into the larger of the two communities, Father James W. Kelly obtained land on the east end of Kloman Avenue from the Republic Iron Co. and erected a small frame church. He took up residency in a back room of the church. A rectory was built in 1880.

In 1892, as the membership of the church increased to about 200 families, the original structure proved too small and it was replaced by a second church built across the street.

In the fall of 1906 the original church was razed and the present rectory built in its place. A third church in Quonset-style, was blessed July 4, 1948.

PARISH LIFE. The present church was built in 1963. Ground was broken and construction began in April. Bishop Thomas L. Noa dedicated the completed structure Sept. 15. The new facility was equipped with a full basement and modern kitchen facilities. It is considered "the church that pasties built" because the women of the Altar/Rose Society raised money for construction by selling pasties.

The pasty-making tradition continues and the women host many dinners in the area to raise money for the church. The largest dinner was held in the Thimes Hall in Negaunee for the miners. There were enough members in the group that one crew would begin at 6 a.m. and another would arrive later in the day to serve and clean up.

In 1982, for the first time in the history of the Diocese of Marquette, administration of a parish was assigned not to a priest, but to women religious. Until 1993, Sister Maureen Freeman, CSJ, and Sister Paul Bernadette Bounk, CSJ, served in this capacity at St. Augustine, as well as at Sacred Heart in Champion and St. Agnes in Michigamme. In 1994, Sister Margey Schmelzle, OSF, and Sister Charlotte Wagner, OSF, were appointed pastoral coordinators. Wagner was reassigned in 1997, and Sister Lois Risch, OSF, began sharing the responsibility in 1999.

MISSIONS. From its early history, St. Augustine's served many missions including Diorite, Clarksburg and Humboldt.

PASTORS. Fathers Joseph F. Berube, 1871-1873; Oliver Comtois, 1874; Charles Guay, 1874; Simon Marceau, 1874-1877; James W. Kelly, 1877-1880; Martin A. Fox, 1880-1881; Mathias Orth, 1881-1882; Augustus W. Geers, 1882-1883; John H. Reynaert, 1883-1887; Edward P. Bordas, 1887-1889; John M. Manning, 1889-1892; Francis X. Becker, 1892-1893; Anthony C. Keller, 1893; Alberico Vitali, 1893; Fabian Pawlar, 1893-1894; Fidelis Sutter, 1894-1895; Augustus W. Geers, 1895-1901; John Burns, 1901-1906; Owen J. Bennett, 1906-1907; Joseph L. Hollinger, 1907-1916; George J. Dingfelder, 1916-1917; William B. Stahl, 1917-1942; Anthony P. Schloss, 1942-1946; Charles M. Herbst, 1946-1948; Wilbur Gibbs, 1948-1951; John Vincent Suhr, 1951-1955; August Franczek, 1955-1959; Otto J. Sartorelli, 1959-1970; Charles J. Strelick, 1970-1971; Wayne E. Marcotte, 1971-1975; John J. Shiverski, 1975-1976; Louis Wren, OFM, 1976-1977; Anthony J. Polakowski, 1977; Louis Wren, OFM, 1977-1982; moderator Peter Carli, 1982-1985; moderator William Richards, 1985-1988; moderator Peter Oberto, 1988-1993; James Scharinger, 1993-1994; canonical pastor Gilles Brault, 1994-2000; canonical pastor Msgr. Peter Oberto, 2000-, and sacramental minister James Challancin, 2000-.

St. Mary, Rockland

Father Frederic Baraga organized the people of Rockland and surrounding areas into a parish in the late 1840s, one of the first in what would become the Diocese of Marquette. Larger churches followed the original structure as mining activity increased and the community grew. Following a decrease in mining in later years, parish membership declined, but the people persevered and proudly celebrated the 150th anniversary of St. Mary Parish in 1999. Parishioners with family ties to the first members of St. Mary's have kept the faith tradition strong. The parish also supported the mission church of St. Peter and St. Paul in Greenland for more than 70 years.

St. Mary, Rockland

FOUNDING. During a visit from his post in Assinins, Father Frederic Baraga organized the Catholics of the Minnesota Mine settlement into a parish in 1849. At that time Mass was offered in a boarding house. The first church in Rockland was built in the Irish Hollow location. St. Mary's was dedicated Aug. 17, 1856. A priest from Ontonagon served the mission until three years later when Father Martin Fox built a small house beside the church and took up permanent residency in Rockland.

Shortly after his arrival at St. Mary's, Father Fox also built a church in Greenland and offered regular services to the people of the Norwich and Nebraska mine locations.

As mining operations increased in the area, St. Mary's became overcrowded and the need arose for a larger church. Father Baraga dedicated this second structure Sept. 4, 1859.

PARISH LIFE. A third church was erected and put into regular use in 1899. This, the present edifice, was built in the town proper. The Irish Hollow structure was abandoned permanently and eventually torn down. Parishioners helped build the new church and furnish it. Everything from the altar to pews, stained glass windows and statues, was given to the parish as gifts from its members.

St. Mary's Church purchased the first pipe organ to be brought to the Upper Peninsula. In 1859 Father Fox went to Buffalo, New York to purchase the $700 organ. Another $200 was spent in having it delivered to St. Mary's. A new organ was purchased in 1990.

In 1999, St. Mary parish commemorated the 150th anniversary of the founding of the church in Rockland. Bishop James Garland celebrated an outdoor Mass with the parish Sept. 4.

MISSION. The pastor of St. Mary Parish was responsible for the care of Saints Peter and Paul Mission in Greenland from 1922 until its closure in 1995.

PASTORS. Fathers Martin Fox, 1858-1868; Henry Thiele, 1868-1871; Edward Jacker, 1871-1872; Oliver Comtois, 1872-1873; Anthony Hubly, 1874-1878; William Dwyer, 1878-1882; Charles Dries, 1882-1883; Charles Langner, 1883-1884; Anacletus O. Pelisson, 1884-1885; Joseph Haas, 1885; John Burns, 1885-1887; Michael Weis, 1887-1889; John Henn, 1889-1890; Joseph Boever, 1890; Augustus Geers, 1890; John Reichenbach, 1890-1891; Joseph Haas, 1891-1892; Renatus Becker, 1893-1894; James Lenhart, 1894-1895; Fidelis Sutter, 1895-1896; Edward Bordas, 1896-1897; Renatus Becker, 1897-1900; Frederick Sperlein, 1900-1902; Peter Manderfield, 1902-1922; Bernard Linnemann, 1922-1945; Edward Malloy, 1945-1948; Frederick Hofmann, 1948-1950; John McLaughlin, 1950-1951; Thomas Ruppe, 1951-1958; Frank Hollenbach, 1958-1961; George Pernaski, 1961-1962; Robert Haas, 1962-1963; Norbert LaCosse, 1963-1965; Donald LaLonde, 1965-1967; Raymond Moncher, 1967-1969; Joseph Polakowski, 1969; Lesli Perino, 1969-1970; Raymond Hoefgen, 1970-1973; David Jenner, 1973-1975; Aloysius Ehlinger, 1975-1978; Joseph Carne, 1978-1986; Eric Olson, 1986-1992; Bede Louzon, OFM, Cap., 1992-1993; Ronald Timock, 1993-1995; John Longbucco, 1995-2002; Abraham Kazhunadiyil, 2002-2004; Thomas Thekkel, MST, 2005, and Antony Lukose, 2005-.

ST. JOSEPH, RUDYARD

St. Joseph, Rudyard

Since the time of its founding, St. Joseph Church in Rudyard has shared its prosperity with surrounding communities. By sharing their pastor and supporting mission churches, Rudyard parishioners show their gratefulness to their founders and early missionaries.

FOUNDING. St. Joseph Parish was founded in 1886 by missionary priests who offered Mass in private homes in Rudyard, Pickford, Fibre and Kinross. A church was built in Rudyard in 1902. In 1922 a rectory was constructed and the parish was entrusted with the care of the St. Francis Xavier Mission in Brimley.

PARISH LIFE. The original church was replaced in 1941. The first Mass was offered in the completed structure on Holy Thursday, April 10, 1941.

St. Joseph's cared for the St. Francis Xavier Mission in Brimley until 1965. Holy Family in Barbeau then became its mission. Since 1986, St. Joseph's has been entrusted with the care of the St. Mary Mission in Trout Lake.

On June 28, 1986, Bishop Mark Schmitt celebrated a special Mass marking the 100th anniversary of the founding of the parish. A banquet followed.

A major renovation project was undertaken in 1989 when office space was added to the parish rectory. In 1991 St. Joseph started a library offering assistance for drug and alcohol addiction. The audio cassettes and videotapes, books and other self-help tools makes up the largest collection of its kind in the U.P.

In addition to participating in active parish organizations for worship and liturgy, Christian service and evangelization, the people take part in regular celebrations, such as monthly breakfasts, summer picnics and a fall harvest dinner.

PASTORS. Fathers William Gagneur, 1886-1902; Joseph DeLude, SJ, 1902-1909; Bernard J. Eiling, 1909-1917; Anthony Oehlerer, 1917-1939; Peter Bleeker, 1939-1942; Robert J. Cordy, 1942-1946; James J. Schaefer, 1946-1948; Edward A. Malloy, 1948-1954; Frank J. Gimski, 1954-1965; Norbert B. Landerville, 1965; Kenneth G. Bretl, 1965-1970; Joseph R. Callari, 1970-1975; Allan J. Mayotte, 1975-1980; Robert Polcyn, OFM Cap., 1980-1983; Paul J. Nomellini, 1983-1986; Ronald J. Skufca, 1986-1989; N. Daniel Rupp, 1989-1990; Mark A. McQuesten, 1990-1996; Francis J. DeGroot, 1996-2003, and Cyriac Kottayarikil, 2003-.

Holy Name of Mary, Sault Ste. Marie

Holy Name of Mary Parish, or St. Mary's, in Sault Ste. Marie was the first cathedral of the Diocese of Marquette, originally named the Diocese of Sault Ste. Marie and Marquette. Today the people of the parish take great pride in furthering the faith traditions begun by Jesuit missionaries there more than 350 years ago.

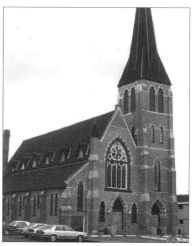

Holy Name of Mary, Sault Ste. Marie

FOUNDING. St. Mary's is the oldest Catholic Church in Michigan. Only two churches in the country are older, in St. Augustine, Fla. and in Santa Fe, N.M.

Sault Ste. Marie's first permanent mission was started in 1668. Jesuit missionaries had served the people for nearly 200 years when Father Frederic Baraga was named bishop of the new Diocese of Sault Ste. Marie and Marquette in 1857.

The present structure is St. Mary's fifth church building. It was constructed in 1881. The present rectory was built in 1922.

PARISH SCHOOL. The first Catholic school in Sault Ste. Marie was started in 1885. The present St. Mary School began in 1937. The elementary school on Maple Street served first through eighth grades for 34 years until its closure in 1971. The school was reopened in 1993 after a 22-year hiatus. The school now serves students in kindergarten through eighth grade.

Prior to 1937, girls in grade school through high school attended the Loretto Academy, opened by the Loretto Sisters in 1896. The Loretto Academy became a co-educational high school in 1945.

In 1971 both the Loretto High School and St. Mary's Grade School were closed due to financial constraints. The Loretto building was sold to the public school system. Until it was reopened as a grade school, St. Mary's was the site of a successful religious education program that served seven parishes including those in Sault Ste. Marie, Brimley, Bay Mills and Sugar Island.

PARISH LIFE. In 1968 the people of St. Mary's had a bell tower constructed that also served as a shrine to the many missionaries who served the church. In 1981 the Tower of History, as the structure came to be known, was given to Le Sault Sainte Marie Historic Sites, which operates the tower as an observation site.

The parish observed the 100th anniversary of the present church in 1981. Bishop Mark Schmitt celebrated a commemorative Mass Oct. 25.

After more than a century in the same church the people were faced with the question of building new or renovating. In the mid-1980s, parishioners voted to renovate and restore their historic church.

From 1985 to 1987, initially due to a furnace breakdown in the church, services were held in the St. Mary school gym. In the meantime, the first part of what would become a three-phase renovation project got under way. Bequests and successful fund-raising efforts made it possible to correct years of wear on the structure and to update the utilities. The second phase of renovations included remodeling the interior space to conform to the new standards set forth by the Second Vatican Council. The restored St. Mary Church was rededicated Sept. 6, 1987.

In January 1996, a third phase of restoration began. Interior plaster and stained glass windows were repaired and the interior was redecorated in the original Gothic-style.

The building was named to the Michigan Register of Historic Places and a marker denoting the designation was erected on the front lawn of the church grounds and unveiled during a May 1990 ceremony.

In addition to supporting extensive improvements to their historic house of worship, the people of St. Mary's also continue to further their spiritual lives. Active parish organizations and spirited adult, youth and hand bell choirs are part of parish life.

In 2005 St. Mary's was linked with St. Francis Xavier Parish in Brimley, Sacred Heart Mission on Sugar Island and Blessed Kateri Tekakwitha Mission in Bay Mills.

PASTORS. Fathers R. Chartier, SJ, 1878-1890; L. T. Garceau, SJ, 1891; Peter Hamel, SJ, 1892-1894; Daniel Donavon, SJ, 1895-1904; J. J. Connolly, SJ, 1895-1900; Edmond Rottot, SJ, 1896-1900; R. Chartier, SJ, 1901-1904; Alexander A. Gagnieur, SJ, 1905-1906; A. Webler SJ, 1906-1907; F. Malone, SJ, 1907-1913; E. T. O'Gara, SJ, 1910-1914; John J. Stenglein, SJ, 1914-1934; Raymond G. Jacques, 1935-1941; John T. Holland, 1941-1945; Joseph Guertin 1945-1954; John G. Hughes, 1954; Robert Monroe, 1954-1974; Terrence Donnelly, 1974-1979; Daniel Zaloga, 1979-1981, and Theodore Brodeur, 1981-.

Nativity of Our Lord, Sault Ste. Marie

Parishioners of Nativity of Our Lord Parish in Sault Ste. Marie began holding regular worship services long before they had a church. The people took great pride in their house of worship once it was finally erected in 1941. They supported many improvements to the church over the years. The Nativity pastor also provided for the parishioners of mission churches and university and high school students in the area.

Nativity of Our Lord, Sault Ste. Marie

FOUNDING. Nativity of Our Lord Parish began as Algonquin Catholic Mission in 1934. The people living in the western section of Sault Ste. Marie struggled to attend Mass at St. Mary's across town and longed for a church of their own.

Finally, it was decided to offer services in the Northwestern Leather Company's recreation hall. The first services were celebrated there on Christmas Day 1934. Father Thomas J. Anderson, assistant pastor at St. Mary's, presided over services there on an irregular basis at first. Then in 1935, permission was obtained to hold regular Sunday Mass at the tannery.

In August 1938, responsibility for the care of the Algonquin Mission was transferred from St. Mary's to Holy Family Parish in Barbeau.

PARISH LIFE. Construction of a church in Algonquin finally moved ahead under the direction of Father Frank Ignatz, who arrived in June of 1940. Father Ignatz abandoned earlier efforts to build a church and designated himself the architect, general contractor and supervisor of the project. Donated labor saved tremendously on costs.

The first Mass was celebrated in the new church March 30, 1941. On May 18 of that year Bishop Francis J. Magner blessed and dedicated the church under the title Nativity of Our Lord. At this time the church was raised to parish status and Holy Family in Barbeau was made its mission. (Five years later responsibility for Holy Family was given to St. Mary's.) A new rectory at Nativity was ready for occupancy in June 1942.

The ensuing 10 years saw the completion of the basement into a parish hall, the decoration of the rectory and church interior, and the finishing of many projects previously undertaken. Property adjacent to the church was purchased and landscaping was carried out. The women of the church worked hard to raise the money to pay for these projects and the men did much of the work.

In celebration of the 25th anniversary of Nativity of Our Lord Parish in 1966, parishioners again supported improvements to their house of worship. A renovation program paid for through the ladies guild and other donations included new altars, interior painting and recarpeting.

At various times throughout the past century, the pastor serving Nativity Parish also cared for the spiritual needs of students at the Lake Superior State University Newman Center and the Loretto High School.

CLOSURE. Nativity of Our Lord was closed July 1, 1996 as a result of the diocese's pastoral planning initiative Fully Alive in '95.

RECORDS. Records for Nativity of Our Lord Parish are kept at St. Joseph Church in Sault Ste. Marie.

PASTORS. Fathers Raymond S. Przybylski, 1938-1940; Frank J. Ignatz, 1940-1946; Thomas P. Dunleavy, 1946; Stephen Wloszczynski, 1946-1951; Charles M. Herbst, 1951-1954; Elmer J. Bares, 1954-1966; Arthur J. Parrotta, 1966-1971; Norbert B. Landreville, 1971-1974; Robert Monroe, 1974-1981; Patrick D. Creeden, 1981-1982; C. Michael Rhoades, 1982-1992, and Paul Manderfield, 1992-1996.

ST. ISAAC JOGUES MISSION, SAULT STE. MARIE

St. Isaac Jogues is a Native American Mission in Sault Ste. Marie. In addition to providing for the spiritual needs of parishioners, the church also plays an integral part in community life.

FOUNDING. Visiting Jesuit seminarians aided the locals in construction of St. Isaac Jogues Church, located on Marquette Avenue. Bishop Thomas L. Noa dedicated the completed structure Sunday, Nov. 27, 1949.

PARISH LIFE. From the time of its founding until diocesan priests took over its care in 1992, St. Isaac Jogues was a mission of the Society of Jesus. The church was named after St. Isaac Jogues, a Jesuit who began the ministry there.

St. Isaac Jogues Mission, Sault Ste. Marie

Between 1958 and 1960 the mission had stained glass windows installed, a statue of the Divine Infant of Prague dedicated, and other interior renovations made to the church and rectory. Also at that time, the church property was increased, bringing the total land owned to two city blocks.

Regular maintenance and upgrades were made throughout the years. In 1967 classrooms for religious education were constructed in the church basement. In the late 1970s a reconciliation room was constructed and the basement hall was modernized. In 1979 a cross made from 70,000 beads and Stations of the Cross depicting a Native Jesus were erected in the church.

The parish celebrated its 25th anniversary in the fall of 1974.

St. Isaac Jogues' facilities are the center of recreation for the youth of the mission and are also used for community events, such as dinners, dances and meetings. The church is so important to its membership that in 1975 and again in 1995, the people were successful in rallying against its proposed closure.

PASTORS. Fathers Leo C. Cunningham, SJ, 1949-1950; Eugene Bork, SJ, 1950; John F. Byrne, SJ, 1950-1952; Joseph Lawless, SJ, 1948-1953 and 1961-1992; James Birney, SJ, 1954-1960 and 1969-1977; Paul Prud'homme, SJ, 1954-1972; Donald Seliskar, SJ, 1975, 1978, and 1980; Henry Gelin, SJ, 1976-1980; Michael Steltenkamp, SJ, 1977-1980; Edward Flint, SJ, 1979; Bernard Haas, SJ, 1979-1986; Thomas Bain, SJ, 1986-1992; Paul Manderfield, 1992-1996; Jeff Johnson, 1996-1998, and John Hascall, OFM Cap., 1998-.

St. Joseph, Sault Ste. Marie

St. Joseph Parish made its first church from a former U.S. Army chapel which was moved and remodeled in 1944. The people wasted no time in establishing their south-side parish, organizing many church committees and beginning their own parochial school. About 20 years after the parish was founded, the people of St. Joseph's banded together to support construction of a new parish complex. With modern facilities and enthusiastic hearts, parishioners continue to build on their faith through parish life.

St. Joseph, Sault Ste. Marie

FOUNDING. Bishop Joseph C. Plagens' decree establishing St. Joseph Parish became effective Jan. 1, 1941. The new church was started because membership at St. Mary's in the same city had grown to excessive numbers. Included in St. Joseph's boundaries would be all those living south of Easterday Avenue between Tenth Street and West Fourth Avenue and south to the boundary of St. Francis Xavier Parish in Brimley. This included about 300 families at the time.

St. Joseph's first pastor was Father Joseph Seifert. Just prior to establishing the parish, the diocese had purchased property for a new church on Minneapolis Street. Building materials and labor were hard to come by during the years of World War II, so construction was delayed until 1944. For the time being, Mass was held at St. Mary's, and Father Seifert lived in a house rented by the parish.

PARISH LIFE. Finally, in September 1944, St. Joseph Parish purchased its first church. A former U.S. Army chapel used by troops at the Sault Ste. Marie Military Area at Fort Brady was moved to the church property on Minneapolis Street. A full-length basement had been dug at the site and the structure was lengthened about 20 feet. Parishioners donated much of the labor for the renovations and made generous gifts for furnishings and other improvements.

The church was dedicated Sunday, Feb. 11, 1945. Immediately, parish life began to flourish, with the organization of many church committees and activities. In 1948 a house was purchased for use as a rectory.

The army chapel served the parish well until 1959, when plans got under way for the construction of a new parish complex to include a multipurpose room, rectory and convent. Groundbreaking for the new church, convent and rectory took place in June 1960. The first Mass was celebrated on Holy Saturday, April 1. The church was officially dedicated May 21. The old church was sold and demolished.

In October 1966, the parish celebrated its 25th anniversary. A commemorative Mass and parish dinner marked the milestone.

By 2000 the parish membership had more than doubled to 629 families. Parishioners dedicate their time and talent to the continued growth of St. Joseph's through participation in many parish organizations and activities.

PARISH SCHOOL. A building fund for St. Joseph's parochial school was started just a few years after the first church was erected. Bishop Thomas L. Noa blessed the cornerstone for the building Oct. 9, 1949. About one year later, on Oct. 1, 1950, the school's dedication ceremony took place.

Initially, the school opened to first through sixth graders. One grade was added in each of the two succeeding years. A second floor was completed in 1954. Dominican Sisters from Adrian, Mich., staffed the school. The women of the order lived in a house on the corner of Fifth and Minneapolis streets until a convent was built as part of the new parish complex in 1960.

In 1971 St. Joseph's School was closed due to financial constraints. The school building continues to be used for religious education programs and is also rented by community organizations. The school gym serves as a parish hall.

PASTORS. Fathers Joseph A. Seifert, 1941-1946; Thomas P. Dunleavy, 1946-1950; Joseph J. Dunleavy, 1950-1952; Thomas P. Dunleavy, 1952-1954; Oliver J. O'Callaghan, 1954-1984; Thomas Wantland, 1984-1985; Donald L. Shiroda, 1986-1993, and Pawel J. Mecwel, 1997-.

Sacred Heart Parish, Schaffer

Despite surviving two devastating fires, the parish of Sacred Heart in Schaffer continued to thrive for nearly a century. In 1995 it was among those that merged to form St. Elizabeth Ann Seton Parish.

Sacred Heart Parish, Schaffer

FOUNDING. Going against the recommendation of the bishop, the people of Schaffer first joined together to build a church of their own in 1899. Before construction of the Sacred Heart Church, Catholics in the area attended Mass in Bark River. Bishop John Vertin didn't think money was available to support another church in the area. But after only one year in existence, the seat of the Schaffer and Bark River dual-parish system moved from St. George's to Sacred Heart, and the Bark River church reverted to mission status. Priests offered services at both churches until 1905, when the two became independent of each other.

On May 2, 1904 a fire destroyed the Schaffer church and rectory. A janitor was reportedly raking leaves and burning brush near the rear of the building when a strong wind spread the fire out of control. The blaze took with it the church and rectory, as well as the public school, a nearby home and a local store. It is said that as the church burned, its treasured bells and steeple toppled across the road. Residents kept pieces of the melted bells as mementoes of the church.

PARISH LIFE. Soon a second church was being planned. Use of a newly-built barn was donated for a chapel while construction of another church began. The second church was more modest than the original, as funds were limited. The one-story and basement structure contained seats purchased from an Escanaba theater.

Tragedy struck again Jan. 17, 1917, when fire destroyed the second church. This time however, the bell tower, which had been built in front of the church, escaped unscathed.

A third church was built the following year. The beautiful, dark red, brick building with a gold-gilded sanctuary, continued to serve parishioners until 1995.

MERGER. As a result of the diocese's Fully Alive in '95 parish planning effort, the Schaffer, Bark River and Perronville churches merged to form one new parish, St. Elizabeth Ann Seton. The first Mass of the new parish was held at the Bark River Senior Center in July 1995.

All three churches were to remain open until a new, central structure was completed. But the doors of Sacred Heart closed early due to the deterioration of the structure. On Dec. 22, 1996, Bishop James Garland offered a closing Mass along with former pastors of the church. More than 300 people gathered to say goodbye to the church.

RECORDS. The records of Sacred Heart Parish are located at St. Elizabeth Ann Seton Parish in Bark River.

PASTORS. M. Gooley, 1899-1900; F. M. Roberfe, 1900; James J. Corcoran, 1900-1904; Joseph A. Mercier, 1904; Thomas Dassylva, 1904-1908; Fabian S. Marceau, 1909-1911; Louis Archille Poulin, 1911-1913; Casper Douenburg, 1913-1914; Louis Archille Poulin, 1914-1915; Auguste Blin, 1915-1921; Frank J. Ignatz, 1921-1922; Philip de Neri Jutras, 1922-1936; William Remillard, 1936-1943; Roland L. Dion, 1944-1946; Wilfred Pelletier, 1946-1949; Joseph H. Beauchene, 1949-1954; John Noel Arneth, 1954-1965; Casimir Marcinkevicius, 1965-1969; Vincent L. Ouellette, 1969-1970; Clifford J. Nadeau, 1970-1974; Gervase Brewer, 1974-1976; Louis Wren,, OFM., Conv., 1976-1977; Paul A. Schiska, 1977-1983; N. Daniel Rupp, 1983-1989; Paul J. Nomellini, 1989-1993, and Alexander K. Sample, 1993-1994.

St. Francis Xavier Mission, Sidnaw

St. Francis Xavier Mission in Sidnaw is one of the smallest church buildings in the Diocese of Marquette. Since it was founded in the late 1930s, the church has been served by pastors of Sacred Heart Parish in Ewen, about 35 miles away.

FOUNDING. Prior to the 1938 founding of Saint Francis Xavier Mission, Catholics in Sidnaw gathered in private homes for Mass. In June 1936 Father Thomas Anderson, pastor of Sacred Heart in Ewen, began making plans for a church in Sidnaw. A grant from the Catholic Church Extension Society helped make the building project successful.

St. Francis Xavier Mission, Sidnaw

Father Anderson's successor, Father Eugene Hennelly, saw the plans to completion. The church was dedicated Oct. 9, 1938. Mass had previously only been offered on the fourth Sunday of the month, and was now held every Sunday.

PARISH LIFE. The St. Francis Guild—made up of women in the church—helped make improvements to the property. In 1962 the seating capacity was increased. Additional improvements included new carpeting and repainting of the interior and exterior in 1981, a new roof in 1986-1987, new siding, an updated heating system and electrical updates in 1987-1988. Also in 1987, the church's old pews were removed and given to parishioners while better ones that were donated by St. Michael's in Ironwood were installed.

The number of registered parishioners is small, but the congregation is joined seasonally by many summer tourists and rifle deer hunters.

PASTORS. Fathers Renatus Becker, 1892-1893; William Joisten, 1893; Hubert Zimmermann, 1893; Joseph Dupasquier, 1893-1894; John Burns, 1894-1895; James Lenhart, 1895-1898; Alexander Hasenberg, 1899-1903; Bernard Eiling, 1903-1908; Charles Diedgens, 1908-1911; Edward Feldhaus, 1911-1912; Anthony Oehlerer, 1912-1917; Joseph Ling, 1917-1934; Gerald Harrington, 1934-1936; Thomas Anderson, 1936-1938; Eugene Hennelly, 1938-1939; Vincent Savageau, 1940-1965; William Richards, 1965-1970; August Franczek, 1970; David Rocheleau, 1970; Donald Hartman, 1970-1971; Raymond Valerio, 1971-1972; Louis Wren, OFM, 1972-1976; Arnold Grambow, 1976-1978; Gary Jacobs, 1978-1984; Francis Dobrzenski, 1984-1999; Thomas Valayathil, 1999-2003; George Kallarackal, MCBS 2003-2004, and Thomas Ettolil, 2004-.

St. Mary Mission, Sobieski

St. Mary Mission, Sobieski

A small group of people gathered together in the early 1900s to form the St. Mary Mission in Sobieski. Members gave generously to make improvements to the facilities. A church rich in the Polish tradition of its founders remained viable until a shortage of priests in the diocese forced its closure in 1995.

FOUNDING. In 1906, five Catholic immigrants from Poland built the mission church of St. Mary in Sobieski. Two years later the humble church was officially dedicated. Responsibility for its administration was given to St. Adalbert Parish in Menominee.

The partnership with St. Adalbert's lasted more than 50 years until 1972. The mission was then attended to by Resurrection in Menominee, 1972-1976; Holy Spirit, Menominee, 1976-1980, and Holy Redeemer, Birch Creek, 1980-1995.

PARISH LIFE. The original St. Mary's did not have a sanctuary or sacristy, but satisfactorily served its members—eight families—until the church was essentially rebuilt in 1945. Parishioners donated all of the labor for the project. A sanctuary and two sacristies were added to the original church. Among additional improvements were the installation of a new heating plant and electrical system, new altars, seating, a choir loft and 14 stained glass windows. In 1980 the interior of the church was repainted and the pews were refinished.

CLOSURE. As a result of the diocese's pastoral planning initiative Fully Alive in '95, St. Mary Mission was closed. Members of the parish tried persistently to maintain ownership of the church in the hope that it could become a museum. But, instead, the building was eventually sold to a private party.

RECORDS. Records for St. Mary Mission are located at Holy Redeemer Parish in Menominee.

PASTORS. Fathers Victor Karch, 1917-1931; Nickolas H. Nosbisch, Charles Fox; co-pastors Norman Clisch and Joseph Gouin, 1972-1976; S. Patrick Wisneske, 1976-1980; Joseph Gouin, 1980-1990; Thomas Poisson, 1990-1991, and Rick Courier, 1991-1995.

Holy Family, South Range

Holy Family, South Range

The founders of Holy Family Parish in South Range worked tirelessly to establish a church of their own. The people have made many sacrifices to maintain the structure's presence in their community. Support of the reconstruction of the church after a fire in the 1930s and contributions to continuing improvements are among the ways the people outwardly have demonstrated their devotion.

FOUNDING. The people of South Range worked for 10 years discussing the possibility and making plans for the establishment a church. Finally, in the summer of 1916, under the devoted leadership of Father Frederick Richter of Atlantic Mine, a building committee was established and soon after church construction commenced. Bishop Frederick Eis blessed the completed edifice in August 1917.

On Jan. 21, 1936, the Holy Family community was devastated when its church was destroyed by fire. Several attempts were made to save the Blessed Sacrament and other precious items but to no avail. Despite the Great Depression, the people remained true to the faith and supported their church. Parishioners wasted no time in rebuilding a house of worship.

It was decided to construct the new church across the street from the original site. This new church, of Spanish Mission design, went up at the intersection of Trimountain and Atlantic avenues. Ground was broken in the spring of 1937 and Bishop Joseph C. Plagens laid the cornerstone on Sept. 26 of that year. The first Mass was held in the completed structure on Easter Sunday 1938.

PARISH LIFE. In the late 1950s, the church was completely redecorated and stained glass windows were installed.

In the spring of 1963, Holy Family Church was raised to parish status and Atlantic Mine became its mission. Father William Oremus was named the first pastor. Care for Atlantic Mine was reassigned to St. Ignatius Loyola Parish in Houghton in 1969.

Father Oremus led parishioners in the excavation of a basement hall project with full kitchen facilities. On July 28, 1965, ground was broken for a new rectory. The structure was ready for occupancy that December.

In 1967, to coincide with the celebration of the parish's 50th anniversary, the sanctuary underwent extensive renovations to meet the new standards for the celebration of the liturgy set forth by the Second Vatican Council. On May 21 of that year, a commemorative Mass was held with a dinner and social afterward.

Catechetical instruction for young people was started during Father Richter's pastorate. He and the women of the church instructed the youth until the 1950s when the Sisters of St. Joseph, serving at St. Joseph and St. Patrick Parish in Hancock, began teaching catechism for the young people of Holy Family as well.

Holy Family has been without a resident priest since 1996. As a result of the diocese's pastoral planning process in 1995, Holy Family began sharing a pastor with St. Anne Parish in Chassell. The missions of Painesdale and Donken were closed and the people were encouraged to join Holy Family Parish. In 2001 Holy Family was linked with St. Ignatius Loyola Parish in Houghton.

PASTORS. Fathers Frederick Richter, 1917-1930; Herman Fadale, 1930-1933; Ovid LaMothe, 1933-1934; Stanislaus Mikula, CP, 1934-1936; Gerald Harrington, 1936-1944; Gino S. Ferraro, 1944-1951; Andrew Shulek, 1951-1953; Casimir Marcinkevicius, 1953-1963; William Oremus, 1963-1964; Frank Hollenbach, 1964-1970; Roland Dion, 1970-1973; Frank Hollenbach, 1973-1976; Raymond Smith, 1976-1996; Bede Louzon, OFM Cap., 1996-2000; Sebastian Ettolil, MCBS, 2000-2001; Thomas L. Poisson, 2001-2002, and John Martignon, 2002-.

St. Francis Xavier, Spalding

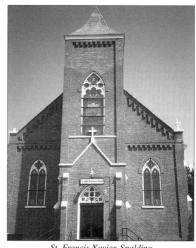

St. Francis Xavier, Spalding

When Father Martin Fox began serving people in the Menominee area in the late 1870s, he chose Spalding as his headquarters. St. Francis Xavier Parish was established in 1878. Despite being served by a long list of pastors who stayed only a short time, the people of the parish maintained a strong Catholic community. In 1995 St. Francis Xavier merged with St. Mary Church in Hermansville to form the new parish of St. John Neumann, but regular services continue in both communities.

FOUNDING. Before the 1878 arrival of Father Fox, sawmill workers in Spalding attended Mass in Escanaba. Father Fox offered services in private homes until he purchased a vacant boarding house for use as a church. The village of Spalding grew quickly, and with the increased population came a need for a larger and more modern church. A rectory was built in 1895. Five years later work on the present church began.

PARISH LIFE. Powers, a sister village of Spalding, vied for the honor of being the site of the new church building, but a popular vote decided in favor of Spalding. Three lots were donated, just east of the original building. The cornerstone was laid in 1902, and formal dedication of the completed structure took place Oct. 11, 1903. The building was of Gothic style and brick veneer construction. Most of the money for the new church was raised by popular subscription. Stained glass windows and two side altars were gifts from parishioners.

In 1922 the interior of the church was repaired and decorated for the first time. A new pipe organ was purchased.

A two-story rectory was built in 1928 at a cost of $10,000. In the early 1940s, repairs were made to the tower and roof, which had been struck by lightning. The entire attic was rebuilt with structural steel. The church was redecorated in 1942.

In 1947, Father Bernard A. Karol began the longstanding tradition of offering Mass to the residents of Pinecrest Sanatorium. In 1961, the facility became Pinecrest Medical Care Facility.

In 1953 the parish marked the 75th anniversary of its founding and the 50th year since the present church was dedicated. To commemorate the milestone, the church was again redecorated. The ceiling of the church was insulated and acoustical tile installed. Repair and painting of the tower also had to be done, because for a second time, the tower had been struck by lightning. At that time, it was lowered 45 feet. A commemorative Mass and banquet were held on Sunday July 29, 1953.

PARISH SCHOOL. From 1940 to 1945, the Sisters of St. Agnes of Fond du Lac, Wis., held a catechetical summer school for the youth of the parish. In 1946 Sisters of St. Francis from Manitowoc, Wis., taught the program, followed by the Sisters of St. Francis, from Silver Lake, Wis.

A parish center was constructed in 1960, complete with classrooms equipped for religious education. In January 1963, a private residence was purchased and converted into a convent for three School Sisters of Notre Dame who would make use of the new classrooms as a parochial school. St. Francis Xavier School, which included grades three through six, was started that fall. There were 67 students the first year. Rising costs made the operation of the school a financial burden on the parish and, regretfully, the school's doors closed in June 1969. A religious education program for the entire parish was then inaugurated. Sisters and lay teachers assisted in the program.

MERGER. In 1995, as a result of the diocese's Fully Alive in '95 pastoral planning initiative, St. Francis Xavier Parish merged with St. Mary's in Hermansville to form the new parish of St. John Neumann. Both parish buildings remain open and are served by the same pastor, who lives in Hermansville.

The parish council is composed of representatives from both churches. Parishioners from both sites join together for all major activities, such as the religious education program, the Disciples in Mission Lenten Bible study, Pinecrest ministries, parish picnic and Mardi Gras Carnival.

PASTORS. Fathers Martin Fox, 1878-1879; Joseph E. Martel, 1881; Theodore Aloysius Majerus, 1881; Edward Bordas, 1881-1882; John H. Reynaert, 1882-1883; Francis X. Becker, 1883-1884; Mathias Orth, 1884-1885; Anacletus O. Pelisson, 1885-1886; Fabian S. Marceau, 1886-1887; Prosper Girard, 1887-1888; Gideon Beliveau, 1888-1890; Alberico Vitali, 1890; Thomas Dassylva, 1890-1891; R. Regis, 1891; Anthony C. Keller, 1892; Joseph Hoeber, 1892-1893; Raphael Cavicchi, 1894; Anthony Molinari, 1894-1896; Frederick Glaser, 1896; Fidelis Sutter, 1897; Julius Papon, 1897; John Henn, 1898; John Burns, 1898-1901; Frederick Glaser, 1901-1908; James J. Corcoran, 1908-1910; Paul Fillion, 1910-1923; Joseph Schaul, 1923-1938; Peter Dapper, 1938-1939; Francis A Seifert, 1939-1947; Bernard Karol, 1947-1952; Walter Franczek, 1952-1966; Raymond Przybylski, 1966-1967; Aloysius Ehlinger, 1967-1970; Thomas Lester Bourgeois, 1970-1978; Ephraem Sitko, 1978-1982; Emmett Norden, 1983-1985; Joseph Polakowski, 1985-1994, and Michael Vichich, 1994-.

St. John Neumann Parish, Spalding/Hermansville

The founding of St. John Neumann Parish of Spalding and Hermansville is the result of a 1995 merger between two separate parishes, St. Francis Xavier of Spalding and St. Mary's of Hermansville. The merger has provided a means of uniting the hearts and spirits of two communities.

St. John Neumann, Hermansville   *St. John Neumann, Spalding*

FOUNDING. Bishop James Garland formally inaugurated the new parish of St. John Neumann July 1, 1995. As part of the diocese's Fully Alive in '95 pastoral planning initiative, parishioners from Spalding, Powers, Wilson and Hermansville were presented with four options. The decision to merge all parishioners into one new parish allowed both church complexes to remain in use full time. The parish has one pastor, one parish council, one finance council and a shared religious education program.

PARISH LIFE. Parishioners joined together in a major way in September 1997 when ground was broken for an expansion of the Spalding church. One of the main goals of the $750,000 project was to enlarge the church, making enough room so that the entire parish could gather for special liturgies. The church had not seen major renovations in many years. During construction Mass was held in the parish hall. The project included the addition of a narthex, which increased the worship area by 1,150 square feet. Mass was celebrated for the first time in the newly renovated church on Palm Sunday, April 5, 1998. Bishop James Garland rededicated the structure Aug. 1, 1998.

In 1990, a long-time treasure of the Hermansville church—a solid brass bell weighing 1,500 pounds—was removed from the tower and put on permanent display on the lawn. The bell had been installed at St. Mary's Church in 1910.

Updates to the Hermansville rectory and the modernization of parish offices at both church buildings were among the renovations made in the 1990s.

Students from the parish's two sites attend religious education classes together under the direction of a single religious education coordinator. Lay catechists come from both sites to staff the program.

PASTORS. Father Michael Vichich, 1990-.

ST. IGNATIUS LOYOLA, ST. IGNACE

The roots of Catholicism in Upper Michigan started on the eastern tip of the peninsula and spread westward. St. Ignatius Loyola Parish in St. Ignace is the second oldest of the diocese's parishes. The Old Mission Church, built in 1837, is the oldest church structure in the state. The structure was moved to State Street adjacent to the burial site of Father Jacques Marquette and is now the Museum of Ojibwa Culture. In the Jubilee Year 2000, Bishop James Garland included St. Ignatius Church among the Baraga Pilgrimage sites.

St. Ignatius Loyola, St. Ignace

FOUNDING. Jesuits started the first permanent mission at St. Ignace in 1671 and named Father Jacques Marquette its first pastor. Father Marquette remained there until 1673, serving the traders and explorers in the "commercial and military heart of the Northwest," as the region was considered at the time. Two years later, on May 18, 1675, Father Marquette died while returning on Lake Michigan near what is now Ludington after having nearly completed a 4,000-mile canoe voyage to the Mississippi River settlements. His remains are buried in St. Ignace.

The first St. Ignace church dedicated to St. Ignatius Loyola was built in 1837. Called the Old Mission Church, the structure was replaced by the present house of worship in 1905. The original church was moved and serves today as the Museum of Ojibwa Culture.

From 1837 to 1873 St. Ignatius did not have a resident priest, but was served through a partnership with Mackinac Island, by priests from Lower Michigan or missionaries in the Upper Peninsula. Father Edward Jacker, the church's first pastor, arrived in November 1873.

PARISH LIFE. The present St. Ignatius Loyola Church was constructed in 1905. A fire in 1942 forced the people to return temporarily to the Old Mission Church for services.

St. Ignatius was enlarged, reconstructed and a basement hall added in 1948 and 1949. Through the devoted sacrifice of parishioners, the $65,000 debt incurred during reconstruction was paid off the following year.

In 1965, the chapel was remodeled to coincide with new regulations set forth by the Second Vatican Council.

In 1985, St. Ignatius began sharing a pastor with Immaculate Conception Parish in Moran and its mission at Trout Lake. The St. Ignace rectory was renovated in 1991 and the pastor continued to reside there.

During the Jubilee Year 2000, Bishop James Garland included St. Ignatius Church among the diocese's Baraga Pilgrimage sites. The tour highlighted shrines to Bishop Frederic Baraga and other churches of historical significance in the diocese.

PARISH SCHOOL. Women religious from the Ursuline Order in Chatham, Ontario, served the religious education needs of young people in St. Ignace for a remarkable 87 years. The Ursuline Academy—a high school for girls—operated from 1897 to 1951 when its status changed to a parochial elementary school.

The parish began paying rent to the sisters for St. Ignatius Elementary, along with covering their stipends and other costs, such as bussing. In 1972, the elementary school and the convent closed, but a few sisters remained to oversee the religious education program at the parish. The last Ursuline Sisters left St. Ignace in 1984.

PASTORS. Fathers Edward Jacker, 1873-1880; Charles A. Richard, 1880-1881; Killian Haas, 1881-1882; co-pastors John F. Chambon and Bishop Ignatius Mrak, 1882; John Chebul, 1882-1885; Francis X. Becker, 1885-1886; John A. Keul, 1886-1887; A. T. Schuettlehoefer, 1887-1888; Edward Chapius, 1888; John H. Reynaert, 1888-1889; Hilary J. Rosseau, 1889-1890; John Henn, 1890-1891; John Chebul, 1891-1893; Joseph Haas, 1893-1894; Joseph P. Kunes, 1894-1897; Adam Doser, 1898-1901; John J. Mockler, 1901-1919; John T. Holland, 1919-1940; George LaForest; 1940-1945; Nolan McKevitt, 1945-1950; Glen Sanford, 1950-1952, Bernard A. Karol, 1952-1974; Norbert Landreville, 1974-1986; Raymond Hoefgen, 1986-1991, and C. Michael Rhoades, 1991-.

BLESSED SACRAMENT, STAMBAUGH

It was the women of the Stambaugh community who led the initiative for establishment of a church of their own. The ladies began building enthusiasm for the endeavor and then worked to raise the necessary funds. Parishioners pitched in money and labor, and in 1948 the hard work paid off. Blessed Sacrament Parish served as the community's house of worship until its closure in 1982.

Blessed Sacrament, Stambaugh

FOUNDING. Before construction of Blessed Sacrament Church in Stambaugh, Catholics in the mining town were first served by priests from Crystal Falls and then Iron River. The ladies of the community had said the distance to travel to Mass at a neighboring parish was too great and that the miles were keeping families from fulfilling their holy obligations.

Thanks to Father George Dingfelder of St. Agnes Parish in Iron River, Mass was said in Stambaugh for the first time on Christmas Day 1943 in the Community Building. Weekly services continued there until 1948 when a church was finally built.

PARISH LIFE. Determined to have a church of its own, the group of women separated themselves from the St. Agnes Guild and started raising funds. In 1944, two lots were purchased on the corner of Seventh and Jefferson streets for an eventual church. A building committee was started in 1948, and a door-to-door fund drive enlisted support from the entire community. The diocesan Home Mission Fund donated $10,000 toward the project. On May 14, 1948, ground was broken and construction began. Members of the parish donated labor, supplies and equipment to the project.

On July 16 of that year, the parish's first pastor, Father Gerard LaMothe, arrived. Soon after, a home was purchased for use as a rectory. The church was of Old English style and had a seating capacity of 225. Generous donations financed the decoration of the church interior. Stained glass windows, statues, furnishings and adornments were among the gifts. Father LaMothe held the first Mass and blessed the new church Feb. 13, 1949. The boundaries of the new parish were Stambaugh and Dover Location south to the Caspian town line, Bates Township, Thunder Road and Ice Lake.

Major renovations were made to the church in the years that followed. Most notable were the modifications made in the 1960s to accommodate changes in the liturgy resulting from the Second Vatican Council.

In 1965, consideration was given to abandoning the church, which was now too small for the growing parish, and building an entirely new church and rectory complex. But those plans did not come to fruition. Instead, the church's interior received a major facelift in 1969. Improvements included new paneling, a new ceiling, remodeling of the main altar, a new heating plant, new furnishings and new Stations of the Cross. At the same time, the parish hall was remodeled. In 1970 a garage was added onto the rectory. All of this work was done by parishioners' donations of labor and money.

From 1949 to 1964, women of various religious orders taught catechetical school at Blessed Sacrament. Service was offered by the Sisters of St. Francis, the School Sisters of Notre Dame, and the Sisters of Saint Joseph of Carondolet, Mo. Beginning in 1964, the young people took part in a western Iron County cooperative program offered by the Dominican Sisters of St. Agnes Parish.

In 1972 a new catechetical program was started for children of grade school age from Blessed Sacrament, Guardian Angels in Crystal Falls, and St. Cecilia in Caspian. Two School Sisters of Notre Dame coordinated the program.

Young people of the parish also attended St. Agnes School in Iron River. From 1957 to 1963, men of the parish volunteered to drive the students to and from the school using a bus purchased by Blessed Sacrament. St. Agnes School closed in June 1970.

In 1973, the parish celebrated 25 years since the completion of its first church, and published a Silver Anniversary booklet.

CLOSURE. After the 1982 death the parish's first pastor, Father Norbert Freiburger, it was decided to close the doors of Blessed Sacrament Church. An economic decline in the area coupled with the diocese's priest shortage, led to the determination. Parishioners were encouraged to join other parishes in the area. The Blessed Sacrament building is being used as a schoolhouse.

RECORDS. Records for Blessed Sacrament Parish are located at St. Agnes Church in Iron River.

PASTORS. Fathers Gerard LaMothe, 1948-1950; Edward Lulewicz, 1950-1951; Norbert Freiburger, 1951-1957; Aloysius Ehlinger, 1957-1963; Casimir Marcinkevicius, 1963-1965; John Noel Arneth, 1965-1973; Raymond J. Smith, 1973-1976; Norbert LaCosse, 1976-1979, and Norbert Freiburger, 1979-1982.

PRECIOUS BLOOD, STEPHENSON

Despite an unsettling start, the Precious Blood Parish in Stephenson has thrived throughout the 20th century. Having overcome many obstacles in the beginning, the people of the parish made many sacrifices and saw their devotion flourish into an eventual church complex measuring a city block. A beautiful church, convent and catechetical center, as well as a new rectory, stand as outward signs of the people's faith and commitment to their parish community.

Precious Blood, Stephenson

FOUNDING. Catholics living around Stephenson first began worshiping together around 1878. Father Martin Fox of Spalding offered Mass regularly in the public school building. In 1879 Stephenson's first church, a small structure located on the present parish property, was built. Priests of St. Francis Xavier in Spalding served the parish with weekly services for the next five years.

Father Francis X. Becker was assigned the first pastor of Precious Blood in August 1883. But Father Becker stayed only a year. Following his departure, the loggers and farmers who made up the new parish struggled to survive the next decade. Being served by more than a dozen priests with short stints from 1884 to 1895 the people struggled in their practice of the faith. However, the arrival of Father Francis X. Barth in November 1895 stirred a revival in the faith community.

PARISH LIFE. Father Barth's first task was building a rectory. By September 1900 Bishop Frederick Eis had laid the cornerstone for a new church. The people of the parish and the community made generous sacrifices so that a new house of worship could be erected in Stephenson. The original church was moved a short distance and used for many years as the parish hall. In its place was built a large Gothic-style, red brick structure. The church was adorned with a rose window, gold leaf cross and two towers. A dedication ceremony was held May 22, 1901.

Missions attached to the early church included Daggett, Ingalls, Wallace, Cedar River and Koss. St. Frederick Parish in Daggett was named an independent parish in 1921. At the same time, responsibility for Holy Rosary Mission in Cedar River was given to St. Frederick's.

The next decade at Precious Blood saw the decorating of the church's interior. In keeping with the high standard of the exterior, a Milwaukee art firm was hired to do the work inside.

Father Albert Treilles did much to improve the church and parish grounds. He purchased additional property and in 1943 had erected a grotto, a replica of Our Blessed Mother of Lourdes in France. Bishop Francis Magner dedicated the shrine on Aug. 15. Parishioners donated statues of The Blessed Virgin Mary, St. Bernadette and Christ the King. The grotto has been the site for summer weddings, special services and for devotion and prayers. Each summer the parish holds a picnic at the site.

The parish celebrated a golden jubilee on Oct. 15, 1950, marking 50 years since the blessing of the church's cornerstone.

Upgrades to the church in the early 1950s included renovating the basement into a modern parish hall. In 1951 Ursuline Sisters arrived at Precious Blood to teach religious education classes. A convent was constructed on property south of the grotto. Bishop Thomas L. Noa dedicated the structure Aug. 15. In 1968 a catechetical center was constructed immediately behind the sisters' home.

Prior to the 1980 centennial year, the parish constructed a memorial room off the east entrance of the church. The space is used as a conference room, gathering space and winter chapel. It is named in honor of the former pastors who served Precious Blood.

A July 6, 1980 Mass, celebrated by Bishop Mark Schmitt, was the culmination of the parish's centennial celebration. Also in the centennial year, a complete parish history was printed.

In 1987 a new rectory was constructed on the south side of the church. In 1999 a new entrance on the west side replaced cement steps.

PASTORS. Fathers Francis X. Becker, 1883-1884; F. X. Weninger, 1884; Mathias Orth, 1884; F. X. De Langie, 1884-1888; Prosper Girard, 1888; John Burns, 1888-1889; Anacletus O. Pelisson, 1889; Michael Weis, 1889-1890; Peter P. Mazuret, 1890; Alberico Vitali, 1890; Joseph Hoeber, 1890-1891; Joseph A. Sauriol, 1891; Paul Datin, 1892-1893; William Joisten, 1893; Fidelis Sutter, 1894; John Henn, 1894-1895; Thomas Dassylva, 1895; Francis X. Barth, 1895-1911; Carl B. Liedgens, 1911-1924; Joseph Dufort, 1924-1931; Joseph Beauchene, 1931-1940; Philip de Neri Jutras, 1940; Albert J. Treilles, 1940-1952; Aloysius Hasenberg, 1952; Msgr. Glen Sanford, 1952-1968; John V. Suhr, 1968-1971; Conrad E. Suda, 1971-1978; John McArdle, 1978-1985; Raymond Zeugner, 1985-1997; Raymond Hoefgen, 1997-2002, and Mathew Perumpally, 2002-.

Sacred Heart, Sugar Island

Sacred Heart, Sugar Island

Bishop Frederic Baraga visited Catholics living on Sugar Island often in the mid-1800s. Of the four churches that had been erected on the island, Sacred Heart is the only one at which regular services are still offered. A priest from Sault Ste. Marie offers Mass and a group of parishioners takes care of the business of the parish and maintains the building.

FOUNDING. Located east of Sault Ste. Marie in the St. Marys River, Sugar Island was visited by Bishop Frederic Baraga between 1854 and 1864. The four churches erected on the island were: Holy Angels at Payment—regular services were offered from 1857 to 1953; St. Joseph at Ishkonigan near Gem Island—operated from 1861 to 1930; St. Theresa at Six Mile Road—founded in 1893, moved to Wilwalk in 1943, renamed St. John and St. Anne in 1950 and closed in 1960; and Sacred Heart at Baie de Wasai (now referred to only as Sugar Island).

PARISH LIFE. Sacred Heart Mission was founded in 1911 by Jesuit missionary Father William Gagnieur. Before construction of the church, Mass was offered in a private home, the log schoolhouse or Thibert's store. The church was blessed Sept. 8, 1928. Mass continues to be offered every weekend at Sacred Heart. Since 1982 one Mass also has been offered at the Holy Angels Church, usually in the summertime. That church is a Michigan Historic Site.

Father Joseph Lawless, SJ, began assisting with the Native American missions of the diocese in 1946. Under Father Lawless' leadership a basement hall was dug under the Sacred Heart church. For decades a ladies' guild helped raise money for necessary improvements to the church. A new altar was erected in 1969. In the early 1970s the church acquired additional property. Renovations in the mid-1970s included the construction of a reconciliation room, roof replacement and interior painting. In 2003 a pipe organ was dedicated.

A core group of parishioners maintains the church and conducts the regular business of the mission. The pastor from St. Mary Parish in Sault Ste. Marie travels to the island by ferry for the weekend Mass. Many summer tourists join the 40 families of the parish for worship. An annual picnic had previously been a parish tradition.

Jesuit missionaries served the people of Sacred Heart Mission for most of the 20th century. In honor of his 40 years of generosity, commitment and outstanding contributions to the people of the region, Father Lawless was named the 1990 Sugar Island Citizen of the year.

PASTORS. Fathers William Gagnieur, SJ, 1911-1937; Paul Prud'homme, SJ, 1937-1946 and 1953-1972; Joseph Lawless, SJ, 1946-1953 and 1959-1992; James Birney, SJ, 1954-1960 and 1968-1977; Henry Gelin, SJ, 1976-1980; Michael Steltenkamp, SJ, 1977-1980; Edward Flint, SJ, 1979; Bernard Haas, SJ, 1980-1986; Thomas Bain, SJ, 1986-1992; Theodore Brodeur, 1992-1995; Jeff Johnson, 1995-1997, and Theodore Brodeur, 1997-.

St. Rita, Trenary

The small parish of St. Rita in Trenary began as a mission of Rapid River and grew through the first part of the 20th century to warrant its own pastor. Today, the church continues to serve the people of the farming communities in the central Upper Peninsula.

St. Rita, Trenary

FOUNDING. French-Canadian Catholics settling in the lumbering community of Trenary in the early 1900s were served by priests from Munising. Around 1910 a priest from Rapid River would come to celebrate Mass one or two weekdays per month in private homes. A former saloon was even used for Mass prior to the building of St. Rita Church, which was dedicated Aug. 17, 1924. For 15 years a priest from Rapid River came by railroad to offer Mass. In 1933 a log cabin house was built to provide a residence for the visiting priest.

PARISH LIFE. By 1947 farming had replaced logging as the main occupation of the region, and additional Catholic families had moved to the community. On June 6 of that year, St. Rita's was separated from Rapid River and received its first pastor. Within a few months a parish hall was built and a home across the street from the church was purchased for a rectory.

Improvements to the church complex came in the mid-1970s when the rectory was repainted and new carpeting installed. The church was partly remodeled, lighting was upgraded, the interior painted and new carpeting installed. In 1981 parishioners constructed an addition, which includes an enlarged vestibule with a cry room and a reconciliation room. Additional improvements were made to the rectory in 1988.

PASTORS. Fathers Andrew Schulek, 1947-1951; Edward Mihelich, 1951-1953; Gervase Brewer, 1953-1958; Aloysius Hasenberg, 1958-1966; Michael Hale, 1966-1968; Robert Haas, 1968-1970; John Ryan, 1970-1971; Louis Wren, OFM Conv., 1971-1972; co-pastor Terrence Donnelly, 1972-1974; co-pastor Peter Minelli, 1972-1974; John Patrick, 1974-1977; William G. Richards, 1977-1981; Raymond Zeugner, 1981-1983; Robert Polcyn, OFM Cap., 1983-1985; Darryl J. Pepin, 1985-1988; Dino Silvestrini, 1989-1991; Richard C. Schaeffer, 1991-1993; Gregory R. Heikkala, 1993-1997; Sebastian Kavumkal, 1997-2000; Thomas J. Thekkel, MST, 2000-2005, and Jacek Wtyklo, 2005-.

St. Mary Mission, Trout Lake

St. Mary Mission, Trout Lake

Throughout the years, pastors serving other parishes in the diocese have also cared for the St. Mary Mission in Trout Lake. But responsibility for the upkeep of church buildings and property, as well as for maintaining the spiritual vigor of church members, lies with the people who make up the congregation. Since the mission was founded in 1911, the people of St. Mary's continue to maintain the vitality of their faith community.

FOUNDING. St. Mary Mission, located 18 miles northwest of Moran, was founded in 1911 as a mission of Engadine. The Moran pastor carried out the responsibility of caring for St. Mary's from June 1941 to 1986. The mission has since been assigned to St. Joseph Parish in Rudyard.

PARISH LIFE. The original church structure served the people for 60 years. The altar society and the Holy Name Society helped support the mission. Regular attendance more than doubles in the summer months.

Ursuline Sisters serving at St. Ignatius Loyola Parish in St. Ignace provided a summer religious education program for the youth of the mission. The church saw somewhat of a spiritual renewal among members in 1966 spurred on by the formation of the grade school girls' choir. A new church building was constructed in 1970. The structure was dedicated March 21, 1971.

PASTORS. Fathers Joseph H. Beauchaine, 1911-1912; Joseph Dufort, 1912-1915; William J. Remillard, 1915-1916; Bernard LeFebre, 1916-1917; Herman N. Gagne, 1917; Francis Geynet, 1918; Edward J. Testevin, 1918; Peter Bleeker, 1918-1922; Joseph Guertin, 1922-1923; Charles Fox, 1923-1931; Raymond Bergeron, 1931-1935; Joseph Seifert, 1935-1937; Thomas P. Dunleavy, 1937-1939; James J. Schaefer, 1939-1941; Thomas Lester Bourgeois, 1941-1943; James McCarthy, 1943-1946; Charles J. Reinhart, 1946-1949; Gervase Brewer, 1949-1951; John H. Ryan, 1951-1953; Edward Mihelich, 1953-1955; Patrick Frankard, 1955-1960; Donald Hartman, 1960-1963; Kenneth Bretl, 1963-1965; Norbert Landreville, 1965-1969; David Rocheleau, 1970-1973; John Chrobak, 1974-1981; Peter Oberto, 1981-1985; Norbert Landreville, 1985-1986; Ronald J. Skufca, 1986-1989; N. Daniel Rupp, 1989-1990; Mark A. McQuesten, 1990-1996; Francis J. DeGroot, 1996-2003, and Cyriac Kattayarikil, 2003-.

St. Barbara, Vulcan

St. Barbara, Vulcan

In the last half of the 20th century, the faith community of St. Barbara Parish in Vulcan increased in size as parishioners from the former mission churches of Loretto and Faithorn joined its ranks. A magnificent building in central Vulcan was erected to replace a much more modest structure that was destroyed by fire in 1925. The people of the parish worked hard and made many sacrifices to see the new church erected. Throughout its century-long existence, the parish has continued to overcome obstacles and provide a foundation in faith for the population of the area.

FOUNDING. The first church in Vulcan was built in 1882 near the Vulcan border with Norway. For the first five years, priests from Norway would offer Sunday Mass. Then, on Oct. 8, 1887, Father Dominic Vento was assigned as the first resident pastor. In subsequent years a rectory was built and the church grounds updated.

On Holy Thursday 1925, tragedy struck when the original church was destroyed by fire. Plans for construction of a new church began immediately. In the meantime, Mass was offered in the town hall.

The new structure was erected in the center of the community on land leased from the Penn Mining Co. The cornerstone was laid in 1925 and construction was completed in 1930. In order to cut down on costs, the men of the parish did much of the work.

PARISH LIFE. St. Barbara's celebrated its centennial June 26 and 27, 1982. Bishop Mark F. Schmitt presided over a thanksgiving Mass and a family barbecue. Live music and dancing was held on the church grounds, and a display of historical photographs of the church helped mark the milestone.

In the late 1990s parishioners supported several major improvements to the parish plant. Renovations were made to the church sanctuary and to the rectory to include more office space. Additional parking space was created and the basement hall and kitchen were remodeled and updated. The gathering space was dedicated in the name of the late Father William Callari.

In 1965 St. Barbara Parish entered into a cooperative arrangement with St. Mary Parish in Norway to support the Holy Spirit Catholic Central School. The collaborative effort continued to thrive in 2000.

Parish organizations include the St. Barbara's League of Women, St. Vincent de Paul Society and the Legion of Mary. The parish is proud of the many young men and women of St. Barbara's who have pursued religious vocations over the years.

MISSIONS. Priests from St. Barbara Parish also served regularly at St. Mary Parish in Faithorn until that chrch was closed in 1995 and parishioners joined the St. Barbara parish community.

In 1966 the priest serving St. Barbara Parish also began administering to St. Stephen Parish in Loretto. In 1971 the Loretto church was destroyed by fire and, instead of rebuilding, it was decided St. Stephen parishioners would join the faith community in Vulcan.

PASTORS. Fathers Dominic Vento, 1887-1889; Anacletus Pelisson, 1890-1891; Alberico Vitali, 1892-1893; Anthony Molinari, 1893-1894; Joseph Pinten, 1894-1895; Joseph Haas, 1895-1897; Benjamino Berto, 1897-1898; William Shea, 1898-1899; John Kraker, 1899; Raphael Cavicchi, 1899-1906; Alexander Wollny, 1906; John Stenglein, 1906-1909; Anthony Molinari, 1908-1920; Alexander Wollny, 1920; George Stuntebeck, 1920; F. Louis Kania, 1920; Dennis Babilewicz, 1920; Constantine Dzuik, 1920-1921; Albert Treilles, 1921; Constantine Dzuik, 1921-1925; Simon Borkowski, 1925-1939; George LaForest, 1939-1940; Casper Douenberg, 1940-1945; William Schick, 1945-1947; Raymond Przybylski, 1947-1966; Thomas Ruppe, 1966-1971; Gervase Brewer, 1971-1972; Stephen Mayrand, 1972-1984; Raymond Hoefgen, 1984-1986; James Hebein, 1986-1994; Jerome Nowacki, 1994-1995; Arnold Grambow, 1995-1996; Mark McQuesten, 1996-1997; William Callari, 1997-2004, and Joy Joseph Adimakkeel, 2004-.

Immaculate Conception, Wakefield

Immaculate Conception Parish in Wakefield was started as a mission of Bessemer. Following a terrible fire in 1909, the people rebuilt the church into an independent parish. The pastor of Immaculate Conception was responsible for recruiting women religious to take over operations at the Wakefield hospital in the 1940s. Two mission churches were also started from Wakefield. Significant improvements to the church building helped the people celebrate Immaculate Conception's 75-year anniversary in 1986.

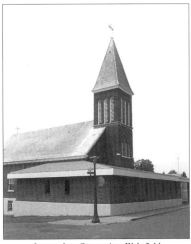

Immaculate Conception, Wakefield

FOUNDING. The establishment of the Catholic Church in Wakefield dates back to 1886 after a church was established in nearby Bessemer. The Bessemer pastor traveled to Wakefield to offer monthly services in private homes or in the schoolhouse. The first church in Wakefield was built in 1892 and dedicated in honor of St. Joseph. The church was served as a mission of Bessemer until 1905.

On St. Patrick's Day 1909, St. Joseph Church was destroyed by fire. Having no money set aside, eager parishioners—led by their pastor—got to work on rebuilding almost immediately.

The people cleared away the charred debris that had been their church, and by June, construction had begun on a new house of worship. Bishop Frederick Eis laid the cornerstone for the new structure on July 18, 1909. A parish bazaar raised several thousand dollars toward the project.

Mass was said in the church basement beginning in October 1909. Three years later, on Sept. 1, 1913, Bishop Eis returned to dedicate the new structure to the Immaculate Conception of the Blessed Virgin Mary, or St. Mary's, as it is commonly referred to. A new rectory was built in 1925.

PARISH LIFE. The 15-year pastorate of Father Thomas Drengacz began in July 1936. While in Wakefield, Father Drengacz did much to improve the Immaculate Conception facilities. He is also remembered for enhancing the spiritual lives of parishioners. Under Father Drengacz's leadership, an annual novena was started and new parish organizations begun, such as the Knights of Columbus, Daughters of Isabella and a unit of the Third Order of St. Francis.

Father Drengacz also instituted a summer catechetical program for the young people of the parish. Franciscan Sisters of St. Cunegunde, Chicago, started the school in 1937. The Franciscan Sisters of Christian Charity from Manitowoc, Wis., taught from 1940 to 1945.

Father Drengacz was also instrumental in getting the Sisters of St. Joseph of the Third Order of St. Francis, from Stevens Point, Wis., to take over ownership of the Divine Infant of Prague Hospital in Wakefield.

Seventy-five years after the construction of the present church, the Immaculate Conception parish broke ground for a significant renovation project. A 30-year dream was realized in 1986 with the completion of barrier-free access to the church, complete with a circular driveway and canopied entrance. The former convent became a parish rectory with a garage, and the church interior was redecorated. The new addition and church entry were dedicated Sunday, Nov. 2.

MISSIONS. Catholic men living in nearby Ramsay and Mikado (later called Verona) donated the funds for construction of a mission church of their own in 1903. The women of the community held fundraising events, while men did the work to clear the site. The structure was completed in May 1905 and dedicated Sacred Heart. Services there were discontinued in 1921 and the church building was razed in 1934. In 1940 Father Drengacz blessed a new church in Ramsay. The mission was cared for by Wakefield until it received its own resident pastor in 1948.

Immaculate Conception assumed responsibility for the care of St. Catherine Mission in Marenisco from 1950 to 1967 and again since 1973.

PASTORS. Fathers Theodore Bateski, 1909; Bernard Linnemann, 1909; John Stenglein, 1910; Emmanuel V. Kopietz, 1913; Casper Douenburg, 1914; Sebastian Maier, 1915; Jerry Schneider, 1915; Charles Szygula, 1915-1930; Mark Hoskins, 1930-1931; Cronan Flynn, 1931-1936; Thomas A. Drengacz, 1936-1952; Francis E. Krystyniak, 1952-1954; Charles Daniel, 1954-1966; Roland Dion, 1966-1969; Robert Chisholm, 1969-1971; Joseph Kichak, 1971-1980; Edward Wenzel, 1980-1982; David C. Jenner, 1982-1985; Allan J. Mayotte, 1985-1990; John Maloney, 1990-1995; Allan J. Mayotte, 1995-2000; Chacko Devasia Kakaniyil, 2000-2004, and James Roetzer, 2004-.

Immaculate Conception, Watersmeet

Started as a mission of Ewen in the 1880s, Immaculate Conception Parish in Watersmeet has been independent since 1916. The original wooden church was replaced by a modern structure in 1957. The parish was blessed with the 44-year pastorate of Father Samuel Bottoni.

Immaculate Conception, Watersmeet

FOUNDING. The original Immaculate Conception Church in Watersmeet was built around 1890. In 1916, a rectory was constructed and the first resident pastor arrived.

Dominican Sisters of Sinsinawa, Wis., taught summer religious education classes for the youth of the parish during the late 1940s and through the 1950s.

PARISH LIFE. The parish was blessed with the 44-year pastorate of Father Samuel Bottoni, who served from 1952 to 1996.

Shortly after his arrival in Watersmeet, Father Bottoni led the parish in construction of a modern church building. The original church was moved farther back on the grounds and used for services until the basement of the new structure was completed. The new church was dedicated July 7, 1957.

In 1958, the original church and rectory were moved eight miles south to Camp Plagens on the shore of Moon Lake. The church was renamed for St. Don Bosco and is known in the area as St. John's Chapel. Camp Plagens was sold in 1996. The chapel now houses the Watersmeet Historical Society.

The people of Immaculate Conception supported additional improvements from 1999 to 2001. Faith formation classrooms were constructed in the basement of the rectory. The parish hall was renovated, the plant was made handicapped accessible and the church interior was painted and new carpeting installed. The parish office and rectory were also redesigned.

PASTORS. Fathers Adam Doser, 1916-1933; John Kraker, 1937-1942; Peter Bleeker, 1942-1945; Casper Douenberg, 1945-1951; Charles Reinhart, 1951-1952; Samuel Bottoni, 1952-1996; Francis Dobrzenski, 1996-1999; Thomas Valayathil, 1999-2003; George Kallarackal, MCBS, 2003-2004, and Thomas Ettolil 2004-.

St. Anthony of Padua, Wells

With little fanfare but much faith, the parish family of St. Anthony of Padua in Wells has worked and prayed and thus nurtured the growth of its village church over the last 50 years.

FOUNDING. Wells was considered a rural community in 1946 when Bishop Francis J. Magner decided a mission church was needed there. Before that time, people living in the area took a streetcar to Mass in Escanaba.

Begun as a mission of St. Joseph Parish in Escanaba, St. Anthony's first church was formed in an adapted garage donated by the Shepeck Dimension and Lumber Co. The original chapel could seat only 130 people.

St. Anthony of Padua, Wells

On July 15, 1947, St. Patrick Parish in Escanaba assumed responsibility for the mission in Wells. That year parish organizations, such as a choir, ladies' guild, Catholic Youth Organization and Holy Name Society, were formed. On Oct. 21, 1948, Father Ralph J. Sterbentz, chaplain of St. Francis Hospital, was appointed administrator of St. Anthony's.

Finally on Feb. 13, 1949, St. Anthony's officially became a parish. Later that year, Father Sterbentz was relieved of his duties at the hospital and took up residence in Wells. A planning committee was formed and fundraising efforts began for a new church building.

PARISH LIFE. Ground was broken for a new church May 10, 1955. Bishop Thomas Noa dedicated the facility Dec. 11. In 1959, a rectory with downstairs classrooms was built and then later expanded. Prior to the organization of CCD classes by the women of the church, the Sisters of St. Dominic from St. Patrick Parish in Escanaba offered religious education classes to the young people.

The parish celebrated its 25th anniversary in June 1974 with a Mass celebrated by Bishop Charles A. Salatka.

Each year the parish hosts a volunteer dinner and a picnic that is both a popular community event and an important parish fundraiser.

PASTORS. Fathers Ralph Sterbentz, 1949-1954; Msgr. O'Neil D'Amour, 1954-1957; Norbert Freiburger, 1957-1973; Arthur J. Parrotta, 1973-1993; Richard L. Schaeffer, 1993- 2004, and Rick Courier, 2004-.

ST. JUDE, WHITE PINE

Despite a devastating decline in the area's economy, which forced many White Pine residents to leave to find work elsewhere, St. Jude Parish has remained a stable house of worship for the Catholics remaining in and around the community. Partnering with its mission church of St. Ann in Bergland, and grateful for financial assistance from All Saints Parish in Gladstone—its "twin" parish, St. Jude's offers religious education and formation and regular opportunities for faith, fellowship and service.

St. Jude, White Pine

FOUNDING. St. Jude Parish was established in 1953, the same year that the White Pine Copper Co. mining project got under way. The first Masses were celebrated by Father Thomas Ruppe of St. Mary Church in Rockland in a building that later became the White Pine Inn. In November 1953, services were transferred to the White Pine Elementary School auditorium. It has been recalled that Father Ruppe heard confessions behind the piano in the auditorium.

PARISH LIFE. Construction of the parish's first church began in October 1955. The cornerstone of the Cedar Street church was laid on March 11, 1956. Bishop Thomas L. Noa dedicated the completed structure May 20.

In 1962 a rectory was constructed and St. Jude's was elevated to parish status. The pastor was also given responsibility for the care of St. Ann Mission in Bergland.

St. Jude's and the White Pine community were hit with hard times when the copper mine saw severe cutbacks in later years. A St. Vincent de Paul food pantry and thrift shop opened in White Pine to support the thousands of people who found themselves out of work.

Improvements were made to the church building in the late 1960s and early 1970s. Stained glass windows were installed, the church was repainted and new carpeting was installed. Native copper and wood were used in making custom sanctuary furnishings.

By the 1990s parish membership numbered around 80 families. Fund-raising programs were started, such as an annual harvest dinner and Millionaires' Party. Young people of the parish traveled to World Youth Day in Denver, Colo., in 1994. The next year two members participated in Mission Honduras. A parish retreat with Holy Family in Ontonagon was held in 1996.

In 1998, St. Jude Parish was "adopted" by All Saints Church in Gladstone. The Gladstone church tithes a percentage of its income to the White Pine parish. St. Jude's had a new bell system installed in 1998, paid for by donations from parishioners. Plans were started for the new St. Martha's Parish Hall, which was dedicated on June 3, 2001. In 2005 St. Jude's was linked with Ontonagon and Rockland.

PASTORS. Fathers Thomas Ruppe, 1953-1958; Frank Hollenbach, 1958-1961; George Pernaski, 1961-1966; S. Patrick Wisneske, 1966-1972; Glen Weber, 1972-1975; Wayne Marcotte, 1975-1980; Allan Mayotte, 1980-1985; Edward Wenzel, 1985-1991; John Longbucco, 1992; Michael Woempner, 1992-2002; Thomas Ettolil, 2002-2004; Abraham Kazhunadiyil, 2004-2005; Thomas Thekkel, MST, 2005, and Antony Lukose, 2005-.

Priests and Men Religious who have Served in the Diocese of Marquette

Abler, Larry, OFM Cap., 80
Adasiewicz, Casimir, 37, 156, 166, 182, 197, 228,
Adimakkeel, Joy Joseph, 162, 168, 322
Andary, Thomas M., 148, 152, 162, 228, 230, 253, 266, 286, 287, 289
Anderson, Thomas J., 117, 146, 180, 199, 222, 228, 258, 297, 304
Andolshek, Andrew
Arneth, John N., 130, 156, 164, 303, 314
Atfield, Thomas, 117, 176, 186, 209, 255
Avinshek, Steve, OFM, 180
Babilewicz, Dennis, 322
Babnik, Ferdinand
Bain, Thomas, 90, 239, 299, 318
Balluff, Ignatius, 243
Banach, John
Baraga, Frederic E., xii, xiii, 1, 2, 4, 33, 45, 58, 61, 79, 139, 175, 185, 215, 216, 220, 227, 233, 234, 242, 268, 275, 292, 295, 317
Baranowski, Stanislaus, 207, 251
Barcome, Earl
Bares, Elmer J., 90, 275, 286, 298
Barrette, S. M., 90
Barron, Joseph, 199, 232, 243, 276,
Barth, Francis X., 115, 142, 143, 315, 316
Bassett, Ronald, 123, 150, 160, 39
Bateski, Msgr. Theodore G., 1228, 129, 133, 166, 324
Baxter, Thomas A.
Bayer, Augustine OSF, 243, 262
Beauchene, Joseph H., 106, 115, 135, 152, 192, 209, 271, 272, 273, 303, 316, 320
Becker, Francis X., 115, 117, 125, 150, 160, 164, 186, 193, 209, 232, 243, 258, 275, 286, 291, 309, 312, 315, 316
Becker, Renatus, 146, 170, 209, 271, 276, 293, 304

Beliveau, Gideon, 258, 276, 309
Belot, John, 131, 162, 168, 180, 277
Bennett, Owen J., 119, 164, 276, 291
Berendsen, Eugene, O.Praem
Berens, Cyprian, OFM, 112
Bergeron, Raymond, 78, 125, 135, 162, 320
Berto, Benjamino, 190, 322
Bertsch, Luke, 105
Berube, James F., 239
Berube, Joseph F., 116, 117, 239 257, 258, 291
Beyer, Emil J., 38, 271, 281, 289
Bienarz, John C., 207, 251
Bifarini, Ugolino, OFM, 190
Birney, James, SJ, 95, 133, 299, 318
Black, Jordan, CP, 277
Bleeker, Peter, 102, 103, 117, 135, 152, 156, 211, 258, 294, 320, 325
Blin, Auguste J., 303
Bodenschatz, Ronald, TOR
Boehman, Bradon, OFM
Boever, Joseph, 246, 276, 293
Boissonnault, Joseph, 106, 175, 209, 211, 258, 271
Bonny, Francis C., 173
Bontempo, Henry, SJ, 108
Borca, Dennis L., 262
Bordas, Edward, 99, 100, 117, 129, 136, 150, 160, 170, 209, 211, 226, 258, 291, 293, 309
Borke, Eugene, SJ, 299
Borkowski, Simon, 322
Borman, Leslie
Boss, Joseph 97
Bottoni, Samuel T., 40, 235, 325
Bourgeois, Thomas Lester, 148, 176, 195, 230, 259, 260, 264, 286, 309, 320
Bourion, Honoratus, 192, 209, 253

Boyle, Faran H., OFM, 214
Bracket, Louis P., 100, 114, 162, 168, 256
Brault, Gilles, 117, 258, 291
Breault, Diendonne Joseph, 93, 175, 228
Bretl, Kenneth G., 90, 103, 143, 152, 260, 294, 320
Brewer, Gervase J., 84, 88, 180, 188, 260, 266, 303, 319, 320, 322
Brockhuis, Antonine, OFM
Broda, Leopold, 197
Brodeur, Theodore J., 95, 103, 162, 166, 168, 182, 296, 318
Brown, Howard J., 237
Brown, John, 105, 209, 232, 243, 275, 285, 286
Buchholtz, Henry A. (P.A.), 38, 100, 205, 209, 243, 262, 269
Budzik, Gratian, OFM
Buescher, Gabriel, OFM, 140
Burenz, John
Burion, Honoratus, 269, 286
Burke, Walter E.
Burns, Edward F.
Burns, John, 93, 105, 115, 125, 146, 170, 186, 209, 234, 258, 260, 264, 276, 291, 293, 304, 309, 316
Buschle, Francis, OFM, 140
Butkowski, Michael
Butler, Thomas, 258
Buttermann, Eugene, OSF, 8, 50, 140
Butzman, Felix, FSC,
Byrne, John J., SJ, 299
Callari, Joseph R., 39, 90, 144, 150, 160, 178, 294
Callari, William P., 121, 184, 321, 322
Calme, Dominic S., OFM, 140
Cangiano, Victor E., 190
Cappo, Louis C., 102, 130, 138, 188, 228, 243, 287
Capyak, Michael, 134
Carli, Peter, 88, 117, 258, 269, 275, 279, 286, 291
Carmody, Charles J., 143
Carne, Joseph, 83, 100, 131, 170, 186, 293

Casanova, Arnold L., 84, 237, 241
Cavicchi, Raphael, 147, 148, 188, 190, 309, 322
Centner, Alexius, OFM, 164
Challancin, James P., 77, 102, 211, 291
Chambon, John F., 10, 103, 129, 132, 166, 167, 182, 312
Chambon, Joseph, 132
Chapuis, Edward, 124, 125, 175, 199, 312
Charlebois, Joseph
Chartier, R. SJ, 10, 296
Cebul, John, 105, 125, 135, 150, 160, 168, 193, 199, 234, 271, 275, 276, 286, 312
Chisholm, Msgr. Robert J., 83, 186, 213, 237, 255, 324
Chrobak, John J., 214, 232, 260, 320
Chrobok, Valentine, 197, 283, 284
Ciupka, Fortunatus, 108, 114, 158
Cleary, Dennis, 199, 254, 255
Clisch, Norman A., 114, 119, 125, 197, 199, 214, 249, 305
Coignard, Alphonse C., 282
Coleman, Thomas B., 131, 277
Colin, J. H., 228
Comtois, Oliver, 170, 239, 243, 255, 276, 291, 293
Connolly, J. J., SJ, 296
Corcoran, James J., 93, 136, 176, 193, 209, 234, 255, 276, 286, 303
Cordy, Robert J., 93, 103, 241, 269, 271, 279, 281, 294
Cornelius, Leonard, OFM
Cotter, Raymond, 152
Courier, Rick L., 144, 246, 264, 305, 326
Craig, Richard
Creeden, Patrick, CICM, 298
Crocker, John, 180, 262, 309
Cunningham, Leo C., SJ, 299
D'Amour, Charles O'Neil, 32, 275, 282, 325
Daniel, Charles W., 114, 158, 180, 282, 324
Dapper, Peter, 117, 135, 258, 309

Dassylva, Thomas, 115, 121, 150, 160, 164, 175, 192, 209, 211, 228, 258, 303, 309, 316
Datin, Paul, 93, 115, 121, 150, 160, 226, 289, 316
David, A. L., 105
De Langie, F. X., 115, 125, 316
DeGroot, Francis J., 90, 249, 294, 320
DeHaan, William, 152
DeLude, Joseph, SJ, 294
Deschamps, Adrien, 152, 289
Desrochers, Joseph W., 76, 78, 188
Desrochers, Timothy H., 39, 76, 78, 85, 102, 160, 262
Diedgens, Charles, 146
Diedgens, Charles, 304
Dietrich, Casimir, 105
Dilmore, Michael, SDS,
Dingfelder, George J., 38, 119, 156, 199, 208, 209, 228, 291, 313
Dion, Roland L., 106, 152, 162, 168, 226, 253, 303, 307, 324
Dishaw, Conrad J., 130, 135, 138, 150, 152, 156, 158, 160, 253, 289
Dittman, Joseph F., 180, 261, 262, 269, 271, 279
Dobrzenski, Francis G., 141, 146, 188, 226, 304, 325
Doherty, Francis R., CSP, 209
Donavon, Daniel, SJ, 296
Donnelly, James L., 39, 150, 160, 195, 226, 266, 289
Donnelly, Terrence, 85, 162, 168, 232, 296, 319
Dooley, Erasmus, 140, 176, 219, 275
Doser, Adam J., 100, 129, 130, 164, 168, 193, 199, 224, 232, 243, 276, 286, 312, 325
Douenburg, Casper, 37, 80, 88, 102, 175, 303, 322, 325
Douglas, Marian, OFM, 105, 140, 226, 324
Dries, Charles, 170, 209, 243, 276, 293
Drengacz, Thomas A., 97, 153, 154, 168, 186, 235, 283, 284, 323, 324

Driege, Raymond
Drolet, Howard V., 121, 131,197, 277
Dufort, Joseph, 115, 121, 135, 150, 152, 160, 192, 228, 271, 281, 289, 316, 320
Dufresne, A. L., 78, 102, 125
Dugas, M. T., CSV
Dulude, J., SJ, 103
Dunleavy, Joseph J., 93, 205, 241, 301
Dunleavy, Thomas P., 93, 114, 135, 156, 158, 162, 256, 297, 301, 320
Dunne, Lawrence, 276
Dupasquier, Joseph, 130, 146, 258, 304
Duquette, Joseph F., 228, 264, 289
Duroc, Sebastian, 139, 140, 149, 150, 160, 209, 243
Dwyer, William, 170, 232, 276, 293
Dzuik, Constantine, 322
Eddy, Anthony
Eddy, Corbin T.
Ehlinger, Aloysius E., 88, 129, 131, 133, 156, 170, 264, 271, 281, 293, 309, 314
Eiling, Bernard A., 103, 145, 146, 152, 168, 186, 271, 294, 304
Eis, Frederick, xiii, 5, 46, 47, 51, 84, 87, 99, 100, 101, 105, 107, 109, 124, 125, 126, 142, 151, 155, 157, 175, 185, 196, 200, 029, 225, 229, 243, 254, 255, 265, 269, 277, 306, 315
Eisele, (First name unknown), 169, 170
Elmer, Charles W.
Erlach, Philip J., 100, 105, 199, 232, 234, 246, 271, 276
Erno, Shaun
Ettolil, Sebastian, MCBS, 112, 121, 214, 271, 276
Ettolil, Thomas, 98, 146, 304, 325, 328
Fabian, Jack
Fadale, R. Herman, 83, 111, 114, 158, 307
Fajt, Fidelis, OFM. Conv.
Faust, Melchior, 37, 80, 88, 97, 105, 124, 191, 192, 198, 234, 244, 246, 255, 286
Feldhaus, Edward N., 146, 275, 304
Felix, Joseph W., 86, 119, 127, 213, 246, 289
Ferland, David, 125

Ferland, David, CP 78
Ferrara, John
Ferraro, Gino S., 119, 156, 190, 264, 307
Filipek, Fidelis, OFM
Fillion, Paul, 150, 152, 160, 193, 282, 309
Fitzpatrick, James, OFM, 105
Fitzsimmons (First name unknown), 209
Flajole, John OFM
Flint, Edward, SJ, 299, 318
Flynn, Cronan, 324
Flynn, Cronan, CP, 235
Fogarty, Joseph C., OP
Fosu, Peter, 95, 103, 119, 154
Fox, Charles, 135 150, 160, 245, 246, 305, 320
Fox, Martin A., 115, 117, 149, 169, 179, 209, 243, 246, 254, 255, 276, 285, 286, 291, 293, 308, 309, 315
Franczek, August, 136, 146, 148, 154, 230, 284, 286, 291, 304
Franczek, Chester J., 76, 78, 97, 100, 114, 130, 166, 182
Franczek, Walter J., 166, 182, 251, 273, 282, 309
Frankard, Patrick W, 180, 241, 260, 320
Freiburger, Norbert A., 131, 171, 234, 277, 314, 326
Gagne, Herman N., 96, 97, 102, 135, 168, 180, 320
Gagnieur, Alexander A., SJ, 296
Gagnieur, William, SJ, 11, 94, 95, 121, 125, 182, 294, 296, 317, 318
Garceau, L. T., SJ, 296
Garcia, Reynaldo A., 232
Gardiner, Christopher B., 85, 91, 118, 119, 152, 273
Garin, Raymond J., 97, 121, 130, 239
Garland, James H., xi, xiii, ixv, xii, 7, 9, 14, 21, 22, 36, 46, 51, 59, 71, 72, 90, 91, 144, 145, 178, 180, 182, 188, 232, 262, 280, 293, 302, 310, 311, 312
Gattin, Michael, SJ, 108
Gausepohl, William, OSF, 140
Gauthier, Lawrence T., 32, 102, 178, 241

Geers, Augustus, 93, 105, 119, 154, 161, 170, 175, 186, 209, 224, 234, 243, 255, 271, 275, 291, 293
Gehring, Owen, OFM
Gelin, Henry, SJ, 117, 129, 133, 258, 299, 318
Genovesi, James, 117, 130, 188, 207, 258
Genseler, Casper, 105
George, Augustin, 80, 88, 228
Gerstle, Fabian, OFM, 140
Geynet, Francis, 111, 135, 152, 253, 273, 320
Gherna, Raphael, 148, 230, 286
Gibbs, Wilbur M., 38, 232, 271, 281, 291
Gimski, Francis J., 103, 121, 154, 273, 284, 294
Girard, Prosper, 115, 117, 120, 121, 129, 150, 160, 168, 309, 316
Glaser, Frederic
Glaser, Jerome
Godina, Joseph
Goerner, Basil S.
Gonchar, John J., OFM
Gondek, Joseph A., 75, 76, 77, 78, 125, 168, 222
Gooley, M., 303
Gouin, Joseph O., 148, 180, 220, 246, 249, 305
Grambow, Arnold J., 142, 143, 146, 148, 152, 164, 226, 275, 286, 304, 322
Greco, Francis
Guay, Charles
Guertin, Joseph E., 135
Guilmin, T. S.
Gustafson, George
Haas, Bernard D., SJ, 299, 318
Haas, Joseph 100, 124, 164, 170, 199, 224, 228, 271, 276, 293, 312, 322
Haas, Killian, 232, 243, 312
Haas, Robert A., 85, 129, 130, 133, 156, 170, 249, 253, 293, 319
Hafertape, Angelus, 105
Hafner, Christopher, OFM, 80, 81
Hale, Michael F., 85, 123, 130, 156, 188, 266, 319

Hale, Michael F., 224
Hamel, Peter, SJ, 296
Handtmann, Isidor, 232
Hanisko, Brother Martin
Harrington, Bertin, OFM,
Harrington, Ethelbert, OFM, 105
Harrington, Gerald F., 98, 146, 221, 222, 262, 304 307
Harris, David T., 178, 276
Hartman, Donald P., 114, 117, 123, 134, 146, 154, 258, 260, 266, 284, 304, 320
Hascall, John S., OFM, Cap., 80, 90, 299
Hasenberg, Alexander, 116, 117, 146, 258, 304
Hasenberg, Aloysius J., 32, 84, 115, 199, 316, 319
Haus, Joseph, 228, 234
Hawelka, J. S., 129, 271
Healy, James P.
Healy, Terrence
Hebein, James M., 76, 78, 123, 130, 131, 148, 188, 266, 277, 322
Heckler, Alphonse, OFM Cap.
Heikkala, Gregory R., 71, 85, 228, 319
Held, Gerald, OFM, 105, 214
Heliard, Francis, 226, 255
Henkes, Donald E.
Henn, John, 100, 1115, 117, 150, 160, 170, 180, 1999, 223, 224, 228, 234, 258, 264, 275, 276, 293, 309, 312, 316
Henn, Joseph 277
Hennelly, Eugene T., 146, 156, 180, 199, 304
Hennessy, John 99, 100, 204
Henry, John C., 243
Hens, Maurice, OMC, 239
Henze, Basil, 105
Henze, Julius, OFM, 105, 140
Heppner, Sylvester, OFM
Herbst, Charles M., 276, 291, 298
Hernandez, Ricardo
Higdon, Coleman, OFM
Hoff, Alphonse, OFM
Hodnick, Anthony, 100, 193, 264, 286,
Hoeber, Francis, OFM, 175

Hoeber, Joseph, 115, 121, 130, 309, 316
Hoefgen, Raymond, 131, 154, 170, 232, 260, 264, 271, 273, 284, 289, 293, 312, 316, 322
Hoelscher, Hilary, 105
Hofmann, Frederick L, 83, 121, 148, 168, 170, 173, 180, 230, 286, 293
Hogan, Camillus F., OFM, 214
Holland, John T., 97, 121, 243, 255, 296, 312
Hollenbach, Frank A., 83, 123, 131, 170, 207, 269, 277, 279, 293, 307, 328
Hollinger, Joseph, 119, 164, 180, 205, 209, 271, 275, 276, 291
Hopkins, Carnell 97
Hoskins, Mark, 324
Hruska, Timothy W., 134, 162, 171
Huber, Kilian, OFM
Hubly, Anthony, 117, 170, 276, 293
Hubly, Joseph A., 117
Hudack, Michael, 108
Huet, L. Z., 192
Hughes, John G., 219, 220, 286, 296
Hukenbeck, Juniper, OFM, 214
Ibach, William, SJ
Ignatz, Frank J., 84, 90, 102, 158, 166, 182, 207, 246, 284, 297, 298, 303
Ile, Robert A.
Jacker, Edward, 80, 104, 105, 128, 150, 160, 170, 174, 185, 186, 209, 232, 243, 276, 293, 311, 312
Jacobs, Gary
Jacques, Raymond G., 138, 192, 239, 253, 289, 296
Jaklic, Francis
Jaksztys, Stanislaus, 277
Jani, Peter, 190
Jenks, Robert
Jenner, David, 88, 98, 112, 117, 131, 166, 170, 173, 182, 235, 258, 273, 293
Jeruzal, Joseph, OFM Cap.
Jiranek, Francis, 207
Jodocy, Mathias N., 93, 102, 160, 238, 239, 243, 289
Jodocy, Mathias J., 101

333

Jogues, Isaac, SJ, 1, 10, 267
Johnson, Jeff G., 95, 103, 222, 237, 299, 318
Joisten, William, 100, 115, 146, 228, 232, 251, 275, 304, 316
Joseph Barron
Joseph, George, 304
Joseph, Roy, MST
Jurkovich, Robb M.
Jutras, Philip De Neri, 78, 115, 125, 271, 303, 316
K.F., Thomas
Kaczmarek, James A., 190
Kadavil, Anthony
Kain, Rev. Michael L., O.Praem,
Kakaniyil, Chacko, 80, 88, 228, 235, 324
Kallarackal, George, MCBS, 80, 88, 146, 304
Kania, F. Louis, 246, 322
Karch, Victor A., 246, 250, 251, 305
Karol, Bernard A., 117, 258, 308, 309, 312
Karottekunnel, Paul, MST, 143, 168, 271, 281
Kasenberg (First name unknown), 246
Kasuboski, Walter, OFM Cap., 80
Kattayarikil, Cyriac, 294, 320
Kavumkal, Sebastian, MST, 85, 129, 133, 166, 182, 319
Kazhunadiyil, Abraham, 276, 293, 328
Keating, Richard, OFM Cap.
Kehoe, Martin, 45, 100, 204, 205, 209, 243, 275
Keller, Anthony, 175, 246, 291, 309
Kelly, James W., 186, 291
Kelly, Senan, OFM
Kennedy, Robert
Kennedy, Thomas A., 121, 143, 232
Kenney, Gerald 78, 125
Kenny, John C., 232, 243, 286
Keul, John, 125, 192, 209, 232, 243, 286, 312
Kichak, Joseph A., 88, 110, 135, 201, 235, 266, 324
Kilfoyle, Bonaventure, OFM, 214

Kirchner, Jerome, OFM, 105, 140
Kizhakedan, John, CMI
Klafkowski, Romanus, 165, 166
Klinger, Boniface, OFM, 214
Klopcic, Lucas, 110
Konopka, Urban S.
Kopietz, Emmanuel, 324
Kopleter, Aloysius, 186
Korb, Joseph A., 102
Korty, Leon, OFM
Kossbiel, John, 175
Kottayarikil, Cyriac, MCBS
Kovalsky, John A., 108, 166
Kozlowski, Alphonse, 277
Kraker, John, 125, 166, 182, 193, 322, 325
Kraker, Joseph, 100
Kraszewski, Boniface, OFM
Kreis, Vincent 97
Krempel, Matthew, OFM, 214
Krezesniak (First name unknown), 251
Krmpotic, Martin, 108
Kron, Henry, 155, 156, 208, 209, 289
Krotkiewicz, Lech
Krystiniak, Edmund, OFM, 277
Krystyniak, Francis E., 100, 154, 197, 273, 284, 324
Kulczyk, John F., 154, 197, 284
Kulleck, Gerald J., SSSR
Kummert, Philip, 243, 258
Kunes, Joseph P., 75, 77, 78, 100, 124, 125, 193, 234, 255, 286, 312
Kuppayil, George, MST, 119, 154
Kurtz, Jeffrey, 91, 93, 134
Labinski, Bertrand, OFM, 140
LaCosse, Nobert, 86, 127, 170, 220, 293, 314
LaFontaine, Pierre
LaForest, George, 123, 138, 153, 183, 186, 192, 219, 220, 253, 273, 282, 312, 322
Lally, Rev. Walter
LaLonde, Donald, 170, 214, 293
LaMothe, Gerard F., 106, 153, 162, 168, 180, 253, 313, 314
LaMothe, Ovid J., 83, 262, 289, 307

LaMotte, Joseph, 170, 173, 276
Landreville, John, 214, 237
Landreville, Norbert B., 98, 202, 235, 260, 294, 298, 312, 320
Landreville, Raphael
Langan, Joseph, 143, 209, 243
Langner, Charles, 140, 149, 150, 160, 170, 175, 186, 209, 269, 276, 278, 293
Lango, Aloysius, ISCB, 190
Lannert, Maxim, OFM
LaPlante, Joseph A., Ch. Major
Larsen, Jerome L., 97, 119, 130, 265, 266
LaViolette, Mathias H., 152, 164, 278
Lawless, Joseph C., SJ, 11, 80, 81, 94, 95, 133, 299, 317, 318
Leary, Dunstan, OFM, 214
Leary, Edward, OFM, 140
LeBre, William
Leckman, John J., 86, 97, 108, 127, 130
LeFebre, Bernard, 135, 320
LeGolvan, Paul, 150, 160, 211, 289
Lehman, John J.
LeLievre, David, 102
Lemagie, Charles 80
Lenhart, James, 146, 157, 170, 198, 199, 258, 293, 304
Lenz, Frank M., 123, 129, 133, 152, 166, 182, 266
LePine, Clement J., 76, 78, 135, 211
Letellier, Michael, 106, 192, 211, 226, 252, 253, 255, 264
Liedgens, Carl, 86, 115, 228, 316
Linck, Lawrence
Linfert, Gabriel, OFM, 214
Ling, Joseph J., 90, 146, 232, 304
Lings, Francis, OSF, 140
Linneman, Bernard, 170, 293, 324
Litzner, Corey J.
Long, Lawrence, 105
Longbucco, John L., 90, 95, 98, 103, 276, 293, 328
Longlean, Philip, 119
Lopez, Alfred A. Brichta, OP
Louzon, Bede, OFM Cap., 121, 131, 170, 277, 293, 307

Lukose, Antony, 276, 293, 328
Lulewicz, Edward J., 148, 166, 182, 197, 230, 286, 314
Lyons, Matthew, 243
Maciarcz, Francis, 207, 251
Magner, Francis J, 6, 31, 35, 76, 132, 193, 221, 240, 256, 297, 316
Maier, Sebastian M., 138, 164, 172, 173, 244, 266, 275, 324
Mainville, Moise, 232
Majerus, Theodore Aloysius, 105, 140, 209, 233, 234, 243, 309
Maki, George S., 123, 160, 237, 266, 271, 281
Makowski, Mariusz, 134, 171
Malloy, Edward A., 103, 170, 282, 293, 294
Malone, F., SJ, 296
Malone, Timothy, 103
Maloney, John M., 129, 133, 166, 182, 235, 324
Maloney, Malcom, OFM Cap.
Mancini, Felix, 111
Manderfield, Paul 88, 102, 103, 105, 201, 205, 298, 299
Manderfield, Peter 168, 170, 244, 261, 262, 264, 289, 293
Manderfield, R.P.
Mannie, Stephen Robert, OFM Cap.
Manning, John, 135, 136, 164, 186, 199, 270, 271, 291
Manon, Cletus, CP, 121
Maramattam, Jose Joseph
Marceau, B. Simon, 239, 291
Marceau, Fabian, 106, 117, 121, 138, 150, 160, 168, 199, 209, 211, 226, 239, 243, 258, 264, 303, 309
Marcinkevicius, Casimir J., 83, 162, 168, 303, 307, 314
Marcotte, Wayne E., 98, 112, 117, 130, 174, 258, 282, 291, 328
Marcucci, Hilarious, 114, 158
Marquette, Jacques, SJ, 1, 311
Martel, Joseph E., 137, 138, 239, 309
Martignon, John E., 123, 160, 186, 256,

Martignon, John E. (*continued*), 266, 307
Matchett, Robert
Matejik, Ambrose C., 102, 201
Mathew, Hubby, MST, 119, 154
Maurice (First name unknown), 243
Mayotte, Allan J., 90, 98, 121, 226, 235, 282, 294, 324, 328
Mayrand, Stephen L., 76, 136, 138, 255, 322
Mazuret, Peter P., 115, 263, 264, 316
Mazuret, Peter P., 316
McAllister, Nilus, 125
McAllister, Nilus, CP, 78
McArdle, John F., 86, 98, 108, 112, 115, 127, 130, 188, 214, 215, 289, 316
McArron, Patrick, OFM, 140
McCammond, James
McCarthy, James N., 83, 97, 119, 186, 190, 260, 320
McCloy, M. , 243
McDevitt, Hugh, 243
McGee, William, 103, 121, 131, 183, 184
McGowen, J.B. 100
McKeon, William
McKevitt, Nolan B., 122, 123, 150, 160, 243, 266, 312
McLaughlin, John, 148, 170, 230, 286, 289, 293
McNaughton, James
McQuesten, Mark A., 90, 275, 294, 320, 322
McQuire, Peter, CP, 277
Mecwel, Pawel J., 162, 168, 301
Medin, Joseph, 108
Megnée (First name unknown), 243
Melican, Martin B., 38102, 143
Menapace, James L., 103, 171, 234
Menard, Peter, 105, 138, 226, 255
Menard, Renee 80
Menet, Jean Baptiste, 10
Mercier, Henry L., 76, 78, 88, 129, 133, 144, 174, 226
Mercier, Joseph A., 303
Meskenas, Vincent
Metzger, Clement, SJ

Micelich, Edward, 83, 84, 175, 260, 319, 320
Mikula, Stanislaus, CP, 199, 307
Miller, James A., 130, 188, 199, 228, 232, 243
Mineau, David, Lt. Col.
Minelli, Peter A., 85, 123, 138, 234, 266, 271, 319
Mlynarczyk, W. Anselm, 129, 165, 166, 168, 199, 206, 207, 251
Mockler, John, 143, 168, 193, 286, 312
Molinari, Anthony, 111, 261, 262, 309, 322
Moncher, Raymond F., 85, 170, 239, 262, 271, 281, 293
Monroe, Robert J., 100, 256, 296, 298
Moriarty, Jeremiah B., 102, 143, 205, 235
Morin, Joseph M., 121, 150, 160
Mott, Allen P.
Moyce, Patrick, 276
Mozina, Luke 105, 150, 160, 209, 275, 286
Mrak, Ignatius, 4, 140, 149, 159, 209, 225, 239, 243, 254, 255, 269, 275, 312
Mulhern, Raymond F., 103, 281
Mupparathara, Abraham J., MCBS, 105
Murphy, C., 209
Murphy, Patrick E., 154, 162, 168
Nadeau, Clifford J., 88, 135, 138, 226, 253, 287, 303
Naessens, Philip, OFM Cap., 88
Nagaroor, Joseph, 9, 141, 143, 144, 282
Nayl, E., 266
Neault, George J., O.Praem, 212
Neibling, Joseph, 232
Neuhaus, John 114, 158
Neuhaus, William H.
Neumair, Joseph E., 129, 164, 224, 244, 246, 273
Neurenberg, John 117, 153, 154, 258
Neurohr, Gilbert N., 282
Newland, Ronald A., USAF
Niebling, Joseph, 117, 140
Nirappel, Antony, 282
Nirappel, James

Nivard, Michael A., 97, 130, 175
Noa, Thomas L., 6, 12, 16, 18, 20, 39, 44, 49, 51, 52, 53, 55, 62, 64, 84, 87, 89, 95, 112, 114, 125, 131, 144, 152, 156, 158, 171, 177, 179, 198, 199, 200, 206, 215, 220, 230, 231, 246, 262, 270, 290, 299, 300, 316, 327
Noe, Marius, OFM Cap., 121
Nomellini, Paul J., 90, 93, 154, 222, 241, 284, 294, 303
Norden, Emmett M., 78, 91, 144, 154, 174, 197, 201, 205, 249, 273, 282, 284, 309
Nosbisch, Nickolas H., 114, 158, 193, 199, 205, 224, 243, 286, 305
Nowacki, Jerome A., 148, 322
Nussbaum, Paul J., 5, 128, 208, 274
Nyman, Matthew G., 39, 93, 162, 168, 201
O'Connell, Peter, 209, 232
O'Gara, E. T., SJ, 296
O'Keefe, J.
O'Neil, Dennis, 186
O'Neill, Joseph
Oberto, Peter, 117, 209, 237, 258, 260, 291, 320
O'Callaghan, Oliver J., 117, 256, 258, 301
Oehler, Benjamin, OFM, 214
Oehlerer, Anthony, 103, 146, 246, 294, 204
Oldegeering, Bede, 105
Oldegeering, Bede, OFM, 140
O'Leary, Dennis D., 119, 121, 129, 131
Olivier, Charles E., 239, 269, 279
Olivier, John H., SS
Olivier, Stephen
Olson, Eric E., 131, 170, 188, 226, 293
Oniskiewicz, Mieczyslaw T., 134, 171, 211
Oremus, William C., 83, 88, 224, 239, 306, 307
Orth, Mathias, 115, 275, 286, 291, 309, 316
Otis, Ignatius, 105

Ouellette, Vincent L., 62, 85, 211, 213, 228, 237, 241, 262, 303
Paganini, A., 150, 160
Pakiz, Marcus, 110
Papon, Julius, 246, 250, 251, 309
Papp, Christopher, U.S. Air Force
Paquet, James Alderic, 102, 106, 114, 158, 173, 180
Paquet, Louis, 239
Parella, A., 243
Parenti, Wenceslaus, 111
Paris, Benedetto J., 129, 133, 166, 178, 182
Parrotta, Arthur J., 76, 78, 111, 134, 136, 256, 298, 326
Paruleski, Robert J., 103, 119, 154, 273, 281
Patrick, John E., 102, 164, 241, 319
Paulantonio, Joseph W.
Pawler, Fabian, 100, 105, 117, 119, 125, 186, 205, 207, 234, 251, 255, 264, 291
Peeters, Ambrose J., O.Praem
Pelissier, Albert C., 114, 121, 158, 192, 193, 195, 221, 227, 303
Pelisson, A. O., 234, 243
Pelisson, Anacletus, 150, 160, 170, 276, 293, 309, 316, 322
Pelisson, Anatole, 115, 117, 129, 186, 199, 227, 228, 239, 253
Pelletier, Wilfrid, 76, 78, 106, 121, 123, 131, 135, 150, 160, 211, 277, 303
Pepin, Darryl J., 85, 102, 190, 203, 319
Pepin, James A., 143, 150, 160, 226
Perino, Lesli, 150, 160, 170, 293
Pernaski, George A., 98, 119, 162, 168, 170, 173, 273, 293, 328
Perumpally, Mathew, 264, 316
Petranek, Carl J., 125, 173, 200, 201
Petroske, Peter, 123, 150, 160, 233
Pfalzer, Juvenal, OFM
Pfalzer, Miles, OFM, 140, 214,
Pfalzer, Roman, OFM
Pinten, Joseph G., 36, 38, 129, 164, 190, 228, 240, 243, 322
Piontek, Cyril, OFM, 197

Piret, Andrew D.J.
Pirron, Sigismund, 105
Plagens, Joseph C., 5, 40, 107, 213, 300
Plappallil, Joseph, 162, 168
Poisson, Thomas L., 150, 160, 186, 228, 246, 264, 305, 307
Polakowski, Anthony J., 117, 166, 170, 182, 197, 258, 309
Polakowski, Joseph C., 201, 232, 264, 291
Polcyn, Robert F., OFM, Cap., 85, 90, 117, 258, 294, 319
Polic, Joseph, 107, 108
Poulin, Louis Archille, 106, 150, 160, 192, 211, 253, 264, 303
Powers, John, 186
Pradarutti, Charles
Presern, Joseph
Proulx, E., SJ, 211
Prud'homme, Paul M., SJ, 11, 80, 81, 94, 95, 132, 133, 299, 318
Przybylski, Raymond S., 90, 152, 154, 251, 273, 280, 284, 298, 309, 322
Pulvermacker, Claude, OFM Cap., 121
Rancinger, Francis, 108
Raphael, Charles, 199
Rausch, Joseph F., OFM, Cap., 130, 232, 281
Raymond, Napoleon Joseph, 209, 225, 226, 232
Reding, J., 258
Regis, R., 120, 121, 309
Reichenbach, John, 170, 271, 293
Reinhart, Charles J., 156, 173, 174, 175, 228, 260, 320, 325
Reis, Henry J., 164, 209, 223, 224
Remillard, William J., 90, 114, 135, 158, 303, 320
Reszka, Raymond
Revello, James
Reynaert, John H., 117, 125, 192, 228, 234, 258, 275, 286, 291, 309, 312
Rezek, Antoine, xi, xiii, xvii, 82, 83 100, 125, 164, 185, 186, 187, 234
Rhoades, C. Michael, 129, 133, 150, 160, 171, 234, 260, 298, 312

Rhomberg, Elvan, OFM
Ricca, Francis J.
Richard, Charles A., 312
Richards, William G., 39, 117, 146, 232, 258, 269, 275, 279, 286, 291, 304, 319
Richter, Frederick, 82, 83, 96, 224, 277, 306, 307
Ricke, Peter, OFM
Rinkowski, Fridolin, OFM, 197
Roberfe, F. M., 303
Roberts, Armour
Rocheleau, David H, 134, 146, 148, 149, 180, 260, 304, 320
Roetzer, James M., 100, 235, 324
Rogosz, Stanislaus, 277
Rohr, Louis F., OFM, 105
Ronkowski, Francis X., 156, 207
Rosseau, Hilary J., 149, 150, 160, 209, 239, 243, 253, 274, 275, 286, 312
Rothen, Bennet, 105
Rottot, Edmond, SJ, 296
Rouleau, Kenneth, OFM,
Roy, William T., 186, 239
Rupp, N. Daniel, 85, 154, 162, 164, 168, 271, 281, 284, 294, 303, 320
Ruppe, Thomas G., 86, 127, 170, 205, 213, 230, 293, 322, 327, 328
Russell, William P., 121, 129, 133, 269, 279
Ryan, John H., 86, 117, 121, 123, 127, 258, 260, 266, 319, 320
Salatka, Charles A., 6, 18, 33, 81, 126, 174, 180, 181, 237, 247, 326
Sample, Alexander K., xi, xii, 7, 71, 93, 237, 284, 303
Sanford, Glen F., 115, 118, 119, 123, 150, 160, 190, 243, 312, 316
Sartorelli, Otto J., 114, 158, 226, 239, 246, 291
Saulnier, Donald, Ch. Capt. USAF
Sauriol, Joseph, 102, 115, 125, 135, 136, 150, 160, 187, 188, 228, 243, 258, 264, 288, 289, 316
Savageau, Paul, 97
Savageau, Vincent, O.Praem, 122, 123,

Savageau, Vincent, O. Praem, 146, 150, 159, 160, 266, 304
Savinshek, Stephen, OFM Conv., 111
Scanlon, Lambert, D.
Schaefer, Adain, OFM
Schaefer, James J., 39, 97, 102, 103, 123, 130, 135, 150, 160, 162, 244, 277, 294, 320
Schaeffer, Richard C., 85, 129, 133, 141, 166, 182, 319, 326
Schafer, Francis, OFM, 175
Scharinger, James G., C.Ss.R, 117, 258, 291
Schaul, Joseph F., 158, 164, 244, 246, 289, 309
Scheetz, Antonine, OFM
Schelhamer, C. F., 209, 228
Scheringer, Francis M., 171, 228, 233, 234, 242, 271, 289
Schevers, Bernard J., O. Praem, 136, 161, 162, 233
Schick, William F., 86, 90, 125, 156, 158, 211, 232, 246, 322
Schiska, Paul A., 93, 117, 134, 136, 174, 228, 239, 258, 271, 281, 303
Schlimgen, Bernardin, OFM, Cap., 80
Schlimgen, Bernardine, H.
Schloss, Anthony, 75, 168, 289, 291
Schmidlin, Dunstan, OFM
Schmidt, Gerald, OFM Cap.
Schmied, Thomas, OFM Cap.
Schmitt, Mark F., 7, 11, 21, 63, 72, 77, 120, 171, 178, 186, 203, 239, 264, 271, 279, 294, 316, 321
Schneider, Adolph F., 82, 83, 100, 168
Schneider, Alban, OFM, 214
Schneider, Chris, OFM
Schneider, Jerome, OFM, 197
Schneider, Jerry, 324
Schneider, Stephen, OFM, 140
Schuettlehoeffer, A. T., 192, 224, 286, 312
Schulek, Andrew C., 307, 319
Sedlock, David, 123, 144, 160, 233, 289
Seifert, Francis A., 86, 114, 125, 127, 135, 158, 162, 190, 205, 300, 301, 320

Seifert, Joseph H., 86, 88, 102, 126, 127, 135, 193, 219, 200, 264, 309
Seliskar, Donald, SJ, 299
Shanley, Michael
Shea, William H., 276, 322
Sheedlo, Walter, 134, 140, 211, 282
Shiroda, Donald L., 112, 125, 184, 190, 228, 237, 301
Shiverski, John J., 102, 117, 241, 258, 269, 279, 291
Silvestrini, Dino F., 85, 125, 249, 319
Silvioni, Anchetto, 111
Simonson, James Wilfred, CSC
Sinopoli, Peter, 189, 190
Sitko, Ephraem J., 112, 123, 136, 266, 309
Skufca, Ronald J., 123, 140, 141, 143, 246, 248, 266, 294, 320
Smietana, Alexander, 100
Smith, William
Smith, B. Neil, 162, 168, 287
Smith, Raymond J., 76, 78, 129, 135, 154, 197, 273, 277, 284, 307, 314
Somers, Adrein, 114, 158
Sommers, Martin C., 209, 232, 271
Soulard, William, 289
Sparapani, Daniel, 134
Spelgatti, David P., 31, 40, 102, 209
Sperlein, Francis, 93
Sperlein, Frederick, 170, 234, 263, 264, 293
Sprajcar, Peter, 110, 201
Srebernak, Frank P.
St. Onge, Donald
Stahl, William B., 93, 68, 119, 154, 234, 291
Stanek, Leander, OFM
Stariha, John N., 207
Starika, Most Rev. John N., 269
Steber, Michael J., 119, 129, 133, 138, 154, 166, 182
Stehlin, Neil Martin, 93, 102, 173
Steltenkamp, Michael, SJ, 299, 318
Stenglein, John J., SJ, 114, 148, 157, 158, 293, 322, 324
Sterbentz, Ralph J., 88, 135, 264, 265, 326

Stetz (First name unknown), 96
Stoffel, Elmer, OFM Cap., 81
Stolarik, Cyrill M., TOR
Stolwyk, Francis, SDS
Stout, T. CP, 102, 168
Strelick, Charles J., 102, 117, 178, 209, 258, 291
Stropher, Lawrence P., 229, 230
Struif, J. E., 124, 199, 243
Strumski, Matthew, 76, 78
Stuntebeck, George A., 117, 121, 147, 148, 173, 180, 229, 230, 258, 264, 275, 286, 322
Sturek, Angelus, OFM
Suda, Conrad E., 115, 154, 170, 273, 282, 284, 316
Suhr, John V., 115, 131, 277, 289, 291, 316
Sullivan, Dennis, 164
Sutter, Fidelis, 115, 119, 125, 129, 150, 160, 163, 164, 168, 170, 175, 228, 271, 291, 293, 309, 316
Swagers, Daniel, 117
Swift, Francis H., 232
Swoboda, Charles J., 99, 100
Szczykowski, Jan, 134, 171
Szoka, Edmund, 72, 213, 236, 237
Szygula, Charles, 207, 324
Teehan, William, 232
Telles, Jordan J., OFM, 105, 130, 140, 214
Terhorst, Gerhard, 79, 80, 87, 105, 227, 228
Testevin, Edward, 102, 135, 152, 154, 168, 170, 282, 320
Thekkel, Thomas Joseph, MST, 85, 276, 293, 319, 328
Theoret, Glenn J., 162, 168, 171, 234
Thiele, Henry L., 105, 169, 215, 216, 243, 276, 293
Thompson, Arnold E., 39, 123, 144, 150, 156, 160,183, 222
Thoren, Guy, 178, 228, 232
Thottackara, Daniel J., CMI
Thundy, Zacharias, CMI

Timock, Ronald K., 123, 130, 131, 150, 160, 170, 173, 188, 237, 266, 273, 293
Tittel, Clarence, OFM, 214
Treilles, Albert J., 106, 113, 114, 115, 157, 158, 316, 322
Troik, Raymond
Trottenberg, Theodore A., 209, 243
Tubin, P.G., 23,
Tuomey, Michael 97
Turajski, Dominic, OFM
Turnbull, John, OFM
Turner, Thomas, 243
Ulrich, Stephen, 201
Valayathil, Thomas, 146, 304, 325
Valerio, Raymond A., 76, 78, 83, 119, 146, 148, 162, 168, 180, 186, 264, 273, 304
Valhovic, Vladimir, OFM Conv.
Van Damme, Larry P., 121, 129, 133, 166, 182, 184
Van Paemel, Angelus 80
Van Straten, M. J., 117, 199
Vandannoor, Joseph, MST, 246, 248
Vanitvelt, Milton H., 213, 244, 246
Varickamackal, Thomas Joseph, 123, 160, 266
Vella, Joseph C.
Vento, Dominic, 192, 321, 322
Vermare, Anthony, 106, 121, 239, 289
Vertin, John, 4, 8, 16, 48, 51, 52, 82, 92, 100, 104, 109, 111, 115, 124, 130, 139, 163, 186, 209, 223, 243, 252, 261, 269, 285, 302
Vichich, Michael T., 76, 78, 91, 154, 180, 309, 310
Villaire, Terry, 103, 184
Vissers, A. A., O.Praem, 123, 152, 273
Vitali, Alberico, 115, 117, 199, 232, 258, 291, 309, 316, 322
Vlahovic, Vladimir, 108
Von Gumpenberg, Julius Baron, 175, 276
Von Tobel, James E., SJ, 239
Waechter, Anthony, 37, 80, 88, 102, 170,
Waechter, Anthony, 172, 173, 175, 273
Wagner, Eusebius, OFM, 140

Wagner, Joseph
Wallace, Joseph C., 129, 228, 234, 264
Wallner, George, 184
Walloch, Albert, 197
Walsh, Edmond, 243
Wantland, Thomas A., 184, 301
Waraxa, Gabriel B., 153, 154, 273, 284
Weakland, B. M. 78, 125
Weakley, Robert, OFM, 105
Weber, Glen (John Glen), 83, 98, 102, 121, 138, 186, 328
Weber, Richard V., OP
Webler, A., SJ, 296
Wehr, Humbert, 105
Weier, Rev. Thomas, OFM, Cap., 121
Weis, Michael, 115, 150, 160, 170, 245, 293, 316
Weissmann, Paul, OFM, 277
Welling, Peter, 105
Wendling, Lery, OFM
Weninger, F.X., SJ, 115, 243, 316
Wenzel, Edward J., 37, 80, 83, 88, 98, 117, 148, 166, 180, 182, 186, 188, 235, 258, 282, 324, 328
Wheelock, Robert, OFM Cap.
Wick, Leander, OFM Cap.
Wilberding, Alphonse, OFM, 140
Williams, James M., 162, 168, 232, 271
Winterheld, Pax, 105
Wirth, Justus, OFM
Wisneske, S. Patrick, 130, 156, 230, 248, 286, 305, 328

Wloszczynski, Stephen, 111, 190, 197, 277, 298
Woempner, Michael A., 98, 222, 328
Wolf, James, OFM Cap.
Wollny, Alexander, 108, 175, 322,
Wren, Louis E., OFM, Conv., 85, 117, 146, 258, 291, 303, 304, 319
Wtyklo, Jacek S., 129, 133, 166, 182, 282, 289, 319
Wypasek, Ludwik
Yaroch, Paul, OFM Cap., 80
Zachman, Clarence, Ch. Major, USAF
Zadra, Leon
Zadra, Dominic A., 239, 271, 281
Zagar, Anthony, 150, 159, 160, 243
Zaloga, Daniel S., 78, 195, 296
Zalokar, Joseph, 110, 175
Zanon, Donald, 184
Zeug, Herculan, 105
Zeugner, Raymond J., 85, 115, 119, 125, 127, 154, 264, 273, 284, 316, 319
Ziegler, Otto, OFM, 228
Ziegler, Rupert
Ziminski, James C., 39, 80, 88
Zimmermann, Hubert, 130, 146, 187, 188, 199, 304
Zimmer, Ellis J.
Zryd, Joseph L. (P.A.), 101, 102, 240, 241, 269, 279
Zuvic, Anton, 108